D1551754

The Rakish Stage

Studies in English Drama, 1660–1800

ROBERT D. HUME

Southern Illinois University Press
Carbondale and Edwardsville

Library of Congress Cataloging in Publication Data

Hume, Robert D.
The rakish stage : studies in English drama, 1660–1800.

Contents: Content and meaning in the drama—Restoration comedy and its audiences, 1660–1776 / Arthur H. Scouten and Robert D. Hume—Otway and the comic muse—[etc.]
Includes bibliographical references and index.
1. English drama—18th century—History and criticism—Addresses, essays, lectures. 2. English drama—Restoration, 1660–1700—History and criticism—Addresses, essays, lectures. 3. English drama (Comedy)—History and criticism—Addresses, essays, lectures. I. Title.
PR708.C6H8 1983 822'.009 82–16984
ISBN 0–8093–1100–3

86 85 84 83   4 3 2 1

For
Kit Hume

Contents

Preface

The plan for this book was first conceived in 1973 when I was still at work on *The Development of English Drama in the Late Seventeenth Century* (published in 1976). My concern in that book was with generic developments in the first fifty years of the period. Specifically, I wanted to escape from simplistic generalizations while attempting to trace more accurately the changes and permutations to be found in play types, taking the corpus of plays *in toto* rather than selectively. Early in the process of writing that book I became convinced that though close reading of some of the plays had produced useful results, such an approach had led to a critical dead end. The present essays, written between 1971 and 1981, represent an attempt to find different and more fruitful ways of dealing with the drama. My object throughout has been to seek approaches which are neither restricted to the verbal confines of particular texts nor heedless of texts. As a critic concerned with "affective impact" I am certainly interested in readers and audiences, but exclusive preoccupation with the reader breeds a subjectivity which I cannot accept. Neglecting the text seems to me just as foolish and counterproductive as ignoring the audience which interprets it and responds to it.

The connecting thread in the present essays is a pervasive concern with the values to be found in the plays and the impact they seem designed to have on an audience. Three sorts of work are represented in this volume:

1. Generic study. Chapter 7 ("Multifarious Forms") is an attempt to sketch a more adequate set of subgenre descriptions for comedy throughout the eighteenth century. Chapter 10 ("Goldsmith and Sheridan") is an attack on longstanding clichés about the dominance of "sentimental comedy" in the later eighteenth century.

2. Critical analysis. Chapters 2, 4, and 8 are devoted to investigation of the design and impact of problem plays by Otway, Lee, and Gay respectively.

3. Contextual study. Under this heading I include not only investigation of the plays' values, ideology, and subject matter, but also studies of the plays' relationship to changing audiences and to the theatrical context in which they were produced. Chapter 1 ("Content and Meaning") explores some broad theoretical questions and offers guidelines for the would-be interpreter of ideology and real-life content. Chapter 2 ("'Restoration Comedy' and its Audiences," written in collaboration with A. H. Scouten) considers the relationship of a changing audience to the best known of the late seventeenth-century plays. Chapters 5 ("The Myth of the Rake") and 6 ("Marital Discord") investigate the treatment of controversial subject matter in a large number of plays. Chapter 9 ("The London Theatre from *The Beggar's Opera* to the Licensing Act") analyzes background in the 1730s—a particularly interesting and neglected period in English drama.

I believe that important work remains to be done in all three realms—genre, impact, and values/content/context. A fourth possibility, analysis in the context of theatrical performance, seems to me to offer great possibilities for a fresh kind of interpretation. I have left it out of account in the present collection because I am now at work in collaboration with Judith Milhous on a book taking this approach to the drama—*Producible Interpretation: Eight English Plays, 1675–1707* (to be published by Southern Illinois University Press).

One general question demands attention at the outset of this enterprise. What should an interpreter want to *do* with this drama? My answer is that there are a variety of useful tasks to be attempted. The plays seem to me to differ considerably in the kinds of meaning they possess and in the sorts of challenges they offer to an interpreter. Every play has a story (seldom in need of much clarification), an affective design (sometimes confusing), and a set of implicit or explicit values and ideological assumptions (sometimes in need of elucidation, often not). Some of the plays—a significant minority—also have a "meaning" which goes beyond questions of affective impact and gets us into the realm of ideas and commentary upon real-life material. Much of chapter 1 is devoted to an analysis of how we may identify and analyze such meaning. My position is that we should try to move beyond the kinds of interpretation based upon close reading which have become prevalent in the last thirty years, but that in doing so we must neither lapse into relativism nor abandon the lessons to be learned from generic and historical context.

These essays present an overview of the drama of this period (concentrating on comedy) focussing on matters of content, ideology and values, impact, and genre. I have tried to make a case for some fine but neglected plays, to demolish some misleading clichés, and to offer a view of the plays unwarped by inherited assumptions or personal preferences. One of the oddest twists in the tangled critical history of "Restoration comedy" has been the determination of some recent scholars to see it as more sexually and socially radical than it actually is. Several of my essays have proved controversial, but none more so than "The Myth of the Rake." To many critics of past generations, the sexual matter in some of the plays seemed shocking, or worse. Ironically, we now find critics wishing to read the plays as embodiments of rebellion against marriage and as manifestos of sexual liberation. This they are not.

I would hardly advocate going to the other extreme and trying to claim that the plays are morally upright demonstrations of Providential justice and Christian ethics. The plays vary a good deal, in point of fact. Speaking for myself, I would be happy to find the plays more socially and sexually radical than they actually seem to me to be—but my preferences really ought to be beside the point. I hardly think that I have "sold out to Aubrey Williams" (as a friend once accused me of doing), but nor do I wish to fall into the trap of reading into the plays a fundamental rebellion against social and religious codes now found obnoxious.

I have assembled this collection of essays (three of them previously unpublished) in the belief that they represent a coherent approach to the plays, and in the hope that they will prove provocative. I will be content if my arguments serve to focus future debate, whether they are accepted, rejected, or modified by later writers. The crucial point to these studies lies more in the kinds of questions they ask than in the particular answers I am able to supply.

Grateful acknowledgment is extended for permission to reprint material in altered form from the following copyright sources:

" 'Restoration Comedy' and its Audiences, 1660–1776," by Arthur H. Scouten and Robert D. Hume: *Yearbook of English Studies*, 10 (1980), 45–69; by the kind permission of the editors and the Modern Humanities Research Association.

"Otway and the Comic Muse," by Robert D. Hume: *Studies in Philology*, 73 (1976), 87–116; by the kind permission of the editor and the University of North Carolina Press.

"The Satiric Design of Nat. Lee's *The Princess of Cleve*," by Robert D. Hume: *Journal of English and Germanic Philology*, 75 (1976), 117–38; by the kind permission of the editors and the University of Illinois Press.

"The Myth of the Rake in 'Restoration Comedy,' " by Robert D. Hume: *Studies in the Literary Imagination*, 10 (Spring 1977), 25–55; by the kind permission of the editor.

"Marital Discord in English Comedy from Dryden to Fielding," by Robert D. Hume: reprinted from *Modern Philology*, 74 (1977), 248–72; by permission of The University of Chicago Press. © 1977 by The University of Chicago. All rights reserved.

"The Multifarious Forms of Eighteenth-Century Comedy," by Robert D. Hume: pp. 3–32 of *The Stage and the Page: London's "Whole Show" in the Eighteenth-Century Theatre*, ed. Geo. Winchester Stone, Jr., copyright © 1981 by The Regents of the University of California; by the kind permission of the University of California Press.

"Goldsmith and Sheridan and the Supposed Revolution of 'Laughing' against 'Sentimental' Comedy," by Robert D. Hume: pp. 237–76 of *Studies in Change and Revolution: Aspects of English Intellectual History, 1640–1800*, ed. Paul J. Korshin; this collection © 1972 by The Scolar Press Limited; by the kind permission of The Scolar Press Limited.

For assistance with checking and preparation of the Index I am grateful to William Burling.

Works Frequently Cited

Parenthetical page references to play texts are to the first printed London quartos unless otherwise specified.

Fujimura	Thomas H. Fujimura, *The Restoration Comedy of Wit* (Princeton: Princeton Univ. Press, 1952).
Hume, *Development*	Robert D. Hume, *The Development of English Drama in the Late Seventeenth Century* (Oxford: Clarendon Press, 1976).
Loftis, *Comedy and Society*	John Loftis, *Comedy and Society from Congreve to Fielding* (Stanford: Stanford Univ. Press, 1959).
The London Stage	*The London Stage, 1660–1800.* Part 1: 1660–1700, ed. William Van Lennep, Emmett L. Avery, and Arthur H. Scouten (Carbondale: Southern Illinois Univ. Press, 1965). Part 2: 1700–1729, ed. Emmett L. Avery, 2 vols. (1960). Part 3: 1729–1747, ed. Arthur H. Scouten, 2 vols. (1961). Part 4: 1747–1776, ed. George Winchester Stone, Jr., 3 vols. (1962). Part 5: 1776–1800, ed.

	Charles Beecher Hogan, 3 vols. (1968).
The London Theatre World	Robert D. Hume, ed., *The London Theatre World, 1660–1800* (Carbondale: Southern Illinois Univ. Press, 1980).
Nicoll	Allardyce Nicoll, *A History of English Drama, 1660–1900*, rev. ed., 6 vols. (Cambridge: Cambridge Univ. Press, 1952–59).
Sherbo	Arthur Sherbo, *English Sentimental Drama* (East Lansing: Michigan State Univ. Press, 1957).
Smith, *The Gay Couple*	John Harrington Smith, *The Gay Couple in Restoration Comedy* (Cambridge: Harvard Univ. Press, 1948).
Sutherland	James Sutherland, *English Literature of the Late Seventeenth Century*, Oxford History of English Literature (Oxford: Clarendon Press, 1969).

I

Content and Meaning in the Drama

Critical study of English drama in the period 1660–1800 still leaves a great deal to be desired. Since neither generic study nor more close reading seems likely to advance our understanding of the plays much further, I propose to consider here the possibilities of another approach, one concerned with the "content" rather than with the form or designed effect of the plays.

I am convinced that the values and ideas in the plays offer us important interpretive possibilities, but only if we approach them with considerable caution and due attention to establishing a valid methodology. My aims in this essay are therefore theoretical and methodological. Specifically, I want to address three central questions: 1) What kinds of "content" (beyond stock devices) does this drama really possess? 2) How is such content best studied? 3) How much does study of content help us with interpretation? My argument is applicable to the drama of other periods and countries, but for convenience and the sake of specificity I have based my case on plays in a limited time span.

One of our key problems as critics is confusion about what these plays "mean." When critics of the old school say that the plays present no social problems, no philosophy, and no serious values, they are simply wrong. But when some recent critics transform the plays into philosophical disquisitions they ignore the realities of text and theatre history. The difference is not "intellectual" versus "anti-intellectual" readings; this is a false dichotomy.

We are not dealing with an all-or-nothing case. The plays do reflect the ideas and values of their day, and many of them contain topical references to political and social issues. The practical problems of dealing with content, however, are formidable. The plays are many and for the most part highly formulaic. Content is hard to pin down, especially when underlying values rather than politics or personal satire are at issue. Trying to separate a play's affective design from its values and its references to real life is a tricky business. But difficulties notwithstanding, we cannot afford to ignore the interpretive uses of content. This essay is an attempt to establish valid aims and procedures for such study.

The Problem: Making More Sense of the Plays

I must explain bluntly at the outset that I am primarily concerned with what E. D. Hirsch, Jr., calls "meaning" as opposed to "significance." Or in Lucien Goldmann's terms my object is to "comprehend" a play's structure, not to "explain" it.[1] When I get into ideology I am on the borderline, but basically my concern is with the comprehension of particular works via their ideas and allusions. I am happy to grant that there remain important studies of this drama to be written by Marxists, structuralists, and reader-response critics, but their concerns are markedly different from mine.

To understand even just the meaning of the plays we need to try to comprehend them in four distinct ways: 1) as self-contained literary structures, 2) as works in generic context, 3) as vehicles for theatrical performance—still a little-studied subject, and 4) as reflections of their contemporary world. Trying to deal with all four matters at once is impracticable. Realistically, the literary historian must deal with a more limited problem.

1. E. D. Hirsch, Jr., *The Aims of Interpretation* (Chicago: Univ. of Chicago Press, 1976), esp. pp. 2–13. "'Meaning' refers to the whole verbal meaning of a text, and 'significance' to textual meaning in relation to a larger context, i.e., another mind, another era, a wider subject matter, an alien system of values, and so on" (pp. 2–3). Lucien Goldmann, "Genetic-Structuralist Method in the History of Literature," rpt. in *Marxism and Art: Writings in Aesthetics and Criticism*, ed. Berel Lang and Forrest Williams (New York: McKay, 1972), pp. 249–50.

Almost every attempt to approach "Restoration" comedy, in particular, has been complicated by its messy critical history. Hostility to the moral codes presented in some of the plays has provoked a long series of defenses, many of them designed to remove the plays from the realm of serious moral questions. To the readings of Palmer, Lynch, and others, L. C. Knights retorted that the plays were trivial, gross, and dull. This in turn generated defenses claiming more philosophical profundity for the plays than most readers can find in them.[2]

General characterizations of both comedy and serious drama have proved unsatisfactory, but to date close reading has generated little more than confusion. Current opinion on Wycherley's *The Country-Wife* is a good example: critics see the play as anything from a savage assault on corrupt society to a hymn in praise of sexual liberation.[3] But if critics can make half a dozen radically contradictory cases and support them all "from the text," where do we stand? Conceivably, of course, Wycherley was being deliberately ambiguous in the fashion of *Le Misanthrope*. Critics, however, have not seen the play in such terms.

If close reading leads only to confusion, the first logical ground of appeal is generic context. Here we have definitely made some progress in recent years. The clichés so long standard (and by no means dead)—comedy of manners, sentimental comedy, heroic tragedy, pathetic tragedy—have provoked a series of vigorous debunkings from John Harrington Smith's *The Gay Couple in Restoration Comedy* (1948) to A. H. Scouten's "Notes Toward a History of Restoration Comedy" (*PQ*, 1966) and my own *The Development of English Drama in the Late Seventeenth Century* (1976). Clichés have been exploded and easy generalizations proved unsound. But though such "atomistic history" (in R. S. Crane's phrase) offers us some sense of subgroups within chronological change, its aim is to avoid the imposition of arbitrary *ex post facto*

2. For a fuller discussion of the entangled critical history see my *Development*, pp. 63–72.

3. For some account of the manifold confusions in current Wycherley criticism see my "William Wycherley: Text, Life, Interpretation," *Modern Philology*, 78 (1981), 399–415.

categories. While the approach is not hostile to the delineation of subgenres or explanation of why change occurred, it is not really designed to handle such matters. Atomistic history—"annals" in Dryden's term—can help free us from false assumptions and can show us what is there, but it can do little to make much sense of the plays or tell us why they are as they are. The history of this drama is not so tidy as we were once led to believe. Well and good, but what next?

One obvious possibility is to look for a single, all-encompassing generic theory of the sort Brian Corman has recently called for.[4] This is certainly an attractive idea, but can it be meaningfully done? Corman is talking about a period of half a century and some five hundred plays. He is looking for an all-illuminating theory that will make *ex post facto* sense of this multitude of plays, even though its principles were never recognized by the authors of those plays. This strikes me as a large order. As Judith Milhous observes, "I am not aware that a theory has yet been proposed in such circumstances for any period in the history of drama, and I have trouble imagining any theory not hopelessly general fitting the plays at issue."[5] A useful general theory would be a wonderful thing to have, but I am skeptical about the prospects. Realistically, I think we need to turn to less grandiose schemes.

If neither close reading nor genre will serve as a reliable way of interpreting these plays, then we must look to something else. A logical choice is content. Under that general heading fall two quite different things: a) specific allusion—direct or disguised—to politics, individuals, and contemporary issues; and b) the ideas and values which underlie the plays. A number of scholars have already done important work in these realms, particularly John Loftis (*Comedy and Society from Congreve to Fielding, The Politics of Drama in Augustan England*), John Harrington Smith (*The Gay*

4. See Corman's "Toward a Generic Theory of Restoration Comedy: Some Preliminary Considerations," *Studies in Eighteenth-Century Culture,* 7 (1978), 423–32, and "What Is Restoration Drama?" *Univ. of Toronto Quarterly,* 48 (1978), 53–66.

5. "Studies in Restoration and Eighteenth-Century Drama, 1978," *Philological Quarterly,* 58 (1979), 403–28, esp. 425–26.

Couple), G. S. Alleman (*Matrimonial Law and the Materials of Restoration Comedy*), Susan Staves (*Players' Sceptres: Fictions of Authority in the Restoration*), and Eugene Waith (*Ideas of Greatness: Heroic Drama in England*). All of these studies, however, have basically seized upon single subjects and followed them in relevant plays. What emerges is a sense of attitudes on particular subjects (for example, heroism or libertinism) or an understanding of how writers draw on a given body of material (for example, Hobbesian ideas or matrimonial law). The authors are rarely concerned with the whole play or the significance of the content to the play's overall meaning and impact. The methodological problems posed by the study of content remain, therefore, largely unaddressed.

Dealing with Content and Meaning: Some Theoretical Considerations

What does *Hamlet* mean? *As You Like It*? Does *Othello* mean that jealousy is bad? That wives should look well to their linen? That the proofs should be mathematical before jealousy proves tragical? Plays are not as a rule reducible to abstract propositions, and treating them as oranges to be juiced is seldom a good idea. Many fine plays have rather little intellectual substance (*The Alchemist*); contrariwise, some rather dreary ones come heavily freighted with ideas (*Back to Methuselah*). I have no wish, Rymer-like, to lay waste to the dramatic landscape from Dryden to Sheridan. Before we invest heavily in the critical and historical machinery that will allow us systematically to strip-mine ideas and topical materials from the drama, some reflections on objects, principles, and limitations seem in order.

Types of Meaning in the Plays

Almost every play written for professional production in England between 1660 and 1776 is constructed from the proven materials of popular drama. These should loom reasonably large in any attempt at an overall analysis. The obvious constituent elements of a large majority of the comedies and tragedies throughout the period are stock characters, plots, and affective devices. The meaning-mongers who dive deep into *The Country-Wife* or *The Man of Mode* without realizing the degree to which these plays are formulaic simply make fools of themselves, as do those champions of Goldsmith and Sheridan who have never bothered to read the numerous laughing comedies of the 1760s. No doubt philosophy too can be derivative, but seldom as thoroughly so as works concocted for the commercial theatre. We must never forget that we are searching for "meaning" in works full of proven theatrical clichés. And the conclusion that there is earth-shattering significance in boy getting girl should be drawn with caution.

An interpreter of plays can legitimately concern himself with the events and characters, with the designed effect on the audience, with underlying values and outlook, or with the ideas communicated. For my purposes in this study "meaning" is basically restricted to explicit ideas. I would thus distinguish study of materials, effect, and intellectual background from analysis of meaning. In a basic way we can differentiate between works with a message and those without one. This need not be a value judgment: *Tom Thumb* is a wonderful play, and *The London Merchant* is a pretty awful one.

Very few of the plays in this period are even arguably "drama of ideas": they lack the questioning of values and the basic challenge to the audience's world view demanded by Eric Bentley and others who have worked out relevant definitions.[6] Their meaning tends, therefore, to be less explicit than an interpreter could wish. One can attempt to determine the affective impact of any play, but "meaning" in a more intellectual sense may or may not be present in a given play. For the interpreter concerned with ideas, the first problem must be to determine whether the play has any.[7]

6. See, for example, Vivian Mercer, "From Myth to Ideas—and Back," *Ideas in the Drama*, ed. John Gassner (New York: Columbia Univ. Press, 1964), pp. 42–70, and more generally Eric Bentley, *The Playwright as Thinker* (1946; rpt. New York: Harcourt, Brace and World, 1967).

7. I have discussed "The Problem of Meaning" in the comedies in my *Development*, pp. 144–48.

The materials from which the plot is constructed are one thing; the "content" that contributes to meaning as we are discussing it here is quite another. For analytic purposes, I think we can fairly say that plays display content in one of three common fashions, which I will subdivide a little further here. The interpreter of meaning will be principally concerned with the third, fourth, and fifth types of content.

Commonplace
   1. literary
   2. intellectual/social/political
General Ideology
   3. values or outlook which provoke thought
Real-life Specifics
   4. topical commentary
   5. overt didacticism

Let me try to illustrate these distinctions. 1) Farquhar's *The Stage-Coach* (1702?) is a delightful and effective little play, but its presentation of young lovers, the threat of a forced marriage, country boobies, and so forth, is so totally stereotypical that I would call its treatment of these subjects literary commonplace. 2) I would put Garrick's *Lethe* (1740) at the level of social commonplace, a work designed to amuse the audience with gibes at standing butts—fops, pushy cit wives, and others. As a political example we might take Crowne's *Charles VIII of France* (1671), a workmanlike imitation of Dryden's heroic mode which gives us thoroughly predictable and unexceptionable examples of good and bad kingship. 3) Some plays which clearly give the audience—at least the original one—food for thought are *The Man of Mode* (1676), *The Way of the World* (1700), *The Beaux Stratagem* (1707), and *The Clandestine Marriage* (1766), to name only some famous examples. Farquhar's play borders on the next category, but the treatment is sufficiently light that the play is usually performed and enjoyed as nothing more than a happy-ending romp. 4) Of plays with overt (often topical) commentary Dryden's *Marriage A-la-Mode* (1671), Gay's *The Beggar's Opera* (1728), Fielding's *Historical Register*

(1737), Crowne's *City Politiques* (1683), Lee's *The Princess of Cleve* (1682), and Macklin's *The Man of the World* (1781) are good illustrations. 5) Overt didacticism (political or social) is well represented in Dryden and Lee's *The Duke of Guise* (1682), Southerne's *The Wives Excuse* (1691), Lillo's *The London Merchant* (1731), and Steele's *The Conscious Lovers* (1722). Obviously I am including in this group both problem plays and those designed as exempla. There is a considerable difference in affective aim and strategies, but this classification is based entirely on the explicitness with which content is presented. Part of the distinction between the fourth and fifth categories lies in the degree to which the author insists that the audience *must* confront or accept the ideas. *City Politiques* can be staged as a pure romp; *The Wives Excuse* cannot. Likewise, however hostile to Walpole we may find *The Beggar's Opera*, it does not thrust an explicit political position on us as *The Duke of Guise* does. These categories are far from being absolute, and readers might well want to argue over the assignment of particular plays. I am simply trying to suggest that in dealing with content we have a spectrum to consider.

We must not demand what the plays do not provide. There are some plays with explicit themes or definite statements about their subject matter, but a great many more offer us no abstract point beyond the commonplace. A Marxist critic—among others—would of course object that the social attitudes (conscious or unconscious) of a play like *The Man of Mode* are vital to an understanding of its reflection of historical reality. I would agree, but I would insist that such issues get us into the realm of "significance." If we are looking for "meaning" of an overt intellectual sort, we will do well to remember that it is not to be found in many of the plays.

Using Content to Interpret the Plays

Content-study in the broadest sense is basically of two kinds.

1. Plays can be used as historical documents. This is a speculative proceeding, since plays are not photographically exact reproductions of real life. They stand in changing and unstable relation to the society they reflect. But with some caution and due allowance

for inevitable error they can be usefully quarried by the historian. Southerne's *The Wives Excuse* can be taken as evidence of concern about bad marriages and the lack of a divorce law. Steele's *The Conscious Lovers* shows us part of a widespread revulsion against dueling and the increasing acceptance of merchants in polite society. It also shows us, to be sure, a set of class structures and social attitudes which are extremely revealing. These matters seem to me, however, to take us beyond textual interpretation and into the realm of historical sociology.

2. Context can be used to help understand the content of the play or its impact on the audience, though the relevance of the imported context is rarely beyond dispute. Here we quickly get hung up on the degree to which a play is "about" something. We must differentiate between a play which is quite explicitly a commentary on a social or political issue and one which simply contains topical ideas or problems. The theoretical borderline is fuzzy, but in practice the difference is usually evident enough. The attack on sale of court places in Edward Howard's *The Change of Crownes* (1667), or Sheridan's biting military commentary in *The Critic* (1779) are quite different from the responses to libertinism mirrored in *The Country-Wife* or the conflicting codes of obligation embodied in *The Conquest of Granada* (1670–71).

My concern here is solely with the sorts of problems posed in the second possibility. In the first realm Lawrence Stone can usefully search the plays for attitudes toward the family, sex, and marriage, as John Loftis can for attitudes toward the merchant, or Susan Staves for concepts of authority. Done with care, this approach can show us an interrelationship between the ideas in the plays and the overall social and intellectual climate of the time. My objects have to do with the interpretation of plays. I want to see how we can use content—ideas, values, and real-life specifics—to help us read the plays with more confidence.

One obvious problem in the use of context to interpret content is the familiar puzzle known as "the limits of veracity." Plays are art, not inedited slices of life. And though so fine a critic as Fujimura can speak in an unguarded moment of "photographic realism" in late seventeenth-century comedies,[8] I hardly need to belabor the degree to which even the soberest English-set comedies and tragedies depart from historical reality. Consider, for a start, plays that rely on tricked or illegal marriages.[9] An audience which did not turn a hair at the illegalities in *Love for Love* or *The Beaux Stratagem* simply cannot have expected realism. For the historian to whom the plays are grist for the mills of historical context, veracity is a major problem, though not necessarily an insuperable one. As John Loftis observes in a judicious study, the "refractive index" can be allowed for by an expert interpreter, and a corrective judgment applied in deducing historical or sociological data from a play.[10]

A second major difficulty lies in judging the audience and its assumptions. If twentieth-century audiences can respond in radically different ways to the same play (*Who's Afraid of Virginia Woolf* or *The Homecoming*, for example), then why should a seventeenth-century audience not respond just as variously to *Love's Last Shift* or *The Provok'd Wife*? As A. H. Scouten and I have concluded, "We see no reason to suppose that a seventeenth-century audience was any less able to enjoy a play for different reasons from different vantage points than a twentieth-century one."[11] Even in the 1660s and 1670s the best evidence available suggests considerable social, political, and moral diversity in the audience.[12] There is no doubt some truth in the longstanding equation of the moral code found in numerous comedies of the 1670s with that of a "court coterie" which formed one small part of the audience at that time. But since some of those plays held the stage unaltered for almost a century, long after the disappearance of the original audience and that coterie, we must suppose that the plays continued to hold a different

8. Fujimura, p. 52.

9. For some details see my *Development*, pp. 49–54.

10. "The Limits of Historical Veracity in Neoclassical Drama," *England in the Restoration and Early Eighteenth Century*, ed. H. T. Swedenberg, Jr. (Berkeley: Univ. of California Press, 1972), pp. 27–50.

11. See ch. 2, sec. "Carolean Plays and Their Original Audience," below.

12. See Scouten and Hume, "'Restoration Comedy' and its Audiences" (ch. 2, below), and Harold Love's excellent study, "Who Were the Restoration Audience?" *Yearbook of English Studies*, 10 (1980), 21–44.

but nonetheless potent appeal for altogether different audiences. Given the success of numerous late seventeenth-century plays on the eighteenth-century stage, we simply cannot presume that audiences demanded and got current representations of their own values and prejudices. Few pastimes are riskier than the derivation of audience values from contemporary plays.

If content-study is to be anything more than an exercise in self-delusion, two general principles must be accepted. These are recognition of 1) *pluralism* in values at all times, and 2) rapid *change* throughout the period. The dangers of uniformitarian assumptions (even within a single period) are amply illustrated by the Robertsonian school of medievalists.[13] In the realm of seventeenth-century drama we might point to scholars as otherwise diverse as Kathleen Lynch, L. C. Knights, and Aubrey Williams. Not all writers of comedy in the Carolean period despised the country, approved of fornication, sneered at cast mistresses, and believed fervently in the Tory view of the Exclusion Crisis. As soon as we start to say that libertines were admired and fallen women despised in the late seventeenth century, we are adopting a set of blinders which hamper us in dealing with plays like James Howard's *The English Mounsieur* (1663), Behn's *The Revenge* (1680), or Durfey's *The Campaigners* (1698). Chronologically, Dryden's *Amphitryon* and Shadwell's *Bury-Fair* come right together; in their values they are a world apart. Nor will we do much better to rely on tidy dichotomies: Tory versus Whig, cynical versus exemplary comedy, and so forth. The interests and values of playwrights are not so neatly defined in the seventeenth and eighteenth centuries, any more than in our own day. The idea that all members of the audience in the 1670s (for example) would respond the same way to a given situation is *ipso facto* ridiculous, and is belied by a multitude of reports of disagreements about particular plays (between Ladies and Wits, pit and gallery)—but critics continue to refer to the assumptions of the Restoration audience with sublime assurance.

13. For a cogent exposé of its methodological inadequacies, see R. S. Crane, "On Hypotheses in 'Historical Criticism': Apropos of Certain Contemporary Medievalists," *The Idea of the Humanities*, 2 vols. (Chicago: Univ. of Chicago Press, 1967), II, 236–60.

The principle of change seems even more self-evident than that of diversity. I would hardly need to argue to convince the reader that in values and outlook the plays of the late 1970s are substantially different from those of the late 1960s, yet if I make the same assertion with respect to the 1660s and 1670s I am likely to get no more than doubting acquiescence. In fact, the whole political and moral climate changes almost beyond recognition between 1668 and 1678. We move from the bright foolery of Dryden's *An Evening's Love* to the ugly sexual satire of his *Mr. Limberham*, from the flowery artificialities of Orrery's *Tryphon* to the fetid world of Rochester's *Lucina's Rape*, from the fizzy social satire of Etherege's *She wou'd if she cou'd* to the bitter reconsiderations of Shadwell's *Timon*. Similar contrasts could readily be drawn for most of the ten or fifteen year spans in the period at issue—for example, 1695 versus 1710, 1735 versus 1750. Any student of content not prepared to allow for considerable topicality in allusion and values is quickly mired in all sorts of trouble. Obviously there are many constants in both plays and conduct books between (let us say) 1675 and 1700, but casually to apply the conduct book of 1700 to the play of 1675 (or vice-versa) is at best risky, at worst direly misleading.

Always remembering, then, that the plays are vehicles written for the professional theatre, and that they display content in degrees ranging from the insignificant to the prominent and central, what can we hope to accomplish by studying the content? First, most specifically, content can help us interpret particular plays with greater confidence. The moral and marital debates of the 1670s will not tell us what *The Country-Wife* "means," but they can certainly give us some sense of how various parts of the original audience might have responded. In a similar way we can study the political impact of *Venice Preserv'd* (1682) or Henry Brooke's *Gustavus Vasa* (1739). More broadly, content study can help us see nongeneric groupings—marital discord comedy, epicurean comedy, Roman tragedy, and so forth. It can also help us understand some kinds of subgenres—gay couple comedy and reform comedy, for example. In these instances the defining feature is essentially generic (a plot device and a plot structure respectively), but making sense of the form requires an appeal to values.

I will be developing and illustrating the possibilities in the next two sections. But for the moment let us consider some of the problems. Content study offers us real possibilities but also dangerous temptations. We must not assume that because content seems to fit it should therefore be applied. The sort of contextual reading practiced by Martin Battestin can be treacherous. How do we *know* that *Joseph Andrews* should be read in the matrix supplied?[14] Even in the realm of approval or disapproval, context is a shaky criterion. One may say that a flock of rake-protagonists in the 1670s seems designed for audience empathy and conclude that Horner must be too. But this is at best a probability, and not necessarily one valid for the whole audience. When a play takes a position on a real-life subject we can usually find a good handle on it. Judging meaning or values from ideological bases extrinsic to the play is far trickier.

We must also beware of wanting to use content for purposes to which it is not suited. Here any sense of a parallel with generic study must be scrutinized with care. There is a generic history, "concerned with the changing forms of Restoration comedy," Maximillian E. Novak tells us, "but there is another history of drama in the Restoration—a history that will examine the content of the plays in terms of an intellectual milieu such as existed when *Marriage a-la-Mode*, *Epsom Wells* and *The Country Wife* were offering their audiences a glance at two different ways of life."[15] Content history is a beguiling idea, but in my opinion not one likely to work. Unlike generic study, content study cannot be usefully applied to all plays. All plays have genre, but not all plays have significant content. To establish a content-focus for a study is to exclude many plays and to grant prominence to those works which "fit," however weak or atypical they may be. One could write an account of social

14. See Battestin's *The Moral Basis of Fielding's Art* (Middletown: Wesleyan Univ. Press, 1959). I am deliberately taking an example of contextual interpretation which a great many scholars have found highly persuasive. For a counterview see Arthur Sherbo, *Studies in the Eighteenth Century Novel* (East Lansing: Michigan State Univ. Press, 1969), ch. 5.

15. "Margery Pinchwife's 'London Disease': Restoration Comedy and the Libertine Offensive of the 1670s," *Studies in the Literary Imagination*, 10 (Spring 1977), 1–23; quotation from p. 23.

attitudes, or views of marriage or morals, or politics. More specifically, one could focus on rakes, or stoicism, or use and views of the law. All of these represent useful and viable possibilities, but they would be highly selective. In each case the emphasis is on the ideas, rather than the plays. Content does not offer the continuity and comprehensiveness that genre does. If one set out to write a "content history" of English drama one would wind up writing a history of content, which is a very different matter.[16]

My assertion that "not all plays have significant content" probably needs clarification and amplification. I am speaking of ideas and real-life allusions deliberately built into the "meaning" by the author. Here again the meaning/significance distinction is crucial. Cuckolding, for example, is a widespread phenomenon in late seventeenth-century comedy. It rarely seems to mean much in a particular play, but its prevalence in these plays is clearly significant to any assessment of audience taste and values. I would, therefore, tend to study it phenomenologically rather than under the heading of "content." Durfey's *A Fond Husband* (1677), for example, seems to me to have nothing of import to say about cuckolding, but by implication quite a lot to say about the taste of Charles II, with whom it was a favorite.

Tentatively, I would suggest a) that content study cannot be usefully applied to all plays, and b) that we often cannot be certain whether the "fit" between play and extrinsic context is sufficiently good to make the appeal to context valid. Ten plays may hold a fallen woman in contempt, but this is no guarantee that the eleventh will too. With these cautions in mind let us proceed to a consideration of ideology (as opposed to topical commentary) in the drama.

Commonplace and Ideology in the Drama

Broadly speaking, I have suggested, content of three kinds is to be found in this drama: 1) commonplace (both literary and intellec-

---

16. For an overview in our period see John Loftis, "Political and Social Thought in the Drama," in *The London Theatre World*, pp. 253–85.

tual); 2) general ideology; and 3) real-life specifics. Neither close reading nor generic study offers us a good method for dealing with content, and thematic study is heavily dependent on the presence of particular subjects in any given play. (Thus a play without a gay couple is a problem for John Harrington Smith.) Clearly we need to find ways to describe values and outlook in more general terms.

Any ideological characterization of the plays (let alone the people) of a period must inevitably be a simplification and a falsification. The principle of diversity makes nonsense of our generalizations, hedge them how we may. Even if we limit our consideration to a brief period (for example, 1660–85) the heterogeneity of values is hard to ignore. As opposed to Winston Churchill and Bertrand Russell, no doubt Dryden, Bunyan, and the first earl of Shaftesbury share some common intellectual ground, but what they do not agree upon is impressive.

There is something enormously attractive in the sort of facile characterization presented by Lovejoy in his much-cited essay "The Parallel of Deism and Classicism" (1932).[17] You make a tidy checklist of nine points (uniformitarianism, rationalistic individualism, antipathy to enthusiasm and originality, intellectual equalitarianism, a negative philosophy of history, and so forth) and *voilà*, you have a characterization. The problem is that as soon as you juxtapose this account of ideology with historical particulars, contradictions start to appear. Dryden believed in progress. Was Swift an "intellectual equalitarian"? Did Pope believe in "rationalistic primitivism"?[18] Insofar as this kind of general characterization of outlook can be valid and useful, it must draw upon a precisely defined period and groups of writers or works (points on which Lovejoy falls down badly). And we must use such a characterization to suggest differences from the norm in a particular work we are trying to interpret, *not* to impose a reading on it. This restriction is frustrating but necessary. The process by which we develop a general ideological characterization is empirical, and its general validity is

17. Rpt. in A. O. Lovejoy, *Essays in the History of Ideas* (1948; rpt. New York: Capricorn, 1960), pp. 78–98.
18. I have discussed the problems of this particular characterization in *Dryden's Criticism* (Ithaca: Cornell Univ. Press, 1970), pp. 158–62.

no guarantee of its applicability to particular cases. To make the process circular—deriving the ideology from a set of plays and then reading it back into them—is obviously unsound. But quite aside from the difficulty of using the general characterization wisely, we have a considerable problem just in developing the ideological characterization.

Even if we restrict ourselves to the values to be found in plays, the problems are formidable. Ben Ross Schneider, Jr., for example, has offered us an account of *The Ethos of Restoration Comedy* which is nothing if not a salutary warning to his successors.[19] The first methodological error in this book lies in its attempt to categorize eighty-three plays over a period of some sixty years, a clear violation of the principles of diversity and change. The result is a blurring—indeed, almost an eradicating—of the traditional Restoration/sentimental dichotomy. And while I detest those terms, there does seem to be genuine difference between the values of Wilson's *The Cheats* (1663) and those of *The Conscious Lovers* (1722). Schneider manages to prove that a wide variety of plays express approval of generosity, liberality, courage, plain-dealing, and love, while taking a relatively dim view of avarice, cowardice, double-dealing, and self-love. I am not aware, however, that anyone has ever imagined the contrary. Where does a coward or a miser come off well in any play in this period? Schneider has laboriously discovered not the "ethos" of this comedy but a number of its commonplace assumptions.

The distinction between commonplace and ideology (a term I prefer to "ethos") is a simple one.[20] Commonplace is belief ingrained at the level of unexamined assumption. Sophocles does not have to argue that incest is frightful: his audience will assume exactly that. On a more everyday plane Carolean dramatists assume the audience's approval of courage, generosity, young love, and so forth. (Here we see a difference between life and literature: plenty

19. Urbana: Univ. of Illinois Press, 1971. For my review see *Philological Quarterly*, 51 (1972), 631–32.

20. For a good discussion see Michael McKeon, *Politics and Poetry in Restoration England* (Cambridge: Harvard Univ. Press, 1975), pp. 36–38.

of parents in the audience would presumably have taken a dimmer view of young love and elopement in actuality than they did of them as stage conventions.) Ideology, in contrast, is a matter of conscious and examined belief, something not believed by everyone. Ideology is a term used in many ways (often with a negative connotation), but I mean nothing grander than what John Plamenatz calls "a set of closely related beliefs or ideas, or even attitudes, characteristic of a group or community."[21] As Plamenatz goes on to say, "A set of this kind can be restricted to a very few persons or shared by many." We are concerned here with values and outlook at the level of potential disagreement. Convictions are not thought through with care and argued with vigor unless they are under attack.

Critical insistence in recent years upon the diversity of the plays has tended to set such ideological accounts as we have had of this drama in disrepute. Any monolithic approach will suffer this fate. A great many of the general characterizations of "Restoration comedy" are ideologically inclined, though they do not employ any such terminology. Critics have tended to see the plays as expressions of a libertine Court Wit ethos, a fairly direct reflection of a coterie audience. Such characterizations have generally been based on a very small sample of the plays and a simpleminded view of the relationship between theatre and audience. L. C. Knights would have us believe that the comedies are "entirely dominated by a narrow set of conventions," the first of which is contempt for marriage. As I have argued elsewhere, this is untrue.[22] Virginia Ogden Birdsall would have us believe that libertines "are exemplary of the Hobbesian thinking which prevailed in court circles after the Restoration."[23] Our first response to this astonishing idea must be to ask what Charles II, his courtiers, and his supporters thought of Hobbes. Dryden's serious plays are full of Hobbes—who serves as his source of a rationale for villains who scheme unsuccessfully to overthrow

21. John Plamenatz, *Ideology* (New York: Praeger, 1970), p. 15.
22. "The Myth of the Rake in 'Restoration Comedy'" (ch. 5 below).
23. *Wild Civility: The English Comic Spirit on the Restoration Stage* (Bloomington: Indiana Univ. Press, 1970), p. 39.

the legitimate authority in whose defense Dryden writes. Are we to conclude that the court coterie believed in Hobbes in comedy but not in tragedy?

A serious ideological characterization is going to have to start from some principles: 1) acceptance of the limitations imposed by diversity and change, 2) recognition of the difference between ideology and commonplace, 3) acknowledgement of the uncertainty of the application of any general characterization to any specific work, and 4) refusal to make easy equations between art and life. We may presume that most of the audience which flocked to *Nero* (1674) would have been less enthusiastic about watching actual torture and murder. We should not assume that the audience would have been comfortable if the sex and schemes of the comedies were translated into reality. As E. E. Stoll has argued, "Literature reflects the taste of the time rather than the time itself, and often the two are widely different. . . . We get not a faithful presentation of the men of the Restoration but a specimen of the entertainment they delighted in." [24] Taste itself is some characterization of the time, but it is an imperfect reflection and is not to be accepted uncritically. Delight in cuckolding need not be taken as evidence that it was widespread at the time or that the audience approved of it in reality.

A confusion of commonplace with ideology must inevitably break down distinctions necessary to interpretation. Crudely put, commonplace is what Dryden and Shadwell agree upon; ideology is where they generally part company. The simplest way to study commonplace is to examine the stock materials of the drama. If we ask what values late seventeenth-century plays hold in common, the answers are obvious but not terribly revealing: honesty, liberality, other ordinary decencies, the desirability of love and marriage, and the necessity of submission to just authority. In comedies and tragedies of both Whig and Tory persuasion we find a general sense of meaning and order: the moral clarity of almost all endings seems testimony to this belief. Where it is lacking (as at the end of Otway's *The Atheist*) its absence is felt with a force both terrible

24. "Literature No 'Document,'" *Modern Language Review*, 19 (1924), 141–57, esp. pp. 141 and 150.

and demoralizing. Recent critical attempts to read some of this drama as seventeenth-century "theatre of the absurd" foist twentieth-century assumptions on a drama to which they are foreign. These plays sometimes pose problems for which there was no available solution (for example, *The Wives Excuse*), but short of *The Beggar's Opera* almost every play exhibits a conviction that there *is* an order to things and that life has clearly defined meaning.

The place of religious values must be considered at this point. Particularly with regard to "Restoration comedy" critics have been far too ready to see a "post-Christian universe" in the plays, one which is "secular" and lacking "any sense of cosmic orderliness." Aubrey Williams has recently provided a welcome corrective to such views.[25] As he points out, an overwhelming majority of playwrights and playgoers throughout this period were professing Christians. That numerous serious plays, especially in the eighteenth century, overtly represent "Providential Justice" is simply a fact. Some of the Carolean Court Wits dabbled in Hobbesian and Epicurean ideas, but they did not write plays essentially hostile to a Christian view of the world. The real question is the extent to which Christianity affects the values of the plays and colors the response of the audience.[26]

Granted, the writers were Christians. They did not, however, put much Christianity directly into the plays. And the audience did not automatically judge events in plays by the standards of real life. The essence of Williams' position assumes the applicability of extrinsic standards. Were they, in fact, applied? Williams finds the presence of religious language (such terms as Providence, salvation, damnation, and grace) in Congreve's plays a signal that such values were being invoked. These terms may have worked this way for some part of the audience. But as Harriett Hawkins suggests,

25. See particularly Williams' "Of 'One Faith': Authors and Auditors in the Restoration Theatre," *Studies in the Literary Imagination*, 10 (Spring 1977), 57–76, and *An Approach to Congreve* (New Haven: Yale Univ. Press, 1979). On "secular" accounts of Congreve in particular see p. ix of the book.

26. For specific responses to Professor Williams see "'Restoration Comedy' and its Audiences" (ch. 2, below), and my review, *English Language Notes*, 17 (1980), 222–26.

seventeenth-century libertine poetry is full of religious imagery, and we cannot discount the possibility of irony.[27] Critics since Norman Holland have seen a serious religious dimension to the end of *Love for Love*, for example. Curiously enough, Jeremy Collier saw it too, finding it outrageous and distasteful. And when Congreve replied to Collier's attack, he did not choose to couch his defense in religious terms.[28] Indeed, we have remarkably little contemporary evidence of positive response to comedies in religious terms.

Religion falls at the level of commonplace in the comedies of the period, and as a result matters of Christian faith and judgment rarely seem to affect the generic conventions of the comedies. Even in the serious drama, where religion is a more frequent and explicit issue, Christianity is rarely much thought about. Where invoked, it is treated as a verity to be acknowledged or demonstrated, not as a debatable proposition. Argument can occur only where there are alternatives. Consequently religion is rarely an important ideological factor in this drama.

The key to ideology is not commonplace but factional conviction. The Tory verities of the Carolean period make no sense as isolated phenomena; they are necessary and significant only if there is a counterview. To define ideology we must seek its basis in differences of outlook. In comedies of this period views of sex and marriage are generally paramount; in tragedies government and kingship or codes of personal obligation tend to be crucial to the plays' underlying sense of order and purpose. The differences are usually obvious enough. The political outlook of *Don Sebastian* (1689) is not that of *Tamerlane* (1701); the values of *Love and a Bottle* (1698) are decidedly not those of *The Funeral* (1701). We are talking here not about genre, not about affective design, and not even about a conceptual meaning which the audience is supposed to notice or deduce. Rather, we are concerned with those assumptions which

27. *Likenesses of Truth in Elizabethan and Restoration Drama* (Oxford: Clarendon Press, 1972), pp. 105–7.
28. See *Amendments of Mr. Collier's False and Imperfect Citations, The Complete Works of William Congreve*, ed. Montague Summers, 4 vols. (Soho: Nonesuch, 1923), III, 169–206.

ultimately govern the play's tone and feeling—and more broadly, the perception it embodies of the nature of its world.

Some attempt at an outline of the ideological bases to be found in this drama seems in order. By definition, one cannot validly characterize a *single* ideology for any period, however restrictively defined. If "Restoration drama" includes both Dryden and Shadwell, then it does not reduce to a single ideological base. Acknowledging the principles of diversity and change compels us to admit that we will always find two or more competing ideologies, and that we must define and explain the subperiods in which we propose to work.

Drama is topical enough that one can trace its response to history closely from decade to decade, and even at times from year to year. But where outlook in a broader sense is at issue, I would distinguish three overlapping eras covering the period 1660–1800, each of which presents distinctive ideological characteristics. These are (I) The Stuart Court World, 1660–1714; (II) The Whig Mercantile Supremacy, 1688–1789; and (III) The Age of Unrest, 1763–1832. The Restoration returned the country to a divine-right monarchy, but nothing could really restore confidence in that form of government. Prevailing views of the structure of the world, the nature of authority, and the natural order were fundamentally altered by the Civil War and the beheading of the king. No successor could sit altogether securely on the throne, and there must always have been a sense that Humpty-Dumpty's heirs could come off the wall too. The Exclusion Crisis of 1678–83 is testimony to a new sense that the succession could be subject to parliamentary acquiesence. Charles staved off the challenge, but when in 1688 William of Orange was invited to displace James II, the country confirmed a radical alteration of its concept of authority.[29] The more limited monarchy established under William and Mary was reconfirmed in 1714 when a foreigner became king in circumstances which made growth

29. For a good discussion of the effects of the Civil War on concepts of authority and obligation in the state see Susan Staves, *Players' Scepters: Fictions of Authority in the Restoration* (Lincoln: Univ. of Nebraska Press, 1979), chs. 1 and 2.

of parliamentary authority inevitable. The Whig supremacy that flourished under Walpole had no definite terminus, but had clearly passed by the start of the French Revolution. It gave way gradually to what I am choosing to call The Age of Unrest. I take as a starting point 1763 (the Peace of Paris), as an endpoint the Reform Bill of 1832. The strains evident in Burke's *Thoughts on the Present Discontents* (1770) become more serious during the years of the colonial insurrection. What would have happened without a French Revolution we cannot be sure. That event, and the Napoleonic Wars, created an intensely repressive climate in England in which public protest against the existing order was severely discouraged.

The evil effects of the Licensing Act make the reflection of these eras in the drama after 1737 less clear than might otherwise have been the case, but we may fairly say that English drama reflects these historical divisions. Carolean drama (1660–85) is markedly different from that of the nineties and later. The changeover becomes pronounced in the late eighties, just as the transition into the Whig era begins. A great deal remains unchanged: theatre is an inherently conservative business, and its dependence on stock repertory reinforces that conservatism. But just in the handling of cuckolding actions we can see a marked shift between 1675 and 1695. The "Restoration stereotypes" (as John Loftis dubs them) survive substantially intact until about 1710 and do not really get "displaced" until the 1730s,[30] but we can nonetheless see a decisive shift in values by the mid-nineties. There is another great shift in the 1770s and 1780s. That one is really beyond my scope here, but we may say in brief that it stems from a quickening social activism (muted by censorship) and a move toward subjectivity in dramatic character reflecting the social, political, and cultural movements evident in England at the end of the eighteenth century.[31]

For the purposes of this study I am primarily concerned with two periods. The first starts with exceptional precision in 1660, begins to fade as the Whig era dawns in 1688, and reaches a clear

30. Loftis, *Comedy and Society*, 4 and 5.
31. For the best discussion of this complex transition see Joseph W. Donohue, Jr., *Dramatic Character in the English Romantic Age* (Princeton: Princeton Univ. Press, 1970).

terminus in 1714. The second commences with the Glorious Revolution and flourishes during the first half of the eighteenth century, finally suffering a decisive eclipse with the social and political changes attendant upon the French Revolution.

The key factor in any ideological differentiation is obviously the Revolution of 1688. The central tenet of a very large number of serious plays in the Carolean period is chivalric obligation, a sense of authority and duty which the eighteenth century replaces with concepts derived from contract law.[32] The difference is that between the Stuart theory of divine-right kingship and the limited monarchy established in 1688. The rhymed heroic play, essentially a phenomenon of the 1660–78 part of the Carolean period, has recently been described by J. Douglas Canfield in such terms. "The rhymed heroic play is closely identifiable with the Restoration proper. These plays are politically reactionary. They are anti-Republican, anti-Puritan, as well as anti-Hobbist, anti-Epicurean. . . . They are also Re-storation in the sense that they are a re-storying of the feudal, hierarchical, Classical-Christian *Weltanschauung*. . . . These playwrights . . . sought to rearticulate the code which gave aristocracy validity, the code which portrayed society as essentially patriarchal, united . . . by the bonds of obligement."[33] The much more specifically political plays written during the "Crisis of Confidence" 1678–83 are largely Tory, and for the most part continue to uphold the Stuart verities. But shortly after the revolution a new sort of play starts to appear. Bancroft's(?) *King Edward the Third* (1690) is an example—one of many plays suggesting that a tyrant can legitimately be overthrown. Susan Staves calls such plays "democratic romances," a term I do not care for. The point is not democracy but limited monarchy: the assumption is that a king has obligations to his people and that he forfeits his position if he fails to meet them. The Tory plays of the Carolean period are divine-

32. John Wallace is at work on an important book on this subject. For the present see his "John Dryden's Plays and the Conception of an Heroic Society," *Culture and Politics From Puritanism to the Enlightenment*, ed. Perez Zagorin (Berkeley: Univ. of California Press, 1980), pp. 113–34.

33. "The Significance of the Restoration Rhymed Heroic Play," *Eighteenth-Century Studies*, 13 (1979), 49–62.

right drama; the Whig counterpart after 1688 might be dubbed political libertarian drama. Numerous plays right through the century preach the message that tyranny must not be tolerated and that even those who die in vain rebellion have died gloriously, as Southerne suggests in *The Fate of Capua* (1700).[34]

The social changes engendered by the Glorious Revolution are less quick to develop and harder to trace, but the gradual alteration in the stereotypes of merchants and the treatment of commerce traced by Loftis between 1688 and 1737 are clearly part of a concomitant change in comedy. More fundamental yet is a basic alteration in the predominant view of human nature. The difference is evident in the long-standing distinction between cynical and sentimental comedy— a distinction for which I prefer the terms harsh and humane comedy. The change is paralleled in comic theory in the move from contemptuous to sympathetic laughter so well traced by Stuart Tave.[35]

If I may be permitted a grandiose generalization, I would suggest that late seventeenth-century plays tend to present "problems" in their dramatic action which are external, while in the eighteenth century many of the plays deal with problems internal to the characters and hence soluble by a change of mind or heart. Contrary examples are easy to find: *The English Mounsieur* (1663) turns on true love dictating reform, and plenty of eighteenth-century comedies (for example, Centlivre's *The Busie Body*, 1709) rely on purely external blocking factors. Nonetheless, I would assert that circa 1688 playwrights start to move increasingly toward a view of character which assumes that man can be good, and that a great many of life's problems are solved by his learning to recognize and act on the virtuous impulses of his heart. This idea underlies the "reform comedy" subgenre which flourishes during the eighteenth century. The distinction comes down to belief or disbelief in the intractability of human nature. One of the most obvious ideological splits in this drama occurs over this issue, and is perhaps clearest in the

34. For a brief account of some of these plays see Clement Ramsland, "Britons Never Will be Slaves: A Study in Whig Political Propaganda in the British Theatre, 1700–1742," *Quarterly Journal of Speech*, 28 (1942), 393–99.

35. *The Amiable Humorist: A Study in the Comic Theory and Criticism of the Eighteenth and Early Nineteenth Centuries* (Chicago: Univ. of Chicago Press, 1960).

difference between those marital discord plays which see no solutions (*The Wives Excuse, The Provok'd Wife*) and those which offer us resolution and reconciliation based on a change of heart in the protagonists (*The Lady's last Stake, The Provok'd Husband*).[36]

Generalization is all very well, but proving a difference in outlook between *The Country-Wife* and *The Recruiting Officer* is no great trick. More to the point, how do we distinguish ideologically between plays close together in time? I would suggest that the reader consider some pairings of plays in light of the following questions. What motivates the characters? (Is motivation much of an issue?) Is progress possible?—or failing that, decency? Are the ways of the world protested by the author? Accepted? Accepted happily? Is the view of human nature harsh and satiric? Humane and tolerant? Crusading and monitory? What seems to be the source of order and meaning in the world of the play? What are the characters' assumptions about social class or legitimate authority? What is the nature of the "problem" which underlies the play's action?

The following groupings are set up to suggest both ideological similarity (second column) and sharp ideological differences (third column).

Marriage A-la-Mode (1671)	*Love in a Wood* (1671)	*Epsom-Wells* (1672)
The Spanish Fryar (1680)	*The Loyal Brother* (1682)	*Lucius Junius Brutus* (1680)
Amphitryon (1690)	*Sir Anthony Love* (1690)	*Bury-Fair* (1689)
The Twin-Rivals (1702)	*The Modish Husband* (1702)	*The Lying Lover* (1703)

At later dates one might contrast *The Provok'd Husband* with *The Beggar's Opera* (both 1728), or *The School for Guardians* (1767) with *False Delicacy* (1768).

I see no reason to get into a point-by-point demonstration. The values of *Amphitryon* are not those of *Bury-Fair*, and the chivalric

36. For a discussion see "Marital Discord in English Comedy from Dryden to Fielding" (ch. 6, below).

assumptions of *The Spanish Fryar* are a world apart from the celebration of the founding of a republic in *Lucius Junius Brutus*. Where commonplace is often just about invisible, a matter of the dog *not* barking during the night, ideology is much more explicit. And while I am not convinced that we can safely or usefully characterize large groups of plays in ideological terms, I would maintain that we ought to be able to identify the values of most single plays, especially in contrast with others of markedly dissimilar outlook. Is appetite, principle, or money the dominant motive? Are we in a harsh world or one in which kindness and decency can prevail? Does the play show us an ugly world? An unchangeable world? A decent world?

The reader may well ask why, if such derivation of values is feasible, critics have had so hard a time with many of the plays. One answer is simply that some celebrated plays (*The Plain-Dealer*, *The Man of Mode*) are relatively ambiguous. I suspect, however, that much of the problem lies with the critical methods employed. Scholars have been concerned primarily with genre, or affective impact, or a meaning to be derived from close reading. Values are not meaning. Another reason that scholars have had problems identifying the values in this drama is simple prejudice. Moral hostility (or skittishness) so blinded whole generations of critics that they mistook the presence of libertine elements for approval of them. And to assume that Carolean comedy (for example) is a direct reflection of the real world is a good way to mix up the implicit and explicit values of the comedies with those of that hypothetical coterie audience.

The whole issue of "What would the original audience have thought of this?" is, in my opinion, largely a red herring. Some knowledge of social and stage conventions is an advantage to a reader and may indeed be vital if the author's irony is to be correctly understood. However, Richard Levin's conclusions for Renaissance drama seem to me valid in our period as well: "The ideas and attitudes necessary to guide our response are established in the plays themselves." Indeed, Levin goes so far as to ask whether there is "any major English Renaissance drama where we would go seriously wrong in our interpretation without a special knowledge of

some idea of the time."[37] The system of internal rewards and punishments common throughout late seventeenth- and eighteenth-century comedies and tragedies, and the writers' habit of making disapproval or ridicule explicit, should not leave us in much doubt about what is approved and what disapproved. Subtle readings create complexities essentially foreign to most of these works as stage plays. I would conclude, therefore, that the ideological assumptions of most of these plays should not be unduly difficult to define.

Real-Life Specifics in the Drama

When we turn from general ideological outlook to real-life specifics (including topical commentary that reflects ideology) we face a new set of problems. Plays can, of course, be written about a recognizable real-life subject in the fashion of Hochhuth's *The Deputy* or Brecht's *Galileo*. But this is rare in any period and exceedingly so in the one at issue here. Beyond a few plays, we are going to have to look for less conspicuous and clear-cut forms of specific content. Our first task, then, must be to identify the forms in which such content appears in these plays. The possibilities are basically fourfold: 1) focus on an abstract theme, 2) overt concern with topical or social issues, 3) direct representation of real-life particulars within a literary context (with or without disguise), and 4) allegory or parallelism. These will be the subjects of the next four subsections. In each case my object will be to point out some plays which possess the kind of content at issue and to consider briefly how it can be identified and discussed with profit.

Specific Content 1: Themes

No critical method has been more abused in the last twenty years than "thematic reading." The critic seizes upon a play, determines that it must be "about" some central theme (appearance ver-

37. *New Readings vs. Old Plays* (Chicago: Univ. of Chicago Press, 1979), p. 166.

sus reality, avarice, disorder, self-discipline, social hierarchy, true faith, or what have you), and proceeds to demonstrate (after a fashion) that the play does indeed display this central idea. Few plays, in fact, are actually designed and written to illustrate abstract propositions, and the contradictory discoveries promulgated by the thematicists are more bewildering than illuminating. Renaissance drama has been the principal hunting ground for thematic study, but many of the weakest and least useful studies of drama in our period have employed this technique. A quick survey of recent readings of *The Country-Wife*—a celebrated tangle already referred to—shows just how unproductive the approach proves. The play has been variously read as a Hobbesian view of the world, an anatomy of masculinity, a comment on impotence and self-destruction, a satire on folly, a demonstration of the difference between love and lust, an analysis of marriage, a satire on selfishness, an account of "the question of freedom," a satire on jealousy, and an anatomy of lust (among other things).

The unsatisfactoriness of thematic reading has been well argued by Richard Levin, a demonstration I need not repeat here.[38] The crucial question, obviously, is whether the play is "about" its characters and action or "about" an idea. This is not to deny that many plays present characters and actions in which ideas are implicit, or to claim that those plays which do exist primarily to communicate ideas do not need characters and actions to carry them out. R. S. Crane explains the distinction cogently in his well-known discrimination of "plots of action," "plots of character," and "plots of thought."[39] All plays have some "thought" component, but it rarely takes precedence over action and characters. Where the action and characters seem to exist primarily as a way of displaying an idea, then we have a special sort of drama, one in which a central theme may indeed be the heart of the play. There are such plays. Levin points to the moralities. At the risk of provoking an irrele-

38. See Levin, *New Readings*, esp. ch. 2. This book incorporates several important articles, including Levin's widely cited "Some Second Thoughts on Central Themes," *Modern Language Review*, 67 (1972), 1–10.

39. "The Concept of Plot and the Plot of *Tom Jones*," *Critics and Criticism* (Chicago: Univ. of Chicago Press, 1952), pp. 616–47.

vant argument, I would suggest that *Waiting for Godot* and *The Iceman Cometh* are plays essentially designed to communicate a central idea.

Plenty of writers in the 1600–1800 period are fond of pulling tidy morals out at the end of a play. Almost all of these morals, however, are commonplaces—the virtue of honesty or true love, the folly of lust or avarice, or what have you. These are by no means central themes. Only a few of the plays are even arguably designed around such a theme. Otway's savage *Friendship in Fashion* (1678) does genuinely seem to me such a play—put together specifically to show up the mores of high society in London.[40] A number of Shadwell's plays seem to me to verge on thematic design, perhaps preeminently *The Squire of Alsatia* (1688) with its extensive comparison of "country" and "city" schemes of education.[41]

Specific Content 2: Social Commentary

Social commentary is an altogether commoner phenomenon in these plays. I am making a two-way distinction here. What a play like Wycherley's *Love in a Wood* (1671) says about cits, rakes, love, and avarice, or Cibber's *The Careless Husband* (1704) about marital fidelity, does not transcend the commonplace. Topical problems or prejudices are invoked, but only to help elicit predictable responses. Plays with genuine social commentary (*Epsom-Wells* or *The Beaux Stratagem*, in direct contrast with the previous pair) either contradict the commonplace or at least ask the audience to think more seriously about it. Social commentary is neither commonplace nor specific historical allusion. Hence my second distinction. A play which presents historical particulars (whether generalized as the sequestration committee or individually in "personated" characters) is very different from one which simply offers a viewpoint on a fairly general topic like Jacobites or fallen women.[42]

40. I have discussed the play at length in "Otway and the Comic Muse" (ch. 3, below).

41. For an analysis, see my *Development*, pp. 78–86.

42. A similar kind of distinction is often made between burlesque (general take-off on a form) and travesty (specific parody of a literary work). The latter depends upon an absolutely specific target.

The commonest subjects for social commentary are libertinism and marital discord. The commentary is occasionally so explicit that there is no missing it, as in Steele's *The Lying Lover* (1703) or Cibber's *The Lady's last Stake* (1707). More often, one needs some sense of context to see that a serious statement is being made. Consider Otway's *The Atheist* (1683). Anyone can see that Otway is telling us something about libertinism and failed marriage in Courtine and Sylvia. But for the couple's distress to work for us, we need to have seen their courtship in Otway's popular *The Souldiers Fortune* (1680). And the play makes fullest sense in the context of a debate about marriage which had raged throughout the 1670s.[43]

Dryden's *Marriage A-la-Mode* (1671) and Shadwell's *Epsom-Wells* (1672) are among the well-known plays taking a clear-cut position on the marriage debate, but they are by no means alone, even in the 1670s. Edward Howard's *The Womens Conquest* (1670) and *The Six days Adventure* (1671) are bad plays which deserved their failure. Both attempt, however, a serious presentation of the problem of women's rights, and the former even tackles the vexed matter of divorce law. Many of the plays containing social commentary are problem plays. Southerne's *The Wives Excuse* (1691), Vanbrugh's *The Provok'd Wife* (1697), and Fielding's *The Modern Husband* (1732) come to mind. Others, more didactic, attempt explicit answers: Shadwell's *The Scowrers* (1690), Steele's *The Tender Husband* (1705), Johnson's *The Wife's Relief* (1711).

One of the oddities in the history of criticism of this drama is the lack of attention to social commentary in the plays. Many critics, to be sure, have assumed that the comedies are so artificial as to be largely irrelevant to anything but their own separate reality—a problem which haunts Kathleen Lynch's *The Social Mode of Restoration Comedy* (1926). Even so, we might have expected a major book to appear by now called *Social Criticism in Restoration Comedy*. Curiously enough, we have had to wait into the 1980s for

43. For relevant background see Lawrence Stone, *The Family, Sex and Marriage in England, 1500–1800* (New York: Harper & Row, 1977), and more particularly Joseph L. Greenberg, "English Marriage and Restoration Comedy, 1688–1710,"

the first serious study of moral questions in this drama, a desideratum finally supplied by John T. Harwood.[44] Going beyond meaning and into significance, I cannot forbear pointing out the obvious need for a book to be called something like *The Sociology of Restoration Comedy*—a study which might best be written by a Marxist-trained critic who has grown disenchanted with his dogma.

Specific Content 3: Contemporary Particulars

The representation of contemporary particulars remains a neglected subject. A few cases are well known, most notably the lampooning of Walpole in *The Beggar's Opera* and *The Historical Register*, Shaftesbury's appearance as masochist and foot-fetishist in *Venice Preserv'd*, and Dryden's appearance as Bayes in *The Rehearsal*. As a rule such matters are categorized under the general heading of "satire." We are, in fact, dealing with three distinguishable phenomena: general political satire, personation, and literary satire. Some plays manage two or even three of these at once, but for analytic purposes the distinction is convenient.

1. Political smears were risky at best. Author and actors risked suppression and occasionally physical violence. In consequence, open derogation is rare. For Sir Robert Howard to trample (*ex post facto*) upon the sequestration policies of the Puritans in *The Committee* (1662) was safe enough and at that date popular with his Cavalier audience. But for Edward Howard to put Asinello, a country gentleman come to town to buy a place at Court, in *The Change of Crownes* (1667) got the play suppressed, even though it is technically set in Naples.[45] The angry Charles II also silenced the King's Company and imprisoned John Lacy, who had played Asinello. Had the king turned a blind eye (or been out of town) we might assume

---

Diss. Princeton Univ. 1976, esp. chs. 1 and 2, and Novak's "Margery Pinchwife's 'London Disease.'"

44. *Critics, Values, and Restoration Comedy* (Carbondale: Southern Illinois Univ. Press, 1982).

45. The play was of course not printed and only came to light in manuscript in 1946. See *The Change of Crownes*, ed. Frederick S. Boas (London: Oxford Univ. Press, 1949).

the satiric intent, but we would lack the validation of contemporary reaction. In this case we are really dealing with a parallel, and only the violence of the response elicited makes it discussable in more than hypothetical terms.

Most comedies indulging in serious political satire, personation, or a combination thereof take care to wrap them in a distracting context, often a literary one. *The Rehearsal, The Historical Register,* and *The Critic* all work this way. One of the few which does not, John Tatham's *The Rump* (Spring 1660), savages a variety of Commonwealth leaders, but does so at a time when the individuals involved were increasingly discredited and there was no strong government in London to regulate theatrical activity.[46] When Aphra Behn rewrote the piece as *The Roundheads* (1681) she was making a more typical political use of the material. Deriding Puritans during the Exclusion Crisis was a pretty safe business, indulged in by many of the Tory writers. Here the attack is almost indirect: the audience understood that Puritan cits stood for Whigs, and prologues and epilogues touted the plays' "loyalty"—a code word understood by everyone.

2. Personation was one of the recurrent games played by dramatists in this period. It was done for literary and political reasons as well as for purely personal ones. The first two times Pepys saw Shadwell's *The Sullen Lovers* (1668) he found it "tedious" and "very contemptible," but on the third occasion, informed that "by Sir Positive At-all is meant Sir Robert Howard," he was suddenly "well pleased with it" (5 May 1668). The personal satire on Sir William Coventry and Sir John Duncomb in Sir Robert Howard and Buckingham's *The Country Gentleman* (banned before performance in 1669) is attested to by the public uproar which got the angry victims thrown in prison and by Pepys' detailed account of the whole imbroglio. Within the play itself, however, there is nothing which ordinary playgoers could seize upon to make the identification. Sir Cautious Trouble-all and Sir Gravity Empty are no more

---

46. On *The Rump* see my *Development*, p. 239, and Gunnar Sorelius, "The Early History of the Restoration Theatre: Some Problems Reconsidered," *Theatre Notebook*, 33 (1979), 52–61.

than good butts.[47] Here again the identification depends upon someone's tipping the audience about the key.

There is a real possibility that the audience (or some members of it) will apply the wrong key and will find that it "works." Etherege's *The Man of Mode* (1676) might well have been viewed by its original audience as an *à clef* composition, and a number of later commentators (notably Dennis) suggest that Dorimant represents Rochester. Yet within a week of the premiere Peter Killigrew wrote to his sister that everyone was trying "to discover the persons meant by it. I find the general opinion will have Sr Fopling to be Mr. Villers, Ld Grandisons eldest son. Mr. Batterton under the name of Dorimant means the Duke of Monmouth & his intrigue with Moll Kirke, Mrs. Needham, & Lady Harriott Wentworth."[48] Few scholars accept these identifications, but on what grounds could we decide to do so?

Is Nat. Lee aiming at Rochester in *The Princess of Cleve* (1682)?[49] Crowne admitted only to pillorying Titus Oates as Dr. Sanchy in *City Politiques* (1682); he received a severe cudgeling for satirizing Rochester in the same play. But where I would see Florio as the offending character, John Harold Wilson opts for Artall.[50] Is Bartoline to be identified with Sir John Maynard? or Aaron Smith? Is Craffy an attack on Samuel Pordage? Is the Lord Podesta a satiric depiction of Sir Robert Clayton? We might presume that Codshead in *The Triumphant Widow* (acted in 1674) represents Elkanah Settle, because the angry Settle tells us so in his preface to *Ibrahim* (1676), but we cannot afford to forget Gay's snide remark about satire: " 'Tis so pat to all the tribe, / Each cries 'That was leveled at me.' "[51]

47. See *The Country Gentleman*, ed. Arthur H. Scouten and Robert D. Hume (Philadelphia: Univ. of Pennsylvania Press, 1976).

48. Joseph Spence, *Observations, Anecdotes, and Characters of Books and Men*, 2 vols., ed. James M. Osborn (Oxford: Clarendon Press, 1966), II, 638.

49. For a fuller discussion, see "The Satiric Design of Nat. Lee's *The Princess of Cleve*" (ch. 4 below).

50. *City Politiques*, ed. John Harold Wilson (Lincoln: Univ. of Nebraska Press, 1967), p. xvii. For contemporary comments recently printed by Michael de L. Landon, see *Theatre Notebook*, 31 (1977), 38.

51. *The Beggar's Opera*, Air XXX.

Perhaps Dryden was after Lauderdale (or someone else?) in *Mr. Limberham* (1678). Very possibly Otway was sniping at Shadwell in *The Atheist*. We know that personation was common, but we can seldom be certain of such identifications. With Samuel Foote, who made a whole career of such hits, we more or less know where we are. But even with Fielding certainty does not extend very far. In principle we might suppose that personation should be easier to prove than broader parallels. In practice this turns out not to be true—in part because a crucial element in most personations lies in the acting.[52]

3. With literary satire we are on surer ground. We have not yet solved all the puzzles in *The Rehearsal* (1671), but we are in no doubt about the authors' views of the 1660s plays it ridicules. Perhaps Davenant was the butt of the "1665" version (unstaged and lost). George McFadden has argued convincingly for a significant admixture of political satire, largely directed against Lord Arlington.[53] Indeed, *The Rehearsal* is a good example of the problems context can pose in determining extraliterary meaning. The literary allusions are numerous and mostly obvious, but personal identifications in this realm are much less so. Given the political nature of Bayes' drama we would be foolish not to check the possibilities of political satire by parallel. And ever mindful of Fielding's habit of hiding a political butt under a literary one, we must watch out for that in the earlier play. Knowing Buckingham's intense involvement in Court politics and parliamentary intrigue, one must surely investigate possible parallels from his activities—and given the six or more year span of composition we must be alert to holdovers, perhaps fragmentary ones, in the 1671 version.[54]

52. Consider Pepys' report of "great factions at Court," 15 January 1669. "It is about my Lady Harvy's being offended at Doll Common's [Katherine Corey's] acting of Sempronia [in a revival of Jonson's *Catiline*] to imitate her—for which she got my Lord Chamberlain, her kinsman, to imprison Doll; which my Lady Castlemayne made the King to release her, and to order her to act it again worse then ever the other day where the King himself was. And since it was acted again and my Lady Harvy provided people to hiss her and fling oranges at her."

53. "Political Satire in *The Rehearsal*," *Yearbook of English Studies*, 4 (1974), 120–28.

54. The rehearsal play (and more broadly those commenting on the theatre) represent a whole subgenre. For a descriptive account see Dane Farnsworth Smith,

Literary satires range from the personal smears of *The Female Wits* (1696), an attack on Manley, Pix, and Trotter, to the highly sophisticated efforts of Fielding and Sheridan, aimed at multiple targets (including political ones) and based on serious principles. Joseph Arrowsmith's *The Reformation* (1672?) is a splendid lampoon on Dryden; its basis is moral objections to *Marriage A-la-Mode*—based on a misreading of Dryden's play, in my opinion, but none the less biting and amusing for that. To this tract Duffett's raucous burlesques of Dorset Garden spectaculars make a sharp contrast. *The Mock-Tempest* (1674) and *Psyche Debauch'd* (1675), in particular, are wonderfully effective travesties. In the eighteenth century Gay, Fielding, and Foote are distinguished contributors to this mode.

Specific Content 4: Allegory and Parallelism

Direct allegory is an extreme rarity in this drama. Dryden's *Albion and Albanius* (1685) is the only prominent example, an opera designed to hymn the Restoration and Charles II's safe passage through the tumult of the Exclusion Crisis. Indirect allegory is a different matter, and a vexed one. As John Wallace has observed: "The attempt to understand the relation between history and literature in the seventeenth century encounters the problem of allegory immediately. The more closely we read certain plays and non-dramatic poems, the more they seem to be offering covert advice on contemporary politics, and the greater is the temptation to translate their figures (in both senses) into topical allusions." [55] The plays are full of seeming parallels to contemporary figures and events. How are we to interpret these apparent allusions with confidence? Wallace proceeds to argue (very convincingly) that seventeenth-

Plays about the Theatre in England from 'The Rehearsal' to the Licensing Act in 1737 (London: Oxford Univ. Press, 1936), and Dane Farnsworth Smith and M. L. Lawhon, *Plays about the Theatre in England, 1737–1800* (Lewisburg: Bucknell Univ. Press, 1979).

55. "Dryden and History: A Problem in Allegorical Reading," *ELH*, 36 (1969), 265–90, and his "'Examples Are Best Precepts': Readers and Meanings in Seventeenth-Century Poetry," *Critical Inquiry*, 1 (1974), 273–90.

century authors leave readers to draw their own precepts and parallels, that we tend to misread works with a "historical" basis because we ignore the capacity for extrapolation "which Dryden took for granted" in his readers. We are, Wallace suggests, both "too cautious" in exploring the historical relevance of a work, and "too quick" to seize on topical "allegories." We should be less worried about whether political references are "in" a work or whether "we have put them there"; since "construction of parallels was the most popular game of the century," we should assume that writers expected it. But merely "to allegorize the historizing poems is to defeat the purpose for which they were written" if in doing so we "insist that the historical view is . . . merely a metaphorical account of recent events with an implied moral." If Wallace is correct in seeing historical works as deliberately contrived to give the reader "pleasure" which "lies in inferring a relevance the poet never stated," then we must try to revise our twentieth-century assumptions about proof of allusion.

That numerous plays, especially in the late seventeenth century, allude fairly directly to contemporary events cannot be doubted. Crowne's *The Misery of Civil-War* (1680) and *Henry VI* (1681), coming at the times they do, could not be anything but warnings against toppling Charles II's government. Shadwell's *The Lancashire Witches* (1681) was heavily cut by the censor because of its presentation of a rogue priest. A year earlier Dryden's *The Spanish Fryar* and Settle's *The Female Prelate* had passed unscathed, but the political situation had changed rapidly and by late 1681 open hostility to Catholicism constituted a partisan statement. The audience was certainly alert to the likelihood of parallels, and Dryden's bland disclaimers notwithstanding *The Duke of Guise* (1682) could hardly be taken as anything but a slam at the Whigs in general and Monmouth in particular. Southerne's *The Loyal Brother* in the same year, despite its Persian setting, is a blunt defense of the loyal and much-maligned brother of a king beset by ambitious traitors. Not many members of the audience could have been too dense to make the application. Dryden's *Cleomenes* (1692), with its noble king in exile, is by no means an allegorical representation of James

II: a close set of historical parallels would unquestionably have got the play banned. Instead Dryden reminds the audience of the deposed king, hoping that his noble portrayal of Cleomenes will carry over.

Otway's *Venice Preserv'd* (1682) makes an interesting test case. The subtitle (*A Plot Discover'd*) is an open signal to the audience to hunt for parallels. Many scholars have viewed both Renault and Antonio as hostile depictions of Shaftesbury, which his biographer K. H. D. Haley takes as "a *reductio ad absurdum*." I must agree with John Loftis, however, that since Otway is not writing systematic allegory, such double portrayal is perfectly plausible.[56] Any attempt to read *Venice Preserv'd* as a direct parallel breaks down immediately: the corrupt Senate of Venice cannot be read as a flattering account of the Tories and Charles II. The point for the seventeenth-century reader would seem to be that plotting against the government, even one so corrupt and inefficient as that represented by Antonio, is destructive and counterproductive.

What are we to make of a case such as Tate's *Richard the Second*? Announced by the King's Company in December 1680 and immediately banned, it was staged a month later disguised as *The Sicilian Usurper*. The disguise was soon penetrated and the lord chamberlain promptly silenced the company. When the play was published Tate complained indignantly that he should not be held accountable for parallels drawn by others. Tate did indeed raise and ennoble Richard, while turning Bolingbroke into a seditious rabble-rouser. But to show a king (however wise, kind, and sinned-against) deposed and murdered proved unacceptable to the authorities. Quite possibly Tate, a Whig sympathizer, had hoped to slip an example of regicide past the censor. The succession to the throne was always a touchy subject, as John Banks found to his cost. *The Innocent Usurper* (ca. 1683?), about Lady Jane Grey, was banned in the eighties and refused again by the authorities in 1694. *The Island Queens* (1684), about Mary Queen of Scots, was finally performed in 1704 with alterations. Banks' denial of any "intent to pattern with these

56. "Political and Social Thought in the Drama," esp. pp. 261–62.

Times" in his preface to the former may be perfectly honest: his interest lay in pathos, not politics. But the response of the authorities to these plays suggests the prevalence of parallel-mongering.

Because parallel-drawing was more a seventeenth- than an eighteenth-century game, there is no eighteenth-century equivalent to the flock of 1680s political plays. The "Majesty misled" theme is common in Walpole-era tragedies and could at times provoke the censor's wrath, as it did for Thomson's *Edward and Eleonora* (1739). The plays which did best were usually those which offered sufficient ambiguity to put them above clear party bias. Addison's *Cato* (1713) is the famous example; Thomson's *Tancred and Sigismunda* (1745) is another.

In some instances the parallelism is beyond reasonable argument. That Bevill Higgons' *The Generous Conquerour* (1702) expresses Jacobite views is self-evident, and we have extrinsic testimony to the unusual nature of the audience which flocked to its first night.[57] But with many an apparent parallel there is no way to determine whether the author foresaw it and hoped that the audience would draw it. Watching Sir Robert Howard's *The Duke of Lerma* Pepys was distressed: "the play designed to reproach our King with his mistresses, that I was troubled for it, and expected it should be interrupted. . . . Its design I did not like of reproaching the King" (20 February 1668). Coming from Howard such an allusion is not unthinkable, but we have no other evidence of such a reaction. *The Maid's Tragedy* was played regularly throughout the 1660s and 1670s, apparently without unflattering parallels being drawn, but then it was an old play.[58] Few critical problems in this drama are as frustrating as the matter of parallelism. It occurs, but we may suspect it oftener than we can prove it.

Reflecting on the various guises in which specific content appears in plays of this period, one should be struck at once by how rarely any play depends centrally upon such extrinsic material. Even *The Rehearsal* is general enough to have survived a century in the

57. See *A Comparison Between the Two Stages* (anon., 1702), ed. Staring B. Wells (Princeton: Princeton Univ. Press, 1942), esp. p. 45.

58. On this curious case see Robert D. Hume, "*The Maid's Tragedy* and Censorship in the Restoration Theatre," *Philological Quarterly*, in press.

theatre after most of its targets were long forgotten. *Albion and Albanius* makes little sense without a detailed knowledge of late seventeenth-century history, but just about everything else can stand on its literary or theatrical merits. One should also note that no great number of plays are involved. By my own rough count, about 10 percent of the plays performed between 1660 and 1700 fall in one of these categories, and perhaps half that number are arguably borderline. Not having read every performed play between 1700 and 1800 I cannot offer an exact count for that period, but my impression is that the figures would be lower. We are, therefore, talking about a figure under one play in five, and in my opinion well under. Third, a surprisingly high proportion of the plays at issue have "content" which rests on inference and is not susceptible of hard proof. That the presence of real-life specifics in a play makes a substantial difference to its meaning is clearly true, but we must have reasonable proof of the extrinsic allusion before we start to get dogmatic about interpretation.

Content and the Meanings in Drama

At the start of this essay I said that I wanted to ask how much the study of content can help us with interpretation. Any answer must be predicated on a prior answer to a more basic question: what do we want an interpretation to do for us? The most obvious answer is "tell us the meaning." But what kind of meaning does a late seventeenth- or an eighteenth-century play have?

By "meaning" most interpreters of plays seem to understand "some sort of idea," as Richard Levin phrases the point.[59] This idea is derivable from the play; it is not usually the same thing as the ordinary sense (story); it is not the underlying values or outlook. For many interpreters "meaning" is a kind of message to be derived from the play. Harcourt and Alithea represent a "right way"; Horner shows us a "wrong way" (Norman Holland). Dorimant is a Truewit and hence to be admired (Fujimura). About the best one

59. Levin, *New Readings*, p. 2.

can say for much of this drama is that if this is what the authors were trying to do, they were damnably unclear about it, not to mention trivial and simpleminded. Some of these plays do offer us a "message," but by no means all of them do, and if we demand what is not there, we will either be very frustrated or wind up foisting "meanings" upon texts which do not actually convey them. In dealing with a formulaic popular drama, the interpreter needs to define his purposes less restrictively.

A full interpretation of "meaning" (as opposed to an account of the content or an exploration of "significance") generally needs to do at least four things: 1) Put the work in generic context. 2) Define its values and ideological assumptions (= put it in ideological context). 3) Explain its affective design. 4) Analyze its real-life allusions and meaning, such as they may be.

The point to establishing generic and ideological contexts is simply to help the critic decide with confidence what sort of play is involved and what sorts of comparisons may prove fruitful to illustrate both similarities and differences between plays. Both kinds of context have obvious bearing on the third point, affective design, and that in turn is important to the successful communication of an explicit meaning, supposing that there is one.

Any serious attempt at the interpretation of a play written for professional performance must reckon with its impact in the theatre. Not to do so is to ignore the obvious in favor of a "meaning" which may be completely obscured or actually negated in performance. There is a legitimate distinction to be made between reading and theatre production: an interpretation may be valid for a reader which is improbable or impossible in performance. Dryden tells us as much in his 1681 preface to *The Spanish Fryar*.

> In a playhouse, everything contributes to impose upon the judgment: the lights, the scenes, the habits, and, above all, the grace of action, which is commonly the best where there is the most need of it, surprise the audience, and cast a mist upon their understandings; not unlike the cunning of a juggler, who is always staring us in the face, and overwhelming us with gibbrish, only that he may gain the opportunity of making the

cleaner conveyance of his trick. . . . But as 'tis my interest to please my audience, so 'tis my ambition to be read: that I am sure is the more lasting and the nobler design: for the propriety of thoughts and words, which are the hidden beauties of a play, are but confusedly judged in the vehemence of action.

But whatever the possibilities for the reader ensconced in his study, an interpreter owes us a clear sense of whether his reading is stageable or not.

If we are looking for "meaning" we must be prepared a) to delimit the search precisely—just what is it we are looking for?—and b) to accept the fact that different plays have different kinds and amounts of meaning. Following I. A. Richards for the sake of a clear definition, I would suggest that the plays are constructed more for effect than they are for denotative sense beyond the story. If we are willing to include impact in meaning, we should have no great difficulty with interpretation in most comedies. But if, with most critics to date, we want to stick to denotative sense, a "real meaning" beyond the obvious, then we have a problem. How many of the plays have such a meaning?

I have argued in the last section that even if we restrict our concept of meaning to *specific presentation of ideas or real-life subjects* we will find a considerable number of plays exhibiting such meaning. The percentage is not high, but it is not insignificant.

The guises in which this sort of meaning emerge have been illustrated in the section "Real-Life Specifics in the Drama." They include abstract themes (*The Squire of Alsatia*), social commentary (*The Wives Excuse*), personation (*The Country Gentleman*), and political commentary (*The Duke of Guise*). There are two gray areas which deserve consideration: general ideological commentary and the "morals" which become increasingly common in the eighteenth century. With a play like *Edward the Third* (1690) we are probably sufficiently close to topical political commentary that we are justified in treating it that way. But what about something like Dryden's *The Conquest of Granada* (1670–71)? Here there is no immediate topical application, but the play is obviously designed to raise explicit questions about the nature of obligation and authority. In consequence, I would be inclined to treat it as an instance in which theme is significant, even if it would not predominate in performance. The tag-morals to be found in a multitude of eighteenth-century tragedies (and even comedies) are another matter.

> Let this story teach unbridled Youth,
> Honor can only be secured by Truth.
>> Charles Johnson, *Caelia* (1732)

> Oh! *Leolyn*, be obstinately just;
> Indulge no passion, and deceive no Trust:
>
> .   .   .   .
>
> The first crime, past, compells us into more,
> And Guilt grows Fate, that was but Choice before.
>> Aaron Hill, *Athelwold* (1731)

The former seems to me no more than a *pro forma* gesture in the direction of moral preachment (in what happens to be a rather effective tragedy). The latter is a direct statement of a serious theme in the play and hence ought to be given more weight in an interpretation. The problem with such tags is the seriousness of the message and its relationship to impact. When at the end of *The Fair Penitent* (1703) Rowe tells us "By such examples are we taught to prove / The sorrows that attend unlawful love," we are certainly given an explicit message, and it is indubitably part of the play's meaning. The message, however, is swamped by the emotional heat of the play: it helps return us to emotional normalcy, but it seems remote from the affective impact of what we have witnessed.

We must not demand what a play does not provide. This is a good motto for critics, but a frustrating one. People want to know "What is this play about? What does it *mean*?" To reply that it is about a couple falling in love, and that it does not mean anything very much in particular is hardly impressive. It may be a wonderfully amusing or moving play, but what is the message? Of course one can easily concoct an appropriate message: the triumph of true love over libertinism, acceptance of the higher social good, endorsement of truth, beauty, or you name it. But plays rarely *say* this, and in fact critics tend not to like those eighteenth-century plays which do. Our problem lies in our lusting after a particular kind of interpretation-of-meaning which many of these plays happen not to accommodate very well.

The Man of Mode (1676) is a good example of what tantalizes critics.[60] The play may or may not be about Rochester, but it definitely presents us a glamorous libertine and lots of his rakish outlook. The temptation to conclude that Etherege is writing "about" libertinism is very great. But what is the message? Is Dorimant a hero to be admired, a brutal fop, a satanic machiavel, a satirized Don Juan figure? What is Etherege trying to say about libertinism? Dale Underwood complains of the lack of an "adequate set of values" within the play by which we might judge it.[61] A variety of appeals to extrinsic standards of judgment has produced little but contradiction and confusion. The reason for this, very simply, is that Etherege is not writing "about" libertinism, and hence there is no message as such. James Sutherland seems to me to hit the point exactly right when he says that in the play Etherege succeeds "in expressing an attitude to life which informs many of the more thoughtful comedies of the time. That attitude is a development from seventeenth-century libertinism."[62] *The Man of Mode* is full of ideas, libertine attitudes, and glancing commentary on issues of the time. But it makes no overall statement, and it has no message. If it did, critics would long ago have worked it out. Most such messages, like most of the satire in this drama, are not overly subtle.

I am sure that some readers will be unhappy with my limitation of "meaning" to explicit ideas and real-life allusions. I do not mean this restriction as an attempt to invalidate sociological, structuralist, or phenomenological studies of this drama. I would welcome more such work. My concern here, however, has been with "content" and how it contributes to authorial meanings built into texts: I have tried to provide a rigorous investigation of a fairly

60. I have discussed this play in some detail in my *Development*, pp. 86–97. For a counterview—making the play overly serious, in my opinion—see Brian Corman, "Interpreting and Misinterpreting *The Man of Mode*," *Papers on Language and Literature*, 13 (1977), 35–53.

61. *Etherege and the Seventeenth-Century Comedy of Manners* (New Haven: Yale Univ. Press, 1957), p. 92.

62. Sutherland, p. 106.

narrow kind of interpretation. Studies of "significance" are a very different matter.

What are we to conclude? One of my initial questions was how study of content can help with interpretation. My answer is that it can help quite a lot with *some* of the plays, provided that we do not exaggerate its importance or try to regard it as a panacea. As a kind of short key to the use of content study—a summation of all my doubts and cautions—I would like to offer the following set of general interpretive principles for use in dealing with this drama.

1. Effect outweighs meaning unless proven otherwise.

2. Meaning—beyond the obvious level of the story—should not be demanded of all plays, or even most of them.

3. The Wallace principle: in many instances we cannot be certain that we are dealing with allusion specifically intended by the author.

4. A performance uncertainty principle: some of the more complex plays have no single "meaning" (even in terms of designed impact), and hence are susceptible of a variety of "valid" production interpretations.[63]

None of these principles is likely to be popular with literary critics. Few critics have wanted to worry overmuch about effect in the theatre, and to deny that there is a message-meaning in a majority of the plays is to deprive them (from many critics' point of view) of their status as serious literature. The Wallace principle has its attractions in allowing us to postulate significant parallels without having to worry about whether they were "intended," but how many critics are prepared to live with the concomitant conclusion that such interpretations cannot be "validated" in the usual ways? (Journals do publish such speculations, but as a rule only if they are duly garbed in phenomenological trappings.) The uncertainty principle is even less welcome, serving as a reminder that we are

63. This raises an interesting question: what sort of validity does an interpretation have if it is *not* communicable in performance? For a vigorous presentation of the position that "no interpretation . . . [of a play] is valid unless proved workable in performance; that is, unless it can be clearly communicated to the audience by the actors and the staging," see Michael R. Booth, "Theatre History and the Literary Critic," *Yearbook of English Studies*, 9 (1979), 15–27.

dealing with playscripts, not with literary texts uncontaminated by the exigencies of the theatre. I offer these principles not to spoil the fun of those critics hell-bent on finding tidy themes and meanings in the drama (I only wish I could), but rather in the hope of encouraging more serious and careful use of content in interpretation. Content-study applies usefully only to a minority of the plays, but it does offer us important possibilities not yet fully exploited.[64]

64. I am indebted to Maximillian E. Novak and Susan Staves for cogent critiques of an earlier draft of this essay. In somewhat different form I presented this material as a lecture at the Folger Shakespeare Library on 23 February 1981.

2

"Restoration Comedy" and its Audiences, 1660–1776

Arthur H. Scouten and Robert D. Hume

The nature of the audience in "Restoration" theatres has been much disputed. Scholars hostile to risqué comedy have tended to follow Macaulay in supposing that debauched courtiers feasted upon fictionalized accounts of their own misdeeds. Believers in a genteel "comedy of manners" have propagated the myth of a courtly coterie audience. Recent scholarship has demolished both suppositions and left us new hypotheses in their place. John Harrington Smith points to a "change" in comedy in the 1680s and 1690s which he attributes to the influence of the "Ladies" in opposition to the "Gallants" who had the ascendance in the 1670s. John Loftis has traced the growth of bourgeois and mercantilist ideology in the drama from 1690 to 1737 as a gradual response to changes in audience composition. Both of these studies are, broadly speaking, "correct," and yet some knotty problems still await our attention.

How uniform were the tastes or beliefs of the "original" Restoration audience at any given time between 1660 and 1700? How significantly did audience outlook shift between 1675 and 1695, or, in other words, between the heyday of Wycherley and that of Congreve? What happened in the critical years around 1700 when the shift to "sentimental" comedy allegedly took place? If the new bourgeois audience rejected all the "Restoration stereotypes" after 1700, why did the work not only of Congreve but of his contemporaries and predecessors remain enormously popular for more than half a century?

These are large and complicated subjects, and we cannot pretend to offer more than tentative answers. We hope, however, to call some common assumptions into doubt and to suggest that the relationship between "Restoration comedy" and its changing audience is more complicated than critics have wanted to admit. For a long time people made assumptions about the "Restoration audience" based on hostile readings of the bawdier comedies. Modern research has demolished those assumptions. But how did the heterogeneous audience we now know to have filled the theatres view the comedies served up for their delectation or instruction? And contrariwise, our view of the audience has changed: what does our new sense of the audience imply about the plays?

Carolean Plays and Their Original Audience

For an astonishingly long time, most accounts of "Restoration comedy" and its original audience were derived from readings of a very few plays. In the last quarter-century we have come to see that we must not uncritically lump the plays of the 1670s with those of the 1690s. We have likewise come to recognize the very considerable diversity of play-types popular at any given time during the late seventeenth century.[1] The whole notion of a dominant "comedy of manners" turns out to be a critics' chimera. Anyone surveying the popular comedies from the years 1662 to 1678 with something like an impartial eye would find it difficult indeed to deduce a set of social or ethical views which transcend the thumpingly commonplace: approval of wit and young lovers, disapproval of forced

1. See particularly A. H. Scouten, "Notes Toward a History of Restoration Comedy," *Philological Quarterly*, 45 (1966), 62–70; Hume, *Development*, chs. 2 and 3; John Loftis, Richard Southern, Marion Jones, and A. H. Scouten, *The Revels History of Drama in English*, Volume V: 1660–1750 (London: Methuen, 1976), Part 3.

marriage and avarice, and so forth.[2] Only a tiny handful of plays present (let alone support) the sort of libertinism for which "Restoration comedy" was long notorious.[3] If we were to look even just at the first years of the 1660s, when the audience was as homogeneous as it ever was to be in London, we would find little evidence for ideological uniformity in the popular new plays. In 1663 audiences flocked to see both John Wilson's crude, coarse *The Cheats*, and Samuel Tuke's chaste, high-flown *The Adventures of Five Hours*. We might imagine that different groups patronized these plays, had not Etherege contrived to combine everything from smutty farce to pseudo-heroic verse melodrama in a single play, the tremendously popular *The Comical Revenge* (1664). Indeed only a methodological simpleton would seriously suppose that you can construct a precise characterization of an audience by extrapolation from popular texts. Delight in Noel Coward and Neil Simon does not preclude delight in Pinter. Likewise we have ample testimony that the same audiences supported both *The Conquest of Granada* and *The Rehearsal* in the 1670s. In short, the plays are extremely disparate in type, tone, and outlook, and we cannot even assume that different parts of the audience supported different sorts of plays.

The whole theory of a coterie audience, long dominant, seems to have no better foundation than the limited knowledge and moral prejudices of later commentators. The many critics whose views are summed up in K. M. P. Burton's peculiar assertion that the audiences consisted principally of "courtiers, hangers-on, and prostitutes"[4] cannot have read Pepys with any attention, and cannot have read the prologues and epilogues from the period. We may agree with Marion Jones that the longstanding Cavalier attitudes of the comedies reflect the political and social values of what was soon a "small . . . minority" of the audience,[5] but we must not neglect the crucial implication in this statement: there must have been a lot of noncourtiers in that audience. A moment's reflection on financial reality tells us why this would have to be so. Two theatres operated

2. See Schneider, *The Ethos of Restoration Comedy*.
3. See "The Myth of the Rake in 'Restoration Comedy'" (ch. 5 below).
4. *Restoration Literature* (London: Hutchinson, 1958), p. 63.
5. *Revels History*, V, 131.

on most days of the week in the 1660s and 1670s. At a rough approximation we may say that 200 spectators were needed at each theatre just to make "house charges" (about £25 per day in this period). And to make the profits which would pay "sharing actors" an income, the two theatres would need to attract well over 500 people per day between them.[6] The population of London was about 400,000 at this time, making the percentage of theatre attenders each day quite small. But 500 is a considerable number of people. Would even 250 courtiers, hangers-on (whoever they may be), and prostitutes have patronized the theatre daily? This seems extremely improbable. We need to ask, in short, both "Who were the Restoration audience?" and "What did they expect or demand of a play?"

The social and political heterogeneity of the audience even in the 1660s has been convincingly demonstrated by Emmett L. Avery.[7] Avery's case is made even more impressive by the limitations in his methodology: working from Pepys, he was of course restricted to information about people Pepys recognized, which naturally gives undue prominence to celebrated persons and those in Pepys' own circle. Considered more broadly, the composition of the audience must appear even more diverse, as the work of Harold Love has amply proved.[8] If we try to look for identifiable subgroups within the audience we find some, but whether we are greatly the wiser for doing so is to be doubted. One obvious source of such distinctions is prologues and epilogues. Working from them Pierre Danchin offers a breakdown: royalty, quality, gallants, citizens, whores.[9] Fair enough, but of course the rhetoric of addresses to the

---

6. For figures underlying these estimates see Judith Milhous, "The Duke's Company's Profits, 1675–1677," *Theatre Notebook*, 32 (1978), 76–88; and Robert D. Hume, "The Dorset Garden Theatre: A Review of Facts and Problems," *Theatre Notebook*, 33 (1979), 4–17.

7. See "The Restoration Audience," *Philological Quarterly*, 45 (1966), 54–61.

8. Love's earlier studies are summed up and extended in his admirable essay, "Who were the Restoration Audience?" *Yearbook of English Studies*, 10 (1980), 21–44.

9. "Le Public des théâtres londoniens a l'époque de la Restauration d'après les prologues et les épilogues," in *Dramaturgie et Société*, ed. Jean Jacquot, 2 vols. (Paris: Editions du Centre National de la Recherche Scientifique, 1968), II, 847–88.

audience must be taken into account, and allowances made for the possibilities of deliberate distortion for effect. Fops, for example, make an inviting target for raillery—but how many fops went to the theatres on an average day, and by whose definition were they fops? So broad a category as "quality" must encompass both the roistering duke of Buckingham and the grumpy, moral John Evelyn. "Citizens" must include everything from wealthy merchants to petty tradesmen to apprentices. Servants evidently found the theatre excessively expensive, but toward the end of the seventeenth century Christopher Rich hit on the bright idea of allowing footmen free entry into the second gallery, making them an acknowledged bloc, and a force in favor of crude entertainments.[10]

We cannot, however, assume that given groups responded in simple and direct ways to dramatic representation of themselves. John Wain, for example, would have it that courtiers delighted in put-downs of pushy cits.[11] No doubt there is some truth in this, but let us consider a test case: Ravenscroft's *The Citizen Turn'd Gentleman*, a vastly successful play which does an especially thorough job of ridiculing the pretensions of a "cit." It received its premiere in the spring of 1672, at just the time when the Third Dutch War was taking quality and gallants out of town and (according to a string of prologues and epilogues) leaving the theatres much more dependent than usual on citizens for patronage. The play was performed, moreover, at Dorset Garden, the theatre more associated with citizens than gallants and men of quality, for whom Bridges Street and later Drury Lane were easier to get to. A similar puzzle attaches to *The London Cuckolds* (1681), a play performed for some seventy years and long a favorite with cits. Unless we presume that the citizens were masochists or self-hating dupes of courtiers' values (no doubt some were), we must grant the group some sophistication in its response to what is technically a hostile picture of itself.

One of the most curious problems for historians of the Restoration audience is its failure ever to sort itself out by patronizing

10. See Cibber's complaint, *An Apology for the Life of Mr. Colley Cibber*, ed. Robert W. Lowe, 2 vols. (1889; rpt. New York: AMS, 1966), I, 233.

11. "Restoration Comedy and its Modern Critics," *Essays in Criticism*, 6 (1956), 367–85, esp. p. 370.

different kinds of entertainments at different theatres. Looking at a large number of plays, John Harrington Smith distinguishes "cynical comedies" from those which embody an "anti-Restoration spirit in comedy." These, he suggests, were championed by "gallants" and the "Ladies" respectively.[12] The group-designations are from prologues and epilogues of the 1680s when there was definitely a split in taste between bawdy, cynical comedy, and more moral romances. Had this division in taste occurred a decade earlier, perhaps we would have seen the King's Company champion one, the Duke's Company the other. The collapse of the King's Company in 1682 made such a neat division impossible until the reestablishment of a second company in 1695. But even then the theatres made no systematic attempt to appeal to separate clienteles.

Consider a list of some of the most successful stock comedies from the Carolean period: *The Committee, The Comical Revenge, Sir Martin Mar-all, An Evening's Love, Sir Salomon, The Rehearsal, The Citizen Turn'd Gentleman, Epsom-Wells,* the 1674 *Tempest, The Country-Wife, The Man of Mode, The Plain-Dealer,* Part 1 of *The Rover, A Fond Husband.* All of these seem to have been stock plays for a good number of years, many of them for several decades. To look for significant common elements among them is essentially futile. In practice, as in theory, "Restoration" comedies exhibit great variety.[13] We may usefully ask, however, what the audience thought it saw in a comedy staged in the contemporary Carolean theatre. At least three answers deserve consideration.

1. A realistic presentation of contemporary society. Both moral zealots and defenders of the plays have taken this position. Brett-Smith and Fujimura both believe that major Restoration comedies exhibit something very near "photographic realism." An appeal to either logic or historical sociology ought, however, to cast grave

12. See John Harrington Smith, "Shadwell, the Ladies, and the Change in Comedy," *Modern Philology,* 46 (1948), 22–33; and *The Gay Couple.* For a reconsideration of Smith's account of the transition, see Hume, " 'The Change in Comedy': Cynical versus Exemplary Comedy on the London Stage, 1678–1693," *Essays in Theatre,* in press.

13. For a detailed discussion of this point see Hume, *Development,* chs. 2 and 3.

doubt on such a notion. Are the events of *The Country-Wife* or *The Plain-Dealer* the stuff of daily life in London in the 1670s? *The Man of Mode* was widely thought to be an *à clef* production (though people could not settle on the key), but the whole point is that it purports to be a glimpse of a special aristocratic world by an insider. *An Evening's Love* is a quite unrealistic "Spanish romance," and so (at one generic remove) is *1 Rover*; *Sir Salomon*, *Sir Martin Mar-all*, and *A Fond Husband* are formulaic schemes and intrigues comedies. Quoting Rapin, Dennis can say (in 1722), "*that Comedy is as it ought to be, when an Audience is apt to imagine, that instead of being in the Pit and Boxes, they are in some Assembly of the Neighbourhood, or in some Family Meeting, and that we see nothing done in it, but what is done in the World.*" [14] If so, few if any of the comedies listed above are as they ought to be. They are too formulaic, too obviously exaggerated for effect. We may usefully draw a comparison with the modern detective story. Many writers of such tales rely heavily on "realistic" details, and there is usually a very clear-cut morality, but one cannot safely draw sociological or ethical conclusions from Dorothy Sayers or Rex Stout.

2. Cloud Cuckooland. This is the opposite extreme. Lamb's defense against moral condemnation is superbly effective, but is it accurate? (And if accurate, at what cost in meaning for the plays?) No doubt we must grant that some comedies come closer to realism, others to Cloud Cuckooland. Equally we must grant that some theatregoers were probably more able than others to see a play as something separate from real life. But to suppose that even a majority of the comedies exist in a separate realm is difficult. Too many of them employ London settings and topical references. To divest them of all ordinary grounds of moral judgment they would have much more clearly to be based upon a fantasy setting and a different society. Very occasionally a writer tries this, as Edward Howard did (without much success, popular or literary) in *The Womens Conquest* (1670) and *The Six days Adventure* (1671). But most

14. "A Defence of Sir Fopling Flutter," in *The Critical Works of John Dennis*, ed. Edward Niles Hooker, 2 vols. (Baltimore: Johns Hopkins Univ. Press, 1939–43), II, 248.

comedies visibly adapt the manners and mores of contemporary English society. The amount of serious and semiserious commentary on contemporary institutions (especially marriage) would make it extremely hard to see *no* relationship between comedy and life.

3. A partially separate aesthetic reality. That audiences saw *some* relationship between comedy and life seems evident in moral protests from theatregoers (as opposed to rampaging *readers* like Jeremy Collier) as early as the 1660s and 1670s. If the comedies showed Cloud Cuckooland, such protests would be totally misguided. We find it very significant that no contemporary playwright or critic takes this line of defense. Conversely, however, we should note the extremely *un*realistic presentation of clandestine marriage and divorce in a large number of comedies throughout the period.[15] Audiences did not demand conformity to either law or reality, which seems to us another extremely significant point. An audience demanding conformity to the events and standards of real life would certainly have choked on many of these plays, from the flying spirits of *The Lancashire Witches* (1681) to the airy "divorce" at the end of Farquhar's *The Beaux Stratagem* (1707). Likewise we may say with assurance that no more than a tiny minority of the audience either approved of or attempted to practice the bedroom-farce antics of *A Fond Husband* or *The London Cuckolds.*[16]

Logic tells us, indeed, that most members of the audience ought to have been able to make some distinction between life and art. The problem is to determine how and where they did so. What would they tolerate as dramatic convention? What standards did they apply to plays? Professor Aubrey Williams has recently argued that we must take into account "the one thing that contemporary playwrights and audiences had most in common: a shared upbringing and schooling in the basic doctrines and precepts of the Christian religion."[17] This reminder is very much to the point: to imagine

15. See Gellert Spencer Alleman, *Matrimonial Law and the Materials of Restoration Comedy* (Wallingford, Pa.: privately printed, 1942).

16. For some account of predominant social attitudes, see Lawrence Stone, *The Family, Sex and Marriage in England, 1500–1800.*

17. "Of 'One Faith': Authors and Auditors in the Restoration Theatre," *Studies in the Literary Imagination,* 10 (Spring 1977), 57–76.

that late seventeenth-century writers and theatregoers were at heart happy heathens is certainly the height of folly. The number of people in the audience who did not consider themselves good Christians must have been functionally nil.[18] Near unanimous belief in Christianity does not, however, prove that any great number of theatregoers systematically applied the precepts of their religion to the comedies they saw. (Nor does it allow us to deduce religious attitudes from plays. Would we try to infer Victorian religious beliefs from *The Importance of Being Earnest*?) Professor Williams wishes to argue that they would have done so and that they would in particular have looked for signs of "Providential justice." This seems to us to force the case beyond its limits. There are, to be sure, a fair number of tragedies which do quite explicitly preach the doctrine of providential justice. Congreve's *The Mourning Bride* (1697) is a good example. Several critics (most notably Rymer and Dennis) tout this formula. But very few *comedies* make the notion of providential justice explicit, and not many more seem particularly suitable vehicles for this kind of moralization. Only if we take the rewarded protagonist with a fair amount of seriousness is a providential reading very plausible.

A few hints of "conversion" can perhaps be found in Etherege's Dorimant, but we suspect that most readers prepared to apply serious Christian standards to him would condemn him with Steele rather than rejoice in his transformation. The rhetoric of conversion can, indeed, be read as satiric. Only with a case like Valentine in *Love for Love* (1695) can a strong providential case be made from the terms of the text.[19] We do not altogether accept this case, but we grant its cogency and coherence. The question is whether Congreve so designed the play, and whether it was so taken

18. We should not, however, suppose that audience members could agree on much else about their religion. A generation later, when religious passions had cooled a bit, Jonathan Swift satirizes the "one faith" argument by having "a Ball of new-dropt Horse's Dung," floating in the gutter with some apples during a rainstorm, greet a pippin thus: "*See Brother, how we Apples swim*," in "*On the Words—Brother Protestants, and Fellow Christians*" (1733), *The Poems of Jonathan Swift*, ed. Harold Williams, 2nd ed., 3 vols. (Oxford: Clarendon Press, 1958), III, 809–13.

19. See Aubrey Williams, *An Approach to Congreve*, ch. 8.

by his audience. We may note that when Jeremy Collier denounced the play, Congreve defended it in terms far removed from those of the reading proffered by Professor Williams.[20] Perhaps, to be sure, this was merely a matter of rhetorical caution. The key question here is whether, *in performance*, the overt religious terminology of the final pages would make the audience respond to a romance on a religious plane. Our best guess is that it might have done so for some portion of the audience, but that few theatregoers would have looked to a comedy with the dominant tone of this one for serious moral or religious edification. A reader, undistracted by the glitter and bustle of performance, might well reflect on the providential moral which adorns this tale. We see, indeed, a significant difference between performance and reading in this respect.

We may agree that writers and playgoers were believing Christians without supposing either 1) that many of them looked to comedy as a serious moral vehicle, or 2) that they would have responded with anything like unanimity in cases where most of them did consider moral issues to be seriously involved. Given the great range of contemporary assumptions about the nature of comedy, and the wide variety of types and tones of particular comedies, we are inclined to conclude that there are no simple answers here. The audience was heterogeneous; the plays are heterogeneous. Even within the narrow confines of the Carolean period before the Popish Plot (that is, 1660 to 1678) there is no tidy way to characterize the relationship between audience and plays. The audience obviously demanded lively action and entertainment from comedies. What some of its members got from these plays beyond entertainment is essentially a matter for conjecture. Ingenious modern critics have found *The Country-Wife*, for example, everything from a nightmare vision of moral chaos and degradation to a triumphant celebration of the life force. Critics at both extremes admire the play. We see no reason to suppose that a seventeenth-century audience was any less able to enjoy a play for different reasons from

20. *Amendments of Mr. Collier's False and Imperfect Citations &c.* (1698), rpt. in *The Works of William Congreve*, ed. Montague Summers, III, 169–206, esp. p. 200.

different vantage points. We are, in sum, simply not able to make assured statements about what Carolean comedy meant even to its original audience. This is a chastening state of affairs.

The Watershed Years, 1678–1688

The shift in taste which ultimately was to produce what has been vaguely and misleadingly termed "sentimental" comedy took place only very gradually over a period of many years. In order to understand the transition to "Augustan" comedy, we must go back to its origins in the Carolean period. Throughout the 1690s the "old" and "new" forms of comedy compete, and the "humane" comedy which is the norm in the early eighteenth century by no means represents a simple triumph of sentimentalism over "Restoration" cynicism.[21] John Harrington Smith was certainly right in pointing to Shadwell's *The Squire of Alsatia* (1688) and other plays at the end of the eighties as indicative of a new trend, but by no means did that trend spring up suddenly. Without being excessively schematic, we may say that both 1678 and 1688 represent crucial turning points in the history of "Restoration" play-types as they reflect audience taste.

The boom in sex-comedy which had been escalating through the mid-1670s suffered a severe setback in the spring of 1678. Behn's *Sir Patient Fancy* (January), Dryden's *Mr. Limberham* (early March), and Shadwell's *A True Widow* (late March) all failed to enjoy the success anticipated for them. This does not necessarily mean that the audience had simply had its fill of smut and was now turning away, sated. Bawdy comedies were written in the next fifteen years, and some of them prospered in the theatre: *The Souldiers Fortune*, *City Politiques*, and *The Old Batchelour* spring to mind. Perhaps, indeed, the concatenation of failures in the spring of 1678 is essentially an accident. Behn's play was attacked at least partly on the

21. See Shirley Strum Kenny, "Humane Comedy," *Modern Philology*, 75 (1977), 29–43; and Hume, "The Multifarious Forms of Eighteenth-Century Comedy" (ch. 7 below).

ground of its female origin; Dryden's was suppressed by government order, perhaps because of personal satire.[22]

We must certainly distinguish between genuine libertine sex-comedy and the kind of farce represented by Durfey's *A Fond Husband* (1677) which continued to be popular. *The London Cuckolds* (1681) is of the latter variety. The distinction is by no means absolute. Dryden said sourly of his *Limberham* while writing it, "It will be almost such another piece of businesse as the fond Husband, for such the King will have it."[23] The difference is, however, evident enough to a modern reader of the two plays, and it seemed so to Shadwell, who includes a brilliant burlesque-travesty of *A Fond Husband* in the playhouse scene in Act IV of *A True Widow*. In his dedication Shadwell complains of "Poetasters of the fourth rate" who "hold, that Wit signifies nothing in a Comedy; but the putting out of Candles, kicking down of Tables, falling over Joynt-stools, impossible accidents, and unnatural mistakes." And in his note to the reader Shadwell adds, "Some, I believe, wish'd all the Play like that part of a Farce in it; others knew not my intention in it, which was to expose the Style and Plot of Farce-Writers, to the utter confusion of damnable Farce, and all its wicked and foolish Adherents."

Whatever the reasons, playwrights were evidently given pause by the failure of major efforts from top writers. The plays of the next four years show a definite drawing back from the libertine formulas which had flourished briefly in the three years after *The Country-Wife* (January 1675). We have, indeed, good evidence that Wycherley's play generated protests which then snowballed as other plays of its ilk were brought upon the stage. Wycherley acidly reports objections to *The Plain-Dealer* (1676) by the "Ladies of stricter lives" in his ironic dedication to the procuress Mother Bennet. In Act II of the later play he proceeds to satirize such objections to

22. We have no conclusive evidence. See Susan Staves, "Why Was Dryden's *Mr. Limberham* Banned? A Problem in Restoration Theatre History," *Restoration and Eighteenth Century Theatre Research*, 13 (May 1974), 1–11.

23. *The Letters of John Dryden*, ed. Charles E. Ward (1942; rpt. New York: AMS, 1965), No. 5.

The Country-Wife in a cutting depiction of Olivia. John Harrington Smith calls the apparent boycott of *The Country-Wife* by the "Ladies" after the first day the first appearance of the "Ladies" as a moral force in the theatre.[24] Strictly speaking, this is probably not true. As early as 2 January 1667 Richard Legh attended *The Custom of the Country* (1620) and reported that the play "is so damn'd bawdy that the Ladyes flung their peares and fruites at the Actors."[25] Probably there were some other instances of moral objections in the sixties and early seventies. Downes says of *The Reformation* (1672) that "the Reformation in the Play, being the Reverse to the Laws of Morality and Virtue; it quickly made its Exit, to make way for a Moral one."[26] Given the content of Arrowsmith's play, we may guess that Downes confused it with something else. There were a few increasingly risqué plays at both houses between 1668 and 1675. One doubts that the Ladies cared for John Dover's(?) *The Mall* (1674), but it quickly failed, and we have no record of protest. Basically Smith's point holds: *The Country-Wife*, a very successful play, was the first recorded instance of systematic moral protest.

The uproar attendant upon the Popish Plot and the Exclusion Crisis naturally bred a spate of political plays, and there are relatively few comedies to study between 1678 and the collapse of the King's Company in May 1682. Shadwell turned to safer and more romantic play-types in *The Woman-Captain* (1679) and *The Lancashire Witches* (1681). Otway scored a major success with his bawdy *The Souldiers Fortune* (1680), clear proof that in some guises sex-comedy was still acceptable, as is *The London Cuckolds* a year later. Shadwell's quick move away from cuckolding-comedy does seem significant, though of course it is in line with his long-standing personal preferences. Nonetheless, he had enjoyed great success in *Epsom-Wells* (1672) and *The Virtuoso* (1676), and his principle was always to supply the audience with what it wanted. Another sign of the times is *The Revenge, or A Match in Newgate* (1680),

24. *The Gay Couple*, p. 132.
25. Cited in *The London Stage*, Part 1, p. 100.
26. *Roscius Anglicanus* (London: H. Playford, 1708), p. 33.

an adaptation of *The Dutch Courtezan*, probably done by Aphra Behn.[27] The serious treatment of a prostitute, and the romantic nobility of the lead-characters, seem unthinkable in a London comedy five years earlier. We do not know how the play fared, and there is no definite record of a revival until 1704, but evidently Mrs. Behn was in search of an inoffensive formula.[28]

The reluctance of the United Company to risk money on mounting new plays makes evidence from that source very sparse between 1682 and 1688. The most obvious trend is a boom in farce with increasingly fancy staging: *A Duke and no Duke, Sir Hercules Buffoon, The Devil of a Wife, The Emperor of the Moon,* Mountfort's *Doctor Faustus.* We will find some very lightweight comedies, some a bit smutty (*Cuckolds-Haven*), some not (*Sir Courtly Nice*). Only once, however, do we find a genuine libertine sex-comedy: Sir Charles Sedley's *Bellamira* (1687). We can scarcely be surprised to learn that it roused objections. The source (Terence's *The Eunuch*), Sedley tells us, necessitated

> some expressions or Metaphors, which by persons of a ticklish imagination, or over-quick sense that way, seem'd too lascivious for modest Ears; I confess after the Plays I have seen lately Crowded by that fair Sex: the exception did not a little surprise me; And this suddain change of theirs made me call to mind our English weather, where in the same day a man shall Sweat in Crape, and wish for a Campagn Coat three hours after. I am very unhappy that the Ice that has borne so many Coaches and Carts, shou'd break with my Wheel barrow.[29]

27. For analyses see Leo Hughes and Arthur H. Scouten, "Some Theatrical Adaptations of a Picaresque Tale," *University of Texas Studies in English* (1945–46), pp. 98–114, and Douglas R. Butler, "A Critical Old-Spelling Edition of Aphra Behn's *The Revenge,*" Diss. Pennsylvania State Univ. 1982.

28. However in 1702 *A Comparison Between the Two Stages,* ed. Staring B. Wells, reports that "the Stage has been dishonoured" with the play "many a time" (p. 11), so we may guess that it had been fairly popular in the preceding twenty years.

29. "The Preface to the Reader," *The Poetical and Dramatic Works of Sir Charles Sedley,* ed. V. de Sola Pinto, 2 vols. (1928; rpt. New York: AMS, 1969), II, 5.

Indeed (though Sedley downplays the bawdiness of the comedy) there is some truth to this. The climate evidently had changed, and had done so a number of years earlier. Not since Nat. Lee's *The Princess of Cleve* (1682) had a new play like this been brought to the English stage. And Lee's play—a failure—is at least arguably a sharply negative satire on the behavior it presents, which Sedley's is not.

Two earlier plays show a clear and deliberate attempt on the author's part to placate the moral element in the audience. John Harrington Smith rightly calls attention to Ravenscroft's prologue for *Dame Dobson* (1683).

> His *London Cuckolds* did afford you sport.
> That pleas'd the Town, and did divert the Court.
> But 'cause some squeamish Females of renown
> Made visits with design to cry it down,
> He swore in's Rage he would their humours fit,
> And write the next without one word of Wit.
> No Line in this will tempt your minds to Evil,
> It's true, 'tis dull, but then 'tis very civil.
> No double sense shall now your thoughts beguile,
> Make Lady Blush, nor Ogling Gallant Smile.
>   But mark the Fate of this mis-judging Fool
> A Bawdy Play was never counted Dull,
> Nor modest Comedy e're pleas'd you much . . .
> In you, Chast Ladies, then we hope to day,
> This is the Poets *Recantation* play
> Come often to't that he at length may see
> 'Tis more than a pretended Modesty:
> Stick by him now, for if he finds you falter,
> He quickly will his way of writing alter;
> And every Play shall send you blushing home.

The London Cuckolds had enjoyed great popularity, but evidently it roused enough objections to make Ravenscroft back off. *Dame Dobson*, however, was no success, perhaps because it simply is not a good play. The second instance of authorial self-purification, Durfey's *The Banditti; or A Lady's Distress* (1686) provoked catcalls, despite its appeal to the Ladies in the prologue to support it against the preferences of gallants in the pit. There is an obvious conclusion to be drawn from the new plays of the 1680s: the moral element in the audience (the Ladies, as they are usually called) was effectively crying down what it regarded as smut in new plays, but it was failing to support plays overtly presented for its delectation. Perhaps better plays would have met a kinder fate, but what we see here is negative influence.

Authors were not much pleased with this state of affairs. Back in 1678 Aphra Behn admitted that *Sir Patient Fancy* had suffered "loss of Fame with the Ladies," and angrily protested against the charge that the play *"was Baudy"* and that *"from a Woman it was unnaturall."* Bawdiness, she complains, is "the least and most excusable fault in the Men writers." Eight years later she was considerably more distressed by the uproar attendant upon *The Lucky Chance.* The amount of fuss caused by this gamey sex-farce is made clear by the author's lengthy and indignant "Preface," rebutting "the old never failing Scandal—That 'tis not fit for the Ladys." Ill-natured playgoers, she says, "wrest a double *Entendre* from every thing."

> When it happens that I challenge any one, to point me out the least Expression of what some have made their Discourse, they cry, *That Mr.* Leigh *opens his Night Gown, when he comes into the Bride-chamber*; if he do, which is a Jest of his own making, and which I never saw, I hope he has his Cloaths on underneath? And if so, where is the Indecency? I have seen in that admirable Play of *Oedipus*, the Gown open'd wide, and the Man shown in his Drawers and Waist coat, and never thought it an Offence before. Another crys, *Why we know not what they mean, when the Man takes a Woman off the Stage, and another is thereby cuckolded*; is that any more than you see in the most Celebrated of your Plays? as the *City Politics*, the Lady Mayoress, and the Old Lawyers Wife, who goes with a Man she never saw before, and comes out again the joyfull'st Woman alive, for having made her Husband a Cuckold with such Dexterity, and yet I see nothing unnatural nor obscene: 'tis proper for the Characters. So in that lucky Play of the *Lon-*

don Cuckolds, not to recite Particulars. And in that good Comedy of *Sir Courtly Nice*, the Taylor to the young Lady— in the fam'd Sir *Fopling* Dorimont and Bellinda.[30]

Very true: *The Lucky Chance* is no bawdier than a host of long-popular plays. But what the audience was evidently willing to tolerate in stock comedies it would not as willingly accept in new productions. We should certainly note, however, an important distinction. A significant part of the objection was to *verbal* indelicacy rather than to sex or cuckolding as such. Objections to copulation in new plays soon developed. Within ten years writers could no longer have a protagonist cuckold someone and then reward such a "hero" with fortune and heroine.

This rather peculiar distinction between actual sex and double entendre is made plain by Shadwell's *The Squire of Alsatia* (1688), whose appearance signals the rise of the "new" style in comedy. Shadwell's prologue makes explicit his awareness of changes in the audience ("Our Poet found your gentle Fathers kind"), his moral purpose ("He to correct, and to inform did write"), and his determination not to offend ("Baudy the nicest Ladies need not fear, / The Quickest fancy shall extract none here"). Double entendre Shadwell does indeed avoid, but his hero, Belfond Junior, seduces, abandons, and pays off a basically virtuous girl in the course of the play. We learn also that he has a child by another mistress. And yet Shadwell loudly trumpets the young man's reform, and explicitly holds him up as a model gentleman. The really significant fact about this avowedly moral play is that it was a tremendous success. The earlier plays written as a concession to the moral group in the audience seem to have fared indifferently at best. Standards *were* changing. As Sedley and Behn complain, what had been acceptable would no longer sit with the audience. By no means, however, had prevailing standards become those touted by Steele fifteen years later. Belfond Junior is scarcely a close prototype for Steele's early

30. *The Works of Aphra Behn*, ed. Montague Summers, 6 vols. (1915; rpt. New York: Phaeton, 1967), III, 185–87. We have altered some of the italics for clarity.

protagonists, let alone Young Bevil in *The Conscious Lovers* (1722). But the balance has tilted and in *The Squire of Alsatia* we see the rudiments of the "reform" pattern common after 1700.[31]

John Harrington Smith comments that there were two basic "forces in opposition [to "cynical" comedy] before 1690." These he defines as 1) "the competition of 'sympathetic' drama," and 2) the conscious opposition of the moralists led by Shadwell.[32] We cannot entirely accept this description of the situation. Shadwell had little influence in the theatre between 1679 and 1688: indeed, he was more or less excluded from it after 1681. And the number of successful "sympathetic" comedies written before *The Squire of Alsatia* is close to nil, no matter how you define that term. Smith's examples come very late in the decade: Carlile's *The Fortune Hunters* (no great success), Durfey's *Love for Money*, and Shadwell's *Bury-Fair*, all date from 1689. One may see in *Dame Dobson* and *The Banditti* a tentative groping in that direction. In Southerne's *The Disappointment* (1684) we may espy a hint of psychological problem-drama. But as we see the situation, "sympathetic" (that is, quasi-exemplary) comedy evolves as a way of avoiding objections to bawdry, especially of a verbal sort. These objections soon extended to the explicit presentation of sex, and at the same time dramatists began to discover the potentialities of a more positive presentation of character. The "sympathetic" formula was naturally agreeable to Shadwell, who had favored something of the sort back in the 1660s and had only grudgingly succumbed to fashion in the early 1670s. But in *The Squire of Alsatia* Shadwell is not

31. Records of revivals are so sketchy in these years that we hesitate to try to draw any conclusions from them. The number of pre-1660 comedies revived by the United Company after 1682 (for example, *Rule a Wife*, *The Jovial Crew*, *The Scornful Lady*, *The Northern Lass*, *The Humorous Lieutenant*, *The Silent Woman*) may suggest a move toward purity in comedy. It might also be taken as a sign that the United Company was seeking variety in its repertory without going to the expense and risk of new plays by taking the cream off the stock of plays formerly belonging to the King's Company. In any case, these plays were very acceptable to the audience, and the decision in 1684 to revive *The Mistaken Beauty* (1661), a chaste play which had evidently dropped out of the repertory in the 1660s, suggests the change in atmosphere.

32. *The Gay Couple*, p. 131.

exerting pressure on the audience; rather, he is responding to a changing climate of opinion.

The Cranky Audiences of 1697–1703

According to long-standing critical dogma, a key transition occurred in the years around 1700, one which saw increasingly bourgeois audiences reject the harsh verities of "Restoration comedy" in favor of the new "sentimental" comedy. The facts are quite different. Audiences continued to support stock plays, but for reasons which we do not pretend to understand completely they damned practically all the *new* plays mounted by both companies. This rejection extends to tragedy as well as comedy, to humane and reform comedies as well as satiric ones. If this calamitous rate of failure among new plays were paralleled by rejection of the stock Carolean comedies, we might hypothesize that writers were simply reacting too slowly to changes in taste. But since the old plays continued to hold the stage, we cannot draw any such easy conclusion.

Scanty performance records before 1705 are a problem. Until then we cannot be certain how many times any given play was performed, even in its first run, and no doubt we altogether lack records of many revivals. Any assessment of "success" is usually at least partly subjective, derived from comments in the preface or dedication of a published quarto, or from a scrap of contemporary commentary. The anonymous *A Comparison Between the Two Stages* (1702) is a great help, but the grumpy author is demonstrably too free with his usual dismissal, "Damn'd." We must also beware of a tidy, uniform formula for "success." Scholars sometimes take six nights in the initial run (including two benefits for the author) as proof of "success." This is unsound. An expensive opera like Durfey's *The Wonders in the Sun* (1706) ran for six nights, but was regarded as a disastrous fiasco: it would probably have had to run three times as long to make back the company's investment. For the purposes of the present investigation "success" has been estimated by Mr. Scouten. Slight differences of opinion or judgment will be found in Mr. Hume's *Development of English Drama*, and in the work of Shirley Strum Kenny. A much more detailed play-by-play survey (in terms of theatrical success) can be found in *Thomas Betterton and the Management of Lincoln's Inn Fields, 1695–1708* by our *London Stage* colleague Judith Milhous, a study to which we are indebted throughout this section.[33]

In the spring of 1702 the author of *A Comparison Between the Two Stages* observed, "I am sure you can't name me five Plays that have indur'd six Days acting, for fifty that were damn'd in three."[34] This is no great exaggeration. Our figures show fifty-seven failures against fifteen successes for the entire six seasons from 1697 to 1703. We should point out right away that this depressing record of failure did not commence in 1698 after Jeremy Collier's blast. His denunciation no doubt hurt the theatres, but the highest rate of failure occurred in the acting season 1697–98, when fifteen out of seventeen new plays failed. The audience revolt was in full swing prior to Collier's attack.

We cannot emphasize too strongly that the audience was not simply rejecting the theatre and the established corpus of English drama. A few new plays were highly successful (witness Farquhar's *The Constant Couple* in 1699), and had audiences really been deserting the playhouses, one or both of the two acting companies would have closed down. As both companies survived, we know that they attracted large enough audiences to pay the fixed house charges and at least "reduced" (or partial) salaries to the actors.

Leafing through the pages of *The London Stage* one can observe which of the older plays were being acted. If we can trust John Dennis, *Coriolanus* (in the Folio text) was played at least twenty times in the 1698–99 season; in the following season *1 Henry IV* was a smash hit; and *Julius Caesar* was acted so frequently that both pirated and authorized quartos of the play were being printed.[35] Adaptations were also popular in these years: Tate's *Lear*, Shad-

33. Carbondale: Southern Illinois Univ. Press, 1979.
34. *A Comparison Between the Two Stages*, p. 2.
35. See John Velz, "'Pirate Hills' and the Quartos of *Julius Caesar*," *Papers of the Bibliographical Society of America*, 63 (1969), 177–93, and Arthur H. Scouten, "*Julius Caesar* and Restoration Shakespeare," *Shakespeare Quarterly*, 29 (1978), 423–27.

well's reworking of *Timon*, and the 1674 "operatic" *Tempest* were offered frequently, as were older plays from other writers—Jonson's *Volpone* and Fletcher's *Rule a Wife* in particular.

From the Carolean period we find *The Comical Revenge*, *The Lancashire Witches*, *Marriage A-la-Mode*, *The Committee*, *The Plain-Dealer*, *The Amorous Widow*, *The Virtuoso*, *The London Cuck-olds*, *The Country-Wife*, *Cutter of Coleman Street*, and *The Rover*, among other plays. In tragedy we find *The Rival Queens*, *The Or-phan*, *Venice Preserv'd*, and the Dryden-Lee *Oedipus* regularly revived.

These then were the chief older plays which were keeping both the young Drury Lane company and the prestigious older group at Lincoln's Inn Fields in business. What can we learn from them? If we were to pretend to be market advisers and study the perform-ance records throughout this period of 1697 to 1703 in order to recommend what works Rich and Betterton should offer to the public at their rival theatres in the next season, we would be led to say that the audiences did not want weepy moralizing plays, but would prefer high comedy. Indeed, one of the most "sentimental" plays, Richard Steele's *The Lying Lover*, failed in the autumn of 1703 at Drury Lane. However, *The Way of the World* was decidedly not a smash hit at Lincoln's Inn Fields in 1700. We find an audience un-willing to accept either extreme of contemporary comedy.

The failure of so many new plays reflects the authors' inability to find any formula which would please the audience. Had "re-form" comedy been prospering we would surely have seen a flood of such plays. The audience rebellion could not have been pre-dicted. The triumph of *Love for Love* at the opening of Lincoln's Inn Fields in April 1695 suggests the possibility of boom times, at least for the older actors. A lot of plays failed in 1695–96 and 1696–97, but then both theatres had enjoyed smash hits as well: *Oroonoko*, *Aesop*, *Love's Last Shift*, and *The Relapse* at Drury Lane; *The Mourning Bride*, *The Provok'd Wife*, and Ravenscroft's *The Anatomist* at Lincoln's Inn Fields. In 1697–98, however, the crash came. All eight new plays at Drury Lane failed, and seven new dramas failed at Lincoln's Inn Fields, leaving only two plays throughout the entire season which definitely achieved six performances. The percentage of failures was unprecedented in late seventeenth-century drama. No single reason can be given to explain the failures. We can note that many of the playwrights were relative novices: there had been a very limited market for new plays during the years of the United Company (1682–95), and the older generation of professional writers had largely died off or retired. Many of the plays which failed in 1697–98 are poor stuff; consequently it may be more profitable to focus on the following five seasons to learn what sorts of plays the audience was rejecting.

While the failures of the 1697–98 season may possibly be explained by poor plays from inexperienced authors, the longer period contains repeated failures by prominent dramatists, writers who had years of success behind them, or, like Farquhar, were to enjoy great success. Mrs. Centlivre, Cibber, Crowne, Durfey, Farquhar, Rowe, Settle, Southerne, and Vanbrugh all experienced failures during these years. The range of play-types is striking. Starting with opera, we will find that Settle's *The Virgin Prophetess* and Oldmixon's *The Grove* were expensive losses, expecially since operas cost so much more to mount than plays. Representing the older heroic drama, Boyle's *Altemira* and Hopkins' *Friendship Improved* both failed, together with Southerne's *The Fate of Capua*, which deserved a better reception. Of the newer "neoclassical" tragedies, Boyer's *Achilles*, Dennis' *Iphigenia*, and Gildon's *The Patriot* all failed. So too did the pathetic tragedies, *Fatal Friendship* by Mrs. Trotter and *The False Friend* by Mrs. Pix. The dramatists were experimenting with a new language for tragedy, as we see in Durfey's two-part *The Famous History of the Rise and Fall of Massaniello*, but like Mrs. Pix's *The Czar of Muscovy*, it failed. Tragicomedy was no more successful, as we see in the failures of Higgons' *The Generous Conquerour* and Smith's *The Princess of Parma*. Neither great actresses nor veteran dramatists nor experiments in prose would save tragedy, for English tragedy was very nearly dead. Insofar as present records inform us, there was not a truly successful new tragedy between Congreve's *The Mourning Bride* in 1697 and Ambrose Philips' *The Distrest Mother* in 1712 (with Addison's *Cato* to appear the following year). Three or four tragedies had reached a second benefit, but never went into repertory. Dr. Trapp's *Abra-Mule* was well received in the 1703–4 season, achieving a total of fourteen performances, but like a number of plays to be discussed later, it did not go into stock and was not revived until 1710. Rowe's *Tamerlane* was a moderate success in 1701–2, but years passed before it was picked up for annual performance on King William's birthday. The dismal fate of tragedies in these years helps to explain the tremendous excitement in London over the reception of *Cato*: theatre-goers had not seen so successful a tragedy in many years.

Season by season, the total record looks like this:

Season of 1697–98
LIF Successes: Hopkins, *Boadicea*; Granville, *Heroic Love*
    Failures: *The Unnatural Mother*; Ravenscroft, *The Italian Husband*; Pix, *The Deceiver Deceived*; Dilke, *The Pretenders*; Motteux, *Beauty in Distress*; Trotter, *Fatal Friendship*; Pix, *Queen Catharine*
DL Successes: none
    Failures: Oldmixon, *Amintas*; Powell, *Imposture Defeated*; *The Fatal Discovery*; Crowne, *Caligula*; Walker, *Victorious Love*; Phillips, *The Revengeful Queen*; Gildon, *Phaeton*; Durfey, *The Campaigners*
Totals: 2 successes; 15 failures

Season of 1698–99
LIF Successes: none
    Failures: Crowne, *Justice Busy*; Dennis, *Rinaldo and Armida*; Cibber, *Xerxes*; Harris, *Love's a Lottery*; Smith, *The Princess of Parma*; *Feign'd Friendship*; Pix, *The False Friend*
DL: Success: *The Island Princess* (semi-opera)
    Failures: Farquhar, *Love and a Bottle*; *Love without Interest*; Durfey, *Massaniello*
Totals: 1 success; 10 failures

Season of 1699–1700
LIF Success: Congreve, *The Way of the World* (marginal)
    Failures: Hopkins, *Friendship Improved*; Dennis, *Iphigenia*; Corye, *A Cure for Jealousy*; Manning, *The Generous*

Choice; Gildon, *Measure for Measure*; Pix, *The Beau De-feated*; Southerne, *The Fate of Capua*

DL Successes: Farquhar, *The Constant Couple*; Vanbrugh, *The Pilgrim*

    Failures: Boyer, *Achilles*; Cibber, *Richard III*; Oldmixon, *The Grove*; Burnaby, *The Reform'd Wife*; *The History of Hengist* (probably not a new play); Craufurd, *Courtship à la Mode*

Totals: 3 successes, 13 failures

Season of 1700–1701

LIF Success: Granville, *The Jew of Venice*

    Failures: Rowe, *The Ambitious Step-mother*; Burnaby, *The Ladies Visiting-Day*; Pix, *The Double Distress*; Pix, *The Czar of Muscovy*; Gildon, *Love's Victim*; Johnson, *The Gentleman Cully*

DL Successes: Cibber, *Love Makes a Man*; Baker, *The Humours of the Age*

    Failures: Centlivre, *The Perjured Husband*; Trotter, *Love at a Loss*; Trotter, *The Unhappy Penitent*; Farquhar, *Sir Harry Wildair*; Settle, *The Virgin Prophetess*; Durfey, *The Bath*

Totals: 3 successes, 12 failures

Season of 1701–1702

LIF Success: Rowe, *Tamerlane*

    Failures: Wiseman, *Antiochus the Great*; Boyle, *Altemira*; Centlivre, *The Beau's Duel*

DL Successes: Steele, *The Funeral*; Farquhar, *The Inconstant*

    Failures: Higgons, *The Generous Conquerour*; Burnaby, *The Modish Husband*; Vanbrugh, *The False Friend*; Dennis, *The Comical Gallant*

Totals: 3 successes, 7 failures

Season of 1702–1703

LIF Success: Centlivre, *Love's Contrivance*

    Failures: Centlivre, *The Heiress*; Oldmixon, *The Governour of Cyprus*; Burnaby, *Love Betray'd*; *The Fickle Shepherdess*; Boyle, *As You Find It*; Rowe, *The Fair Penitent*

DL Successes: Baker, *Tunbridge Walks*; Estcourt, *The Fair Example*

Failures: Manning, *All for the Better*; Cibber, *She wou'd and She wou'd not*; Gildon, *The Patriot*; Farquhar, *The Twin-Rivals*; Durfey, *The Old Mode and the New*; Wilkinson, *Vice Reclaim'd*

Totals: 3 successes, 12 failures

The diversity in type of the successes and failures on this list is striking, though on the whole plays were not prospering at either extreme. We may fairly say, however, that the long line of witty plays which gave a hard, searching look at English society, from *The Alchemist*, through *The Plain-Dealer*, *The Man of Mode*, and on to Congreve's popular *The Old Batchelour* (1693), was definitely on the wane. The reception met by *The Way of the World* in March 1700 was evidently a shock to both playwright and theatre company. Dryden reported it a "moderate success," from which we would deduce that it achieved at least a sixth night and quite possibly more.[36] Nor did the play immediately disappear from the boards: it was revived at least briefly around January 1702 and again in 1705.[37] Nonetheless, this reception for a play by the author of *Love for Love* and *The Mourning Bride* was taken as a humiliating failure and a deliberate rebuke to the author.

Just before the premiere of Congreve's last play, William Burnaby, a new dramatist working very much in the tradition of satiric comedy, brought out the first of his three comedies in this mode. All of them proved complete failures. Farquhar's *Love and a Bottle* fared almost as badly. However, those plays which took a softer view of human nature (perhaps best termed "humane comedy") did no better.[38] Durfey's *The Old Mode and the New* and Mrs. Centlivre's *Beau's Duel* failed. Manning's *All for the Better*, in the long-popular mode of Spanish romance, did not succeed. Such plays as Boyle's *As You Find It* and Wilkinson's *Vice Reclaim'd*, which are

36. *Letters*, No. 74.
37. See Robert D. Hume, "A Revival of *The Way of the World* in December 1701 or January 1702," *Theatre Notebook*, 26 (1971), 30–36.
38. See Shirley Strum Kenny, "Humane Comedy."

in the new "reform" style, experienced the same fate. The audience apparently rejected the soft didactic plays as readily as they rejected satiric pictures of London life. Even the Shakespearean adaptations were unsuccessful. Gildon's *Measure for Measure* and Burnaby's *Love Betray'd* (a mangled version of *Twelfth Night*) both vanished from the boards immediately. We may not be surprised at these verdicts; more startling is the failure of Colley Cibber's flashy revision of *Richard III*. Cibber tells us that the play did not bring five pounds above the fixed house charges on his benefit night. Yet this famous adaptation went on to become one of the best known renditions of Shakespeare for the next two centuries.[39]

A skeptical reader could, up to this point, argue that most of the failures were mediocre plays, or were perhaps the victims of special circumstances: excessive expectations (*The Way of the World*) or the censor's axe (*Richard III*). Even that pair of cases is surprising. Congreve's play, after a brief revival in 1715, was acted almost every season from 1718 to the end of the century, many times at both patent houses. Cibber's adaptation was revived for the author's benefit in April 1704, but not again until January 1710. For the next century and a half it was the most frequently acted of any "Shakespearean" play. The tremendous theatricality of Cibber's version has even won it some twentieth-century admirers: indeed, it influenced the Olivier film.

Consider some other striking cases. 1) Rowe's *The Fair Penitent* (1703): from the popularity in these years of Banks' "She-tragedies," Southerne's *The Fatal Marriage*, and Otway's tragedies, one would suppose that a play centering on a beautiful heroine in distress, developing into a drama of the passions, would certainly be attractive to the taste of the time. Yet *The Fair Penitent* sank without trace. This pathetic tragedy, so influential on Richardson and the direction of the English novel, was not accepted by its first audience.[40] Twelve years later, Rowe's tear-jerker was revived and promptly became one of the top-drawing cards of the London theatre for the rest of the century. 2) Farquhar's *The Twin-Rivals* (1702):

39. The play did initially labor under a special disadvantage: the censor removed Act I in its entirety.

40. See the *Revels History*, V, 282–83.

this comedy failed at its premiere and disappeared until November 1716, when it was revived. It stayed in the repertory until 1780. 3) Vanbrugh, *The False Friend*: this comedy failed at its opening in 1702, and disappeared until March 1710, when it was played twice. It had three performances in 1715. But in 1724 it went into the repertory and was acted regularly until mid-century, with its final performance in March 1767. 4) Cibber, *She wou'd and She wou'd not*: Cibber tells us that his comedy reached six nights on its initial run in 1703, but the audience on the sixth night was so small that the company did not make its house charges. As a result, the play did not go into repertory. It was revived for one performance in April 1707. Finally, it was revived in 1714, and rapidly became very popular. It was acted at both patent houses for the rest of the eighteenth century, and held on in stock until the mid-nineteenth century. It is close to the top of all eighteenth-century comedies in both longevity of performance and total performances.

Cases like these are potent evidence for a strange audience revolt in the period from 1697 to 1703. In at least half a dozen instances we can show from performance records that plays which initially failed to enter the repertory (at best) were revived over several generations for a wide variety of audiences. Indeed, these plays loom large among the small group of "perennial favorites" (in Shirley Kenny's phrase) from the late seventeenth-century period. Nothing like this pattern of later acceptance can be found in the Carolean period, or in other periods of English drama. None of the neglected or rejected plays from the "early Restoration" is known to have returned to the repertory in such manner.

To say that the audience had turned against "Restoration" stereotypes and that the writers failed to adapt to changed taste simply will not do. Let us look at the plays revived during the season of 1703–4, when the audience revolt began to slacken. The number of known performances is given in parentheses.

Crowne, *Sir Courtly Nice* (3); Crowne, *The Countrey Wit* (2); Shadwell, *The Sullen Lovers* (first revival in twenty-five years); Jonson, *The Silent Woman* (3); Congreve, *The Old Batchelour*; Behn, *The Rover* (4); Behn, *The Emperor of the Moon* (7); Shadwell, *The*

Woman-Captain (2; second revival in sixteen years); Shadwell, *The Lancashire Witches* (6); Jonson, *Volpone* (4); Wycherley, *The Plain-Dealer*; Fletcher, *Rule a Wife*; Congreve, *The Double-Dealer* (2); the 1674 *Tempest* (2); Shadwell, *The Squire of Alsatia* (12; first revival in twelve years); Etherege, *The Comical Revenge* (3); Fletcher-Buckingham, *The Chances*; Fletcher, *The Scornful Lady*; Tate, *A Duke and no Duke* (3); Betterton, *The Amorous Widow* (3); Caryll, *Sir Salomon* (6); Fletcher, *The Humorous Lieutenant* (2); Brome, *The Jovial Crew* (3); Jonson, *Bartholomew Fair* (3); Etherege, *The Man of Mode*; Mountfort, *Greenwich-Park* (2); Etherege, *She wou'd if she cou'd*; Congreve, *Love for Love* (2); Howard, *The Committee* (2); Shadwell, *The Miser* (2); Durfey, *A Fond Husband* (2; first revival in five years); Jevon, *The Devil of a Wife* (2); Lacy, *Sauny the Scot* (first revival in four years); Dryden, *Secret-Love*; Durfey, *Madam Fickle*; Behn, *A Match in Newgate*; Ravenscroft, *The London Cuckolds*; Newcastle-Dryden, *Sir Martin Mar-all*

We see very clearly here that the theatres were staying in business by performing classic English comedies, the majority of them leading examples of the "Restoration stereotypes."

Why audiences were so difficult in the years around 1700 we frankly do not know. Authors were baffled: in prologue after prologue they lamented the fickleness of the audience, and in prefaces and dedications they tended to blame actors and managers for their misfortunes. If authors were puzzled and indignant, managers were frantic. They imported foreign singers at inflated prices, tried entr'acte dancers, animal acts, acrobats, and vaudeville turns. They cannibalized favorite scenes from plays and popular operas. They kept changing the starting time of performance (most unusual in an institution as conservative as the theatre). Competition from concerts was severe: they met it with a flood of interpolated songs and instrumental entr'actes.[41]

Established professionals simply did not know what to do. Betterton's management of Lincoln's Inn Fields has been criti-

41. For a fine study of the encroachment of music on the theatres in this period, see Curtis A. Price, "The Critical Decade for English Music Drama, 1700–1710," *Harvard Library Bulletin*, 26 (1978), 38–76.

cized,[42] but he can scarcely be blamed for a situation in which the audience was rejecting almost all of the new plays at *both* theatres. Congreve's decision to withdraw from the theatre at the age of thirty has been lamented—but what could he do? He had seen the audience turn away from Southerne's comedies in the 1690s, and reject the talented William Burnaby outright in the first years of the new century. Congreve had responded to a cool reception for his second play, *The Double-Dealer* (1693), by trying again and altering his formula. But when *The Way of the World* met a similar fate he evidently could see nowhere to turn next. It is scarcely an accident that his principal ventures after 1700 were in musical forms: *The Judgment of Paris* and *Semele* (the latter unhappily remaining unperformed). Plays of all types were failing outright with dismal regularity, and Congreve evidently felt no inclination to subject himself to further rejections by a sour and captious audience.

We are left with a rather disturbing paradox. "Restoration comedy" shows no signs of losing its popular appeal in the theatre in the years around 1700, but the new plays descended from it were having a very bad time indeed. To some observers (Vanbrugh chief among them) the growing craze for music suggested that opera might be the salvation of the theatre. As Vanbrugh was soon to discover to his great cost, however, Italian opera was a sinkhole rather than a goldmine.[43]

The Judgment of Posterity, 1700–1776

Underlying most studies of late seventeenth-century drama are two assumptions, implicit or explicit. 1) "Restoration comedy" was written to appeal to a coterie audience; 2) the disappearance of that coterie forced the theatres to turn to a new, more bourgeois audience which demanded more "sentimental" comedy after 1700.

42. For example, by Shirley Strum Kenny in "Theatrical Warfare, 1695–1710," *Theatre Notebook*, 27 (1973), 130–45.

43. For details of Vanbrugh's ill-fated venture into opera, see *Vice Chamberlain Coke's Theatrical Papers, 1706–1715*, ed. Judith Milhous and Robert D. Hume (Carbondale: Southern Illinois Univ. Press, 1982).

The point of this brief concluding section is simply to ask what we can deduce from the history of late seventeenth-century plays on the eighteenth-century stage. To do justice to the subject would require a book-length study based on detailed statistical analysis of the records available in *The London Stage*. Here we hope merely to indicate some suggestive patterns of evidence, drawing on the admittedly tentative work of pioneers in the field.

The crucial fact is glaringly obvious: many seventeenth-century plays *were* popular on the eighteenth-century stage. We can scarcely present this as a fresh discovery, and yet its importance must not be missed. Reading most of the half-century's-worth of critics descended from the schools of Bernbaum and Nicoll, one would suppose that so drastic a change in audience taste and standards as allegedly occurred around 1700 would quickly have driven the older plays from the boards. To be sure, the types of new plays did shift in the period 1688 to 1708, and the audience quirkiness we analyzed in the last section certainly contributed to the impression that audiences were turning away from "Restoration" play-types. The supposed "failure" of *The Way of the World* in 1700 has been cited innumerable times as a symptom of a move toward "sentimental" comedy. The readiness of critics to seize upon this "fact" is evidence principally of their lack of interest in studying revivals. Since 1832 we have had Genest at hand, from whose pages any interested party can calculate that *The Way of the World* was performed well over 200 times in London during the eighteenth century. Let us consider some evidence of this sort, long available, but not much used during the past twenty-five years.

Congreve, so often cited as an example of what the "new bourgeois audience" rejected, is (happily) the subject of the fullest and most meticulously careful study yet done of any playwright save Shakespeare whose work was revived on the eighteenth-century stage.[44] In this study Professor Avery reached a number of conclusions. Principally these are 1) that Congreve's plays flourished until the Garrick era; 2) that Garrick's indifference to Congreve signifi-

44. Emmett L. Avery, *Congreve's Plays on the Eighteenth-Century Stage* (New York: Modern Language Association, 1951).

cantly diminished the number of performances of his plays in the 1740s and 1750s; 3) that nonetheless they continued to be successful (in part at Covent Garden) until the 1760s; 4) that after a brief flurry of performances around 1776 in revisions mounted by Sheridan at Drury Lane, the plays largely disappeared from the boards. The following table is adapted from Avery's figures. It shows the total percent share held by Congreve's plays in the year-round repertory at all London theatres.

1700–1701 to 1704–5	2.1
1705–6 to 1709–10	2.7
1710–11 to 1713–14	4.0
1714–15 to 1719–20	4.7
1720–21 to 1728–29	5.1
1729–30 to 1736–37	5.5
1737–38 to 1740–41	6.2
1741–42 to 1746–47	5.0
1747–48 to 1755–56	5.2
1756–57 to 1765–66	3.6
1766–67 to 1775–76	1.3
1776–77 to 1783–84	3.4
1784–85 to 1791–92	2.4
1792–93 to 1799–1800	1.0

Several notes and observations are in order. Avery subdivided unequally to reflect events affecting the theatres: for example, the Licensing Act, and Garrick's assuming the management of Drury Lane. Performances of *The Mourning Bride* are included, which accounts for a significant part of the performances of Congreve's plays in the 1780s and 1790s.[45] The figure for the first five years of the century must be regarded as meaningless; the records are too incomplete to generate significant statistics.

This table very clearly tells us, however, that Congreve *gained* popularity steadily over a period of some forty years, achieving his

45. During the eighteenth century Avery counts 435 performances of *Love for Love*, 300 of *The Old Batchelour* (all but 50 before 1747), 285 of *The Way of the World*, 150 of *The Double-Dealer*, and 245 of *The Mourning Bride*, whose greatest period of popularity was the fifteen years after 1747.

greatest share in the repertory around 1740, a quite astonishing 6.2 percent of all performances in London (excluding operas and foreign-language productions). In fairness we must add the qualification that the abrupt falling off in new play productions following the Licensing Act in 1737 probably helps to account for Congreve's reaching a peak in the years immediately after it, but he had been above 5 percent for the preceding fifteen years, and stayed there twenty years afterward. John Loftis is perfectly correct in saying that during the 1730s the "Restoration stereotypes" disappeared from new plays,[46] but Avery's figures suggest that for some twenty years beyond the Licensing Act those stereotypes remained welcome and popular on the eighteenth-century stage.

In a review of Avery's book Alan Downer questions the suggestion on page 1 that "the reception of [Congreve's] plays should illuminate the status of Restoration comedy as a whole, especially the work of such comparable authors as Wycherley, Etherege, and Vanbrugh."[47] To ask the question is reasonable, but we find that with minor qualifications Avery's claim holds up. Consider, for example, the fortunes of *The Rehearsal* (1671). It was performed during most seasons from 1704 (when records become fairly full) to 1778, when it was condensed to a three-act version.[48] Its period of greatest popularity was from 1739 to 1742 (another reflection of the influence of the Licensing Act, in our opinion); the 135 performances in nine seasons from 1739 to 1747 are a result, in part at least, of its serving as a popular vehicle for both Theophilus Cibber and David Garrick as Bayes.[49] We should probably observe at this point that the fortunes of any one play (or even one writer) in a given term of years must inevitably reflect the preferences and predilections of leading actors. A play which made a good vehicle for Garrick (or in earlier years for Colley Cibber) would be performed a lot.

46. *Comedy and Society*, ch. 5.
47. *Philological Quarterly*, 31 (1952), 258–59.
48. Competition with *A Peep Behind the Curtain* and later with *The Critic* helped to drive *The Rehearsal* off the stage.
49. See Emmett L. Avery, "The Stage Popularity of *The Rehearsal*, 1671–1777," *Research Studies of the State College of Washington*, 7 (1939), 201–4.

Consider the case of Wycherley's *The Country-Wife* and *The Plain-Dealer*. Both plays enjoyed their greatest popularity on the eighteenth-century stage in the years 1725 to 1742 (averaging about five performances per annum each). Both fell badly out of favor during the later 1740s and 1750s. *The Country-Wife* was reduced to a two-act version by Lee in 1765, and rewritten as *The Country Girl* by Garrick in 1766; *The Plain-Dealer* was revamped by Bickerstaff in 1765.[50] Surveying eighteenth-century responses to Wycherley, Avery concluded that the falling-off in popularity of his plays after the early 1740s resulted from a slowly rising tide of moral opinion which became genuinely dominant in the 1760s and 1770s. Wycherley's share of the total repertory was 1.9 percent in the later 1720s (his peak during the eighteenth century); twenty years later it was down to 0.4 percent and by the 1750s his plays had virtually disappeared from the stage.[51] Obviously Wycherley faded earlier than Congreve; we would suppose that in part this reflects the difference between a genuine Carolean playwright and one who came a full generation later. Etherege, we may note, faded out still earlier, and his plays were not picked up by eighteenth-century revisers. The pattern which we are seeing here is a simple and consistent one: considerable popularity in the 1720s, 1730s, and early 1740s; followed by a falling-off which is more or less rapid depending on how offensive a particular play or author is to the stiffening moral standards of the mid-eighteenth century; followed by outright chopping or rewriting in the 1760s and 1770s. Vanbrugh presents the same history.

Some strong confirmatory evidence is offered by Shirley Strum Kenny in a study of the fortunes of the works of turn-of-the-century playwrights on the eighteenth-century stage.[52] Her figures (performance totals of works by these writers at five-year intervals)

50. For details, see Emmett L. Avery, "*The Country Wife* in the Eighteenth Century," *Research Studies of the State College of Washington*, 10 (1942), 141–72, and "*The Plain Dealer* in the Eighteenth Century," ibid., 11 (1943), 234–56.

51. Emmett L. Avery, "The Reputation of Wycherley's Comedies as Stage Plays in the Eighteenth Century," *Research Studies of the State College of Washington*, 12 (1944), 131–54.

52. "Perennial Favorites: Congreve, Vanbrugh, Cibber, Farquhar, and Steele," *Modern Philology*, 73, No. 4, Part 2 [Friedman *Festschrift*] (1976), S4–S11.

show a major upsurge in popularity between 1715 and 1730, a prolonged peak in popularity between 1730 and 1745, a gradual falling-off by 1760, and greatly diminished significance in the repertory after that. In rough terms, Kenny is able to say that the twenty-five comedies by these five writers constituted 25 percent of the total London repertory (by performance) in the 1740s and 1750s, and frequently accounted for between 40 and 60 percent of all performances of comedy in London in a given year in that period. We may note, surveying Kenny's figures, that Congreve's proportion of the total was tending to fall off in the last twenty-five years. By mid-century, Congreve, who had stopped writing earliest, was the most dated of the writers Kenny surveys.

We are probably safe in suggesting that the continuing popularity of older comedies in the 1740s and 1750s was a side-effect of the Licensing Act: Drury Lane and Covent Garden were mounting few new plays for the simple reason that they did not have to take any risks, being secure in their monopoly. But until 1737 this was not true, and the substantial popularity of the older plays represents genuine theatrical viability. The moral objections of the Collier era had, in fact, very little long-term effect on repertory offerings.[53] Reading criticism as it grew into a major industry in the eighteenth century, one finds that moral objections to older plays *from writers who attended the theatre and supported the drama* became widespread only in the 1750s and 1760s. Edmund Burke's quite hostile view of the older comedy, published in the *Reformer* (No. 2; 4 February 1748), was the precursor of a flood of such attacks. Significant numbers of critics find the older comedies crude or immoral only after mid-century. This is what Avery found in following the fortunes of Wycherley and Congreve; this is the observation of Charles Harold Gray;[54] and this is what our own reading tells us. That *The London Cuckolds* was dropped by Drury Lane in 1751 is no accident: it fits a pattern which goes beyond any single play or writer.

53. See Calhoun Winton, "The London Stage Embattled, 1695–1710," *Tennessee Studies in Literature*, 19 (1974), 9–19.
54. *Theatrical Criticism in London to 1795* (New York: Columbia Univ. Press, 1931).

A significant parallel to the pattern of popularity, disfavor, and adaptation we have noted may be found in the fortunes of Ben Jonson's plays.[55] *Volpone, The Alchemist,* and *The Silent Woman* all held the stage into the middle of the century, and then gave way to altered versions in the 1760s and 1770s. *Every Man in His Humour,* revived only once in the first half of the eighteenth century, and then briefly, was altered by Garrick in 1751 and became a popular stock comedy. By 1773, Noyes remarks in surveying "criticism," "the plays of Jonson were considered thoroughly obsolete."[56] Noyes' researches make abundantly plain another most interesting parallel: the kinds of criticism leveled against Jonson's plays in the 1760s and 1770s are substantively identical to those aimed at Congreve and Vanbrugh. Distinctions which seemed very clear indeed to late seventeenth-century critics had largely disappeared: crude old plays were crude old plays to the reformers of the 1760s.[57]

Where does this leave us? We find several implications in this little survey. 1) The audience revolt against new plays around 1700 was a temporary aberration; it does not in itself signal a basic shift in taste or morals. 2) A much more fundamental shift occurred in the years around 1760, a shift which genuinely did deprive "Restoration comedy" of its popular audience. 3) "Restoration comedy" was not simply an embodiment of the ideology of a coterie audience. To some degree it was that, of course, but not to such an extent that very different audiences could not enjoy it. 4) Not until the middle of the eighteenth century were audiences inclined to take the moral implications of old plays very seriously. 5) A concomitant point: what eighteenth-century audiences saw in the older plays was essentially entertainment. Reviewing Avery's study of Congreve's reputation, Alan Downer concluded that it was "evidence

55. See Robert Gale Noyes, *Ben Jonson on the English Stage, 1660–1776* (1935; rpt. New York: Blom, 1966).
56. Noyes, p. 29.
57. A similar pattern seems to hold true for the plays of Fletcher on the eighteenth-century stage. See Leo Hughes and A. H. Scouten, "The Penzance Promptbook of *The Pilgrim*," *Modern Philology,* 73 (1975), 33–53, and the preface to the 1778 collected edition of the plays of "Beaumont and Fletcher."

that the eighteenth-century focus was on theater, rather than on drama; . . . plays were considered only as vehicles for what really mattered and was interesting, the actor's performance." This seems to us no more than a modest exaggeration. The eighteenth-century theatre was a business, and plays were its raw material. The best of the old plays were high art, but they lasted in the theatre only so long as they continued to entertain a heterogeneous audience.

3

Otway and the Comic Muse

We now think of Otway as a writer of tragedies. The domestic simplicity of *The Orphan* (1680) is often praised, while the flaming
passions and harrowing pathos of *Venice Preserv'd* still have some
power to move us. Articles on Otway's pathos, politics, religion,
and tragic vision abound. Yet he did write some comedies, and about
these there has been a conspiracy of silence. In his own age, Otway
was considered a comic writer of some importance. Even the sple-
netic author of *A Comparison Between the Two Stages* (1702) singles
him out, with Dryden, as a writer who triumphed in both comedy
and tragedy.[1] The reason for neglect of the comedies is not far to
seek, for they are, as the same writer observes, "highly loose and
prophane."

Only two or three modern critics have had a kind word for
Otway's comedies—works which admittedly require a strong stomach. They are not graceful, amusing displays of wit and manners,
but serious, bitter satires whose surface gaiety does little to mask
the author's violent disillusionment and despair. Otway died at the
age of thirty-three, and I would not claim that in his three essays at
comedy he equaled the best of Wycherley, Etherege, or Congreve.
But he was in their league, and his comedies clearly deserve serious,
unbiased analysis. Both for their own considerable merits and as

1. *A Comparison Between the Two Stages*, ed. Staring B. Wells, p. 33.

an aid to understanding Otway's tragic vision, they will repay our attention.

Otway's Comedies and the Critics

Otway has had mixed luck with the critics. *Venice Preserv'd* has always enjoyed a considerable reputation. Its exuberant excesses have been looked on with indulgence; even the Nicky-Nacky scenes have been tolerated as a satiric expression of political opinion. The comedies, though they reflect a similar vehemence, have generally been ignored or denounced. Such writers as John Palmer, H. T. E. Perry, Kathleen Lynch, Thomas H. Fujimura, Dale Underwood, and Norman Holland do not so much as mention Otway's name. Nor does Rose Zimbardo in *Wycherley's Drama: A Link in the Development of English Satire*, though Otway is clearly the most determined satirist among writers of Restoration comedy, and Wycherley's influence on him is unmistakable, extending even to the borrowing of a character. Bonamy Dobrée does list one Otway comedy in the bibliography to his influential *Restoration Comedy* (1924)—because it appeared in a Mermaid edition.

Otway's comedies fell out of the repertory during the first half of the eighteenth century. The wonder is that they lasted as long as they did after the time of Jeremy Collier. *Friendship in Fashion*, tried after a lapse of at least thirty years, provoked a near-riot at Drury Lane (22 January 1750), after which the managers stuck to safer fare. Writing about *The Souldiers Fortune* in 1832, Genest commented: "Otway's merit as a *Comic* writer has not, of late years, been sufficiently attended to—this is an excellent play, but very indecent, particularly in the character of Sir Jolly Jumble."[2] This account cannot have encouraged the Victorians to investigate the subject. Had Macaulay done so, we would have heard less about the evils of *The Country-Wife* from him.

2. *The London Stage*, Part 4, I, 169–70. John Genest, *Some Account of the English Stage*, 10 vols. (1832; rpt. New York: Burt Franklin, n.d.), I, 313.

Twentieth-century commentators have generally been frigidly disapproving. Nicoll discusses Otway under "Farce and Sentimentalism," tagging his discussion of the three comedies onto Otway's translation-adaptation of *The Cheats of Scapin*. He says tersely that they are "Elizabethan in structure and in plot" (whatever that means), "with a fair infusion of Restoration vulgarity." Of Sir Jolly Jumble Nicoll says only that he is "one of those types which display in all their fulness the horror and the degradation of certain aspects of Restoration life." R. G. Ham describes the comedies as pointless, indecent, and inept. John Harrington Smith deals with them briefly and with evident distaste.[3] Worst of all for Otway's critical fortunes, the editor of the standard edition was plainly both horrified and disgusted by the comedies.

> It has been customary to inveigh against his ribaldry. To us of the present generation who are bored rather than shocked by it, to do so would be to harpoon a jelly-fish. An apology would be fitter, so very feeble and unalluring does its stark grossness render it. Of the three comedies that Otway wrote, only one, *The Souldiers Fortune*, achieved popularity and underwent several revivals. The rest were stillborn. The reason of this lies in the essential fatuousness of his comedies, their dull, featureless, purposeless vacuity. They were not meant to instruct or correct, and they do not entertain. Their wit is of a poor quality, their plot and intrigue are the common stage-property of the day, and their characters uninteresting.[4]

This hysterical denunciation, feebly masquerading as aloof indifference, certainly does not invite renewed attention or revaluation.

Only three critics, I believe, have ventured to differ, or to treat these comedies with any seriousness. Montague Summers, in the introduction to his edition of 1926, delivers a ringing endorsement

3. Nicoll, I, 258. Roswell Gray Ham, *Otway and Lee* (1931; rpt. New York: Greenwood, 1969), pp. 99–106, 205–6. Smith, *The Gay Couple*, esp. pp. 40, 97–98, 106–7.

4. *The Works of Thomas Otway*, ed. J. C. Ghosh, 2 vols. (Oxford: Clarendon Press, 1932), Introduction, I, 44. All textual references will be to this edition.

of Otway's power as a satirist and skill as a contriver of comic action and dialogue.[5] That it has gone unheeded is not surprising: the edition is textually worse than worthless (being actually dishonest at times); Summers did not support his praise with analysis; and he has never enjoyed much reputation as a critic. More than forty years later Thomas B. Stroup published what remains one of the best things ever written about Otway, an article which tries to sum up the nature of Otway's outlook on life.[6] Stroup had the good sense and honesty to draw freely on the comedies, though it was no part of his purpose to give a systematic account of them. The only praise for Otway's comedies as comedies since Summers' comes from James Sutherland. "It has been customary to dismiss the three comedies of Otway with impatient contempt. . . . Left to himself, Otway would probably have chosen to write satirical comedy: what he did in fact write, having to please the players and the playgoers, was farcical comedy uneasily streaked with satire."[7] He goes on to deliver two pages of sensible appreciation, though he is obviously a bit uncomfortable with Otway's precarious oscillation between "farce and a disturbing realism," and he does not like the "disconcerting mixture of lewd comedy and satire."

Friendship in Fashion *in Its Context*

To understand these comedies, one must start by realizing that Otway was of the second generation of Carolean writers, and that the context in which his comedies appeared was not that of the early Carolean drama. These works are not wit or manners comedies, displays of genteel artificiality or urbane libertinism. "Restoration comedy of manners" is usually viewed as the product of two short,

5. *The Complete Works of Thomas Otway*, ed. Montague Summers, 3 vols. (Bloomsbury: Nonesuch, 1926), Introduction, esp. I, lxvi–lxviii, lxxxi–lxxxiv.
6. "Otway's Bitter Pessimism," *Essays in English Literature of the Classical Period Presented to Dougald MacMillan*, ed. Daniel W. Patterson and Albrecht B. Strauss, *Studies in Philology*, Extra Series, No. 4 (Chapel Hill: Univ. of North Carolina Press, 1967), pp. 54–75.
7. Sutherland, pp. 141–43.

discrete periods (1668–76; 1691–1700), a construct I have objected to elsewhere.[8] One should not extract a few favorite plays from context. Between 1668 and 1678 there occurred a great boom in sex-comedy, starting with Betterton's *The Amorous Widow* (ca. 1669), and carrying on through such plays as Dryden's *Marriage A-la-Mode* (1671), Dover's(?) *The Mall* (1674), Wycherley's *The Country-Wife* (1675), Shadwell's *The Virtuoso*, and Etherege's *The Man of Mode* (1676). In these years there was a steady escalation in shock tactics. As in the New York theatre of the 1960s, playwrights pushed ever farther with titillating sex. Copulations and cuckoldings abound, which they most decidedly do not in plays of the preceding decade. The difference may be seen in comparing Etherege's suggestive but carefully chaste *She wou'd if she cou'd* (1668) with *The Man of Mode*. Prior to the middle 1670s servants do not enter from the bedroom, "tying up Linnen." Some of these plays have a serious moral basis (*Marriage A-la-Mode*); some do not (*The Mall*); in others the issue has been warmly disputed (*The Country-Wife*). By no means did the stream of sex-comedies stop magically in 1676. It goes right on with such works as Rawlins'(?) *Tom Essence*, Mrs. Behn's *The Rover* (Part 1), and Durfey's *A Fond Husband*—this last a blatantly amoral comedy of cuckoldry which became a favorite of King Charles II.

The spring of 1678 saw the production of Behn's *Sir Patient Fancy* (January), Shadwell's vitriolic *A True Widow* (March), and Dryden's roaring, roistering, scandalous *The Kind Keeper; or Mr. Limberham* (March)—an avowed imitation of Durfey's play which was banned after three nights.[9] Neither of the other two seems to have had a good run: perhaps the audience found that smut had been taken too far to stomach comfortably; perhaps it had merely tired of the ever more blatantly risqué. Modern scholars who suppose that *The Country-Wife* is the acme of Restoration raciness have not read the comedies of 1677 and 1678. At any rate, the sex-boom

8. See A. H. Scouten, "Notes Toward a History of Restoration Comedy." Cf. Hume, "Diversity and Development in Restoration Comedy, 1660–1679," *Eighteenth-Century Studies*, 5 (1972), 365–97, and *Development*, chs. 6–8.

9. *The London Stage*, Part 1, p. 269.

had burned itself out; the onset of the Popish Plot that fall changed theatrical conditions; and writers sought different modes.[10]

Otway's first comedy, *Friendship in Fashion*, appeared in April 1678. Its large doses of raw sex must be partly understood as a perfectly sensible reaction to the triumph of such plays as *The Country-Wife*, *The Virtuoso*, and especially *A Fond Husband*. Otway wrote for bread; he needed to succeed; and just like Dryden in *Mr. Limberham*, he followed the trend. I am going to argue that Otway used the sex-comedy mode for his own serious purposes, but to deny or ignore his place in this mini-tradition would be silly. Ever unlucky, he got onto the bandwagon too late. Other deliberately shocking plays (smutty plays, if you will) were failing, and probably his did too. Langbaine does report it "a very diverting Play . . . acted with general applause."[11] But the defensive tone of the author's preface, lack of any known revival until the eighteenth century, and the lack of any edition after the first all suggest indifferent success.

Otway's background as a writer consisted of three tragedies, one of them a translation, plus a three-act farce, *The Cheats of Scapin*, translated from Molière to serve as an afterpiece for his version of Racine's *Bérénice* (ca. December 1676). Contrary to common report, this translation represents Otway's only significant borrowing from Molière.[12] Otway shifts the action into a nominally English setting, and proves his ability to write brisk, "low" comic dialogue—a far remove from the high-flown diction of the rhymed heroic tragedies which were all he had previously written. But workmanlike though this translation is, it gives no hint of what Otway would do on his own. (In passing, we may note that it was one of the first afterpieces of the Restoration period, anticipating the standard eighteenth-century pattern, and that it continued to be

10. I have given only the barest outline of context here, since I have dealt with the relevant plays more fully in my *Development*.

11. Gerard Langbaine, *An Account of the English Dramatick Poets* (Oxford: West and Clements, 1691), p. 398.

12. See John Wilcox, *The Relation of Molière to Restoration Comedy* (1938; rpt. New York: Blom, 1964), pp. 144–46.

a favorite with audiences into the nineteenth century.) Setting out to write on his own, Otway could of course look to other writers for inspiration. He was very friendly with Shadwell until politics divided them, and Wycherley was plainly his point of departure.

In *Friendship in Fashion* Otway makes the male lead (Goodvile) a vicious scoundrel, his wife a cold-blooded adulteress. Ham complains that the play is "indecent" even by "the standards of its time," branding Goodvile a degraded imitation of Wycherley's Horner. Perhaps so, but with a difference. Critics have squirmed and worried over Horner's "attractiveness," and he has been considered everything from "wholly negative," "an agent of destruction" to "a wholly positive and creative comic hero . . . squarely on the side of health, of freedom, and . . . of honesty."[13] One could not, however, suppose Goodvile to be designed as any kind of comic hero, even a rogue hero like Horner, without making Otway out to be a monster. We start then from an anomaly. Here is a "Restoration comedy" whose protagonist is utterly contemptible, even by the easy standards of the other characters in the play. Plainly we must ask why. What was Otway up to, and what sort of response did he hope to elicit from his audience?

The plot-design of the play is schematically simple. Goodvile neglects his wife, with whom he is bored. He endeavors to seduce Camilla, even though she is engaged to marry one of his two best friends, Valentine. He is somewhat hampered by Victoria, a kinswoman under his protection whom he has seduced and now wishes to be rid of—so he plans to marry her off to his other best friend, Truman. Mrs. Goodvile, who knows all about his doings, affects loving ignorance while she cuckolds him with Truman. Goodvile fails in his attempt on Camilla; Victoria marries Sir Noble Clumsey, a drunken fool. Along the way Goodvile copulates with Lady Squeamish in the dark, thinking her to be Camilla; she had thought *he* was Truman. Goodvile finally catches onto his wife's doings, and tries to surprise her *in flagrante delicto*, hoping thereby to get rid

13. See respectively Anne Righter [Barton], "William Wycherley," *Restoration Theatre*, ed. John Russell Brown and Bernard Harris, Stratford-upon-Avon Studies, 6 (London: Edward Arnold, 1965), pp. 71–91, and Virginia Ogden Birdsall, *Wild Civility*, p. 136.

of her, but the attempt is foiled and at the end of the play he is left
with his horns and his unwelcome wife—poetic justice of a sort.

What object is served in this goulash of lies, plots, hypocrisy
and fornication? Ham sees nothing more than "hectic bustle," and
says flatly that the play had no "purpose" other than "to amuse,"
comparing it to "a series of *fabliaux*." Montague Summers, on the
other hand, calls the play "a mordant social satire" in which Otway scarifies vice and lashes society, without saying how he knows.
We must, I think, reflect both on the conclusion of the play and on
the distinctions Otway gives us among his characters. The persons
of the piece fall into two groups: the three "friends" with their
associated females, versus the minor fools and skunks who populate the plot. All of the latter are thoroughly despicable. Malagene
is the most prominent, an affected, presumptuous fool and coward
who thinks it a great joke to knock over a cripple in the street (I,
371). Caper and Saunter are lesser fops in this degraded Sparkish
mode. Sir Noble Clumsey is a drunken lout. Lady Squeamish (or
her double) we have met already in *The Country-Wife*, and the long
passages of her conversation that Otway gives us do nothing to
improve our view of her. The crew of characters contributes to an
atmosphere of coarse revelry, contemptible affectation, and selfish
sensuality.

The principal characters fall in the realm of gentility and wit—
as Otway chooses to present that world. The title has of course a
sharply ironic double edge to its meaning. 1) This is what *friendship* is in the "fashionable" world. 2) This is the sort of friendship
now in vogue. As we discover almost immediately that the protagonist intends to seduce one friend's fiancée while palming off a cast
mistress as a wife for the other, we can have no illusions about the
harshly negative view Otway took of his subject, all the more so if
we remember that throughout all nine of Otway's full-length plays
runs a prominent theme—the vital importance of true friendship
and the utter vileness of falseness to a friend. No reader of *Venice
Preserv'd*, remembering Jaffeir and Pierre, should be able to imagine that Otway would want us to look on Goodvile with other than
horror and detestation. His self-serving lies and deliberate attempt
to betray his bosom friends (gradually revealed during the play) can

only be seen as the blackest and most despicable kind of treachery. Horner, we should recall, is a scrupulously good friend to Harcourt: we cannot imagine his attempting to seduce Alithea while pretending to further Harcourt's suit.

The subject of the play is fashionable friendship—and the libertine philosophy and social code behind it. Naturally we side with Truman and Mrs. Goodvile, whose adultery yields a punishment to fit Goodvile's crime. Otway never suggests that Truman and Valentine (or even Camilla) have any particular virtues. They represent, evidently, a tolerable if unadmirable way of the world. They are not so stupid or pretentious as the minor fools, nor so evil as Goodvile. They do little, however, to suggest a genuine positive norm in the world of the play.

Goodvile and the minor fools give the work a thoroughly evil flavor. *This*, says Otway, is the fashionable world—and presents us a truly ugly picture of broken friendship. The plot is loaded with intrigue, confusion, and narrow escapes, especially in the wild night garden-scene in Act IV, full of copulation and swordplay. But here these elements of the sex-farce are served up with none of the lively relish of *The Country-Wife* or *A Fond Husband*. As both Sutherland and Summers observe, Goodvile is far too real a person for us to accept him comfortably as a comic convention. As he bills and coos with his wife (who plays up with vigorous insincerity), assures Truman of his devoted friendship, or snaps "I will sooner return to my Vomit" than take back his wife (I, 408), we have to respond with disgust.

Much of the first part of the play is given over to society conversation. In consequence, the plot drags a bit; but Otway does communicate a vivid sense of the vapidity, vacuousness, and triviality of these people and this world. The scandal-mongering Malagene, we are told, "would pimp for his Sister, though but for the bare pleasure of telling it himself" (I, 341), and after watching him for a bit, we believe it. Even Truman and Valentine, the "best" characters in the play, accept the banalities of their squalid world with amused indifference. Watching the fops "attempt" Mrs. Goodvile and Camilla, Truman observes: "Oh, 'twere pity to interrupt 'em;

a woman loves to play and fondle with a Coxcomb sometimes as naturally, as with a Lap-Dog" (I, 361).

The end of the play leaves no doubt as to how it should be taken. Goodvile, assisted by a pair of whores, sneaks back into town to surprise his wife: "some hot-brain'd, Horn-mad Cuckold now would be for cutting of Throats; but I am resolved to turn a Civil, Sober, discreet Person, and hate blood-shed: No: I'l manage the matter so temperately that I'l catch her in his very Arms, then civilly Discard her, Bagg and Baggage, whilst you my dainty Doxies take possession of her Priviledges, and enter the Territories with Colours flying" (I, 423–24). His scheme foiled by the forewarned adulterers, Goodvile is publicly humiliated and then forced to put the best face he can on things. This patching up a pretense of marriage and friendship makes a ghastly parody of the usual comic resolution. Here we find no joy, no forgiveness, no festive regeneration. We are not even allowed to enjoy relief at the averting of exposure, as in *The Country-Wife*. Instead, an intolerably dirty and dishonest status quo is hypocritically patched up with insincere civilities. Goodvile says, "*Truman*, if thou hast enjoyed her [Mrs. Goodvile], I beg thee keep it close, and if it be possible let us yet be friends." To which Truman coolly replies, "'Tis not my fault if we be Foes" (I, 430). Goodvile then gives Valentine some advice about his new wife: "look to her, keep her as secret as thou wou'dst a Murder, had'st thou committed one: trust her not with thy dearest Friend, She has Beauty enough to corrupt him."

With this bleak, raw ending Otway slams home a realization of just how ugly these relations will continue to be. We are shown a brutally unappetizing world—and that is exactly the point of the play. As in some of Hogarth's drawings, vice is depicted, but only to be made unattractive. Horner may seem rather fun to some observers; Dorimant is undeniably glamorous, however reprehensible we may think him. Goodvile is something else again. *Friendship in Fashion* is brilliant, but not fun. Sutherland comments on the distressing realism of emotion and character psychology, especially in Act V. We are given an accurate picture of selfish, licentious debauchees and society whores. Otway did not play these court-wit games in life, and he does not approve them in literary facsimile. (There is some biographical evidence that he had engaged in debauchery and hated himself for it.) We are not supposed to like what we see, or be amused by it. *Friendship in Fashion* is an angry commentary on prevalent social codes in high society, and Otway's point would be entirely lost if we were merely amused or entertained.

The Souldiers Fortune: *A Comic Success*

The Souldiers Fortune (June 1680) is brisker, more amusing, less overweighted with an obtrusive satiric point—factors which probably contributed to its success in the theatre. Downes reports that this comedy and Durfey's *A Fond Husband* "took extraordinary well, and being perfectly *Acted*; got the Company great Reputation and Profit." [14] The main action follows a more standard pattern, allowing us to sympathize with the adulterers as they abuse an old cit. The situation is strictly routine: young Clarinda has been forced to marry rich old Sir Davy Dunce while her true love, Captain Beaugard, has been away at the wars. Upon his return to London they set out to make the old brute a cuckold, and they succeed. In a second plot line Beaugard's friend, Courtine, woos and wins the witty Sylvia, friend to Lady Dunce (Clarinda). What makes the play unusual is the way these elements are handled.

The atmosphere of the work is greatly influenced by three things: the presence of Sir Jolly Jumble, the character of Sir Davy Dunce, and the military background. Sir Jolly is Otway's most memorable comic character—a homosexual pimp and voyeur exhibited among his girls, who are guaranteed to be "lew'd drunken stripping Whores . . . that won't be affectedly squeamish and troublesome" (II, 104).

---

14. *Roscius Anglicanus*, pp. 36, 41. Downes comments particularly on Leigh's excellence as Sir Jolly Jumble. Some of his other roles were Old Fumble in *A Fond Husband*, Pandarus in *Troilus and Cressida*, Dominic in *The Spanish Fryar*, Dashwell in *The London Cuckolds*, Malagene in *Friendship in Fashion*, Sir Patient Fancy, and Oldfox in *The Plain-Dealer*. In short, he specialized in dirty old men and obnoxious fops.

Sir Jolly has horrified the critics. Though impotent, he loves "to know how matters go, though, now and then to see a pretty Wench and a young Fellow Towze and Rowze and Frouze and Mowze; odd I love a young fellow dearly, faith dearly—" (II, 103), and says so with a bright good humor that Nicoll is quite unable to accept with equanimity. Vanbrugh's Coupler is a similar character, presented much more negatively. But Sir Jolly hurts no one and is by no means a bad sort. Aside from his slavering eagerness to "peep," he turns out to be one of the most decent and humane characters in the play—which is surely a very blunt authorial comment.

Sir Davy Dunce is all that a fond cuckold should be: foolish, suspicious, gullible, cowardly, and selfish. His fatuous complacency and nauseating endearments to his wife are to be gloated over rather than pitied. Nicoll thinks otherwise, saying that the "old and betrayed husband . . . is treated by Otway towards the close of the play in an almost pathetic manner." This reaction seems contrary to a great deal of evidence in the play. Before we ever meet Sir Davy, we are given a bitingly unsympathetic view of him. He is "an old, greasie, untoward, ill natur'd, slovenly, Tobacco-taking Cuckold; but plaguy Jealous," who objects to clean underwear and continually eats garlic. Sylvia observes, from a young woman's vantage point, that "'tis an unspeakable blessing to lye all night by a Horse-load of diseases; a beastly, unsavory, old, groaning, grunting, wheazing Wretch, that smells of the Grave he's going to already" (II, 104, 107–8). Nothing in the play should dispose us better toward the cuckold. Sir Davy hires assassins to murder Beaugard, and when he thinks he is stuck with the "body," plants it on the premises of a close friend and neighbor and calls the Watch to find it, hoping to "let my Neighbour be very fairly hang'd in my stead" (II, 187). Why should we have any sympathy for the old swine?

Infinitely more feeling should be elicited by the soldiers' plight. Otway had recently served in Flanders, and knew whereof he spoke. Beaugard is disbanded and broke, paid off in debentures instead of ready money, and left destitute without an occupation (II, 101). Otway goes so far as to include an extraneous scene, explicitly blasting corruption in the army and bewailing the treatment of honorable men (II, 122–24). Poverty is thus made *real* in this play:

unlike the court wits, Otway knew about destitution at first hand. Beaugard is not the usual airy younger son, scrambling to make his fortune; rather, he is a grown man facing a bleak future in a desperately inhospitable world.

The harsh realism of the military background and the psychology of some of the characters may seem to accord oddly with the farcical parts of the play. The stratagems of the cuckolding plot, especially when Sir Davy is made to serve as go-between; the cuckold's agreement to let his luscious young wife try to "revive" the "dead body" of Beaugard; and Beaugard's appearance as his own ghost (II, 185) all smack of Aphra Behn's racy light comedies. This combination of farce and realism certainly raises some questions about the coherence of the play and its overall effect, problems best approached through the relation of the two plots.

Little is made of the actual sex in the cuckolding plot. It is briefly enjoyed, but not dwelt upon or discussed. (Otway does allow some high spirits, as when Sir Davy, erroneously thinking himself horned, roars "I'll run mad, I'll climb *Bow* Steeple presently, bestride the Dragon, and preach Cuckoldom to the whole City"— II, 136.) The real dirt in the play is ancillary, stemming mostly from Sir Jolly and the picture of an unappetizing old husband. That we are to welcome the successful adultery seems clear; but the spirit in which it is presented needs to be understood. John Harrington Smith was able to revel in the boisterous sexual carryings-on in Ravenscroft's notorious *The London Cuckolds* (1681), but seems curiously distressed about them here.[15] Probably the realness of Otway's characters makes acceptance of adultery more difficult. Smith is particularly upset by what he considers "glamorization" of adultery, by which he means the "excuse" of true love and a previous desire to marry. One finds this excuse in a variety of plays, including Mrs. Behn's *The Roundheads*, *The False Count*, and *The Lucky Chance*, and Mrs. Pix's *The Spanish Wives*, for example. But I do not see that Otway is looking for an excuse here, and the play makes much more serious sense if we accept the proposition that Beaugard and Lady Dunce really care for each other. If he is after nothing

15. *The Gay Couple*, pp. 106–7.

more than easy sex, we have merely a coarse farce. But women in this society often *were* forced to marry for money, and in raising the issue Otway is not just seizing on a specious excuse for adultery. The title of the play and the plight of the disbanded soldiers should help us realize that Otway takes the condition and frustrations of the indigent seriously, as well he might. At the end of the play Sir Davy is blackmailed into acquiescence: he accepts his position and horns with a harsh, masochistic gaiety in which there is more self-contempt than forgiveness or resignation. As in *Friendship in Fashion*, nothing is really solved. Stroup comments that the conclusions of Otway's plays establish no moral order, afford no cathartic purgation, provide no satisfying sense of an ending. "No dance or wedding feast concludes the comedies; no hero's body carried off the stage in triumph or heroine crowned in death concludes the tragedies."[16]

For Beaugard and Lady Dunce there can be no satisfactory conclusion. (Unless, of course, Otway were to adopt Farquhar's easy way out and provide a legally impossible divorce.) And the more real we find the characters, the less happy we can be about their circumstances. But the bleak flatness of the play's end is a little disconcerting, especially in view of the "happy" conclusion of the "romance" plot. Courtine and Sylvia are difficult to judge fairly: Otway's savage dissection of their marriage in *The Atheist* inevitably casts a pall over our appreciation of their courtship. John Harrington Smith dismisses it as a "feeble" example of the gay couple love game. From one vantage point, perhaps it is. In their first bargaining scene they banter, but only sourly, agreeing to bicker, belie one another, and reject marriage (II, 120–21). Their exchanges lack bite and gusto (for example, II, 132–34), but their lack of sparkle, and their dubiety about their feelings and about marriage, should be understood as a reflection of real doubt and malaise, not as a witty affectation to be cast aside upon whim. They are mutually attracted, but doubtful of the future. In this respect they are less engaging but much more real than the usual sort of gay couple Smith prefers—Dryden's Celadon and Florimell, for in-

16. "Otway's Bitter Pessimism," p. 74.

stance. The proviso scene (II, 171–77) has little wit or tenderness: the lovers embark upon matrimony, but without confidence in the outcome. Little wonder that joy is not unbounded at the end of the play. In the marriage Otway sees something to hope, much to fear, nothing to celebrate. There is humor in Sir Jolly's response to the news: "In troth, and that's very uncivilly done: I don't like these Marriages, I'll have no Marriages in my House, and there's an end on't" (II, 193). Earlier, he has flatly refused to assist "in the business of Matrimony"; "civil correspondence" is his line, and he will stick to it (II, 156). This is a slightly sick joke, but a pointed one. Nowhere in Otway's comedies are we given any ground for optimism about the institution of marriage.

Superficially, *The Souldiers Fortune* concludes with a conventionally happy ending. Beaugard has enjoyed his conquest; Courtine has won his girl. But a little reflection explains and justifies the sober and dark-tinged conclusion. Beaugard and Lady Dunce are real enough that we may wonder what the future holds—and clearly it is bleak for both of them. Enjoying sex with Lady Dunce certainly does not get Beaugard out of his predicament. The romance plot holds only a little more promise. Obviously, few Restoration comedies will bear any consideration of the future in store for their characters. (What kind of husband will Dorimant make Harriet? What will become of Margery Pinchwife?) But usually the author is careful to maintain the convention of the romantic happy-ever-after marriage, or to treat his characters as puppets to whom we may remain perfectly indifferent. *The London Cuckolds* is a good example of the latter approach. We watch the trio of cuckoldings with amused unconcern, and have no reason at all to consider these doings in the light of real life. *The London Cuckolds* is amusing, pleasant, and frivolous; *The Souldiers Fortune* is amusing, unpleasant, and ultimately serious.

Otway does stick to a basically conventional form, and we can, if we wish, ignore the darker implications in his handling of it. Very probably the original audience did so, just as it did with *Marriage A-la-Mode.*[17] As Dickens chose to do in his revised ending for

17. See ch. 4, sec. "The Satiric Impact of the Play," below.

Great Expectations, Otway leaves us free to evade the issue and romanticize if we insist. To do so is utterly to trivialize the play. Along the way, we are given much to amuse and entertain us, but the harsh brutality of this world, made vivid and real, and the unfestive ending, should not be ignored. Sutherland holds that in this one play "Otway succeeds fully in combining his sense of the actual with the cathartic gaiety of comedy."[18] I see little that is cathartic here, but agree absolutely that *The Souldiers Fortune* has an unusual, effective, and disturbing realism, leavened but not obscured by a conventional plot pattern and a harsh, often obscene comic gaiety.

The Atheist: *An Unsettling Sequel*

The Atheist: or, The Second Part of the Souldiers Fortune is a strange play. It was staged in the late spring of 1683,[19] and proved to be Otway's last dramatic work. Less than a year later he was dead. By this time Otway was in desperate financial straits, and his writing a sequel to the popular *Souldiers Fortune* is clearly an attempt to capitalize on its success. There is no evidence for Summers' assertion that *The Atheist* "met with considerable success." We have no record of any revival; the work was not reprinted; we know nothing of its initial run. Ham sums up the usual view of the play, calling it "an afterthought born of necessity, and, like most sequels, a confession of impotence." Nicoll dismisses it in half a sentence as a weak continuation.[20] No one has ever seen any point to the play. And yet it is, I will try to show, no slovenly potboiler (Ham's term), but rather a harsh, dead-serious play, and above all a truly brilliant experiment.

The play's constituent elements have seemed hopelessly diverse

18. Sutherland, p. 142.

19. *The London Stage*, Part 1, p. 320, guesses at a July premiere. This seems too late in the season, and too close to the publication date (advertised 8 August). An epilogue reference to the conviction of Sir Patience Ward for perjury dates the play after 19 May. I would put the premiere soon after that.

20. *Otway and Lee*, p. 205; Nicoll, I, 258.

and discordant. Ham calls the play a "loose-jointed thing"; John Harrington Smith finds it "an aggregate of cheap romance and cheap farce." This is certainly the impression it gives—a jumble of miscellaneous elements. Summers loyally praises some of the odds and ends, but without claiming any overall purpose or unity in the play. Otway does not, one must grant, altogether succeed in unifying his assemblage, but by no means is it a careless mélange of stale tricks.

There are three main parts to the plot: 1) a romance and swordplay story in which Beaugard and the widow Porcia are united, despite the fierce opposition of her brother-in-law, Theodoret, and his friend, Gratian, who is also in love with her; 2) the title plot, in which Daredevil is shown to be a complete fake—a secret believer; and 3) an ugly depiction of Courtine and Sylvia stuck in an intolerably wretched and unsatisfactory marriage. Drifting on the fringes of all three are Lucrece, who schemes to catch Beaugard for herself, and Beaugard's impoverished old father, a merry gamester who shamelessly lives off his son.

The Atheist should not be damned out of hand for being a sequel. Rather the reverse. Beaugard might almost as well be a new character entirely: he has come into money (via an uncle), and no mention is made of his doings in the earlier play. The only significant carryover is in Courtine and Sylvia. Most of the sequel plays in this period are indeed pretty weak (save *The Relapse*), and as sequels quite pointless. Such plays as Behn's *The Rover* (Part 2) and Shadwell's *The Amorous Bigotte* come to mind. But here Otway has an obvious point: he proposes to show us just what happens *after* the romantic marriage which provides the happy conclusion for so many Carolean comedies. In his view, our satisfaction with such endings is so much dishonest, sentimental slush, and so he gives us the most memorably nasty picture of marital discord before Southerne's *The Wives Excuse* (1691). Marital discord can be largely comic, as in *She wou'd if she cou'd*. We dislike Goodvile too much to be distressed about his marriage in *Friendship in Fashion*. But we rather like both Courtine and Sylvia, which makes their marriage uniquely horrible, especially when we consider her position in it. Had Otway ended *The Souldiers Fortune* with a romantic flourish, the sequel would enjoy some comic incongruity. Ending as soberly as it does, it leaves us no easy way to evade the implications of the upshot. Courtine has quickly come to hate his wife.

> I am forced to call a Woman I do not like, by the name of Wife; and lie with her, for the most part, with no Appetite at all; must keep the Children that, for ought I know, any Body else may beget of her Body; and for Food and Rayment, by her good will she would have them both Fresh three times a day: Then for Kiss and part, I may kiss and kiss my Heart out, but the Devil a bit shall I ever get rid of her. . . . By the vertue of Matrimony, and long Cohabitation, we are grown so really One Flesh, that I have no more Inclination to hers, than to eat a piece of my own. (II, 305)

At times there is a comic edge to the complaints. Courtine has grown a beard: "I wear it on purpose, Man; I have wish't it a Furze-bush a thousand times, when I have been kissing my— . . . Wife.— Let me never live to bury her, if the word Wife does not stick in my Throat" (II, 306). "But wo and alas! O Matrimony, Matrimony! what a Blot art thou in an honest Fellows Scutcheon" (II, 310). But other comments cut deeper, as when Courtine, invited to do a little whoring, replies, "Why then I'll be a Man again. Wife, avaunt, and come not near my Memory; Impotence attends the very Thoughts of thee" (II, 312). The scenes between Courtine and Sylvia (for example, II, 340–43) could be made really distressing in the theatre. "*Courtine.* Oh the unconscionable Importunity of an unsavoury, phlegmatick, cold, insipid Wife! By this good day, she has kiss'd me till I am downright sick; I have had so much of her, that I shall have no stomach to the Sex again this fortnight" (II, 349). Taken out of context (as I am forced to present it here), such a passage may seem funny, but given the horrid sense of entrapment felt by both husband and wife, it cannot be taken so. Otway does a fine job of making us feel sorry for Sylvia while still seeing how intolerably cloying her demands for affection seem to Courtine (for example, II, 353). Not a jot is abated at the end of the play. Following the masked intrigues of Acts IV and V Courtine discovers that he has

unwittingly been trying to help his wife make him a cuckold, and
this is the last we see of them.

> *Courtine.* Your humble Servant, my Dearest! . . . hence-
> forth, my Dearest, I shall drink my drink, my Dearest,
> I shall whore my Dearest; and so long as I can pimp so
> handsomly for you, my Dearest, I hope if ever we return
> into the Countrey, you'll wink at a small Fault now and
> then with the Dairy-Wench, or Chamber-Maid, my
> Dearest.
> *Sylvia.* I always was a Burden to your sight, and you
> shall be this time eas'd on't. [*Exit.*
> *Courtine.* With all my heart! Heav'n grant it would last
> for ever. (II, 395)

There is no resolution, and no prospect of any. Unlike Farquhar in
The Beaux Stratagem, Otway allows us no fairy-tale happy ending.
The result is a crushingly effective demolition of the happily-ever-
after convention.

   The most prominent part of the play's plot is the Beaugard-
Porcia story, but the marital-discord element seems ample justification of the sequel-design. The place of Daredevil in the play is
more problematical. He is an effective humour character, sharply
satirized. As a coward and buffoon he makes a good adjunct to the
intrigue and swordplay parts of the plot. Summers is right in his
praise of the scenes showing Daredevil's "deathbed" penitence, especially the one in which Beaugard's father, "*disguis'd like a Pha-
natique Preacher*," receives his confession (II, 390–92). I shall try
to show in due course that Daredevil fits into a broad theme of
authority and rebellion. Much of his characterization and significance, however, is probably extrinsic to the play. J. C. Ross has
shown that many of the puzzling or apparently irrelevant details
concerning Daredevil make him a satiric caricature of Thomas
Shadwell.[21] *The Atheist* was staged in the aftermath of the Exclu-

21. "An Attack on Thomas Shadwell in Otway's *The Atheist*," *Philological
Quarterly*, 52 (1973), 753–60.

sion Crisis; feeling over such plays as *City Politiques* and *The Duke of Guise* (staged the previous winter) was still running high; and Shadwell was anathema to the Tory writers, with whom he was carrying on a pamphlet war. Little in *The Atheist* after the prologue allusion to *Mac Flecknoe* points directly and obviously to Shadwell, but newspaper controversy in January 1683 adds evidence which makes the identification virtually certain. Removing the play from the context of 1683 makes the intrusion of this attack something of a blot on the play's design, but at least we can now see more clearly what Daredevil is doing in the play.

The courtship plot which ties the play's various actions together gives us a sketchy but not unattractive view of Beaugard and Porcia. Neither starts out with any intention of marrying. The play opens with Beaugard and his father disputing.

> *Beaugard.* Sir, I say, and say again, No Matrimony; I'll not be noos'd. Why, I beseech you, Sir, tell me Plainly and fairly, What have I done, that I deserve to be married!
> *Father.* Why, Sauce-box, I, your old Father, was married before you were born.
> *Beaugard.* Ay, Sir; and I thank you, the next thing you did, was, you begot me; the Consequence of which was as follows: As soon as I was born, you sent me to Nurse, where I suckt two years at the dirty Dugs of a foul-feeding Witch, that liv'd in a thatch't Sty upon the neighb'ring Common; as soon as I was big enough, that you might be rid of me, you sent me to a Place call'd a School, to be slash't and box't by a thick-fisted Blockhead, that could not read himself; where I learnt no Letters, nor got no Meat, but such as the old *Succubus* his Wife bought at a stinking Price, so over-run with Vermin, that it us'd to crawl home after her. (II, 299)

Otway has a sour view of life, let alone marriage. Porcia speaks of the latter from sad experience. "To give you one infallible Argument, that I never will marry, I have been married already, that is, sold: for being the Daughter of a very rich Merchant, who dying left me the onely Heiress of an immense Fortune, it was my ill luck to fall into the Hands of Guardians, that, to speak properly, were Raskals; for in a short time they conspired amongst themselves, and for base Bribes, betray'd, sold, and married me to a—Husband, that's all" (II, 317). Asked where the husband is, she replies, "Heav'n be thanked, dead and buried." But Beaugard finds that he is seriously attracted to her (II, 359), while Porcia decides that she fears her brother-in-law's domination even more than matrimony (II, 364). They agree to marry, and as we like them we are glad, but with the Courtine-Sylvia plot unfolding simultaneously we can scarcely go into sentimental raptures over the projected union. Only the most careless spectator could miss the warning. We are allowed to hope for the best, but cannot forget just how wrong such a marriage can go.

Even viewed thus, *The Atheist* may seem to fly apart into its component pieces. We need to understand, though, that beyond the obvious contrast of romance and marital discord plots, Otway employs other devices to unify superficially disparate material. Inversion is the most important of the techniques he uses: quite literally, we are shown a world upside-down. Ian Donaldson has made a brilliant analysis of this mode of comic vision. "Inversion involves a sudden, comic switching of expected roles: prisoner reprimands judge, child rebukes parent, wife rules husband, pupil instructs teacher, master obeys servant. . . . In *Bartholomew Fair* [Jonson] presents a picture of a farcical and Saturnalian society in which normal social roles are inverted, and normal social functions flouted; and . . . by this means he compels us to attend to questions which are far from farcical, and which are concerned principally with problems about *social order*; with the problems of what Jonson called 'licence' and 'liberty.'"[22] Donaldson does not mention *The Atheist*, but it is a perfect example of what he is talking about. In three main areas Otway radically inverts the usual treatment of a subject. Beaugard and his father have switched roles; Daredevil is

22. *The World Upside-Down: Comedy from Jonson to Fielding* (Oxford: Clarendon Press, 1970), ch. 1, esp. pp. 6, 20 (italics added).

a religious hypocrite who feigns atheism instead of the usual puritan piety; Courtine and Sylvia show us a genuinely intolerable marriage, an interesting contrast to the usual gay couple raillery about it.

By itself, the father-son inversion is quite amusing, but little more than that. The father wheedles money out of his son (II, 302), and spends it on wine, women, and gaming. He says bitterly that Beaugard can take his "swill in Plenty and Voluptuousness—Hickup—while your poor Father, Sirrah, must be contented to drink paltry Sack, with dry-bon'd, old, batter'd Rogues, and be thankful. You must have your fine, jolly, young Fellows, and bonny, buxom, brawny-bum'd Whores, you Dog, to revel with, and be hang'd to you, must you? Sirrah, you Rogue, I ha' lost all my Money" (II, 329). What to do with the old scapegrace? Sounding just like a worried old father, Beaugard hopes "to find him run so far in Debt within this Fortnight, that to avoid the Calamity, he shall be forced to compound with me for his Freedom, and be contented with a comfortable Annuity in the Country" (II, 334). After despicably cooperating with Theodoret against his son, the old man has a change of heart when Beaugard again gets the upper hand: "I have Remorse of Conscience, and am sensible I have been a Rebel: wherefore, if my Liege Son and Heir have recruited his Power, and be once more up in Arms, Loyalty and Natural Affection . . . will work" (II, 376). Informed that he will be hanged for murder, the old gentleman laments: "farewell for ever old Hock, Sherry, Nutmeg and Sugar, Seven and Eleven; Sink-Tray, and the Doublets! Never comes better of rebelling against one's natural born Children" (II, 377).

At the end of the play he makes a striking appeal to his son: "*Jacky*, you Rogue, shall not I have a little spill out of this Portion now, hah? The jolly Worms that have fatten'd so long in this Malmsey Nose of mine with the Fumes of Sack will die, and drop out of their Sockets else. Couldst thou have the Heart to see this illuminated Nose of mine look like an empty Honey-Comb; Couldst thou be so hard hearted?" (II, 397). And Beaugard agrees, "Though you have been a very ungratious Father, upon condition that you'll promise to leave off Gaming, and stick to your Whoring and Drinking, I will treat with you." The father is duly "penitent": "The truth

on't is, I have been too blame, *Jack*! But thou shalt find me here-
after very obedient; that is, provided I have my Terms: which are
these . . . Three Bottles of Sack, *Jack, per diem*, without Deduction,
or false Measure: Two Pound of Tobacco *per* Month; and that
of the best too. . . . Buttock-Beef and *March*-Beer at Dinner, you
Rogue: A young Wench of my own chusing, to wait on no body
but me always: Money in my Pocket: An old Pacing Horse, and an
Elbow-Chair" (II, 398).

This delightful spoof on the penitent prodigal so common in
late seventeenth-century comedy, and the reversal of father and son,
fits neatly into some broader themes in the play—loyalty, authority,
and rebellion. Otway plays mocking games with them in the father-
son relationship, but they enter extensively and explicitly in Porcia's dealings with Theodoret: "*Porcia*. With hopes of Liberty I am
[transported] indeed: it is an English Woman's natural Right. Do
not our Fathers, Brothers and Kinsmen often, upon pretence of it,
bid fair for Rebellion against their Soveraign; And why ought not
we, by their Example, to rebel as plausibly against them?" (II, 379)
Sylvia denies the principle's applicability to husbands, but is sorely
tempted when Lucrece courts her in male attire (II, 367–70). A
stream of references to "the [Popish] Plot" (for example, II, 307)
runs right into the epilogue's denunciation of "the *Spirit of Rebellion*," and ties the themes to relevant topical political concerns. Most
of Daredevil's conversation turns on a denial of conventional authority and restrictions, often in a highly comic way. Thus he ad-
vises Courtine to poison his wife: "what would you with her else,
if you are weary of her?" (II, 325), and proposes an evening's
amusement: "let us fire a House or two, poison a Constable and all
his Watch, ravish six Cinder-women, and kill a Beadle" (II, 335).
He is, of course, a huffing fake. The scenes between Theodoret and
Gratian find them insisting fiercely on the claims of honor and
friendship (for example, II, 337–39), and represent an important
but incongruous contrast in this world of deceit, intrigue, and appetite. The two of them prove, however, thoroughly ineffectual.

The last two acts of the play contain such dizzying twists and
turns that even just the story line is difficult to follow. But if we stop
and reflect on the import of what we have seen, the final speeches

help pull things together. Beaugard has physically overcome his opponents, and proposes to settle matters to suit himself—a *"Victor"* *"with Power in hand"* who has achieved his success by *"Chance."* "All this comes by the Dominion Chance has over us," he says flatly and bleakly (II, 398). Compare the "Providential Justice" so loudly touted by Cibber or Centlivre, and acknowledged even by Dryden and Congreve. Otway has no such faith and finds no cheer even in the good "Fortune" Vanbrugh is willing to enjoy. As the myriad inversions tell us, the world of *The Atheist* is topsy-turvy. Otway looks out on a chaos in which the traditional centers of stability, meaning, and authority seem powerless. The energetic, even manic swordplay and slapstick, the lush extravagance of the "enchanted castle" and its sexual fantasies amuse us, but do not significantly alter the play's despairing depiction of a meaningless world gone mad. Indeed with the benefit of hindsight we can see a grim, central appropriateness to the title. Daredevil is a believer who feigns disbelief; Otway is an unhappy disbeliever who longs to believe.

Idealism versus Pessimism

Throughout Otway's works run two veins of thought—a passionate commitment to high ideals of duty and friendship, and a bitter, all-pervading pessimism. We need not subscribe to the romantic view of Otway to appreciate the power and pathos of this combination. He may or may not have suffered the torments of unrequited love for Mrs. Barry; he certainly did die young and in terrible poverty. But the essentials of his tragic outlook are present in *Alcibiades* (1675), his first play. And the tragic power of the dichotomy is clear even in that crude bloodbath.

Clifford Leech observes that in high tragedy of the Shakespearean variety, the tragic effect stems from pride in man's unavailing but heroic struggle against implacable fate.[23] Such a formula seldom applies to late seventeeth-century tragedies, whose

---

23. "Restoration Tragedy: A Reconsideration," *Durham University Journal,* 11 (1950), 106–15.

authors are usually uncomfortable about poetic injustice. They do present it, but cautiously qualified. The results are generally the fall of a *very* flawed protagonist; villain tragedy; or explicitly pathetic tragedy. Otway wrote a highly effective specimen of the pathetic mode in *The Orphan* (1680). But his usual emphasis in tragedy is less on the implacable decrees of fate than on the agonizing inadequacies of man. Amidst the welter of conflicting critical opinion about *Venice Preserv'd*, there is substantial agreement that the power of the tragedy stems from its painful presentation of man's inability to control himself, much less the world. All of Otway's tragedies bring an obvious craving for inaccessible heroic ideals into conflict with this ineluctable, unpalatable fact.

Stroup emphasizes Otway's "pervasive determinism." "Fortune, Chance, Fate—not men—control. Hence the ultimate pessimism." [24] I would qualify this judgment somewhat. Fate, even a malignant fate, is one thing; chance quite another. One can accept a determinism stemming from an ultimate order, a directing force. But to perceive man's inability to control himself and to think that the forces which kick him about are accidental and aimless is frightening and demoralizing. The comedies express such a perception, and help us understand the existential predicament less clearly embodied in the tragedies. Stroup helpfully catalogues the pervasive expressions of cynicism, frustration, and futility in Otway's plays. Without equating all of them to Otway's personal outlook, we may say that the plays clearly express the author's bitter disgust at the nature of the world as he found it. Men are treacherous: broken oaths are legion in these plays, especially *Friendship in Fashion* and *Venice Preserv'd*. Nowhere in human institutions does Otway find meaningful values. Marriage, friendship, parental feeling, government—all turn out to be unreliable mockeries of the meaning and order they symbolize and burlesque. The amount of ritual ceremony—oaths, greetings, orations—in Otway's plays is staggering. (Stroup counts eighty major instances in nine plays.) The point is that these forms are *hollow*: they cannot be trusted,

24. "Otway's Bitter Pessimism," p. 71.

because they have no relation to any larger sense of meaning and order.

There is much truth in Montague Summers' summation. "He was above all a sentimentalist, and when he found his dreams shattered, his ideals degraded, his friendship betrayed, his love strumpeted and mocked, what wonder that his fair affections turned to gall in his bosom and that his mouth was filled with fierce stinging words? There is no more hot scorner of mankind than the disillusioned sentimentalist. And so he drew [in the comedies] the men and women of his world as he truly saw them, licentious, brutal, false, hard, and above all inordinately self-centred and selfish" (I, lxvi). This view is romantically simplistic in its biographical assumptions. Nonetheless, the account of the overall outlook is borne out by the text of the plays. In this respect the comedies are perhaps a truer indication of Otway's feelings and view of the world than are the tragedies, where conventional elements loom larger. The heroic nobility so well depicted in *Don Carlos* (1676), and to a lesser extent in *Caius Marius* (1679) and *Venice Preserv'd*, distracts from and softens the near-nihilism of the author. Otway does *not* preach nihilism, let me hasten to say: he hates it, fears it, longs for order and meaning—and shows us a world without them. The "happy" ending of *The Atheist* with its bitter acceptance of the power of "Chance" is a quintessentially appropriate conclusion to Otway's dramatic canon.

Assessing Otway's place among writers of late seventeenth-century comedy, one can certainly put him in the ranks of Etherege, Wycherley, Southerne, Vanbrugh, and Congreve. He has, however, a special and effective perspective. He is a poor outsider, and he stays that way. Unlike Shadwell or Wycherley (for example), Otway never made much progress in the fashionable world. (Summers indeed says that Otway could indulge in moral indignation because he was no gentleman!) He does, at any rate, see clearly the brutality and viciousness of the Hobbesian rake, and is roused to a fever pitch of disgust and indignation. Only in Lee's Nemours in *The Princess of Cleve* (1682) does one find in this drama so fierce an attack on the libertine and his philosophy.

Critics often try to find the plays of Etherege, Wycherley, and others "satires," in the belief that this somehow justifies them, or confers significant moral purpose on works of otherwise dubious morality.[25] How satiric *The Man of Mode* and *The Country-Wife* are we need not debate at the moment. But if one wants harsh, unmistakable satire in late seventeenth-century comedy, here it is. Neglect of Otway's comedies is really quite astonishing. *The Souldiers Fortune* was a tremendously popular play; the others were not; but in light of modern attention to *The Way of the World*, we can scarcely justify success in the theatre as our criterion for critical attention. I do not believe that Otway ever quite fulfilled his potential in either tragedy or comedy; but the comedies represent at least as considerable an achievement as the tragedies so often studied and praised.

Friendship in Fashion is perhaps too single-mindedly a play with a point, and its too-heavy speeches weigh it down. *The Souldiers Fortune* is an extraordinarily fine stage comedy, enjoyably racy, and it successfully leavens satiric point with entertainment. *The Atheist*, one must grant, does not quite come off. The intrigues become over-complex; the fantasy elements and "enchanted castle" are extremely disconcerting. (The fantasy is, I think, appropriate to Otway's picture of a topsy-turvy world gone mad, but there is no denying that one stumbles over it awkwardly.) The parts of the play do not work smoothly together. Nonetheless, in concept it is an ambitious and impressive experiment. The marital discord sequel is the work of genius, and it invests the play with a seriousness and honesty rarely found in any comedy. *The Souldiers Fortune* leaves some grounds for optimism; *The Atheist* denies them. Among other writers of seventeenth-century comedy, only Southerne had anything like as coldly bitter a view of the ways of the world. Not too surprisingly, his best comedies—*The Wives Excuse* and *The Maid's Last Prayer*—were indifferently received when they appeared in the early nineties and have been neglected since then.

One reason for critics' avoidance of Otway's comedies has been

25. See Charles O. McDonald, "Restoration Comedy as Drama of Satire: An Investigation into Seventeenth Century Aesthetics," *Studies in Philology*, 61 (1964), 522–44.

their "bawdiness"—a concept which needs some explanation. What *The Country-Wife* treats lightly has been accepted; what *Mr. Limberham* or *Friendship in Fashion* present nastily has not. The coarseness and "prophaneness" of Otway's comedies is partly explained by context: they follow the peak of the sex-boom and precede the reform movement. That Otway makes sex vivid and often ugly is surely justified by the seriousness with which he treats the subject. For John Harrington Smith to enjoy the frivolous sexual games of *A Fond Husband* and *The London Cuckolds* while balking at Otway is most peculiar. One may say that the world he presents is unappetizing; but then that is his point. To say that it really isn't very nice to dwell on the subject is simply moral "ostrichism." The Nicky-Nacky scenes in *Venice Preserv'd* are a magnificently effective smear on Shaftesbury, and a clear extension of Otway's comic art. Imagine putting "Richard Nixon" on stage with a whore circa 1970, playing dog under the table, asking her to spit on him, kick and whip him, and finally begging to be allowed to smell her "dear fragrant foots and little toes" (II, 275). Some spectators would have gloated over the picture; others would have responded with the most violent kind of outrage and disgust.

The real objection to Otway's comedies seems generally to have been in reaction to his cynical outlook. There is plenty of raw sex in *Friendship in Fashion*, and a cuckolding action in *The Souldiers Fortune*, but far more has been tolerated in other plays. In both cases Otway protests against charges of bawdiness. "*Ladies, there's no Bawdy in't, / No not so much as one well-meaning hint,*" he insists in the prologue to his first comedy. This may seem disingenuous or ironic, but, as John Harrington Smith rightly observes, "bawdy" was often used to refer specifically to double entendre in this period. And Otway does not employ such titillating devices. His harsh view of romantic myths and upper-class civilities has a definite shock value, and legitimately so.

Far from being "fatuous" and "vacuous" exercises in routine entertainment (as Ghosh and Ham say), Otway's comedies are almost desperately serious plays. The comedy-world of Etherege or even Wycherley is far from cloud-cuckooland, but the authors are commenting on Restoration society and philosophy at a considerable remove from reality. Otway's comedies are less conventional, closer to the cruel and unpalatable facts of life as he perceived it. In his tragedies Otway permits us a view of soaring hopes and aspirations—dashed, to be sure, but still present. In the comedies he exhibits a bitter despair which is far more deeply disturbing. Using some of the conventional elements of Carolean comedy, but abandoning—and rejecting—most of its values, Otway gives us his vision of the world. The comedies are violent but curiously cold satires: despair has triumphed over indignation. Sutherland is persistently bothered by an "uneasy" mixture of farce, satire, and realism, but the combination is, I think, completely comprehensible. The farce is appropriate to a meaningless world run mad, and Otway laughs at it. The ugly bitterness of marital discord and the selfish callousness of the human animal are horrible, but also horribly funny. So in his comedies Otway presents unvarnished the gritty reality of a bleakly nasty world—onto which he foists a harsh, macabre gaiety which scarcely distracts from the savage picture.

4

The Satiric Design of Nat. Lee's The Princess of Cleve

Scholars have generally found this play baffling, objectionable, or both. Lee started, of course, with Madame de La Fayette's *La Princesse de Clèves*, and he follows its action quite closely in his main plot. The Princess confesses her chaste love for Duke Nemours to her husband, who then nobly expires of love and jealousy. In the novel, Nemours is an attractive and honorable man, though not a wholly blameless one. Lee turns him into a brutal and cynical whoremonger, and onto Madame de La Fayette's delicate and aristocratic tale he grafts an apparently disjunct middle-class cuckolding plot. Even the genre of the resulting play has been sharply disputed. Allardyce Nicoll calls the work a straight "tragedy," as do Harbage and Schoenbaum in the *Annals of English Drama*. Montague Summers cautiously refrains from specifying a type. Thomas B. Stroup declares the work to be the prototype for "sentimental" comedy, while James Sutherland hails it as a "satiric" comedy. In the terminology of its own time, the play is probably best considered, as Langbaine describes it, a "Tragicomedy," since it does comprise a radically split plot.[1] Lee himself sar-

1. Nicoll, I, 419; Alfred Harbage, *Annals of English Drama, 975–1700*, rev. S. Schoenbaum (London: Methuen, 1964), p. 183; Montague Summers, *A Bibliography of the Restoration Drama* (1935; rpt. New York: Russell and Russell, 1970), p. 86; Thomas B. Stroup, "*The Princess of Cleve* and Sentimental Comedy," *Review*

donically dubs the piece a "Farce, Comedy, Tragedy or meer Play" (II, 153).[2]

As might be expected, critical evaluations of the play are wildly varied. For the most part they are extremely derogatory. Nicoll characterizes it as "ineffectual and worthless," considering the plot "chaotic" and the atmosphere "corrupt." He finds "not the slightest hint even of poetic and true dramatic sentiment," and concludes a summary dismissal by likening the play "to a rotting dung-heap" (I, 147). R. G. Ham offers a similar appraisal: offended by "bawdry" he finds "nothing" in the play to recommend it.[3] Genest says that the serious part is "somewhat dull," but that "the comic part is very good," and adds somewhat cryptically, "Nemours is a spirited character."[4] Evidently he enjoyed the "cynical and irreligious" part of the work which so offends Nicoll and Ham. John Harrington Smith says more neutrally that the play "furnishes some of the most brutal free gallantry in the period."[5] To what end it does so Smith does not even hazard a guess, but evidently he considers it a "cynical" comedy. Lee's editors argue both that "this coarseness was an intentional satire upon the immorality of the day," and that in the characters of the Prince and Princess of Cleve and in Nemours' "reform" we have the basis of sentimental comedy. Simultaneously to categorize a play with *The Country-Wife* and *The Plain-Dealer* and to praise its "sentimentalism" strikes me, at least, as something of a paradox. The one intelligently favorable critical appraisal comes in a regrettably brief comment in Sutherland's OHEL volume, where the suggestion is offered that Lee was deliberately debunking a rake hero. This seems to me absolutely correct. I think, however, that we can go considerably further in the play's defense.

Clearly *The Princess of Cleve* presents a number of knotty problems. Most broadly, we need to ask what the point of it is.

---

of English Studies, 11 (1935), 200–203; Sutherland, pp. 143–44; Langbaine, *An Account of the English Dramatick Poets*, p. 324.

2. All references to Lee's text are to *The Works of Nathaniel Lee*, ed. Thomas B. Stroup and Arthur L. Cooke, 2 vols. (1954–55; rpt. Metuchen, N.J.: Scarecrow Reprint Corp., 1968).

3. Ham, *Otway and Lee*, p. 169.

4. Genest, *Some Account of the English Stage*, I, 319–20.

5. *The Gay Couple*, p. 98.

Why does Lee combine smut and sentiment? Why does he travesty his source? We need to know how seriously to take Nemours' reform, whether the two plots are genuinely disjunct, and just what part the recently deceased earl of Rochester has in the play. This last point adds an extrinsic complication to an already formidable tangle of literary problems. I think I can show beyond reasonable doubt that a) the play is—as Montague Summers claims—a fierce though partially disguised satiric attack on Rochester; b) Lee makes skillful and purposeful use of his source; and c) the apparently peculiar double plot is a brilliantly designed satiric debunking of both the libertine ethos of Carolean sex comedy and the heroic and *précieuse* conventions of contemporary tragedy.

Problems of Date and Context

Before we launch into a consideration of the play itself, some historical problems and circumstances demand attention. The date of the play's composition and production have never been determined; it is textually entangled with two other plays by Lee; and in view of Lee's rather drastic change in political outlook sometime after 1680, its sequential place in his canon is of some importance to the interpreter.

We possess no performance records for *The Princess of Cleve*: the evidence that it was in fact performed is a) Dryden's prologue and epilogue, printed in his *Miscellany Poems* of 1684; b) the title page of the first edition (1689), which specifies "As it was Acted at the Queens Theatre in Dorset-Garden"; c) the partial cast printed with that quarto—which unhappily gives no help with the date;[6] and d) John Downes' comment in *Roscius Anglicanus* (1708) that

---

6. The 1689 quarto names only nine of the fourteen principal actors. All of those named were members of the Duke's Company, and Mrs. Betterton is among them. She took few new roles after the union until the Bettertons lost their money in 1691. She did, however, appear in *The Massacre of Paris* when it was finally performed in 1689: probably she had been cast for the play before it was banned. But especially since the cast list is incomplete, it does not prove anything except that on its evidence the premiere could have been before the union of November 1682.

the play succeeded less well than Lee's others. Nicoll's date, "c. September 1681," is nothing more than a blind guess. The editors of the *Annals* are more cautious, saying "1680–1681." *The London Stage* lists the play under September 1680 with the explanation that "a reference to the death of the Earl of Rochester (26 July 1680) suggests that the play probably followed that event rather closely."[7] This reference to the demise of "Count Rosidore," however, is merely a passing insertion and red herring: the play's principal reference to Rochester is in the character of Nemours, and if one accepts the highly plausible notion that the whole play is a posthumous comment upon Rochester, then one must allow several months, at least, for composition and production. A date in the middle of the 1680–81 season seems the earliest possible. Actually, a markedly later date is extremely probable. A copy of Thomas Farmer's music for the play gives the date December 1682,[8] and the first of several songs published from it appeared in the "Fourth Book" of *Choice Ayres and Songs* (1683). In all likelihood then the play was being prepared for production in December 1682 and was staged a little later that season.

The peculiar relationship of *The Princess of Cleve* to Lee's *The Massacre of Paris* makes a relatively late date all the more likely. Consider the sequence of Lee's plays. *Mithridates* appeared in February 1678; *Oedipus*—a collaboration with Dryden—in September 1678; *Caesar Borgia* in the spring or summer of 1679; *Theodosius* probably in early summer 1680. *Lucius Junius Brutus*, ideologically a fiercely Whig play, was banned after three to six nights (authorities differ) in December 1680. In view of these dates, I doubt that Lee was producing yet another play in the spring, summer, or autumn of 1680. His next documented play is *The Duke of Guise*, a militantly Tory play written in collaboration with Dryden, banned in July 1682 but allowed on the stage the following November. Lee's last play, *Constantine the Great*, another Tory manifesto, was staged in November 1683. By the next year he was at least intermittently confined to Bedlam. This leaves 1681 a blank;

7. *The London Stage*, Part 1, pp. 290–91.
8. See British Library Add. MS. 29,283, ff. 79–83, 119–24, 165. Folio 79 gives the date: "T Farmer Decemb: (82)."

it also leaves us wondering where to fit in *The Princess of Cleve* and *The Massacre of Paris*, which must precede it.

Lee's dedication of *The Princess of Cleve* (published in May 1689) is a plea to Dorset, then lord chamberlain, to license *The Massacre of Paris* for production the following autumn—which in fact Dorset promptly did. (Why *The Princess of Cleve* waited so long before publication, at a time when a lapse of no more than a year between performance and print was normal,[9] is a problem to be considered in due course.) This dedication gives us two decidedly helpful pieces of information. First, though Lee was indignant, he was "forc'd" by the "Refusal" of *The Massacre* "to limb my own Child"—that is, to reuse bits of it in other plays. Second, "what was borrowed in the Action is left out in the Print"—which accounts for some rough patches in the published form of *The Princess*.

Looking back to the chronology of Lee's works, we are confronted with two possibilities, without having any hard evidence to determine which is correct. First, Lee wrote *The Massacre* in the spring of 1679 at the height of the anti-Catholic hysteria of the Popish Plot (*ipso facto* likely enough), and then sat on it for two or three years before cannibalizing it. Second, in the spring or summer of 1681, following the banning of *Lucius Junius Brutus*, Lee decided to write a propaganda piece whose "loyalty" could not be called in question, but found to his mortification that the French ambassador had enough influence to get the piece stopped. Despairing of ever getting it staged, Lee then used bits of it when he set to work on *The Princess of Cleve* and *The Duke of Guise* in late 1681 or early 1682.[10] Certainly he seems to link the composition of *The Princess* directly to *The Massacre* when he says in the dedication that the former "was a Revenge for the Refusal of the other."

9. See Judith Milhous and Robert D. Hume, "Dating Play Premières from Publication Data, 1660–1700," *Harvard Library Bulletin*, 22 (1974), 374–405. The reason for the sudden resurrection of *The Princess* and *The Massacre* in 1689 is twofold: the Glorious Revolution of 1688 made the latter acceptable on the stage, and Lee, released from Bedlam in the spring of 1689, needed to support himself. He died a drunkard in May 1692 without doing any more writing.

10. For detailed accounts of the borrowed material in *The Princess of Cleve* and *The Duke of Guise*, see the notes in the Stroup-Cooke edition.

Obviously I incline to the second theory, though from the subject matter one might expect *The Massacre* to be written at the earlier date. Several pieces of evidence make the later date plausible, however. First, there is the apparent linking with the composition of *The Princess*. Second, I doubt that the perpetually indigent Lee would have held a play unperformed for two years. Third, had *The Massacre* already been banned, Lee would hardly have gone on to write the far more obviously objectionable *Lucius Junius Brutus*, especially when he badly needed money and would not have wanted to risk another banning. Fourth, as violently anti-Catholic a play as Settle's *The Female Prelate* was allowed on stage as late as June 1680: why should *The Massacre* have been singled out, among several such plays? Fifth, a related point: until *Lucius Junius Brutus* in December 1680 (stopped *during* its first run), there is no recorded instance of major censorship or refusal of license during the Popish Plot period. After that, excisions and bannings are numerous, as in the cases of Tate's *Richard the Second*, Shadwell's *The Lancashire Witches*, Crowne's *Henry the Sixth* and *City Politiques*, and the Dryden-Lee *Duke of Guise* within the next eighteen months.[11]

Questions of date and sequence are of special import because at some time between *Lucius Junius Brutus* and *The Duke of Guise* Lee performed a remarkable political turnabout. A radical who had consistently written against the divine right of kings,[12] Lee abruptly joined Dryden in a play which fiercely defends Charles II and the Tory view of the succession question. Worse yet, from the Whig point of view, Lee proceeded to utilize mob scenes from *The Massacre of Paris*, inverting their meaning so that what had been defended was now besmirched. Curiously enough, Lee's erstwhile Whig friends, as Frances Barbour observes, "instead of attacking Lee's apostasy . . . charged Dryden with leading Lee astray." In his *Vin-*

11. See Arthur F. White, "The Office of Revels and Dramatic Censorship During the Restoration Period," *Western Reserve University Bulletin*, New Series, 34 (Sept. 1931), 5–45.

12. See Frances Barbour, "The Unconventional Heroic Plays of Nathaniel Lee," *University of Texas Studies in English* (1940), pp. 109–16.

dication of the Duke of Guise (1683), Dryden refutes "the Accusation, that this Play was once written by *another*, and then 'twas call'd the *Parisian Massacre*: Such a Play, I have heard indeed was written; but I never saw it. Whether this be any of it or no, I can say no more, than for my own part of it. . . . I have enquired, why it was not Acted, and heard it was stopt, by the interposition of an *Ambassador*. . . . But that I tempted my Friend to alter it, is a notorious *Whiggism* to save the *broader Word* [lie]."[13] What caused Lee's change of side we cannot say. The Exclusion Crisis reached its peak during 1681, and perhaps Lee, like many others, came to fear the chaos and potential civil war which a forcible change in the succession threatened. He had been friendly with and greatly influenced by Dryden as early as 1677. By late 1681 Lee had written a poem in praise of *Absalom and Achitophel*—though he was initially ignorant of the authorship.

We need not assume that *The Massacre* is wholly the product of Whig partisanship, and hence antithetical to the principles of *The Duke of Guise*. Dryden's *The Spanish Fryar* (November 1680) is, after all, a fiercely anti-Catholic play. The Whigs had no monopoly there. I would hypothesize that Lee wrote the play during early 1681 while his political views were shifting, had it banned, and lifted a pair of key emotional scenes for a new play, *The Princess of Cleve*. Finally despairing of ever getting *The Massacre* performed, he then borrowed more fully from it while working on his parts of *The Duke of Guise* in the first months of 1682. Why *The Princess* was not performed more quickly is easy to explain: the Duke's Company already had a rather full schedule of new productions. January brought *The Royalist* and *Mr. Turbulent* to the stage, February saw *Venice Preserv'd*, March *Vertue Betray'd* and *Like Father like Son*, April *The City Heiress*. The King's Company collapsed in March and merger negotiations occupied the actors' attention. The highly topical *Duke of Guise* was planned for July; otherwise only one new play was tried between April and the full

13. *Dryden: The Dramatic Works*, ed. Montague Summers, 6 vols. (London: Nonesuch, 1931–32), V, 326–27.

union of the two companies in November—the anonymous *Romulus and Hersilia*. Plays from major writers were not usually premiered during the summer.

Whatever the date of *The Massacre of Paris*—and we shall probably never be certain—we may feel reasonably sure that *The Princess of Cleve* was conceived and written in late 1681 or early 1682, at a time when Lee's whole sense of values and ideology had just undergone a violent reversal. I think we can usefully hypothesize that the moral flux in the play, its violence and bitterness, represent not a freakish outburst on Lee's part, but rather reflect the spiritual turmoil and unsettling self-questioning through which Lee must have been suffering. Any man capable of writing as powerfully antimonarchical a play as *Lucius Junius Brutus*, plainly a work of passionate conviction, cannot blithely bow to political expedience and produce a Tory manifesto like *The Duke of Guise*. The process of transition, I believe, brought forth the peculiar and disconcerting *Princess of Cleve*.[14]

Nemours and Rochester

Madame de La Fayette's novel was published in Paris in 1678 and appeared in an English translation the following year. That Lee worked from the translation is demonstrated by his following its error "Cleve" for "Cleves" in the running title. The original is a delicate but impassioned account of extramarital love, concentrating on the intense psychological agony suffered by the principals. The noble prince and his virtuous wife, torn by her conflicting ethical and sexual impulses, are dissected with a cool but sympathetic exactness which leaves them stature while rendering them human.

14. Since this essay was first published, J. M. Armistead has reargued the case for a 1678–79 date for *The Massacre*. See *Nathaniel Lee* (Boston: Twayne, 1979), ch. 7. I continue to find the later date somewhat more likely. For my purposes here, however, the key issue is the date of *The Princess of Cleve*—a point on which Armistead has accepted my conclusions.

Nemours is equally well analyzed, an attractive and honorable man who fails to control a passion which overcomes will and reason. Despite his prominence in the story, Nemours is more an agent brought to bear on the others than a principal. *Motives* are the real subject of the tale—especially as the characters misunderstand and deceive themselves. Should the Princess have confessed her feelings to her husband? A nice problem! Obviously this love-and-ethics-ridden triangle offers straightforward tragic potentialities, and the story was indeed employed by Boursault in a tragedy (lost) staged in 1679. To imagine the passions and conflicts of the novel straightforwardly translated into dramatic form makes clearer how radically Lee chose to depart from the original.

In Lee's play the Prince and Princess are essentially unchanged, but they fade into secondary characters as Nemours becomes the focal point of the work. Madame de La Fayette's original title was *Le Prince de Clèves*; her final title indicates a recognition of the passivity of the Prince as tragic hero, and the importance of his wife's psychology as the key to the story. Lee's play could accurately be entitled: *The Slimy Amours of the Wicked Duke Nemours*. If this strikes the reader as a shocking, flippant, and degrading suggestion—good. That is, I think, exactly the reaction Lee wants. Leaving the Prince and Princess virtuous, noble, and heroic, Lee shunts them to one side and focuses on a much-changed Nemours. In his dedication he gloats over the shock this picture gave the audience: "when they expected the most polish'd Hero in Nemours, I gave 'em a Ruffian reeking from Whetstone's-Park [a whores' hangout]" (II, 153). To any reader of Madame de La Fayette's lovely novel, the shock is indeed considerable.

We are introduced to Nemours on the first page of the play. He is philosophizing to Bellamore, a young man he addresses as "My bosom Dear" and "my sweet-fac'd Pimp." His solemn advice to his young paramour is blunt and to the point. "Sirrah, stick to clean Pleasures, deep Sleep, moderate Wine, sincere Whores, and thou art happy" (II, 157). Nemours' bisexuality is underlined several times in the play, as when he addresses Bellamore: "Thou Dear Soft Rogue, my Spouse, my Hephestion, my Ganymed, nay, if I dye to night my Dukedom's thine" (II, 177), and when he makes explicit his desire to "make a Mistress" of the *Prince* of Cleve (II, 204).[15]

In the first two scenes of the play we learn that Nemours is pursuing the Princess of Cleve, who has just married his dearest friend; he is contracted to marry the noble and beautiful Marguerite; he has seduced and abandoned the unhappy Tournon; Tournon is now pimping for him, and has in prospect Elianor and Celia, wives of two foolish cits. Through the play we follow the complex process of his pursuit of this bevy of females. Nemours is a goatishly insatiable whoremonger. "No new Game[?]" he enquires of Tournon; "thou knowest I dye directly without variety" (II, 160). Friendship, one of the strongest bonds of obligation in Restoration codes, exerts no restraining influence on him.[16] Even Bellamore repines at Nemours' designs on the Princess: "methinks 'tis hard, because the Prince of Cleve loves you as his Life." Nemours coolly replies, "I sav'd his Life, Sweet-heart, when he was assaulted by a mistake in the dark, and shall he grudge me a little Fooling with his Wife, for so serious an Obligation?" (II, 178).

Nemours' ugly lies to Marguerite throughout the play (for example, II, 186) culminate in the scene in which, disguised, she allows him to seduce her, gains his solemn oath never to touch any woman but her, unmasks and reproaches him. To her bitter observation, "Oaths with you Libertines of Honour are to little purpose," Nemours rejoins "Take you your Ramble Madam, and I'll take mine" (II, 201–2). Nemours gloats over the Princess' love for him (II, 183), sends Bellamore off to an assignation in his stead (having accidentally scheduled two for the same time—II, 203), and tearfully assures the Prince of Cleve of his undying love and friendship (II, 206). Nemours is, in short, a monster, though a glamorous and successful one. Nemours has wit, gaiety, brains, and exuberant

15. From the treatment of homosexuality in Otway's *The Souldiers Fortune,* Southerne's *Sir Anthony Love,* Vanbrugh's *The Relapse,* and a host of other plays, we may assume that the late seventeenth-century audience could be expected to find bisexuality thoroughly repulsive. Lee was presumably aware that he was perfectly accurate when he imputed it to Rochester.

16. Compare the violent satire on false friends in Otway's *Friendship in Fashion,* discussed in ch. 3 above.

energy—qualities which in an ordinary comedy would make him very appealing indeed. The original casting would have helped bring out his appeal, since the part was acted by Thomas Betterton, a performer whose heroic overtones must have made an effective contribution to the shocking disparity between Nemours' superficially attractive appearance and his degraded moral reality. Betterton was a great Hamlet, Brutus, Macbeth, Lear (in Tate's version), and Jaffeir (in *Venice Preserv'd*). To send him prancing through Nemours' squalid antics must have produced an effect akin to Twain's "Royal Nonesuch."

Nemours' view of the world is ruthlessly hedonistic: any pretense to another standard he considers hypocritical. The Vidam of Chartres (whose "sowre Morals" Nemours complains of) reproaches him as "the Whores Ingrosser.... Believe me Sir, in a little time you'll be nick'd the Town-Bull." To this criticism of his "Obscenity" Nemours replies:

> Why 'tis the way of ye all, only you sneak with it [a loaded pronoun] under your Cloaks like Taylors and Barbers; and I, as a Gentleman shou'd do, walk with it in my hand. For prithee observe, does not your Priest the same thing? did not I see Father Patrick declaiming against Flesh in Lent, strip up to the Elbow; and telling the Congregation he had eat nothing but Fish these twenty years, yet protest to the Ladies, that Fat Arm of his, which was a chopping one, was the least Member about him? . . . Does not your Politician, your little great Man of bus'ness, that sets the World together by the Ears, after all his Plotting, Drudging and Sweating at Lying, retire to some little Punk and untap at night? (II, 178)

Similar passages could be multiplied *ad nauseam*. Consequently Nemours' closing speech, if read straight, comes as a considerable surprise.

> For my part, the Death of the Prince of Cleve, upon second thoughts, has so truly wrought a change in me, as nothing else but a Miracle cou'd—For first I see, and loath my Debaucheries—Next, while I am in Health, I am resolv'd to give satis-

faction to all I have wrong'd; and first to this Lady [Marguerite], whom I will make my Wife before all this Company e'er we part—This, I hope, whenever I dye, will convince the World of the Ingenuity of my Repentance, because I had the power to go on.

> He well Repents that will not Sin, yet can,
> But Death-bed Sorrow rarely shews the Man.
>   (II, 226)

Much turns on how we read this astonishing speech. Thomas B. Stroup feels that Nemours is "good at heart": "His attempt upon the Princess sobers him and brings him to the realization that he has greatly wronged the faithful Marguerite." But if Lee means this reform to be taken literally, it is left so perfunctory as to be entirely unconvincing. Unlike Stroup, I cannot leave the play feeling that Lee delights in "the repentance of the rake" and means to tout "the natural goodness of man in the character of Nemours." Exactly forty lines before the final speech Nemours replies to the Princess' announcement that she will never see him again: "She Lyes, I'll Wager my State, I Bed her eighteen months three weeks hence, at half an hour past two in the Morning. . . . I know the Souls of Women better than they know themselves" (II, 225). This suggests neither reform nor goodness of heart.

An examination of some key passages will show that there is no sudden change of heart at the end; that Nemours has long been seriously attracted to Marguerite, and does not intend to lose her; and that his "reform" is a carefully devised piece of bait. After a stormy encounter with Marguerite in IV, i, Nemours comments:

> Yet when I see my time I must recall her,
> For she has admirable things in her, such as if I gain not, the Princess of Cleve may fix me to her, without nauseating the Vice of Constancy. (II, 203)

The punctuation in this slovenly quarto is often problematical: delete the comma after "not" and add one after "Cleve," and one gets a different, perhaps a better meaning for this speech. But the determination not to lose Marguerite is clear. A little later Nemours debates with himself—what if the Prince dies? "Shall I Marry the Princess of Cleve, or stick to Marguerite as we are? for 'tis most certain she has rare things in her, which I found by my last Experiment, and I love her more than ever, almost to Jealousie; . . . I'll throw boldly, clear the Table if I can, if not, 'tis but at last forswearing Play, shake off my new acquaintance, and be easie with my reserve" (II, 210). Nemours wants both women. But Marguerite's renunciation of him rouses his jealousy. "Lose her I must not, no, I'll lose a Limb first, [to Tournon] therefore go tell her, tell her the Prince of Cleve's Death has wrought my Conversion, I grow weary of my wild Courses, repent of my Sins, am resolv'd to leave off Whoreing and marry his Wife" (II, 218). He promptly proposes marriage to the Princess, who loves him dearly but sees all too clearly that his affections will soon wander, despite his solemn protestation that "Once to be yours, is to be for ever yours, / Yours only, without thought of other Woman" (II, 223). He threatens suicide, but she departs anyway, whereupon he utters his boast about bedding her in due course, and sets out to regain Marguerite.

> Heark there without, the voice of Marguerite,
> Now thou shalt see a Battle worth the gazing,
> Mark but how easily my reason flings her.
>
> (II, 225)[17]

In short, Nemours' "reform" is nothing more than a cleverly calculated scheme to persuade Marguerite into marriage. He may "love" her (whatever that means by his lights—we have gathered that she is something extraordinary in bed), but the leopard has not changed his spots.

To what end does Lee accomplish this stunning degradation of Madame de La Fayette's "polish'd Hero"? The literary effect will be considered in the next section. But Lee clearly had a more per-

---

17. Stroup and Cooke, II, 588 nn., note that a passage was probably cut just at this point, since "the audience has been prepared for a scene of some length and importance between Marguerite and Nemours, but the quarrel between the two is limited to two lines." I would guess that the material cut was probably an alteration of III, ii, 44–170, of *The Massacre of Paris* (*Works*, II, 26–29). If so, it would not have prepared us any better for the astonishing reversal at the end.

sonal and vindictive motive as well. As Montague Summers points out, Duke Nemours is a stage representation of John Wilmot, earl of Rochester.[18] We know very little about Lee's personal relations with Rochester. On slender evidence R. G. Ham asserts that "to Lee the name of Rochester was almost beyond praise," an opinion founded partly on Lee's rhapsodic dedication of *Nero* (publ. 1675), and partly on the "Count Rosidore" passage in *The Princess of Cleve*.[19] That Lee initially worshipped Rochester is likely enough, but that he continued to do so after about 1677 is implausible. Rochester's "Allusion to Horace," probably written in the winter of 1675–76, calls Lee "a hot-brained fustian fool" who belongs "in Busby's hands, to be well lashed at school." As David Vieth observes, by 1677 Lee had deserted (or been rejected by) the "Rochester-Shadwell" clique, and aligned himself with "the Dryden-Mulgrave axis." Rochester has been exonerated from responsibility for Dryden's Rose Alley beating in 1679, but the hostility between the two camps is notorious.[20]

We may then be surprised to find in *The Princess of Cleve* what Pinto calls "a touching tribute" to Rochester, "clearly the product of genuine affection and admiration."[21] This passage is likewise taken at face value by Ham, Vieth, and others.

> *Vidam.*   He that was the Life, the Soul of Pleasure,
>   Count Rosidore, is dead.
> *Nemours.*   Then we may say
>   Wit was and Satyr is a Carcass now.
>   I thought his last Debauch wou'd be his Death—
>   But is it certain?

18. Montague Summers, *The Playhouse of Pepys* (1935; rpt. New York: Humanities Press, 1964), p. 301. Summers makes the point only in passing.
    19. *Otway and Lee*, p. 49.
    20. *The Complete Poems of John Wilmot, Earl of Rochester*, ed. David Vieth (New Haven: Yale Univ. Press, 1968), p. xxx. J. Harold Wilson, "Rochester, Dryden, and the Rose Street Affair," *Review of English Studies*, 15 (1939), 294–301.
    21. Vivian de Sola Pinto, *Enthusiast in Wit: A Portrait of John Wilmot, Earl of Rochester, 1647–1680*, rev. ed. (London: Routledge, 1962), p. 232.

Vidam.   Yes I saw him dust.
  I saw the mighty thing a nothing made,
  Huddled with Worms, and swept to that cold Den,
  Where Kings lye crumbled just like other Men.
Nemours.   Nay then let's Rave and Elegize together,
  Where Rosidore is now but common clay. . . .
  He was the Spirit of Wit—and had such an art in guild-
  ing his Failures, that it was hard not to love his Faults:
  He never spoke a Witty thing twice, tho to different Per-
  sons; his Imperfections were catching, and his Genius
  was so Luxuriant, that he was forc'd to tame it with a
  Hesitation in his Speech to keep it in view—but oh how
  awkward, how insipid, how poor and wretchedly dull
  is the imitation of those that have all the affectation of
  his Verse and none of his Wit. (II, 162)

Two other, much briefer passages, usually ignored, should be set
beside this glowing tribute.

> [*Nemours.*]   The Fury of Wine and Fury of Women pos-
> sess me waking and sleeping; let me Dream of nothing
> but dimpl'd Cheeks, and laughing Lips, and flowing
> Bowls, Venus be my Star, and Whoring my House, and
> Death I defie thee. Thus sung Rosidore in the Urn. (II,
> 188)
> [*Tournon,* of Nemours].   Go thy ways Petronius, nay, if
> he were dying too, with his Veins cut, he wou'd call for
> Wine, Fiddles and Whores, and laugh himself into the
> other World. (II, 218)

These three passages, together with Nemours' closing speech, clearly
allude to Rochester. And there is a progression from mention of his
death to a sharp query about deathbed conversion.

Pinto, Ham, and others take the first passage as a spontaneous
tribute to Rochester, interpolated into the play as a topical compliment soon after Rochester's death. I propose, rather, that Lee in-

serts it as a device to bring Rochester to mind.[22] Nemours, fatally attractive but vicious, is a portrait of "what Rochester was really like." And in the series of four more or less direct allusions to Rochester Lee moves from high compliment (out of *Nemours'* mouth, we should remember) to what Summers calls the "scorpion sting" of the final couplet. "He well Repents that will not Sin, yet can, / But Death-bed Sorrow rarely shews the Man." Rochester's celebrated deathbed conversion, widely publicized in Robert Parsons' *A Sermon preached at the Earl of Rochester's Funeral* and Bishop Burnet's *Some Passages of the Life and Death of the Right Honourable John Earl of Rochester* (1680), is here viewed sardonically, to say the least.

Rochester, Lee tells us, was a Nemours. Significantly, I think, Lee's 1689 epilogue picks up the notion of "Wit," for which "Count Rosidore" is praised so highly. A question is posed: "What is this Wit which Cowley cou'd not name?" The epilogue concludes: "'Tis like the Comedy you have to day, / A Bulling Gallant in a wanton Play." "Bulling" here means "fraudulent, scheming": put Nemours' praise together with Lee's epilogue, and the result is yet another blunt authorial comment.

Would an attack on Rochester have been timely in 1682? Would anyone have cared about it? Quite by chance, we can answer these questions decisively and affirmatively. On 26 June 1682 the lord chamberlain forbade the acting of a new comedy by John Crowne, *City Politiques*. As with *The Duke of Guise* (forbidden in July), the ban was lifted at the end of the autumn, and the United Company staged the play in January—a savage lampoon on Titus Oates, Stephen College, and the Whig faction. But "Libels may prove costly things," as Crowne notes in his preface, declaiming against "bar-

---

22. In a letter to *TLS* (2 Nov. 1935) Graham Greene backed up Summers' identification of Nemours with Rochester by pointing out that just before the Count Rosidore passage Lee puts into Nemours' mouth a speech ("Nay, now thou put'st me in Poetick Rapture . . ."—II, 161) lifted from the opening of Rochester's version of Fletcher's *Valentinian*. In a reply, W. J. Lawrence (9 Nov.) argued that the passage must be a late addition, since *Valentinian* was not printed until December 1684. But there is evidence that as *Lucina's Rape* (see British Library Add. MS. 28,692) Rochester's play was performed by the King's Company ca. 1675–76.

barous cowardly Assassinates." This reference is explained by a passage in the Morrice Entry Book. "Mr Crowne was cudgled on Wednesday last in St Martin's Lane and hee that beat him said hee did it at the suite of [that is, in behalf of] the Earle of Rochester some time since deceased who was greatly abused in the play for his penetency &c."[23] Exception was evidently taken to Florio, "A Debauch, who pretends to be Dying of the Diseases his Vices brought upon him, and penitent, in love with *Rosaura*." The rakish Artall impersonates him at various points in the play, driving home Crowne's lesson in the sexual success of hypocrisy.

Thus we have another play, written and performed at almost exactly the dates I have hypothesized for *The Princess of Cleve*, in which Rochester is a satiric target. I think we can conclude both that Rochester's debauchery and penitence remained topical in 1683 and that to attack him for them was physically dangerous. This helps account for three puzzling facts about *The Princess of Cleve*. First, Lee is careful not to associate Nemours directly with Rochester, except by implication in the final speech. Second, the obvious and glowing initial reference to Rochester can serve as a shield against criticism—even if it does turn out to be Nemours' view of Rochester, not Lee's. And third, Lee's failure to publish the play in 1683 is entirely comprehensible if we suppose that he reflected on Crowne's experience and hesitated to expose his partially disguised attack to the close scrutiny which print allows.

Heroic Sentiment versus Libertinism

On a personal and historical level *The Princess of Cleve* is a savage attack on Rochester. But the play also functions in a literary frame of reference. Nemours becomes the representative of the libertine ethos so common in the sex comedies of the Carolean period, and in so doing he becomes a touchstone by which we judge the heroic ethos represented by the Prince and Princess of Cleve. There are

23. 27 Jan. 1683. Cited in *The London Stage*, Part 1, p. 318.

two worlds in the play, one courtly and refined, the other crass and bourgeois. Disconcertingly, Nemours bridges the gap, functioning comfortably in both.

The Prince and Princess, painfully noble, honest, and decent, customarily speak in the high-flown blank-verse rhetoric of Restoration tragedy. For example, at the end of the "confession" scene we are given the following exchange:

> *Princess.*   The study of my Life shall be to love you.
> *Prince.*   Never, Oh never! I were mad to hope it,
>   Yet thou shalt give me leave to fold thy hand,
>   To press it with my Lips, to sigh upon it,
>   And wash it with my Tears—
> *Princess.*   I cannot bear this kindness without dying.
> *Prince.*   Nay, we will walk and talk sometimes together,
>   Like Age we'll call to mind the Pleasures past;
>   Pleasures like theirs, which never shall return,
>   For Oh! my Chartres, since thy Heart's estrang'd,
>   The pleasure of thy Beauty is no more,
>   Yet I each night will see thee softly laid,
>   Kneel by thy side, and when thy Vows are paid,
>   Take one last kiss, e'er I to Death retire,
>   Wish that the Heav'ns had giv'n us equal fire;
>   Then sigh, it cannot be, and so expire.
>
> (II, 182)

When Nemours falsely clears himself of responsibility for the dropped letter,[24] the Princess exclaims

> O 'tis too much, I'm lost, I'm lost agen—
> The Duke has clear'd himself, to the confusion
> Of all my settl'd Rage, and vow'd Revenge;
> And now he shews more lovely than before:

---

24. In the novel the dropped letter belongs to the Vidam of Chartres; Nemours allows it to be attributed to him as a favor to his friend—thus unintentionally making the Princess think him false when he is not. Here Lee further blackens Nemours by making him the author, and the disclaimer a lie.

> He comes agen to wake my sleeping Passion,
> To rouze me into Torture; O the Racks
> Of hopeless Love! it shoots, it glows, it burns,
> And thou alas! shalt shortly close my Eyes.
>
> (II, 169)

This is melodramatic bombast, though less inflated than the worst excesses typical of Lee's 1670s style. But, very significantly, Nemours insincerely indulges in the same sort of rhetoric, making it flagrantly bombastic.

> [To the Princess]
> Behold a Slave that Glories in your Chains,
> Ah! with some shew of Mercy view my Pains;
> Your piercing Eyes have made their splendid way,
> Where Lightning cou'd not pass—
> Even through my Soul their pointed Lustre goes,
> And Sacred Smart upon my Spirit throws;
> Yet I your Wounds with as much Zeal desire,
> As Sinners that wou'd pass to Bliss through Fire.
> Yes, Madam, I must love you to my Death,
> I'll sigh your name with my last gasp of Breath.
>
> (II, 212)

In a scene which is not in the original novel, Lee has Nemours and the Prince fight. The Prince declares, "one of us must fall." Nemours replies, "Then take my Life." Provoked into drawing his sword, Nemours disarms the Prince, "gives him his Sword agen," and solemnly announces, "I swear upon the point of Death, / Your Wife's as clear from me, as Heav'n first made her" (II, 205–6). Both men then burst into tears and swear eternal friendship as before. Resemblances to both heroic drama and the duel scene in Steele's *The Conscious Lovers* (1722) are obvious: indeed this scene is carried out with the throbbing melodramatic gusto of John Banks or Elkanah Settle. The audience normally did take such heroics very seriously, and its instinctive reaction would be admiration. And yet *we* know what Nemours really is, even if the Prince does not. And to see the Prince and Princess completely blind to Nemours' hypocrisy casts a deep ironic shadow over the exalted heroic and moral standards they represent.

The ineffectuality of the Prince is made painfully obvious throughout the play. The noble and pathetic love-death of the novel simply seems stupid when Nemours is transformed into a ruttish liar. The Princess fares a little better, since she finally sees part of the truth about Nemours. But her continued love of so worthless a person, and the obvious possibility of a future yielding, are not to her credit. We are also left to wonder how pure and disinterested her "confession" is. Dryden's epilogue calls her, with a lovely double irony, a "saintlike fool." Lee had specialized in villain plays during the seventies, but most of them contain genuine heroes and heroines. The Princess belongs, in type, with the noble Statira in *The Rival Queens*, but in this context she is made to seem foolish rather than heroic or charmingly pathetic.

The omnipresent subplot further degrades the heroic element in the play. St. Andre and Poltrot are doltish cit cuckolds; their wives Elianor and Celia are witty but sex-mad sluts. Sometimes assisted by Nemours, the four of them provide a steady stream of smutty songs (for example, "Phillis is soft, Phillis is plump," II, 163–64) and heavy badinage, as "is the fashion." The husbands' wenching schemes mirror and travesty Nemours' upper-class love-intrigues. Together they try to whore, while each endeavors to cuckold the other. The scene in which the two men unknowingly pay their addresses to their masked wives (III, i) is typical. They boast of their prowess ("we never miss hitting between Wind and Water") and abuse their wives. St. Andre: "mine's so fulsome, that a Goat with the help of Cantharides wou'd not touch her." Poltrot: "Gad, and my Wife has Tets in the wrong place, she's warted all over like a pumpl'd Orange" (II, 189–90). St. Andre's "sleepwalking" speeches and Poltrot's description of catching his wife *in flagrante delicto* (concluding, "I feel something trickle, trickle in my Breeches") are bluntly and joylessly obscene (II, 207–10). This rancid smut is followed instantly by Nemours' announcement that the Prince is dying of a fever brought on by the violence of his love for his chaste but

unloving wife.[25] This juxtaposition is no accident. The report of the
Prince's death comes a little later, at the end of a page on which
Celia justifies her adultery by saying that her "ravisher" had threat-
ened to "rip open" her husband's body. To this Poltrot replies, "And
so thou wert forc'd to consent. . . . I must praise thy Discretion in
Sacrificing thy Body, for o' my Conscience, if they had seen this
Smock-face of mine, I had gone to pot too before my Execution"
(II, 217). This excremental reference from a cowardly cuckold makes
a weird prelude to the announcement of the Prince of Cleve's romantic love-death.

There is no need to multiply examples of smut and ugliness:
they are legion. This profusion presents us with two possibilities.
Either Lee produced a sloppy and pointless amalgam of filth and
heroic sentiment, or he deliberately set out to debase the heroic part
of the play. The intermingling of elements, especially in the presence
of Nemours, makes a satiric interaction inevitable. Split plots *can*
be used for a thematic contrast which supports, rather than undercuts the heroic plane, as in Dryden's *The Spanish Fryar*. Even in the
more ironic *Marriage A-la-Mode* (1671) the heroic is not systematically dirtied, as it is here. What happens in *The Princess of Cleve*
is very simple: in the world of the play, the heroic ethos and its
rhetoric become a ghastly mockery.

The Satiric Impact of the Play

To see the "point" of the satire we need to start by considering the
reactions Lee was seeking to elicit. Nemours is indubitably a scab-
rous swine and the play may indeed be accurately described as a
rotting dung heap. Whatever the original audience made of it,
twentieth-century critics have generally responded with disgust,
nausea, and revulsion. I see no reason to suppose that this is not
exactly what Lee wanted.

25. In his *RES* article Stroup says that "the lovelorn Prince . . . runs upon
Nemours' drawn sword and gets himself out of his friend's way." This is not accurate: the Prince suffers no physical wound. "I have no Wound but that which Honour makes, / And yet there's something cold upon my Heart" (II, 206).

He knew perfectly well what he was doing. "When they expected the most polish'd Hero in Nemours, I gave 'em a Ruffian
reeking from Whetstone's-Park." How does Lee want us to react to
this startling transformation? The next two sentences of the dedication give us a valuable and hitherto ignored hint. "The fourth
and fifth Acts of the Chances, where Don John is pulling down;
Marriage Alamode, where they are bare to the Waste; the Libertine,
and Epsom-Wells, are but Copies of his Villany. He lays about him
like the Gladiator in the Park; they may walk by, and take no notice." Each of these four plays puts a "gentleman's" sexual miscon-
duct in a negative light, though there are considerable differences
in the authors' treatment of the subject. In Buckingham's revision
of Fletcher's *The Chances* (1667), Don John comes off as a reasonably attractive scapegrace, despite some blunt descriptions of his
lying, womanizing ways.[26] Similarly, Dryden's satire in the female-
swapping plot in *Marriage A-la-Mode* can be ignored, and the material taken purely for its titillative value. Indeed an anonymous
contemporary indignantly reports that the members of the audience
completely missed the point of Dryden's "gentile Satyre against this
sort of folly," and contrived to enjoy what should have shamed
them.[27] As Dryden says in his epilogue, using a phrase Lee picks
up, he "would not quite the Woman's frailty bare, / But stript 'em
to the waste, and left 'em there." In fact, Dryden's picture of sexual
infidelity is bluntly negative. And Lee tells us, in so many words,
that he has gone further and been blunter. On the evidence of *Marriage Asserted*, the audience needed to have things spelled out.

Shadwell's *Epsom-Wells* (1672) makes a valuable comparison
to *The Princess of Cleve* because of its use of a multilined plot with
characters at different social levels. At the top, the romantic couples

26. E.g., *The Chances* (London: Langley Curtis, 1682), p. 11:

> "Oaths? What care you for Oaths to gain your ends
> When ye are high and pamper'd? What Saint know ye?
> Or what Religion, but your purpos'd lewdness,
> Is to be look'd for of ye?"

27. See *Marriage Asserted* (London: Herringman, 1674), pp. 75–76; cited by
Harold Brooks, "Some Notes on Dryden, Cowley, and Shadwell," *Notes and Queries*, 168 (1935), 94–95.

(Rains and Lucia, Bevil and Carolina) put up a graceful show of gay-couple wit. A cut below them come the Woodlys, whose adulteries wind up in divorce. Still lower come the contemptible cuckold cits, Bisket and Fribble, and their wives (called respectively "an impertinent, imperious Strumpet" and "a very Whore" in the Dramatis Personae). They are treated with the kind of contempt Lee lavishes on St. Andre and Poltrot. Lowest of all we find the scum—Kick and Cuff ("cheating, sharking, cowardly Bullies") and Mrs. Jilt ("a silly, affected Whore"). By keeping these levels fairly distinct (as Lee deliberately avoids doing) Shadwell is enabled to expend brutal contempt on his cits, while turning a surprisingly indulgent eye on the escapades of his upper class characters, persons of "Wit and Pleasure." Lee was not minded to be so generous. Shadwell's *The Libertine* (1675), a wild and bloody recension of the Don Juan story, and *Timon of Athens* (1678)—though Lee does not name it—make even better comparisons.[28] Both are "satyrical tragedy," in which the moral code of contemporary libertine comedy is imported into a tragic structure. The result in *The Libertine* is a sardonic comment upon both horror tragedy and the ethos of libertine comedy. In *Timon* Shadwell set up contrasts which "compelled [or ought to have] his unsuspecting audience to develop a gradual but unequivocal revulsion for the Hobbesian principles of which they approved in comedy."[29] Lee, I believe, is seeking a very similar result in *The Princess of Cleve*. Very probably the audience refused to listen. This, I presume, is what Lee means by his cryptic remark that the audience "may walk by, and take no notice." If one chooses to treat the action as a diversion in cloud-cuckooland, then one may enjoy the play as a value-free farce, just as John Palmer read *The Country-Wife*.[30] But we have ample evidence that Lee did not want the play taken this way, and to judge by the reactions of most of the critics, he succeeded in making it almost impossible to do so.

28. For a further discussion of these other plays see chs. 7 and 8 of my *Development*.

29. See John Edmunds, "'Timon of Athens' Blended with 'Le Misanthrope': Shadwell's Recipe for Satirical Tragedy," *Modern Language Review*, 64 (1969), 500–507.

30. John Palmer, *The Comedy of Manners* (London: Bell, 1913), ch. 4.

If we look beyond the text of the play for its extrinsic targets, we will find three of them:

1. Nemours is Rochester, and the demolition is devastating, especially where the vaunted deathbed conversion is concerned. Lee's attack is obviously personal and moral; it may also be latently political. Rochester had associated himself with Whig politicians late in life, especially Dorset and Buckingham. And in both literature and politics he had ties to Shadwell, with whom the Tory writers were feuding energetically in 1682 and 1683. *Mac Flecknoe*, the second part of *Absalom and Achitophel*, Dryden's *Vindication of the Duke of Guise*, and Otway's *The Atheist* (ca. June 1683) all belong to this quarrel. Lee's use of sexual innuendo is of course highly suitable to Rochester, and actually it is fairly restrained. Otway's depiction of Shaftesbury in the Nicky-Nacky scenes of *Venice Preserv'd* (February 1682) is far uglier—an attack staged while Lee was probably at work on *The Princess of Cleve*.

2. The heroic/*précieuse* ethos of Restoration tragedy is debunked by association with degraded sexuality. It is not made evil or hypocritical, just ineffectual. Lee had specialized in grand if overheated displays of love, nobility, and heroism. The powerful love-death of Sophonisba and Massinissa in *Sophonisba* (1675), the achingly real feelings of Statira and Roxana in *The Rival Queens* (1677), the searing pathos of Monima and Semandra in *Mithridates* (1678), the still-powerful display of love and sensibility in *Theodosius* (1680) all lead one to expect an exuberant exaltation of the Prince of Cleve. Madame de La Fayette's triangle provided Lee with precisely the sort of situation from which he was accustomed to wring every ounce of pathos, adorned with floods of heroic rant. But in *The Princess of Cleve* Lee's rousing affirmations of the heroic vanish: the love-story suffers from a peculiar flatness which reflects, I suspect, simple lack of conviction. When "reality" is Nemours and the cuckold cits, the exquisite sensibility of the Prince becomes meaningless.

3. Nemours behaves like the rake "hero" of an ordinary Carolean sex comedy—*The Country-Wife*, Durfey's *A Fond Husband* (1677), or Ravenscroft's *The London Cuckolds* (1681). But here we are not invited to sit back, relax, and enjoy the frolic. The con-

tinual and obtrusive presence of the heroic/*précieuse* standard serves as a jarring reminder of Nemours' viciousness. Wycherley's Horner hurts no one who matters; Nemours does, and we cannot forget it, even though Lee is not bent on drumming up sympathy for the victims. As James Sutherland cogently observes, "In the Duke of Nemours Lee seems to be saying to his audience: 'This is the sort of character you admire. Well, take a good look at him, and see what your precious Dorimants are really like.'"[31] Comparison to *The Man of Mode* (1676) is indeed useful here. By most accounts Dorimant is a picture of Rochester, drawn sympathetically by a friend. The portrait was favorable enough to outrage Richard Steele, whose memorable denunciation of the character and the play appears in *Spectator* 65 (1711). Dennis defended the play, a decade later, on the ground that the Carolean audience saw Dorimant's faults and knew him to be no fit pattern for imitation. Nonetheless, Dorimant is glamorous, powerful, and successful, and he is evidently to be rewarded with a beautiful and wealthy wife—whom he wins in a kind of mock-conversion scene. Coincidentally, the part was played by Thomas Betterton. I certainly do not mean to suggest that Lee was writing with an eye on Etherege's play. But clearly Dorimant and Nemours represent opposite poles of opinion about the earl of Rochester, in particular, and about the libertine heroes of contemporary comedy in general. Lee tears away the tinsel and false glamor with icy distaste. He does not preach, and he is wise enough to avoid punishing Nemours—to provide poetic justice would ruin the play's point. Nemours emerges powerful, glamorous, and successful—and all the more horrible for that. The audience ought to feel his attractions just enough to be revolted by its own readiness to tolerate this slippery, goatish scoundrel.

Nothing in the Lee canon prepares one for *The Princess of Cleve*. Consequently the play has seemed an aberration, to be set aside with fastidious distaste or blank incomprehension.[32] I have

31. Sutherland, p. 144.

32. Nineteenth- and early twentieth-century opinion seems typified by Nicoll on the one hand and H. M. Sanders on the other. Sanders reports only that the play "need not detain us," since it "is a tragi-comedy of a flagrant type, and if, as the author tells us, it cost him much pains [actually, this is said of *The Massacre*!], it is

shown that far from being a random assemblage of incongruous materials, the play is in fact a biting three-pronged satire. And if my redating is correct, it comes out of the eighteen-month period in Lee's life in which he somehow swung from Whig rebel to Tory loyalist. The reasons behind this radical shift we are unlikely ever to learn, barring the discovery of hitherto unknown letters or diaries. We know nothing of Lee's earlier views on comedy, though his seething contempt for the libertine ethos comes as no great surprise. Likewise his savaging of Rochester is perfectly comprehensible, on personal, literary, and political grounds. But the bleakly sardonic view of the heroic ethos taken in *The Princess of Cleve* has to come as a shock. I do not think it merely fanciful to say that the play seems to represent the "chaos is come again" stage of Lee's conversion. The ugliness and moral flux so evident in the work reflect, I think, the author's distress about his loss of faith in a heroic value-system which he must have linked, disastrously, to a political outlook he had been forced to abandon. Ham complains, with perfect justice, about the relative "flatness" and lack of conviction in Lee's last two plays—his part of *The Duke of Guise* and *Constantine the Great*. This flatness is not just a sign of diminished poetic fire; rather it is the result of a radical reversal of outlook which seems to have left Lee clinging, rather desperately, to a Tory orthodoxy he could not passionately believe in.

The Princess of Cleve is certainly an unusual work—nasty, ugly, degrading, and meant to seem so. Critics have usually been too repelled to ask *why* it is so. This is odd, since critics have forever been fretting after hard-hitting satire in "Restoration comedies," wanting the likes of Wycherley, Etherege, and Congreve to be the angry moralists traditional comic theory says they ought to be.[33] Well, here is a savage satire. Lee does not just decry libertine comedy, though this is probably the most effective demolition of its premises in the whole period. Nor does he just travesty the heroic drama.

---

a pity his labour was so ill-bestowed." See "The Plays of Nat Lee, Gent.," *Temple Bar*, 124 (1901), 497–508.

33. See, for example, Charles O. McDonald, "Restoration Comedy as Drama of Satire," and Rose A. Zimbardo, *Wycherley's Drama: A Link in the Development of English Satire* (New Haven: Yale Univ. Press, 1965).

Instead, he brings the two value systems together and lets each expose the hollowness and inadequacy of the other. The play is more a despairing than an angry satire: we are not given a comfortable sermon from a superior vantage point, but rather a brutal exposé whose author can find *no* meaningful positive norm. In his final works Lee retreats uncomfortably into the Tory verities, maintaining what shadow of the heroic ethos he can. In *The Princess of Cleve*, which springs from the period of transition, Lee bitterly weighs the two value systems most characteristic of Carolean drama and finds them both horribly wanting. The result is a dizzying and deliberately sickening view into a moral abyss.

5

The Myth of the Rake in "Restoration Comedy"

Reading modern scholarship, one might deduce that "Restoration comedy" is full of unrepentant rakes; that the plays expound a "libertine" philosophy; and that they are essentially hostile to marriage. Sensible critics have realized that the third proposition is ridiculous and that the other two require significant qualification. Nonetheless, the role of the libertine in late seventeenth-century comedy remains the subject of much confusion. I am not trying to argue that there are no rakes in these plays, merely that modern readers—like part of the original audience—have oversimplified and misunderstood them.

Specifically, I shall address six interrelated questions. 1) How many "rakes" are there in exactly what group of comedies? 2) How does the rake change between 1660 and 1710? 3) To what extent do the comedies (or some of them) endorse libertinism? 4) To what extent do they tolerate wild-oats sowing? 5) How uniform is the rake as a character type? 6) How seriously is "reform" to be taken? To avoid misunderstanding, I will say at once that on the basis of late seventeenth-century social standards I do not regard a mistress or two as constituting libertinism, and that to lump all genuine rakes in a single category seems to me to ignore clear and important distinctions. The "polite rake" and the "debauchee" are a world apart. Likewise the "extravagant rake" is very different indeed from the "judicious rake." "Reform" may be anything from a *pro forma* convenience to an occasion for moral preachment. To ignore these distinctions seriously distorts our understanding of the values which underlie these plays.

Libertinism versus Marriage

The idea that "Restoration comedy" champions the libertine while denigrating marriage rises naturally enough from the rhetoric of the gay couple and the prominent examples of a few characters— Horner in *The Country-Wife* and the tom-catting "heroes" of *The London Cuckolds*, for example. Witty railing against the restrictions of marriage is indeed a prominent feature of many plays. *Secret-Love* (1667), *She wou'd if she cou'd* (1668), *Marriage A-la-Mode* (1671), *The Man of Mode* (1676), *The Rover* (1677), *Bellamira* (1687), *The Old Batchelour* (1693), and *The Constant Couple* (1699) come readily to mind, and this list could easily be lengthened. "Goale, that's mariage," grumbles a character in *The Country Gentleman* (1669).[1] That every one of these plays ends with a romantic marriage has given critics remarkably little pause.

Intent upon denigrating his subject, L. C. Knights states flatly that "In the matter of sexual relations Restoration comedy is entirely dominated by a narrow set of conventions. . . . The first convention is, of course, that constancy in love, especially in marriage, is a bore. . . . Appetite, it seems (and this is the second assumption), needs perpetually fresh stimulus."[2] He can indeed cite innumerable derogatory remarks about marriage. Many of them (as he himself admits) are from characters explicitly branded as silly or wicked. Knights argues, however, that such remarks can be paralleled in the utterances of witty and attractive characters. True enough, but he fails to point out that in the latter case we almost invariably get an implicit or explicit recantation in due course.

The charge of libertinism is by no means restricted to detrac-

1. Sir Robert Howard and George Villiers, second duke of Buckingham, *The Country Gentleman*, ed. Arthur H. Scouten and Robert D. Hume, p. 145.
2. "Restoration Comedy: The Reality and the Myth," *Explorations* (London: Chatto and Windus, 1946), pp. 131–49. Originally published in *Scrutiny* in 1937.

tors. Virginia Ogden Birdsall has hailed the comedies of Etherege, Wycherley, and Congreve as honest celebrations of libertinism. In her view, the "typical English comic protagonist" is a "rake-hero" in vigorous intellectual rebellion against the repressive morality of the puritans and the bourgeoisie. "Thus the rake-heroes, both as libertines and as persistent challengers who thrive on controversy, are exemplary of the Hobbesian thinking which prevailed in court circles after the Restoration."[3] Seen thus, "Restoration comedy" is a series of manifestos in favor of skeptical libertinism. This position is extreme, but not without some precedent. As long ago as 1929 Guy Montgomery suggested that we can see in these plays a rebellion against established social and moral standards which parallels the Royal Society's innovations in science. "These comedies, which have emerged from the dramatic chaos and puritanical night, show us a society struggling for adjustment in a newly discovered world. . . . In doing so it proposed new bases for marriage and family life."[4] Are all the happy-ending marriages no more than a facile convention, a betrayal of the plays' underlying values? To my knowledge no one has made this argument, but it seems implicit in the positions of several critics.

I do not mean to dismiss libertine readings lightly. James Sutherland, surely one of the sanest and fairest readers these comedies have ever had, starts his discussion by observing that "Since comedy is traditionally a Dionysiac revel, expressing the unrestrained and unregenerate nature of man, it might be expected that from its first beginnings Restoration comedy would show that libertine spirit which was to become so characteristic of it."[5] And he is entirely correct in observing that "the libertine element in Restoration comedy reached its height in the 1670s." But when he says that during the 1690s "it becomes increasingly clear that the rake-hero is giving way to the man of sense," I want to ask exactly what is meant by

---

3. *Wild Civility*, pp. 6, 39.

4. "The Challenge of Restoration Comedy," *University of California Publications in English*, vol. 1 (Univ. of California Press, 1929), pp. 133–51. Montgomery is thinking largely of gay-couple claims for equality of the sexes.

5. Sutherland, p. 89. Following quotations from pp. 129, 152.

"libertine" and whether all—or even most—of the protagonists of 1670s comedies qualify as "rake-heroes."

The best account of "libertine" philosophy as it relates to these comedies is given by Dale Underwood.[6]

> Philosophically the libertine was an antirationalist, denying the power of man through reason to conceive reality. . . . Accordingly the libertine rejected the orthodox medieval and Renaissance concept of universal order and of man's place and purpose therein. . . . His ends were hedonistic, "Epicurean," and embraced the satisfaction of the senses in accordance with the "reasonable" dictates of Nature—that is, in this case, one's "natural" impulses and desires. . . . At least three philosophic lines of thought are involved: Epicureanism, skepticism, and a type of primitivism or naturalism for which unfortunately there is no other received name.

One cannot deny that such philosophy was in the air, or that scraps of this hedonistic skepticism do appear in many comedies of the time. I am very willing to agree with Sutherland that Etherege "succeeded . . . in expressing an attitude to life which informs many of the more thoughtful comedies of the time. That attitude is a development from seventeenth-century libertinism."[7] But I have shown in some detail elsewhere that Etherege's plays were by no means typical in form or values even of the 1670s comedies.[8] And the presence of a set of ideas by no means proves that a playwright wishes us to accept them. We must consider both source and context. Dryden, after all, puts a great deal of Hobbes into his heroic plays—in the mouths of his villains, as a means of driving us toward a very different set of values. Professor Knights can quote Sir John Brute and Fainall on the horrors of marriage—but I would suppose merely that these characters are being shown up for what they are. Likewise when a playwright has antimatrimonial homilies

6. *Etherege and the Seventeenth-Century Comedy of Manners*, esp. ch. 2. Quotation from pp. 13–14.

7. Sutherland, p. 106.

8. *Development*, chs. 6 and 7.

mouthed by an airy young scapegrace who subsequently falls on his knees before the heroine, I suspect that we should know better than to take the "libertine" protestations at face value. Are we to feel sorrow and regret upon the occasion of the marriage?

The idea that even 1670s comedy is hostile to marriage as an institution is patently absurd. It is, however, quite definitely hostile to marriage of economic convenience, and especially to "forced" marriage. Both were serious problems in upper-class seventeenth-century society. These points have been tellingly argued in an important and neglected article by P. F. Vernon.[9] His conclusions are worth quoting at length.

> John Palmer thought that Restoration dramatists expressed contempt for marriage because they considered that monogamy imposed artificial restrictions on man's natural promiscuity. . . . The comedies do not bear out this view. The majority of heroes and heroines in Restoration comedy . . . never consider the possibility that their love may one day fade. Their only fear is that financial insecurity or mercenary parents may prevent their consummating their love within the bounds of matrimony. . . . What then of those notorious libertine heroes of whom so much is written? . . . It is true that some characters in the comedies do express criticism of monogamy along the lines suggested by Palmer. But these are either cheeky, comic eccentrics (such as Celadon in Dryden's *Secret-Love*, Ascanio in his *The Assignation*, and Philidor in James Howard's *All Mistaken*), whose unconventional witticisms are obviously not to be identified with the considered views of the dramatists, or even of the main characters; or, if heroes with whom we are meant to sympathise more fully, they recant by the end of the play, after their libertine poses have been subjected to the same kind of comic "debunking" that King Ferdinand's prejudices receive in *Love's Labour's Lost*. . . . Usually the dramatists try to demonstrate that the promiscuity of the libertine cannot be successful as a way of living because it is "unnatural." Profes-

9. "Marriage of Convenience and The Moral Code of Restoration Comedy," *Essays in Criticism*, 12 (1962), 370–87.

sor Underwood seems to come to the conclusion that the marriages which end the comedies of Etherege represent a compromise [between "conventionality" and "libertinism"] . . . . It is a strangely onesided kind of compromise! Etherege's hero is only the most subtly drawn of a long line of similar anti-matrimonialists . . . all of whom are eventually forced by their witty female partners to renounce their libertine beliefs. J. H. Smith's study brings out effectively how, far from indicating any disrespect for monogamy, all these heroes are used to reinforce the assumption that a long-lasting, freely-chosen love-relationship is the happiest state of life.

I myself have read every extant comedy performed in the fifty-year period under consideration here, and I have never found a play which seemed to me genuinely to attack marriage as an institution or to envisage any serious alternative. *Marriage A-la-Mode* comes as close as any, but Dryden's conclusion is uncompromisingly conservative.

Dramatists were indubitably interested in discussing the ways in which a sound marriage could be worked out. Male sovereignty in marriage, still deeply entrenched in law, was coming under fire, and the many proviso scenes in these comedies show us a stylized form of agreement upon the pattern of a mutually satisfying marriage. The bad marriages frequently shown—as in *The Wives Excuse* and *The Provok'd Wife*—are a warning and an attempt to expose a genuine social and legal problem. The cuckolding pattern so common in the 1670s expresses hostility to marriage of convenience gone wrong, not to marriage itself.[10] Comedies in which a "libertine" protagonist is left unmarried are quite rare. Philidor in *All Mistaken* is an extreme example of the "extravagant rake" discussed below. Rashley in Durfey's *A Fond Husband* (1677) and the three gallants in *The London Cuckolds* are obvious instances, though they are scarcely more than plot devices in bedroom farces. Horner is the example who will come to every reader's mind. But even in *The Country-Wife* we see conventional marriage upheld in Har-

10. I have discussed these issues at some length in "Marital Discord in English Comedy from Dryden to Fielding" (ch. 6 below).

court and Alithea. I do not agree with the critics who see that couple as a moral norm for the play. But are Harcourt and Alithea somehow shown up or derided? Let the critic prove it who can. *The Wives Excuse* is uncompromisingly bleak, but as a rule even the darkest comedies—Otway's *The Atheist* or Vanbrugh's *The Provok'd Wife*—support marriage as an institution, however horribly wrong it can go.

That libertine ideas are present in the comedies we must agree, but no one has shown that the values of the plays are predominantly libertine, nor does such a demonstration seem possible. We need to ask, at this point, what role the libertine ideas play. Underwood is absolutely right when he tells us that in these comedies we see a clash between "two broadly opposing sets of traditions: on the one hand Christianity and Christian humanism, the 'heroic' tradition, the honest-man tradition, and the tradition of courtly love; on the other, philosophic and moral libertinism, Machiavellian and Hobbesian concepts as to the nature of man, and Machiavellian ethics." [11] I think he considerably overestimates the degree to which even Etherege supports the libertine position, but the conflict he depicts between "epicure" and "stoic" outlooks is plainly present in many comedies.

A similar but sounder sense of the value-dichotomy in these plays has been expounded by C. D. Cecil in an acute and sensitive essay. "Restoration comedy preserves the evidence of a gradual change among the youthful gentry from a libertine ideal to a prudent one based largely on the mid-seventeenth century concept of *honnêteté*. Attributes of this social mode are latent in the polite rake of Etherege and Wycherley, and clearly developed in the typical Congreve hero. . . . Every Restoration comedy that still interests us attempts to realise an ideal personality based on some compromise between libertinism and self-control." [12] The use of the term "*précieux*" in this essay is perhaps misleading, since Cecil is not referring to carryover from the literary habits of the Caroline period. But the terms in which he understands the "polite rake" seem

11. Underwood, p. 8.

12. "Libertine and *Précieux* Elements in Restoration Comedy," *Essays in Criticism*, 9 (1959), 239–53.

to me extremely convincing. "The polite rake knows that the probable alternative to marriage is grotesque—a world of surly old bachelors or, as Wycherley has it in *The Country Wife*, of 'old boys . . . who like super-annuated Stallions are suffer'd to run, feed, and whinney with the Mares as long as they live, though they can do nothing else'. . . . Urbane society tolerates the polite rake because he must eventually surrender to it or pass outside as a buffoon." In Dorimant, Cecil suggests, we may "perceive the future man of sense assumed by the dramatist but outside the action of his play." This view accounts satisfactorily both for the presence of rakes and for the marriage pattern so dominant in these comedies.

If we stop to ask why the figure of the rake has so exercised students of these comedies, at least one reason is obvious—the court of Charles II was full of "literary rakes." Buckingham, Dorset, Mulgrave, Rochester, Sir Charles Sedley, and a host of others were members of a scandalous if loosely-defined circle—the "Court Wits." "The name was as loose as the morals of the assemblage," remarks John Harold Wilson in what remains the best account of this group.[13] The king set an example of promiscuity, and his followers emulated him with enthusiasm, though time and scandal have magnified the Court Wits' reputation for debauchery. Wilson demolishes many juicy anecdotes, but admits unequivocally that "from a modern point of view, the record of debauchery is sufficiently complete. . . . Even in their own day there were outcries from respectable people, who wondered why Heaven withheld its fire." However ludicrously exaggerated the views of nineteenth-century critics of society and drama (Beljame asserts that Congreve's heroes frequent brothels!) the truth is that Charles' court was populated by dashing young libertines. Wilson gives a general characterization of their outlook.

> The Wits have been variously labeled cynics, skeptics, libertines, Epicureans, pagans, and atheists. To a certain extent, some of the terms apply, yet none is strictly accurate. They were cynical (as the King, their master, was cynical) because their limited experience demonstrated that no man was honest and no

13. *The Court Wits of the Restoration* (1948; rpt. New York: Octagon, 1967), p. 5. Following quotation from p. 36.

woman chaste. . . . They were not true skeptics, for they accepted the materialism of Lucretius and Hobbes. They were libertines by instinct (as most young male animals are), but they were libertines by conviction as well, for they saw no ethical values in their world, and no purpose in living save the gratification of their senses. They were Epicureans, not in the philosophical meaning of the term, but only as that title has become confounded with hedonism; they were addicted to the unholy trinity: wine, women, and song. Pagans they were not, for they worshiped no idols and took no joy in Nature. They were atheists only in the eyes of the scandalized clergy, who were prone to use the term to describe any deviation from orthodoxy. Yet they were all members of the Church of England, and gave an easy lip service to its dogmas. (Pp. 16–17)

If this is a fair characterization of the real-life Restoration rake, and I think it is, then we can proceed to ask how well the description fits protagonists in the comedies. The answer is not very well. Of the major writers only Etherege was a Court Wit, though Wycherley was a fringe member. We may say of Horner and Dorimant that "they saw no ethical values in their world, and no purpose in living save the gratification of their senses." We will find many a rake saying something of the sort, but when we stop to consider source and context we will find only a small number of hard-core libertines in these plays—and few of them are kindly treated.

We cannot afford uncritically to read society—and one small part of it at that—into these comedies. In a pedestrian but useful study Donald Clark Wall concludes that "the comedy of this period [1660–85] generally drew little material from the lives of the libertines. Of the ninety-five comedies surveyed, sixty-two (sixty-five percent) either do not present a libertine character or else present one whose actions and attitudes seem to have almost no connection with those of the historical rakes. . . . From the viewpoint of this study, the widely read comedies of Wycherley and Etherege are actually atypical."[14] Wall finds that only sixteen plays seem to contain

14. "The Restoration Rake in Life and Comedy," Diss. Florida State Univ. 1963. Quotation from Abstract.

"accurate representations of contemporary rakes." If anything, he is still overestimating the place of the rake in these comedies, since he makes no attempt to assess context. Otway's *Friendship in Fashion* (1678), for example, does present a full-blown rake in Goodvile, but only as the object of a bitterly serious satiric attack. Only a Macaulay or an Archer could find that a libertine play.

There are indeed some libertines, and many expressions of libertinism in "Restoration comedy." How are we to react to them? In the case of Goodvile or Sir John Brute, quite clearly with loathing. But what of a Dorimant? If we take him as "real"—and his association with Rochester encourages this response—we are more or less forced to approve or disapprove. In this event we join Archer on the one hand or Mrs. Birdsall on the other. In 1927 H. F. B. Brett-Smith insisted that Etherege was "concerned to give an exact picture of fashionable life" and to show "nature as nature was to be seen in the London of 1676."[15] Fujimura goes so far as to speak of "photographic realism" in Restoration comedy.[16] But without retreating into cloud cuckooland, I think we can see these plays as comic fictions. Writing three years earlier than Brett-Smith, E. E. Stoll announced that the misers and cuckolds of Wycherley and Congreve are "ridiculous."

> And so with the Etherege and Congreve philosophy of conduct or "code." It is comical because it is gay—but also, as Lamb would forget, because it is so bold, bad, and different, because so wittily but also so startlingly phrased. It is not the philosophy or code of the period. For it is of the very essence of comedy that it should not express the code of the period, but that Saturnalian spirit of rebellion against this code, in those who nevertheless acknowledge it, which in all ages takes the form of wit and laughter. Comedy is ever in league with nature, and not with virtue. Comedy is under the rule of the Lord of Misrule—a Feast of Fools.[17]

15. *The Dramatic Works of Sir George Etherege*, ed. H. F. B. Brett-Smith, 2 vols. (Oxford: Blackwell, 1927), I, lxx, lxxxiii.

16. Fujimura, p. 52.

17. "Literature No 'Document,'" *Modern Language Review*, 19 (1924), 149.

Stoll sees in these comedies the same kind of dichotomy and tension defined in different ways by Underwood and Cecil. That even the comedies of the 1670s comprise both libertine and "social" or "moral" impulses should be obvious to any unprejudiced reader. With that in mind we are ready to analyze the clash in the plays themselves.

Attitudes toward Cuckoldry and Mistress Keeping

Defining the "ethos of Restoration comedy" is extremely difficult, and indeed impossible unless the group of plays so defined is sharply delimited. No single play can be fairly representative of both the cuckolding comedies of the 1670s and the "reform" comedies written by Cibber and Centlivre in the first years of the eighteenth century. The term "Restoration comedy" is fatally vague, for in general usage it comprises both the works of the Carolean period (1660–85) and many plays written in the "Augustan" mode dominant early in the eighteenth century. The transition between these two norms is accomplished gradually over a twenty-year period starting in the middle eighties, during which time the old and new schools coexist and mix. Properly speaking, the "Restoration rake" is a phenomenon of the Carolean period. Historically, the Court Wit group flourished 1665–78: by 1680 its aging members were scattered, silent, reforming, or dead. And in comedy, as critics from Montgomery to Sutherland rightly observe, the "libertine element" (however defined) reached its height in the mid-1670s. There are rakes aplenty in nineties comedy, but they tend to be viewed with a harshness almost unknown twenty years earlier.

Crudely defined, a rake (short for rakehell) is a *roué*, a licentious or dissolute man. The term carries strong connotations of profligacy, idleness, and waste. Many members of Carolean society would have characterized Buckingham, Rochester, Sedley, and others in these terms or worse. The observations of Clarendon and Evelyn, to name two well-known commentators, are scathing. Insofar as rakes in plays represent something like the Court Wits, much of the audience probably found them both glamorous and shocking. Pepys reacted to the Court Wits this way; alas, the *Diary* stops before he had a chance to comment on any of the major stage rakes.

Determining "society's standards" is difficult at best, if only because they are never uniform. If the scholar turns to the multitudinous courtesy books of the seventeenth century he can find evidence for almost any position. The notorious second part of Francis Osborne's *Advice to a Son* (1658) is often quoted as an index to the dissoluteness of the Restoration—though of course it was written with Cromwell in power. Osborne says flatly that a man is stupid to marry, unless he gains a great estate thereby. Marriage entails loss of freedom, and turns inevitable fornication into sinful adultery. Better just fornicate and avoid the worry and expense of marriage. So says Osborne, and Pepys reports that his *Advice* was one of the most widely read books in England. Of course this is not evidence that its precepts were widely accepted or practiced. Most of the courtesy books are relentlessly moral, which proves nothing either.[18] The difficulty of knowing whom to believe and proving relevance to drama haunts studies which try to rely on this kind of evidence.[19] Two generalities can probably be hazarded with safety. First, in both life and literature a double standard prevailed. Heroines of comedies are invariably spotless and pure. When Nicoll tells us that in the gay couple "the woman [is] as emancipated as the man"[20] he is talking nonsense. Only in rhetoric are heroines ever emancipated. There are only a handful of instances of a fallen woman marrying anyone but a comic butt (Sir Positive At-all in *The Sullen Lovers*) or a gull (Sir John Swallow in *Sir Martin Mar-all*). Exceptions include Phæbe in Durfey's *The Marriage-Hater Match'd* (1692), and Angellica in his *The Campaigners* (1698). In the first case a seducer is tricked into marrying the girl he seduced; in the latter the seducer repents and marries the woman he has impregnated.

18. For a useful survey of such works see John E. Mason, *Gentlefolk in the Making* (Philadelphia: Univ. of Pennsylvania Press, 1935).

19. For example, Jean Gagen, "Congreve's Mirabell and the Ideal of the Gentleman," *PMLA*, 79 (1964), 422–27, and D. R. M. Wilkinson, *The Comedy of Habit* (Leiden: Universitaire Pers, 1964).

20. Nicoll, I, 196–97.

The second generalization is an obvious corollary: men of the upper classes could keep mistresses without much reproach, especially unmarried men. Halifax's well-known advice to his daughter—suggesting that she close her eyes and await her husband's maturity—need not be quoted again here.

In any analysis of libertinism in this drama two quite distinct elements must be distinguished—the simple keeping of a mistress versus cuckolding actions or "free gallantry" (as J. H. Smith describes it) in which we see active and multifarious attempts at seduction. A single play can and often does present both. But the moral impact of a cuckolding play is a much more complicated matter. Nowhere in late seventeenth-century comedy is there serious protest against keeping a mistress. Keepers and wenchers are frequently derided, and around the end of the century the "reform" of the gallant is often acclaimed—but mistresses were regarded as an inevitable part of the fashionable world, probably even more in comedy than in life. Rather than rattle off a long list of largely unfamiliar names and titles, I will try to illuminate the attitude taken with three illustrative cases.

James Howard's *The English Mounsieur* (1663) is the earliest gay couple play. It is lively, like other 1660s comedies quite moral, and entirely lacking any "libertine" tone. The penniless Welbred is courting the beautiful young Widow Wealthy, whom he finally wins after he has both renounced gaming and convinced the Widow of his genuine love. His exuberant financial irresponsibility and his keeping a mistress (Mrs. Crafty) makes Welbred an "extravagant rake." But the Widow never exhibits a jot of concern about the mistress, while Welbred's gaming seriously upsets her. Early in the play Welbred agrees to help Mrs. Crafty trick Frenchlove (a stupid fop) into marriage. Hearing of this, the Widow expresses her satisfaction with such good-hearted generosity (19).[21] The mistress is just not an issue, even in a play as morally decorous as this one.[22]

---

21. For a fuller discussion of *The English Mounsieur*, see my introduction to the Augustan Reprint Society facsimile (Los Angeles, 1977).

22. In Elizabeth Polwhele's *The Frolicks* (1671)—a play by a virtuous virgin who may well have been a clergyman's daughter—the heroine is hugely amused when two of her suitor's ex-mistresses tie a pair of his bastards to his back, and she

A more startling example is Shadwell's *The Squire of Alsatia* (1688). Historically, this is certainly one of the most important plays in the whole period. Shadwell is unabashedly didactic, and in Belfond Jr. he proposes to show us a quasi-exemplary protagonist. We find this young gentleman supporting an ex-mistress (Mrs. Termagant) and a three-year-old bastard. We first meet him as he is climbing out of bed with Lucia, an attorney's daughter he has just seduced. Throughout the play he sweet-talks her, trying to persuade her that she was right to yield, and making her half-promises he has no intention of keeping. All the while he is busy courting Isabella, an heiress. He finally wins his girl (and her fortune), upon which his guardian pays Lucia off handsomely (£1,500) and young Belfond proceeds to swear illogically to her father that she is innocent. Shadwell is all admiration for this gentlemanly generosity. Young Belfond excuses his womanizing quite bluntly: "we may talk of mighty matters; of our Honesty and Moraility; but a young Fellow carries that about him that will make him a Knave now and then in spite of his Teeth" (21). Such admissions notwithstanding, he loudly asserts his determination to "conform . . . for ever" to his heiress, if he can win her. And at the end of the play he is spouting piety in verse.

> Farewel for ever all the Vices of the Age:
> There is no peace but in a Virtuous Life,
> Nor lasting Joy but in a tender Wife.

Nicoll denounces this play as "hopelessly and permeatingly vulgar, brutal and immoral."[23] From his point of view, this is true. But Shadwell seems to have written with real moral conviction, and the play was enormously popular. Nothing in the play suggests that it ought to be subtitled *The Libertine Reclaim'd*. Rather, Shadwell is showing us the maturation process of a virtuous and honorable young man. He certainly does not regard Belfond Jr. as a rake, or consider his conduct reprehensible.

In *The Way of the World* (1700) we find an equally clear case

---

marries him without a qualm. See *The Frolicks*, ed. Judith Milhous and Robert D. Hume (Ithaca: Cornell Univ. Press, 1977).

23. Nicoll, I, 198.

of a protagonist we favor having had a mistress, and continuing to look out for her. Mirabell's relations with Mrs. Fainall have provoked a few moral trumpetings from various critics over the years, but such objections are based strictly on prejudice. Within the play we will find no hint that we should disapprove. Mrs. Fainall herself clearly seems to feel that Mirabell has been decent, honorable, and trustworthy throughout. His continued concern for her in Act V does indeed bespeak decency and honor. In sum, keeping a mistress has nothing to do with libertinism.

Cuckolding actions are a different matter altogether. Here we must distinguish between the farcical sex-romp (*A Fond Husband*) and the genuine display of libertine principles in action (*The Country-Wife*). No doubt the rutting "heroes" of *A Fond Husband* or *The London Cuckolds* say what libertines say, but this is no more than formal motivation for the bedroom antics. Lack of moral outcry about these plays is an accurate reflection of their essential meaninglessness. When we turn to plays where the author takes human implications more seriously—as in Otway's *Friendship in Fashion* or Southerne's *The Wives Excuse*—then the "libertinism" quickly becomes upsetting or unpleasant. A play like *The Country-Wife* manages to be halfway serious while keeping a light tone.

By the standards of comedies written after about 1670 old husbands with young wives are fair game for horning, especially if the wife entered the marriage under duress. Cuckoldom is punishment, and dramatists often mete it out with gusto. Beaugard horning Sir Davy Dunce in Otway's *The Souldiers Fortune* (1680) is an excellent example. The cuckold is a nasty old man with a wretched young wife who could not marry Beaugard because he was poor. Copulation is no real remedy, but it is a measure of revenge, as well as good fun. Here the cuckoldom is an expression of hostility. It may also be an expression of contempt for a foolish, ineffectual, often complacent husband—for example, Congreve's Sir Paul Plyant. Where our attention focuses more on the gallant, the rake can become more than a means to an end. Horner, Dorimant,[24] Shadwell's

24. Dorimant of course makes no cuckolds during the play. But his successful attempt on an upper-class woman is extremely unusual, and belongs with cuckoldry rather than mistress-keeping.

Bruce and Longvil (in *The Virtuoso*), Lee's Nemours (in *The Princess of Cleve*), and a few others are genuine libertines, not merely convenient dramatic devices.

Cuckolding is decidedly not characteristic of 1660s comedy. In *She wou'd if she cou'd* Courtall is given every opportunity to bed Lady Cockwood, but he carefully engineers an escape every time. By the middle 1670s we find no such squeamishness: Lady Gimcrack duly gets bedded by Bruce en route to his marriage in *The Virtuoso*. Courtall, to be sure, talks grandiosely of libertinism, but he does not live up to his own rhetoric. Mrs. Birdsall declares him a "rake, libertine, and skeptic" who delights "in his own wickedness,"[25] but this description seems curiously at odds with what we actually see him do. During the next few years there is a surge in cuckolding actions. Betterton leaves the issue in doubt at the end of his influential *The Amorous Widow* (ca. 1669), and of course Dryden pulls up short two years later in *Marriage A-la-Mode*. But in Shadwell's *Epsom-Wells* (1672), Dover's(?) *The Mall* (1674), and then in a great flood of plays we find explicitly consummated adultery. A significant part of the audience was evidently shocked, or claimed to be shocked, by *The Country-Wife* in 1675.

The boom in explicit sex scenes reached its peak in 1678 with Dryden's notorious *Mr. Limberham*, Otway's *Friendship in Fashion*, and Behn's *Sir Patient Fancy*. After that, there is a rapid decline in cuckolding and free gallantry. John Harrington Smith traces these elements closely through the nineties, and declares that Doggett's *The Country-Wake* (1696) is the last comedy in which the "hero" was "permitted to make a cuckold in the progress of the play, and win the heroine also."[26] Long before this time writers had adopted the expedient of letting a "friend" attend to this part of the plot. Thus in *The Double-Dealer* (1693) Careless, not Mellefont, takes Lady Plyant to bed. After 1682 writers become increasingly careful to show adultery in a bad light (*The Wives Excuse*), to use it as an obviously well-deserved punishment for the cuckold (*City Politiques*), or to treat it so farcically that it roused little ire (*Cuckolds-*

25. Birdsall, *Wild Civility*, p. 71.
26. *The Gay Couple*, p. 167.

Haven). The exuberant sexual pursuits of the seventies almost entirely vanish, and when a writer returned to the old tone, as Sedley did in his rollicking *Bellamira* (1687), the results provoked a storm of audience objections. Indeed we have no reason to suppose that even in 1676 much of the audience approved of, let alone practiced, what it was shown in popular comedies.[27] Analyzing the ways in which free gallantry and adultery were made palatable will take us a long way toward understanding the sorts of rakes presented in these plays.

Extravagant Rakes versus Vicious Rakes and Philosophical Libertines

Four basic strategies for rendering libertinism acceptable on the stage were in common use. Comic exaggeration could take the sting out, as in *The Constant Couple*. The victims could be made contemptible, as in *The Country-Wife*. Libertinism could be harshly satirized, as in *Friendship in Fashion*. Or it could be abolished by a salutary moral reform, as in *Love's Last Shift*. Each mode has an effect on the character of its libertine, a subtlety to be pursued in due course.

The "Rake" is not a single, definable type. This should be self-evident to any reader of the plays just named. In trying to determine the variant forms, one must start with a basic distinction. The "Polite Rake" and the "Debauchee" have almost no connection. The Polite Rake is a young man of wit and breeding. He flouts society's rules, but he is accepted as a member of the best society.

---

27. Susan Staves has objected a) that this analysis of libertinism in the plays does not sufficiently take into account "the importance of representation and decorum," and b) that some of the seventies and eighties plays express "real skepticism" and "malaise" about marriage (*Players' Scepters*, pp. 166–67). I can certainly agree with the second point: my analysis of the skeptical plays (which I would call problem plays) will be found in ch. 6 below. About the first point I am dubious. Professor Staves is correct in saying that the comedies "violate decorum" in presenting things which "seventeenth-century critics" were "upset about." But I doubt the validity of judging the ethos of the plays by appealing to moral objections many of which came from outside the theatre world.

The Debauchee includes several disparate types, all of them contemptible. Principally these are the country blockhead, whoring his way through London (Belfond Sr. in *The Squire of Alsatia*), the hypocritical, wenching puritan (Alderman Gripe in *Love in a Wood*), and old whoremongers (Snarl in *The Virtuoso*). The distinction between Polite Rake and Debauchee is largely a matter of social class and style. Authors are indulgent with genteel young men who carry off their affairs with flair before settling down. The distinction is that between a Truewit and a Witless or a Witwoud. Even among the Truewit class, however, there are at least three major types to be distinguished.

An important contribution to this task has been made by Robert Jordan, who has described and analyzed a type he defines as the "extravagant rake" in some detail.[28] The extravagant rake is characterized by frantic intensity, promiscuity, crazy impulsiveness, cheekiness, reckless frivolity, breezy vanity, and devastating self-assurance. His daffy manner is a key to the type. "He cannot take himself, or anybody else, at all seriously," says Jordan, who concludes that "he is a comic figure" but not "a comic fool." This is an extremely important distinction. We laugh at him, but not with contempt. He knows what he is, and he is what he wants to be. This is not true of the fops and Witwouds who try to be what they are not. The extravagant rake may be an "entertaining puppy"— but he is an immensely amusing and likable puppy. Some conspicuous examples are Philidor in *All Mistaken*, Celadon in *Secret-Love*, Willmore in Part 1 of *The Rover*, "Sir Anthony" in *Sir Anthony Love*, and Sir Harry Wildair in *The Constant Couple*. As this list suggests, the type appears steadily from the first years of the period to the end of the century. After that it quickly withers away.

As Jordan observes, the extravagant rake is *not* regarded as a typical young man or a common type. His companions react as to a unique and startling phenomenon. Common descriptive adjectives include "mad," "airy," "extravagant," "gay," "wild," and so forth. One would not apply such terms to cold calculators like Hor-

28. "The Extravagant Rake in Restoration Comedy," *Restoration Literature*, ed. Harold Love (London: Methuen, 1972), pp. 69–90.

ner and Dorimant. The extravagant rake is regarded by other characters in the play with a combination of astonishment and affection. His "wildness"—sexual, financial, or otherwise—is looked on with indulgence by all but the stuffiest old fathers, and in a good nine cases out of ten he winds up renouncing his former ways and settling down to marriage. Along the way, the extravagant rake does manage to *sound* wild. Libertine tirades are a major characteristic of this type. The extravagant rake in Fane's *Love in the Dark* (1675) delivers himself thus.

> *Trivultio.*   Here are Riches, but Marriage attends it: a Golden Trap. . . . Lying with another Man's Wife is like invading an Enemies Countrey: there's both Love and Ambition in't; 'tis an enterprize fit for a great Spirit. . . . Matrimony! for Heaven's sake name it not. I do not love to hear the sound of Fetters.
>
> *Sforza.*   . . . I think indeed the strictness of it was but a kind of juggle, betwixt the Women and the Fryars.
>
> *Trivultio.*   True, Such a devilish thing could never have been found out else. 'Twas worse than the invention of Gunpowder; and 't has alter'd the course of love, more than the other has done of War. . . . For slavish Offices and things ungrateful, Constraint is necessary, but for the Sweets of Love, To have a Task impos'd; t'have Men, like hir'd Town Bulls, Made amorous by force, and beating to't! Do Men chain up themselves at Dinner to their Tables? . . . are drudgeries the better for being endless? (20–21)

Similar sentiments are to be heard from Willmore in *The Rover*, Ramble in *The Countrey Wit*, Roebuck in *Love and a Bottle*, Sir Harry Wildair, and a score of others. As Jordan observes, however, these pronouncements are made deliberately outrageous. Judging from the amused reactions of other characters, "libertine philosophy in the mouth of such a rake seems designed more to reinforce the sense of hyperbolic extravagance and impertinence than to con-

stitute a serious case seriously advanced."[29] The "libertinism" of
the extravagant rake is largely an affectation and a humour, to be
shed when convenient. Occasionally we are openly told so, especially late in the period when authors worried more about moral
impact. Thus near the outset of Mrs. Trotter's *Love at a Loss* (1700)
the heroine says unconcernedly of her admirer's extravagant philosophy, "I believe there's more Humour and Affectation, than any
serious Reflection in it" (5).

In short, the libertinism of the extravagant rake is comic and
exaggerated. Most of them are far wilder in word than in deed. A
little gaming and a bastard or two were nothing which could not
be expected of a high-spirited young gentleman, let alone an extravagant rake. Moral judgment of "libertinism" in this context is
largely irrelevant. When a dramatist feels constrained to offer an
excuse, he falls back readily on youth. The extravagant rake's escapades are seldom taken seriously by anyone. "I fain would break
him of this humour, because I love him" remarks the heroine of
The English Mounsieur (27), and when a friend puts in a good
word, he points out that Welbred's behavior "is onely a fault and
miscarriage of his youth" (66). Jordan concludes that the extravagant rake fills "a carnival role" in which he "is a one-man *mardi
gras*" providing "therapeutic release." "In him customary restraints
are thrown off with a wild exuberance and an unashamed joy, and
if he does finally dwindle into a husband this could be said to mark
the passing of carnival and the acceptance of responsibility."[30]

Excellent as Jordan's account of the extravagant rake is—and
I am much indebted to it—he seems to me to lose his perspective
when he tries to differentiate this type from others. His "starting-
point" is a "distinction between the extravagant rake and the more
normal rakish gentleman of Restoration comedy such as Dorimant
in Etherege's *The Man of Mode*, Rodophil and Palamede in Dryden's *Marriage à-la-Mode*, Horner in Wycherley's *The Country Wife*,
Longvil and Bruce in Shadwell's *The Virtuoso*, and Truman and

29. Jordan, pp. 74–75.
30. Jordan, pp. 87–88.

Valentine in Otway's *Friendship in Fashion*."[31] I agree with Jordan entirely that the distinction is "largely one of manner or style." The second group, whom he dubs "judicious rakes," are indeed noted for smoothness, social polish, "understanding," and self-control. The differentiation is both real and important. But to call Dorimant and Horner "the more normal rakish gentleman of Restoration comedy" is a very serious error indeed. Dorimant and his ilk—a far smaller group than the tribe of extravagant rakes—are in fact quite atypical of the protagonists of these comedies.

The gentleman who is normally the "hero" of a late seventeenth-century comedy comes in two basic types, the "ordinary rakish gentleman" and the *honnête homme*. Very often a comedy will have one of each, hero and friend. The *honnête homme* type does not become really common until the nineties, though examples can be found much earlier—Worthy and Lovetruth in *The Country Gentleman* (1669), for example, or Raymund in *The Humorists* (1670), Bellamour in *A True Widow* (1678). *Bury-Fair* (1689) typ-ifies the nineties plays in which we see the taming of a dashing young man, Wildish, who talks libertinism but is not really seen practicing it, versus the sober maturity of Lord Bellamy, a man of culture, good sense, and breeding. ("He that Debauches private Women, is a Knave, and injures others: And he that uses publick ones, is a Fool, and hurts himself"—10.) The example and advice of the *honnête homme* reclaiming an incipient rake from his youth-ful follies is of course one of the more tedious clichés of eighteenth-century comedy. But in the less priggish context of pre-1700 comedy, such figures are often attractive and theatrically effective.

The usual protagonist, however, is the gentleman Truewit with a good heart and routinely "libertine" inclinations. He does not go to the behavioral extremes of the extravagant rake, and he is not the hardbitten flouter of the conventional social code that we find in Jordan's "judicious rake." Loveby in *The Wild Gallant* is not really wild enough to be a full-fledged extravagant rake, and he makes a good borderline case. So does Sir Frederick Frollick in *The*

31. Jordan, p. 83.

Comical Revenge. The ordinary protagonist is well-illustrated by Courtall and Freeman in *She wou'd if she cou'd*, Wildish in *The Mulberry-Garden*, Wildblood and Bellamy in *An Evening's Love*, and Ranger in *Love in a Wood*. In Part 1 of *The Rover* (1677) we can see a clear difference between the extravagant Willmore and his friends Frederick, Blunt, and Belvile. Indeed Belvile verges on the *honnête homme*. This list could be carried on at length right into the eighteenth century. My point is simply that the norm is neither Dorimant nor Sir Harry Wildair, and in this context "rake" does not properly apply to the ordinary loose-living young Truewit.

Genuine rakes fall in three major categories, with two additional subsections. The extravagant rake, the vicious rake, and the "judicious rake"—whom I prefer to call the philosophical libertine—are the major types. To them must be added those rakes who populate bedroom romps (Rashley in *A Fond Husband*) and those whose libertinism is really mainly an excuse for loudly touted "reform" (Loveless in *Love's Last Shift*). This last group will be discussed briefly in the last section. The bedroom romp crew require little comment. They do and say rakish things, but in a lighthearted way which renders potentially ugly and obscene doings comically innocuous. *The London Cuckolds* is a splendid example: despite its seamy events, the manner is so lighthearted that even most moralists have been disarmed. Some other plays which seem to me to fall in this category or verge on it are *Tom Essence*, *Sir Patient Fancy*, *The Rambling Justice*, *The Roundheads*, *City Politiques*, and *Cuckolds-Haven*. Congreve's *The Old Batchelour* and Farquhar's *Love and a Bottle* are close to this type—no accident, I think. Both are highly imitative first efforts from talented young writers who plunder the clichés of the seventies with insouciant vigor.

The philosophical libertine and the vicious rake have two major features in common: their libertinism is real, not all airy talk and lighthearted escapades, and it is taken seriously. These types differ in the harshness with which libertine behavior is viewed. Critics may argue over how negatively Dryden presents Woodall's doings in *Mr. Limberham*. But at its extremes the distinction is entirely clear. No one would say that Otway's despicable Goodvile is set in the same light as Wycherley's Horner. Even lumped together, the plays employing such genuine rakes make no long list. We need not haggle over precise boundaries and totals, but by my calculations we are dealing with no more than roughly twenty plays out of more than two hundred.[32] That this list includes two of the three most widely read comedies from this period helps account for the extraordinarily exaggerated reputation of the Restoration rake.

The philosophical libertine both professes and acts in accordance with the Court Wit code outlined in the first section and does so without the comic exuberance which would render it innocuous. The small number of these cases is rather startling. Jordan names Dorimant, Horner, Rhodophil and Palamede, Longvil and Bruce, and Truman and Valentine—these last two in a play dominated by a vicious rake. To this list I would add Dryden's Woodall. Characters in Dover's(?) *The Mall* (1674) and Durfey's *The Virtuous Wife* (1679) and a few others are borderline, lacking the conviction and impact of the greater writers' rakes. The only plays not from the 1670s I would add to this list are Lee's *The Princess of Cleve* and Sedley's racy *Bellamira*, the latter a decided anachronism in 1687. Like the Court Wit, the philosophical libertine is a phenomenon of the 1670s.

Dryden was the pioneer. *Marriage A-la-Mode* (1671) does not contain a Dorimant, but it does provide the first serious presentation and analysis of libertine ideas in Carolean comedy. Characteristically, Dryden considers the issue from the vantage point of the long haul, not that of the youthful roisterer. The play poses a question in its opening song.

32. Plays which seem to me definitely to display libertinism in a serious way are the following. *The Mall* (1674), *The Country-Wife* (1675), *The Man of Mode* (1676), *Tom Essence* (1676), *The Virtuoso* (1676), *Sir Patient Fancy* (1678), *Mr. Limberham* (1678), *Friendship in Fashion* (1678), *The Virtuous Wife* (1679), *The Spanish Fryar* (1680), *The Princess of Cleve* (1682), *Bellamira* (1687), and *The Wives Excuse* (1691). Several of these plays are unabashedly hostile to the libertine they display; others verge on the sex-romp category. Some plays which seem to me borderline cases include *Epsom-Wells* (1672), *A Fond Husband* (1677), *The French Conjurer* (1677), *Sir Barnaby Whigg* (1681), *The London Cuckolds* (1681), *The City Heiress* (1682), *City Politiques* (1683), and *Sir Anthony Love* (1690). Another scholar might wish to include cases like *The English Frier* (1690), *The Old Batchelour* (1693), *Love's Last Shift* (1696), and *Love and a Bottle* (1698)—but I think my point holds.

> *Why should a foolish Marriage Vow*
> *Which long ago was made,*
> *Oblige us to each other now*
> *When Passion is decay'd?*

This is a clear statement of the libertine pleasure principle. Dryden answers not with an endorsement of marriage, but with the conclusion that men are too selfish, and their possessive instinct too strong, for the freedom of open marriage to work. Palamede explicitly proposes "a blessed community betwixt us four," but Rhodophil replies that jealousy makes this impossible, and hence that they must "make a firm League, not to invade each other's propriety" (79). Thus we see would-be libertines retreating from their principles when faced with the realization of their implications. A great many readers do not seem to have taken this conclusion seriously, or choose to regard it as an evasion on Dryden's part. I see it, on the contrary, as an entirely serious answer to the question Dryden starts by posing, and an explicit repudiation of libertine principles on the ground that they are unworkable.

Critics occasionally refer to "the Dorimant-Horner tradition,"[33] and Jordan takes them as the principal exemplars of his "judicious rake." I have analyzed the two relevant plays in some detail elsewhere,[34] but a brief account of these characters is in order, especially as they are by no means identical. Horner is a rogue-hero, a trickster who cuckolds fools; Dorimant is a glamorous seducer of society belles. As rakes, they do share many characteristics. Both are smart, socially polished lovers of intrigue with voracious sexual appetites. Both possess an immense amount of self-control and have a profound understanding of the ways in which people can be manipulated. Both have an exceedingly harsh attitude toward life—they are not flippantly cynical in the extravagant rake manner, and their actions are coolly self-disciplined. As Jordan remarks, "Dorimant is not particularly renowned for scatter-brained lightheartedness." Both are *tough*; they can and will inflict pain, and Dorimant especially has an ugly sadistic streak. Under-

33. Birdsall, p. 180.
34. *Development*, ch. 3.

wood describes Dorimant as a man whose "activities are now explicitly and predominantly the expression of . . . a Hobbesian aggressiveness, competitiveness, and drive for power and 'glory'; a Machiavellian dissembling and cunning; a satanic pride, vanity, and malice; and, drawing upon each of these frames of meaning, an egoistic assertion of self through the control of others." [35] This is true: what keeps Dorimant from seeming a brutal and repulsive figure, a Lord Foppington, is his comic submission to love. The great lady-killer succumbs to love and is tamed by a woman even tougher and more self-controlled than he. Dorimant is glamorous but reprehensible. Horner, though a Truewit, lacks his stature and potency. Horner comes off as king of a rather sordid and definitely unrealistic world. As Cecil remarks, in this amusing fantasy, pregnancy, disease, and the recriminations of husbands and brothers are swept aside. Promiscuity is the way of the world, and here it is managed with style. "For a moment sex is the unalloyed fun that the youthful libertine hoped and pretended it might be. This is the raucous, English statement of an ideal which seems to have been under continual discussion in the salon of Ninon de Lenclos. In *The Country Wife*, as in the legend of that salon, the ideal is achieved." [36] Neither *The Country-Wife* nor *The Man of Mode* can be called a libertine tract. The former is too clearly a comic fantasy, the latter accepts the ways of the world while clearly implying that for the individual maturity must bring change. Nonetheless both plays do indeed present a genuine, hard-nosed libertine without overt disapproval, and the effect upon subsequent characterizations of "Restoration comedy" has been enormous.

Very few genuine libertines in these comedies are presented so neutrally. The harshness of outlook is paralleled in a few of the gamier seventies sex comedies. Lovechange in Dover's(?) *The Mall*, secretly married to the rich Widow Woodbee, blackmails his wife out of half her fortune and brutally forces her to conceal their marriage (61) before he makes the luckless Mr. Easy hand over his lubricious young wife for Lovechange's use. Beauford, in Durfey's

35. Underwood, p. 73.
36. Cecil, "Libertine and *Précieux* Elements in Restoration Comedy," p. 250.

The Virtuous Wife, is a would-be Horner who takes his lumps but finally makes a cuckold before winning an heiress. But both plays are clumsily written, and the libertine emerges as sordid and unconvincing.

Attempts to delineate a "Dorimant-Horner tradition" have failed heretofore, and always will fail. Even critics who look for successors recognize a difference. Thus Mrs. Birdsall qualifies her claim in mid-sentence: "Of all Congreve's comic heroes Bellmour stands most clearly in the Dorimant-Horner tradition, but he possesses their high spirits without their astringency and reveals a philosophical streak which is new." [37] Bellmour does indeed lack bite: he is an epicure, not a machiavellian with sadistic tendencies. The harshness of the seventies libertine is never present in a Congreve protagonist. Valentine has his bastard and Mirabell has had a mistress, but neither is a rake in the sense I am using the term here. One may legitimately say that Congreve's characters have a place in the libertine tradition, but the libertinism of the nineties is philosophically very different indeed from that of the seventies. Reading Underwood, one would almost suppose that libertinism was an organized philosophy, and that it remained static throughout the late seventeenth century. But Maximillian E. Novak has pointed out that this is a serious mistake, and he draws a vital distinction between the Hobbesian libertine (my term, not his) of the seventies and the "refined libertine" (his term) of the nineties.[38] The milieu in which Congreve wrote was not that of the Court Wits—he was a young boy when that era passed. Novak's characterization of the new "libertine" mode is accurate, but comes as something of a shock. "By the end of the century, libertinism had become a gentleman's creed. Moderate pleasure, retirement, love of art and gardens; skepticism, and refinement of manners then became the new libertine ideals." I do not really like to use the term "libertine" to describe the outlook of the Congreve protagonists. They are urbane, witty skeptics, relativists in morals—"neo-Epicureans" rather than libertines in the Court Wit sense.

37. Birdsall, p. 180.
38. *William Congreve* (New York: Twayne, 1971), ch. 1, esp. pp. 42–51.

Urbanity and reflectiveness characterize the neo-Epicurean of the nineties. Many of the "ordinary rakish gentlemen" of nineties comedy are essentially of this sort. They have a basic goodness of heart one simply does not find in the likes of Horner, Dorimant, Lovechange, Beauford, or Dryden's Woodall. A great deal of the difference lies in a change in attitude toward the dramatist's material. Reading Sedley's steely *Bellamira* (1687) in context between Durfey's *The Banditti* (1686) and *The Squire of Alsatia* (1688) tells one just how far the drama has moved from the harsh comedies of the seventies. Sedley's comedy—delightful, but seldom read—is a free adaptation of Terence's *The Eunuch*. Thais is transformed into the wanton Bellamira, kept by the foolish Keepwell, but enjoyed by a wide variety of others. Lionel's successful courtship via rape is the sort of libertine excess "Restoration comedy" has a reputation for, though it is essentially without parallel in the whole period. The gay couple matches Merryman, a hard-drinking old Falstaff of fifty, with witty, cynical young Thisbe. Sedley's witty, sardonic view of his characters, his easy acceptance of promiscuity and worse, express the Court Wit philosophy with devastating clarity. Sedley neither likes nor criticizes the world he shows—he merely accepts it. Even more than *The Country-Wife* this play is genuinely libertine in its assumptions, and it drew a furious storm of protest from the post-Carolean audience.

Dryden said dolefully of *Mr. Limberham* that it gave offence because "it express'd too much of the Vice which it decry'd." [39] Other plays suffered the same problem: audiences reacted to the libertine, not to the way he was presented or the resolution arrived at. In the case of *Limberham*, the audience may have had a point. But *Marriage A-la-Mode* evidently gave offence, though its values are uncompromisingly anti-libertine. Several of the plays which prominently attack a "vicious rake" had little success on the stage. Obviously the writers were trying to make a point, and these plays are often among the most serious and moral comedies of the period.

39. Dedication of *The Kind Keeper, or Mr. Limberham* (pub. 1680).

Nat. Lee's *The Princess of Cleve* (1682) is an excellent illustration of an author taking a Dorimant and deliberately blackening him.[40] Lee systematically travesties his *précieuse* source. In his dedication he gloats over the shock this gave his audience: Nemours is made a bisexual goat, an insatiable liar, intriguer, and whoremonger. Superficially, he is a glamorous and successful Dorimant, a great aristocrat, a Truewit. Throughout the play he spouts and lives up to a ruthlessly hedonistic philosophy. Nemours is a despicable character, but nonetheless a powerful, glamorous, and successful one.

The vicious rake is largely a post-Carolean phenomenon, a reaction against the Court Wit outlook. Goodvile in *Friendship in Fashion* is the first major example.[41] Important instances include Lorenzo in *The Spanish Fryar* (where libertinism is equated to political anarchy), Friendall in *The Wives Excuse*, Sir John Brute in *The Provok'd Wife*, and Richmore in *The Twin-Rivals*. Occasionally a play will present so bitter a view of a vacuous and promiscuous society that free gallantry is made profoundly ugly without resort to a full-fledged vicious rake—as in *The Maid's Last Prayer* (1693). Otway hit on a neat expedient in *The Atheist* by mercilessly showing up a pretended rake as an idle boaster and secret believer. In several of these plays the vicious rake is a husband. This twist allows the dramatist to drum up sympathy for his abused and unhappy wife. In Cibber's hands this leads to a predictable and implausible reform, but in Vanbrugh's it can produce serious, disturbing, and irreconcilable conflicts.

The vicious rake is invariably despicable. Often he is threatening and hateful, capable of inflicting irreparable harm. Farquhar's Richmore has raped and impregnated a virtuous woman, and his "reform" is entirely unconvincing. Vanbrugh's Sir John Brute is little better than a street-bully—the sort of debauchee derided in the persons of Young Ranter, Old Ranter, and Dullman in *The English Frier* (1690), or in some of Shadwell's last plays. The distinction between vicious rake and debauchee is almost entirely one of social position and power. The vicious rake is generally wealthy,

40. For an analysis, see ch. 4 above.
41. For an analysis of this play and *The Atheist*, see ch. 3 above.

well-connected, and a manipulator of others. The debauchee is frequently bankrupt, a carouser who is not in control of his life. The difference between the debauched rake of the nineties and the libertine rake of the seventies is paralleled in some conspicuous changes in fop figures. Little has been said about fops here. Most of them are boasting pretenders to a libertinism they do not practice, from James Howard's Frenchlove to Crowne's Sir Courtly Nice. But in the nineties fops tend to become either completely contemptible or ugly menaces. Cibber's Sir Novelty Fashion, especially as transformed into Lord Foppington by Vanbrugh, is a world away from the innocent gaiety of Fopling. Foppington is smart, tough, and dangerous.

In the nineties the rise of the neo-Epicurean school of thought drove the serious libertine out of business. Comedies continue to display rakish gentlemen and extravagant rakes, while the *honnête homme* enjoys a boom. But where serious libertinism is presented it appears in vicious rakes and debauchees. This change has essentially nothing to do with "sentimentalism," Jeremy Collier, or the rise of "exemplary" comedy. Rather, it represents a change in a minority social code. As Novak well suggests, the Court Wit philosophy had never been more than the scandalous code of a clique. By the nineties the clique was a distant memory, and some features of the code had been subsumed into the attitudes which underlay the ordinary rakish Truewit.

There is no instance in late seventeenth-century comedy in which "libertinism" is presented both seriously and favorably. This may seem a startling assertion, but I believe it will stand scrutiny. In a handful of comedies libertinism is equably accepted as the way of the world—*The Country-Wife* (a fantasy which is near farce), *The Man of Mode* (comically softened), *Bellamira*, and arguably a few others. In perhaps fifteen cases it is employed as a *donnée* in a sexual romp—that is, not seriously. The cits who long flocked to see *The London Cuckolds* would not, presumably, have enjoyed the play had they taken it at all seriously. In a considerable majority of the plays where a real libertine is seriously presented the treatment is unmistakably hostile. That this has been so little recognized is clearly a function of the moral standards of later commentators. If one assumes that to keep a mistress or beget a bastard makes a man a libertine, then late seventeenth-century comedy is crawling with libertines. But by the standards of the time a rake could be a comic extravagant, a contemptible debauchee, or an ugly reality. Only rarely is real libertinism presented even with neutrality.

The Question of "Reform"

So far in this study the various sorts of rakes have been treated as essentially static entities. At this point we need to take a complicating factor into account—changes within a play. A very large proportion of the rakes proceed to "reform" in due course. Some thirty-one years ago David S. Berkeley effectively exploded the once prevalent idea that Loveless' *volte-face* in *Love's Last Shift* in 1696 was some sort of first. He points out twenty-three earlier cases of the penitent rake, his earliest instance coming in 1664.[42] There are few sentiment-laden reforms in the fashion of Centlivre until the eighteenth century. Earlier, especially before the nineties, the manner of reform tends to be quite casual: even where the reformation seems seriously meant (for example, Careless in *The Debauchee*) authors do not try to generate emotional slush for the audience to wallow in.

This restraint should not blind us to an important fact: "reform" is far more widely prevalent even than Berkeley suggests. Indeed, except in romantic elopement comedies and some gulling plays, some sort of reform is more or less customary in comedies of this period. Almost every standard-pattern boy-wins-girl comedy involving a love game requires a settlement which implies acceptance of new restrictions in marriage. At times we are left to assume that agreement to marry is itself a kind of reform. Dryden explicitly says so. Replying to complaints that he makes "debauch'd persons ... my Protagonists" and writes "to make libertinism amiable," he insists that playwrights "make not vicious persons happy, but only

42. "The Penitent Rake in Restoration Comedy," *Modern Philology*, 49 (1952), 223–33. See also Paul E. Parnell, "The Etiquette of the Sentimental Repentance Scene, 1688–96," *Papers on Language and Literature*, 14 (1978), 205–17.

as heaven makes sinners so: that is by reclaiming them first from vice. For so 'tis to be suppos'd they are, when they resolve to marry; for then enjoying what they desire in one, they cease to pursue the love of many." [43] The ordinary rakish gentleman finds himself in love, and romantically or humorously he swears constancy and is accepted. Wildish in *The Mulberry-Garden* is an example of the witty suitor who remains witty—but we are by no means to assume that his declaration is insincere. What makes Belfond Jr. in *The Squire of Alsatia* special and surprising is the didactic seriousness with which his reform is insisted upon, not the reform itself.

Almost all of the extravagant rakes settle down to matrimony. Philidor in *All Mistaken* is an obvious exception, but he is so extreme a comic humour that one never takes him seriously, and Howard's implication at the end of the play is clearly that he and Mirida will agree to marry when they have played their game to the full. Even such determined antimatrimonialists as Behn's Willmore and Farquhar's Mirabel (in *The Inconstant*) duly succumb. Often the denouement is achieved by a proviso scene, a pattern set by Celadon and Florimell in *Secret-Love*, and imitated by a host of writers throughout the century. The flip-flop performed by the extravagant rake is usually so radical as to be plainly comic. In *The Constant Couple* Farquhar's Sir Harry Wildair, told that he must marry Angelica or fight a duel, exclaims: "Here am I brought to a very pretty Dilemma; I must commit Murder, or commit Matrimony, which is best now? A license from *Doctors Commons*, or a Sentence from the *Old Baily*? If I kill my Man, the Law hangs me; if I marry my Woman, I shall hang my self;—but, Dam it,—Cowards dare fight, I'll marry, that's the most daring Action of the two, so my dear Cousin *Angelica*, have at you." [44] The effect of such

---

43. Preface to *An Evening's Love* (pub. 1671).

44. *The Complete Works of George Farquhar*, ed. Charles Stonehill, 2 vols. (1930; rpt. New York: Gordian, 1967), I, 144. These sentiments must have been devised early in the play's spectacular run, for the version of this scene published in the first quarto makes Sir Harry less extravagant and gives him an almost Steelish sensibility. "By Heavens I love her. . . . When you speak, all the Faculties of my charm'd Soul crowd to my attentive Ears. . . . The Day breaks glorious to my o'er-clouded Thought, and darts its smiling Beams into my Soul. My love is heighten'd

reversals is to turn the whole performance of the extravagant rake into a game. It is a phase and a pose, and when these flighty birds have reason to abandon it, they promptly do so. This realization should greatly diminish the impact of their "libertine" sentiments, however loudly delivered. Jordan is quite correct in saying that "most of the really explicit cases [of libertine pronouncements] come from extravagants."[45] If we duly consider the source, we must conclude that the playwrights are not trying to make us take these sentiments seriously.

Genuine libertines often do wind up married, though without full-dress recantation. We see this sort of ending in *The Virtuoso*, *Mr. Limberham*, *The Virtuous Wife* (a strictly cynical marriage?), and even in *Bellamira*. Nemours' reform in *The Princess of Cleve* is clearly a special case. Horner duly holds out—as is customary in sex-romp plays which focus on cuckolding actions (*A Fond Husband*, *The London Cuckolds*, *City Politiques*). Vicious rakes are almost by definition beyond reform. Many of them (Goodvile, Friendall, Sir John Brute) are already married, and their viciousness serves to illustrate the evils of ill-founded marriage. A related category, not previously discussed, is the "apparently wicked rake," introduced specifically for the purpose of engineering his reform. Loveless in *Love's Last Shift* (guaranteed to be "Lewd for above four Acts") is the famous case. Cibber is unconcerned with psychological probability, and asks us to melt with rapture when a man who has spent ten years in utter debauchery renounces his ways for no very good reason. Cibber's penchant for too facile reform is displayed again in *The Careless Husband* (1704), though he treats the subject more seriously in *The Lady's last Stake* (1707), a ponderously didactic play. An early experiment in the rake reforming to marry the girl he has seduced is Behn's(?) *The Debauchee* (1677). There Lord Loveless is made an ordinary rakish gentleman, not a vicious rake, so his turnabout can be made convincing. Shadwell in

---

by a glad Devotion; and Vertue rarifies the Bliss to feast the purer Mind" (47–49 of Q1). The revisions to this key scene first appear in the second edition, published about two months after the premiere.

45. Jordan, p. 74.

The Scowrers and Durfey in *The Campaigners* employ a similar formula, which becomes one of the commonplaces of eighteenth-century "reform" comedy. Susanna Centlivre and Charles Johnson in particular were to exploit it with enthusiasm.

Plays like *The Gamester* (1705) and *The Generous Husband* (1711) invite, even demand, tearful empathy. What makes them so unsatisfactory (from our vantage point) is not the reform, but the implausibility of such reform except as a *pro forma* convention. *The Relapse* is a very effective answer to *Love's Last Shift* largely because of its more realistic treatment of sexual appetite. In ideology the two plays are much closer than critics of Bernbaum's generation supposed. Even the witty reform of the extravagant rake can be effectively debunked, as in Ravenscroft's beautiful travesty of *Secret-Love* in his joking proviso scene in *The Careless Lovers* (1673). But moral complaint and satire aside, we must ask how "reform" is to be taken in these plays.

Lest anyone feel that I am finding "reform" in peculiar places, let me point out that I am not alone in reading the plays this way. Norman Holland says flatly that "without exception, every one of the eleven plays we have considered deals with the reform of the hero, not his reward. His initiation into true love at the end—his 'reward'—marks his reclamation to virtue."[46] To make this claim Holland has to pronounce Harcourt the "hero" of *The Country-Wife*, but no matter. His close reading of the plays of Etherege, Wycherley, and Congreve leads him to conclude that the agreement to marry constitutes and symbolizes a major change in the protagonist. We will do well to recall that Dryden tells us so. Underwood observes that the Fletcherean rake "characteristically sees marriage . . . as merely a 'custom' at odds with his liberty and indulgence. . . . [He] customarily ends his course in marriage. But in terms of the problem of love, there is usually little meaning in his doing so. It is merely a way—presumably to Fletcher's audience an agreeable way—of bringing the play to an end after the author has exhausted the sensational situation arising from the naturalistic pred-

---

46. *The First Modern Comedies* (Cambridge: Harvard Univ. Press, 1959), p. 203.

ilections of the character,"[47] Similar charges might be leveled against some "Restoration" plays—*The Assignation,* or *Sir Barnaby Whigg,* for example—but for the most part marriage is handled more romantically. Compare Buckingham's revision of *The Chances* with the Fletcherean original, or Farquhar's *The Inconstant* with its source. *The Wild Goose Chase,* and this difference is obvious. Shirley's epicures are closer to "Restoration" practice, though their reform tends to be too quick and easy, almost giving one a foretaste of Centlivre. In the better late seventeenth-century comedies we see a genuine conflict between "libertine" inclinations and a love which cannot be denied.

Jordan suggests that when the extravagant rake agrees to marry he is accepting adulthood and social responsibility. Dryden would agree, and Shadwell explicitly affirms the importance of the decision to marry in *The Squire of Alsatia.*

> *Isabella.* How can I be secure you will not fall to your
>   old courses agen?
> *Belfond Jr.* I have been so sincere in my Confessions,
>   you may trust me; but I call Heav'n to witness, I will
>   hereafter be entirely yours. I look on Marriage as the
>   most solemn Vow a man can make; and 'tis by conse-
>   quence, the basest Perjury to break it. (85)

But what do we make of a case like Dorimant? Is he a rake reformed by the love of a good woman? A hypocrite bent on marrying money? An ambiguously attractive libertine comically humbled? John Traugott has suggested that what we see is not recantation but rather the establishment of a new and higher set of values. "The aim of the rake is freedom. . . . From a revolution against earlier values of Christian humanism, the rake has moved through Hobbesian naturalism to a new ethic of communion founded in knowledge of self."[48] I see more renunciation than Traugott does. I cannot agree that "Restoration comedy rings down the curtain with

47. Underwood, pp. 132–33.
48. "The Rake's Progress from Court to Comedy: A Study in Comic Form," *Studies in English Literature,* 6 (1966), 381–407.

the values of the rake unsullied, or, more accurately, uncleansed." Very few comedies in this period leave libertinism unsullied: one of the infuriating things about Traugott's essay is his failure to explain what group of plays he is trying to characterize. He seems to me right, however, in sensing a changed apprehension of life. The "reform" of the rake, the epicure, and the witty gentleman is founded on "witty understanding," not on mere capitulation to a repressive social code. Traugott draws an important distinction between "reform of the rake not through witty understanding as in Etherege and Congreve but through sensibility and compassion." His examples of the latter are *The Beaux Stratagem*, *Tom Jones*, and *She Stoops to Conquer*, but a long list of early eighteenth-century plays falls in this category.

There are relatively few cases of "witty understanding" reform. Novak reads Congreve this way, and I agree with him. The majority of reforms seem to me partly comic, partly a symbolic acceptance of both love and social order as the rake (of whatever persuasion) renounces the rationalistic and individualistic freedom demanded by libertine doctrine. The Carolean rake arrives at a resolution which looks to Steele like disgusting libertinism; the loose-living Augustan protagonist has to submit to a much more restrictive social and moral code. The essential difference is in the social norms of 1675 versus those of 1710. In both cases we see in "reform" a process of maturation and socialization.

If "Restoration comedy" is by Carolean standards so relatively moral, why did its rakes draw the ire of contemporary moralists? This is an obvious objection, and I assume that some readers have been muttering it to themselves or scrawling it in the margins. I would reply first that the outlook of the court circle (which considerably influenced the drama) was not shared by most of the population. Religious zealots and bourgeois prudes paid no attention to the way libertinism was shown; they objected to its being shown at all. And second, let us consider a famous and often-quoted denunciation.

In the *Playes* which have been wrote of late, there is no such thing as perfect Character, but the two chief persons are most commonly a Swearing, Drinking, Whoring, Ruffian for a Lover, and an impudent ill-bred *tomrig* for a Mistress, and these are the fine People of the *Play*.[49]

A year later Shadwell continued his diatribe.

It pleases most [of "the Rabble"] to see Vice incouraged by bringing the Characters of debauch'd people upon the Stage, and making them pass for fine Gentlemen who openly profess Swearing, Drinking, Whoring, breaking Windows, beating Constables, &c.[50]

This certainly sounds deplorable, and such complaints can be closely paralleled late in the period, in the writings of James Wright, Blackmore, and Collier.[51] But in 1668 what exactly is Shadwell attacking? I can find only five plays to which he could be referring: *The Wild Gallant* (a flop), *The Comical Revenge, All Mistaken, An Evening's Love*, and possibly *Secret-Love*. All five involve an extravagant rake of sorts. Shadwell, ever a literalist, is flinging his fits over what are quite clearly designed as comic exaggerations. His sense of decorum was outraged, but this should not lead us to suppose that 1660s comedy is populated with libertines. Shadwell himself, we may note, was soon to make effective use of debauched characters in *Epsom-Wells* (1672).

A generation later Blackmore wailed:

The *Man of Sense*, and the *Fine* Gentleman in the *Comedy*, who, as the chiefest Person propos'd to the Esteem and Imitation of the Audience, is enrich'd with all the Sense and Wit the Poet can bestow,—this *Extraordinary Person* you will find to be a *Derider* of Religion, a great *Admirer* of *Lucretius*, not so much for his *Learning* as his *Irreligion*, a Person wholly *Idle*, dissolv'd in Luxury, abandon'd to his Pleasures, a great Debaucher of Women, profuse and extravagant in his Expences;

49. Preface to *The Sullen Lovers* (1668).
50. Preface to *The Royal Shepherdess* (1669).
51. See especially James Wright, *Country Conversations* (London: Henry Bonwicke, 1694), pp. 1–17.

and, in short, this *Finish'd Gentleman* will appear a *Finish'd
Libertine.*[52]

At the time this was written nearly fifteen years had passed since
any new comedy could legitimately be so described. There are only
a handful of characters in all of late seventeenth-century comedy
who fit Blackmore's fevered account. Of that handful only a few
escape harsh satire. That "Restoration comedy" still suffers from
an unsavoury reputation is tribute to the disordered imagination of
Blackmore and his tribe. Blackmore is irritatingly unspecific about
what plays he finds objectionable. Collier, though he devotes only
a brief discussion specifically to libertinism, does at least cite chapter and verse.[53] All he proves, however, is his complete insensitivity
to tone and context, for he lumps together extravagant rakes, debauchees, and epicureans—making no distinctions at all.

Libertinism was in the air during the Carolean period. The
Court Wits both practiced and preached it, though scandal magnified their wickedness. Libertine philosophy does indeed color a group
of late Carolean comedies, and it is the object of a brilliant and
savage attack by Shadwell in *The Libertine* (1675), a sardonic mock-
tragedy few scholars have read and appreciated. Shadwell takes
naturalistic philosophy to an extreme, and produces a Don Juan
who has killed his own father (among some thirty murders) and
specializes in raping nuns. His friend Lopez has killed his elder
brother to acquire an estate; their comrade Antonio has impregnated his own sister. Throughout the play they butcher, plunder,
and rape with enthusiasm. The result is a diverting travesty of the
libertine philosophy and moral code. But most protests against the
loose-living young Truewit, or the behavior and rhetoric of the extravagant rake, are ludicrously overemphatic, often to the point of
downright hysteria. From Blackmore to Archer ("a stink is a stink")
such protests tells us more about the protesters than about the plays.

Late seventeenth-century comedies contain plenty of sex, and

52. Preface to *Prince Arthur*, rpt. in *Critical Essays of the Seventeenth Century*,
ed. J. E. Spingarn, 3 vols. (1908–9; rpt. Bloomington: Indiana Univ. Press, 1957),
III, 230.

53. *A Short View of the Immorality, and Profaneness of the English Stage*
(London: S. Keble et al., 1698), esp. pp. 140–48.

even smut, but the values which emerge after a balanced reading are by no means libertine values. To say that "the combination of libertinism, wit, and antimatrimonial attitudes was commonplace in the Restoration—a syndrome assumed by every writer of comedy . . . the libertine attitude toward love and marriage [was] present in almost all Restoration comedy" is to misrepresent the plays.[54] To find libertinism in sixties comedies, except from extravagant rakes, would be very difficult. Dryden, Behn, Shadwell, Otway, and Southerne are unanimous in their contempt for genuine libertinism. Wycherley and Etherege present a distinctly qualified, "favorable" picture. Congreve accepts a neo-Epicureanism which is a far cry from the Court Wit outlook. Vanbrugh knows how terribly wrong a marriage can go, but even in *The Provok'd Wife* he ends with a good marriage, and one we applaud. Farquhar moves from the extravagant rake (Roebuck in *Love and a Bottle*) toward the man of sensibility (Aimwell in *The Beaux Stratagem*). The prevalence of "libertine" sentiment and antimatrimonial talk in their comedies is a response to genuine social problems and a reflection of an age-old clash between individual inclination and social demands. The rebellion of the Court Wit outlook against social convention is faithfully mirrored in these comedies—and so is its inevitable failure. Rakes in these plays are seldom anything but comic exaggerations, satiric butts, and bedroom farce conventions. Reputation notwithstanding, "Restoration comedy" gives precious little support to libertinism. Its authors accept a moral code which was anathema to the Victorians and remains so to serious Christians. But they did not endorse libertines nor were they genuinely hostile to marriage.[55]

54. Novak, *Congreve*, pp. 45–47. I have deliberately selected this example from the work of one of the best modern scholars in the field.

55. I am grateful to the late John Harold Wilson for useful criticism and advice.

6

Marital Discord in English Comedy from Dryden to Fielding

Marital discord in English comedy goes back at least as far as Noah's wife and remains a common theme in twentieth-century drama, *Who's Afraid of Virginia Woolf* being an obvious example. Nonetheless the subject has been little studied. We still tend to think of comedy in terms of a boy-gets-girl romance pattern or, more broadly, a structure encompassing a movement from adversity to prosperity.[1] But many "comedies" do not present such a structure (*Volpone*, *Le Misanthrope*), and marital discord is a significant theme in, and even a focus for, a surprising number of plays. This is particularly true in the years around 1700, when a rising debate about the legal status of women and reform of the divorce laws made the subject topical.

The myth is still current that "Restoration comedy" is hostile to marriage. In the common gay couple pattern, both male and female rail against marriage, vowing to remain free—the male insisting on his libertinism, the female on her independence. But even there love usually conquers wanderlust, and witty antagonism is

1. Northrop Frye goes so far as to assert that "comedy" is the name of a structure and that, though the form usually has a predominantly festive mood, any work with such a structure qualifies as a comedy, regardless of its content or our reaction to it. See *A Natural Perspective* (New York: Columbia Univ. Press, 1965), p. 46. For some qualifications and objections, see my "Some Problems in the Theory of Comedy," *Journal of Aesthetics and Art Criticism*, 31 (1972), 87–100.

abandoned for the deeper satisfactions of living happily ever after. Thus romantic convention is almost always served, even when the love-duel is seriously used to suggest the difficulty of making a good and viable marriage. In many plays a proviso scene is used to suggest the working out of a satisfactory marital arrangement—the most famous, of course, being the one in Congreve's *The Way of the World* (1700), in which Millamant wonders if she must "dwindle to a wife." Occasionally, however, a playwright will take a hard look at what happens *after* marriage, as in Otway's bitter *The Atheist* (1683), Southerne's brilliantly nasty *The Wives Excuse* (1691), or Vanbrugh's *The Provok'd Wife* (1697). And after 1700 "reform" comedies focusing on marital reconciliations become increasingly common.

There are two reasons for studying marital discord comedy in the period delimited here. First, several of the most interesting and important plays from the 1660–1737 period have seemed peculiar and even repulsive because scholars have not fully recognized that they represent serious social commentary on contemporary problems. Second, I want to suggest that writers' views on marriage—especially as they are expressed in marital discord comedy—are an important key to the shifting ideological stances which underlie the complicated transition from seventeenth- to eighteenth-century comedy.

Many attempts have been made to trace the transition from "Restoration" to "sentimental" comedy, employing a variety of terms and touchstones. One of the best such studies is John Harrington Smith's *The Gay Couple in Restoration Comedy*.[2] Smith uses the gay couple and its witty love-game as an indicator of authorial outlook as he follows the move toward what he calls "exemplary" comedy. Good though the study is, it suffers from certain inherent limitations. Not all of the early or satiric writers employ a gay couple, and not all of the later ones who fail to do so produce exemplary comedy. Smith, focusing on a courtship ritual, is well equipped to handle romance and even cuckoldry patterns, but he lacks terms in

2. See also his "Shadwell, the Ladies, and the Change in Comedy," *Modern Philology*, 46 (1948), 22–33.

which to discuss marriage comedy with precision. This is doubly unfortunate, since during the 1690s, the crucial period in the transition from what I call "Carolean" to "Augustan" comedy, there is a decided shift in focus "from the unmarried 'gay couple' to the problems of a married couple."[3] In fact, both cuckoldry and the gay couple diminish drastically in importance during the nineties.

How are we to characterize the "new" varieties of eighteenth-century comedy? "Sentimental" is thoroughly discredited as a catchall phrase.[4] "Exemplary" is suggestive as an opposite to "satiric" but reductive: few plays short of *The Conscious Lovers* actually try to present models for emulation. Quite a few do show a "reform" and invest it with enough didactic seriousness that the reform becomes a distinguishing generic feature. One may perhaps speak broadly of hard versus soft comedy, or old versus new. Shirley Strum Kenny has developed a useful concept in "humane comedy" (fl. 1695–1710), which may be contrasted with the relatively harsh, satiric comedy which flourished in the Carolean period. Few scholars still insist on seeing an absolute distinction between the "Restoration" ethos of Vanbrugh and Farquhar and the "sentimental" ethos of Cibber, Steele, and Centlivre—or, worse, condemning the former for showing signs of contamination. Kenny is surely right in seeing all of these writers as representatives of the humane school. And yet this group is by no means homogeneous, as she is the first to admit. There are major differences in tone and moral ideology between plays as disparate as Vanbrugh's *The Provok'd Wife* (1697), Steele's *The Tender Husband* (1705), Farquhar's *The Beaux Stratagem* (1707), and Cibber's *The Lady's last Stake* (1707). All can legitimately be discussed as humane comedies, but we need a vantage point and a vocabulary to make necessary distinctions.

The treatment of marital discord makes a convenient index to the differences. And, though the theme is far from ubiquitous between 1690 and 1730, it is common enough to serve as a useful

3. See A. H. Scouten, "Notes Toward a History of Restoration Comedy," *Philological Quarterly*, 45 (1966), 62–70.

4. See Arthur Sherbo, *English Sentimental Drama*, and "Goldsmith and Sheridan and the Supposed Revolution of 'Laughing' against 'Sentimental' Comedy" (ch. 10 below).

touchstone, just as the gay couple is in the Carolean period. It possesses special utility in this transitional period when the old and new styles of comedy are struggling for supremacy, since marital discord (unlike the gay couple) is a major element in both satiric and reform-oriented comedies. Starting from a survey of the institution of marriage in the period and attitudes toward marriage in the comedies, I shall attempt to show that the two types represent, ideologically, different responses to the same problem.

The Marriage Question in Life and Drama

During the second half of the seventeenth century, writers became increasingly aware of a marriage problem. A woman was little better than a chattel, a condition emphasized by a growing desire to acquire property through marriage.[5] "Matrimony's but a bargain made / To serve the turns of Interest and Trade," wrote Samuel Butler in a satire called "Marriage." Or, as Gay puts the point in *The Beggar's Opera*,

> *Polly.* I did not marry him (as 'tis the Fashion) cooly and
> deliberately for Honour or Money. But, I love him.
> *Mrs. Peachum.* Love him! worse and worse! I thought
> the Girl had been better bred. (10)

The problem with which Richardson was to confront Clarissa was both real and common in the late seventeenth century, a fact reflected in the plots of scores of comedies. Worst of all, once married, a woman had almost no legal recourse against a husband who proved vicious, tyrannical, or unfaithful. Legally, the two were one, but only the husband had any rights. The woman was barred from owning property (all she had passed automatically to her husband)

5. See H. J. Habakkuk, "Marriage Settlements in the Eighteenth Century," *Transactions of the Royal Historical Society*, 4th ser., 32 (1950), 15–30. Habakkuk comments specifically on the "increasing subordination of marriage to the increase of landed wealth, at the expense of other motives for marriage," in contrast to the practice prevailing in the sixteenth and early seventeenth centuries (p. 24).

or making a will. Only a marriage settlement could guarantee a wife an income of her own from her own property—though if the husband failed to pay it the woman had difficulty enforcing the contract. She could not testify in court against her husband, could not stop him doing what he liked with "her" property or even from forcibly separating her from their children.[6]

In short, the subjugation of the woman was just about total. Like the American slave in the nineteenth century, a wife might be lucky in her owner but more likely might not, in which case she was essentially helpless. A traditionalist like George Savile (*Advice to a Daughter*, published in his 1700 *Miscellany*) saw the subordination of women in marriage as a legitimate reflection of inferior and dependent status. A radical like Mary Astell (*Some Reflections on Marriage*, 1694) complained that subordination was one thing, slavery another—and that, if "absolute Sovereignty" was not necessary or desirable in the government of England, as the settlement of 1688 suggested, why should it be so in the family?

No matter how impossibly bad the marriage, divorce was for practical purposes impossible. It was available only through parliamentary decree—a long, difficult, and inordinately expensive process. Only six such divorces were granted between 1660 and 1714, the first of them in 1698. The first to a commoner came in 1701. Naturally there was much talk about them, as there had been earlier about the notorious Lord Roos case in 1670, which was regarded as a trial balloon floated by Buckingham, who hoped to

6. On marriage and the status of women, Chilton Latham Powell's *English Domestic Relations, 1487–1653* (New York: Columbia Univ. Press, 1917) provides useful background information, while Jean Gagen's *The New Woman* (New York: Twayne, 1954) deals with the period under consideration here from a basically literary standpoint. Reginald Haw's *The State of Matrimony* (London: S.P.C.K., 1952) is useful for its investigation of the conflict of ecclesiastical and civil law, despite the author's fierce Anglican bias. The fullest treatment of marriage and law in the plays of the 1660–1714 period is of course Gellert Spencer Alleman's *Matrimonial Law and the Materials of Restoration Comedy*. For an authoritative account of the relevant statutes, one should consult W. S. Holdsworth's *A History of English Law* (London: Methuen, 1903–38). Lawrence Stone's *The Family, Sex and Marriage in England, 1500–1800* has been criticized (for example, by Alan Macfarlane in *History and Theory*, 18 [1979], 103–26), but it is certainly the best general treatment of the subject.

arrange a divorce for the childless Charles II.[7] But legally nothing changed until 1698, when it became somewhat easier for a man—only the man—to gain a parliamentary decree.[8] No woman was granted a parliamentary divorce until 1801. Even for males the process remained slow, costly, humiliating, and legally problematical. The whole problem was not faced squarely until 1753, when Parliament passed Lord Hardwicke's Marriage Law (26 George II, c. 33, effective March 26, 1754), which for the first time broke with canon law doctrine and gave to marriage the modern notion of a purely civil contract.

"Divorce" is often mentioned in late seventeenth-century comedies—for example, in Shadwell's *The Humorists* and *Epsom-Wells*, Rawlins'(?) *Tom Essence*, and Lee's *The Princess of Cleve*. But the modern reader must understand that playwrights casually lump together three quite different things under this heading: 1) separation, either by mutual consent or by order of an ecclesiastical court, with a separate maintenance awarded to the wife; 2) annulment—also in the province of the ecclesiastical courts and in theory available only on the ground of an unrecognized impediment invalidating the original agreement; and 3) divorce by act of Parliament. Only the second and third gave either party the right to remarry. Ecclesiastical courts could theoretically grant separations on the ground of cruelty, but adultery—which had to be "proved"—was the usual ground. And, since many marriages were essentially business deals, dividing property tended to produce acrimony.

In view of this background, the many expressions of hostility to marriage in "Restoration comedy" should be understood as a reflection of an increasingly serious social concern. Thus in Shirley's *The Lady of Pleasure* (1635) we find a wealthy young widow exulting in her freedom, determined not to return to the "fetters" of

7. Winifred, Lady Burghclere, *George Villiers, Second Duke of Buckingham, 1628–1687* (1903; rpt. Port Washington, N.Y.: Kennikat, 1971), pp. 212–13. As Alleman points out (p. 121), the parliamentary bill allowing Lord Roos to remarry was not technically a divorce. He had been granted an ecclesiastical separation and was allowed to remarry in order to prevent the extinction of his peerage.

8. The controversy around that time is reflected in Vanbrugh's *The Provok'd Wife*. See Curt A. Zimansky's introduction to the Regents Restoration Drama Series edition (Lincoln: Univ. of Nebraska Press, 1969), pp. xviii–xix.

marriage—though she does finally reform a rake and decide to marry him.[9] A host of parallels could be listed: some of the ladies succumb to marriage, while others, like Lady Haughty in Newcastle's *The Triumphant Widow* (1674), stoutly and successfully resist. Readers will recall the litigious Widow Blackacre in Wycherley's *The Plain-Dealer* (1676), determined not to marry and thereby lose the right to sue in her own name. "Matrimony, to a Woman, [is] worse than Excommunication, in depriving her of the benefit of the Law," she says (91)—an ugly truth not altogether disguised by her status as a comic butt. "Learned Ladies" are frequently the object of humorously hostile commentary, as in Thomas Wright's *The Female Vertuoso's* (1693; an adaptation of Molière's *Les Femmes savantes*). Valeria in Mrs. Centlivre's *The Basset-Table* (1705) typifies these "unnatural" women—she would rather stick to her microscope than elope with her admirer.

The women in the gay couple tradition serve not only to join their admirers in witty sparring but also to express a serious problem. What can compensate for the loss of freedom? The frequent proviso scenes in these plays serve as a formalized answer to the question, "Where will sovereignty lie in the marriage?" Before marriage, at least according to *précieuse* convention, the woman was a fickle and domineering mistress, the male her abject slave. Would all this come to a quick end? This is the point to the humorous assurance given by Worthy and Lovetruth in Sir Robert Howard and Buckingham's *The Country Gentleman* (1669).

Lovetruth.   You shall always be obay'd.
Worthy.   And your Commission shall not be taken from
    you after mariage, but always command in chief.
Lovetruth.   Go abroad when you please.[10]

9. Her enjoyment of independence anticipates a character like Defoe's Roxana. Defoe is a veritable repository of commentary on marriage and the woman's unsatisfactory status. See Spiro Peterson, "The Matrimonial Theme of Defoe's *Roxana*," *PMLA*, 70 (1955), 166–91, and David Blewett, "Changing Attitudes toward Marriage in the Time of Defoe: The Case of Moll Flanders," *Huntington Library Quarterly*, 44 (1981), 77–88.

10. *The Country Gentleman*, ed. Arthur H. Scouten and Robert D. Hume, p. 85.

Congreve's famous proviso scene in *The Way of the World* (IV, i) is deliciously witty and is leavened with persiflage. But under the banter there is a sharp edge of legal and psychological fact. Millamant's lament for her "dear Liberty," her determination never to marry "unless I am first made sure of my will and pleasure" are serious matters indeed to women in an audience which lived under the marriage laws of 1700.

Very early in the period there are signs that male sovereignty is coming under fire. "H.B." 's *The Female Rebellion* (ca. 1659) is a satire on the Puritan rebellion and government which works by likening them to a community of Amazons torn by internal dissension. The Puritan attack on monarchy is specifically equated with female objections to marriage. (Ridicule of female government goes back, of course, to such earlier plays as Fletcher's *The Sea Voyage* and Cartwright's *The Lady Errant*.) Two Amazonian works by Edward Howard, bad plays but interesting documents, take up the subject even more schematically. *The Womens Conquest* (1670) contrasts two absolutist kingdoms, one female run, one run by males. The conclusion is that a compromise on the English model is best, heavily weighted on the male side. *The Six days Adventure* (1671) treats of a kingdom where men and women take turns governing and asks whether "Matrimony" or "the Law of nature" is responsible for establishing "The Tyranny of men" (27). Predictably, Howard opts for traditional hierarchy and defends the status quo in England.[11] Almost all seventeenth-century comedies arrive at this conclusion one way or another. Thus, in Fletcher's long-popular *Rule a Wife and Have a Wife* (1624), a woman tries to dominate her marriage by laying down radical provisos—which fail to work. Obviously the audience is meant to enjoy watching the male regain his properly dominant role.

To say that "Restoration comedy" is hostile to marriage is simply erroneous.[12] Rather, we may say that it increasingly exhibits an awareness of the drawbacks and possible pitfalls of matrimony. As P. F. Vernon has shown,[13] there are many attacks on marriages of

11. All three plays are well analyzed by Gagen, pp. 170–77.
12. On this issue see ch. 5 above.
13. "Marriage of Convenience and The Moral Code of Restoration Comedy."

convenience which have turned out badly—usually shown in the triumphant cuckolding of an obnoxious old husband. But hostility is directed against the abuse, not the institution. How many of the celebrated "libertines" of this comedy are upheld and left as is? Remarkably few, in fact. Etherege's Dorimant is normal in this respect: despite all his railing against love and marriage, he falls head over heels in love and undergoes at least a perfunctory reform. A Pinchwife or a Sir Jaspar Fidget can be comically punished and Horner allowed to get off scot free in a play like *The Country-Wife*, but even there "good" marriage is upheld in Harcourt and Alithea—and this is certainly the norm. Carolean comedies almost invariably attack arranged marriage of convenience and uphold the virtues and attractions of freely chosen marriage for love. The few exceptions—Philidor in James Howard's *All Mistaken* (1665), for example—usually reflect flagrant comic exaggeration which is plainly not to be taken as a serious expression of authorial opinion.

Forced marriage is a common theme in English drama throughout the seventeenth century.[14] George Wilkins' *The Miseries of Enforced Marriage* (1607) is a good epitome of the type which results from full development of the theme. Aphra Behn (who adapted Wilkins' play in *The Town-Fop*, 1676) makes the theme prominent in more than ten of her plays, remaining from first to last a vehement champion of the right to free choice. In this respect her plays are unusually passionate but by no means atypical. Almost all of the witty antimatrimonialist protagonists in such comedies as Dryden's *The Wild Gallant* (1663) and *An Evening's Love* (1668), Newcastle's *The Humorous Lovers* (1667), Etherege's *The Man of Mode* (1676), Durfey's *The Marriage-Hater Match'd* (1692), and a host of others really protest not marriage but marriage of economic convenience. Little libertinism is upheld for men; for women the problem is to establish a satisfactory basis for marriage on personal faith, since legal protection was lacking.[15] The endings

14. See Glenn H. Blayney, "Enforcement of Marriage in English Drama (1600–1650)," *Philological Quarterly*, 38 (1959), 459–72.

15. For a consideration of female views of sexual appetite, mostly from eighteenth-century diaries and novels, see Patricia Meyer Spacks, " 'Ev'ry Woman Is at Heart a Rake,' " *Eighteenth-Century Studies*, 8 (1974), 27–46.

of plays like *An Evening's Love* and *The Man of Mode* are actually quite unrealistically "romantic." Without perhaps taking the marriages very seriously, we are at least to accept *pro forma* the reformation of the male. One tends to think of reformed rakes as a phenomenon of "sentimental" comedy circa 1700, and indeed "reform" is then increasingly presented in a saccharine way which now simply seems to call attention to the implausibility of it all. In fact, "penitent rakes" are a commonplace from the 1660s on: what changes is rhetoric as writers place a heightened emphasis on "conversion." [16]

"Restoration comedy" basically upholds monogamy and romance-style marriage based on free choice. But a great many marriages of the time were made on the basis of economic considerations, and the dramatists well knew that the majority of marriages brought little happiness, however contracted. What John Harrington Smith calls "cynical comedy" protests economic considerations before (usually) accepting romantic marriage. But what happens *after* a bad marriage has been contracted? In a variety of ways this question becomes a theme in comedy and even a focus for nonromance comedy.

A distinction does need to be made between plays in which marital discord is a significant, perhaps even a defining, theme and those in which it is introduced simply a) for comic effect or b) to justify adultery. Only a small percentage of the comedies containing an unhappy marriage touch seriously on the issues with which we are concerned here. The humorous possibilities of domestic squabbling have long been known: there is a whole Italian Renaissance farce subgenre (the *contrasto*) devoted to the subject; Plautus and Molière make effective use of the device (Molière often with some psychological subtlety, as in *Georges Dandin*); and domestic warfare is a long-standing English farce tradition.

Amusing instances of marital discord are legion in late seventeenth-century comedy. Most of them rely on the appeal of inversion—a domineering wife tyrannizes an ineffectually rebel-

16. See David S. Berkeley, "The Penitent Rake in Restoration Comedy," *Modern Philology*, 49 (1952), 223–33.

lious husband. Sir Oliver and Lady Cockwood in Etherege's *She wou'd if she cou'd* (1668) and Barnaby Brittle and his wife in Betterton's *The Amorous Widow* (ca. 1669) come to mind. Sometimes the emphasis is more on cat-and-dog fight—as in the cit subplots in Shadwell's *Epsom-Wells* (1672) and Lee's *The Princess of Cleve* (1682). The woes of an "imaginary cuckold" may be dwelt upon, as in Elizabeth Polwhele's *The Frolicks* (1671). Or a whole play may be focused on a long-suffering wife who finds a way to turn the tables on her tormenter, as in Shadwell's *The Woman-Captain* (1679) or Betterton's *The Woman Made a Justice* (1670; lost)—if it is indeed based on Montfleury's *La Femme Juge et Partie*. A splendid example of a delightfully ridiculous play dealing almost exclusively with marital discord is Jevon's *The Devil of a Wife* (1686), perennially popular in various eighteenth-century adaptations. But the piece is nothing more than a farcical "taming of a shrew," with a bit of convenient magical transformation thrown in. In none of these cases is *marriage* considered seriously, the institution or the laws regulating it criticized, or the emotions of the participants analyzed with any real feeling.

Marital discord as a provocation for adultery is somewhat harder to disentangle from marital discord comedy properly so called. The question is whether the author is interested in studying the marriage or accomplishing the copulation. Otway's marvelous *The Souldiers Fortune* (1680) is a good borderline example. Captain Beaugard's true love has been forced to marry rich old Sir Davy Dunce while the impoverished captain was off at the wars. The marriage Otway shows us is disgusting, and, though the successful cuckolding action solves nothing, we enjoy it anyway. But what is criticized is enforced marriage, not marriage itself. Indeed in a second plot line Courtine and Sylvia, after many doubts and a proviso scene, embark upon matrimony. In popular plays like Durfey's *A Fond Husband* (1677) and Ravenscroft's *The London Cuckolds* (1681), we are really concerned only with the mechanics of cuckolding plots: bad marriages are simply a convenient motivating donnée. In the 1680s writers will often add to a bad marriage the excuse that the adulterers were engaged but forcibly separated, for example, in Behn's *The False Count* (1681) and *The Lucky Chance*

(1686). As in the Pinchwife/Margery part of *The Country-Wife*, we are never in such cases centrally concerned with marriage and its problems. Consequently I have simply ignored the dozens of plays which contain bad marriages, choosing to focus on those few in which marital discord becomes a problem sufficiently emphasized to help define the play's basic impact.

Before we plunge into an account of marital discord in particular plays, at least one explanation is in order. I have no desire to reduce plays to trite little sermons by announcing that they are "about" some centrally defining "theme"—avarice, jealousy, human folly, marital discord, or what have you. I think, however, that we can usefully pay attention to reiterated problems, subjects, and ideas in comedy. Otway's *The Atheist* is not a sermon "about" marital discord, but one can scarcely deny that its presence profoundly affects the play's impact on us.

To ignore such material or to suppose that it has a purely literary significance is to trivialize some fine plays. One of the clichés about "Restoration comedy" is its remoteness from real life, its "artificiality." Dougald MacMillan has argued, indeed, that only at the end of the eighteenth century, in such writers as Inchbald, Holcroft, and Reynolds, do we start to get a drama which makes a "serious" attempt "to present contemporary life and social problems."[17] This is basically true, and yet, in a few marital discord comedies, we can see serious, even impassioned attempts to make comedy serve such a function a full century earlier.

Problem Plays

What happens when a writer cannot overlook social reality or chokes on blithe literary solutions to marital problems? The romance assumptions of Carolean comedies, which suggest that marriage is a guaranteed happy ending, have seemed shallow and facile to many twentieth-century readers. To suppose that Dorimant can change

---

17. "The Rise of Social Comedy in the Eighteenth Century," *Philological Quarterly*, 41 (1962), 330–38.

his ways is to imagine that the leopard can change his spots. Marital discord reform plots—popular in the plays of Cibber, Johnson, and others after 1700—are even less convincing, though in fact they rest on the same assumptions. Both romance endings and marital reform solutions are sharply challenged by icily skeptical satirists, who approach these matters with a refreshing dose of realism.

Otway's brutal *The Atheist* (1683) is a forceful demolition of romance norms.[18] This play is a sequel to *The Souldiers Fortune*, in which we saw Courtine and Sylvia cast discretion aside and determine to marry. Here Otway sets out to show us what happens *after* one of these lovely romance endings. After a year or so of matrimony, Courtine is nauseated by his wife's endearments, irritated by her demands for attention, and made impotent by the very thought of her. She, for her part, is infuriated by his indifference and quite interested in looking elsewhere. Marital discord can be made very funny—as in *She wou'd if she cou'd* or *The Devil of a Wife*—but here it is almost unrelievedly distressing and depressing. We *like* both husband and wife; their mutual boredom, entrapment, and resentment is made memorably vivid; and Otway relents not a whit at the end of the play. The couple ends more bitterly than it began, and only the death of one of them will resolve a truly intolerable situation. To judge from critics' responses to the play, they would prefer witty irrelevance to social and psychological realism made so inescapably unpleasant.

Other plays treat troubled marriages in a variety of tones. Otway's *Friendship in Fashion* (1678) is certainly one of the ugliest satires in the period, delivering a truly nasty view of husband and wife deceiving each other with close friends. At the end Otway puts together a grating parody of the usual happy ending, with marriage and "friendships" insincerely patched up with hypocritical civilities. Lee's complex *The Princess of Cleve* (1682) contains humorous marital discord and cuckolding involving two cit couples, but its real marital point lies in the love-death of the Prince of Cleve. In Mme. de La Fayette's original, this tragic event is taken absolutely

---

18. This brilliant but nasty comedy has been almost universally misunderstood and condemned. For a full analysis see ch. 3 above.

seriously: Lee rings it round with ironic juxtapositions which drastically undermine its heroic-romantic legitimacy.[19]

At the opposite extreme from this pseudo-*précieuse* pathos, one finds something like Joseph Harris' *The City Bride, or The Merry Cuckold* (1696), an adaptation of Webster's *A Cure for a Cuckold* (ca. 1625; printed 1661). Captain Compasse, presumed dead three years, arrives home to find that his wife, Peg, has been adding to the family in his absence—with the help of the merchant Ventre. But Compasse treats the matter as a huge joke, says he will do the same for Ventre if Ventre's wife is willing, and cheerfully takes a lawyer's advice: "Make a flat Divorce between your selves, be you no longer her Husband, nor she your Wife: Two or three Hours after meet again, salute, woo and wed afresh, and so the base Name of Cuckold's blotted quite" (31). This breezy trifle has plenty of fun at the expense of its characters but is an effective satiric reflection upon the desperate seriousness with which cuckoldom and even unintentional female infidelity are taken in this drama. Readers will recall the tragic denouement of a similar plot in Southerne's *The Fatal Marriage, or The Innocent Adultery* two years earlier.[20] A direct satiric attack on conjugal reform appeared a decade later, around the height of the reform boom. *The Roving Husband Reclaim'd* (anonymous, 1706) is a sardonic burlesque, allegedly written by "a Club of Virtuous Ladies, in Vindication of Virtuous Plays." It was not performed and was probably not intended to be, but it remains amusing reading, providing all the elements of tearful didacticism in a deliciously flippant way.[21]

The best-known "reply" to the romantic verities in general and sentimental reform in particular is Vanbrugh's *The Relapse* (1696), written in response to Cibber's popular *Love's Last Shift*, performed early that year. In most respects, Cibber's play is a very

19. For a detailed account see ch. 4 above.

20. For an interesting analysis, see Julia A. Rich, "Isabella of Southerne's *The Fatal Marriage* (1694): Saint or Sinner," *Restoration*, 5 (1981), 88–99.

21. A less satiric but somewhat similar play is Charles Molloy's *The Perplex'd Couple: or Mistake upon Mistake* (1715), a lively, good-humored intrigue-farce which runs forced marriage and comic marital discord plots in parallel. No reform is needed, since all the strife was the result of misunderstanding—a neat turn.

ordinary "Restoration" comedy, but in Act V, aiming at the "Ladies," he pours on emotional slush.[22] Stunned by Amanda's virtue, Loveless performs his highly implausible *volte-face* and announces that henceforth he will be a model husband, since "sure the nearest to the Joys above, / Is the chast Rapture of a Vertuous Love" (103). From a man who has abandoned his wife for ten years while he whored and gamed his way through his fortune, this is not very convincing. Vanbrugh's play suggests that Loveless' reform will not last and that even Amanda's virtue may not be proof against temptation. By no means is the play a savage attack upon sentimental comedy by an outraged, hard-line satirist. Cibber was delighted by the play and took a lead role in it. Loveless does manage an adulterous copulation with Berinthia, but Amanda holds out against Mr. Worthy, and, in a highly melodramatic scene, he is so taken with her virtue that he finds that "the Coarser Appetite of Nature's gone" (I, 93) and desists.[23] Worthy adds, "How long this influence may last, Heaven knows"—but the emotionalism of the conversion is not so far from Cibber's norms. Vanbrugh is skeptical about marital fidelity and neatly deflates Cibber's overpuffed reconciliation. The cloying lovebirdism in I, i, of *The Relapse* obviously cannot last. If anything, though, the Lovelesses' marriage looks relatively viable in contrast to the parallel "romance" plot, in which Young Fashion cuts out his brother, Lord Foppington, to marry the wealthy Hoyden, an oversexed country slut. At the end of the play, Foppington ironically compliments his brother on his choice—"You have Marry'd a Woman Beautiful in her Person, Charming in her Ayrs, Prudent in her Canduct, Canstant in her Inclinations, and of a nice Marality" (I, 99–100). Here Vanbrugh issues a crunching reminder that one pays a price in marrying strictly for money.[24]

22. See the analysis by Paul E. Parnell, "Equivocation in Cibber's *Love's Last Shift*," *Studies in Philology*, 57 (1960), 519–34.

23. References to all Vanbrugh plays (including *The Provok'd Husband*) are to *The Works of Sir John Vanbrugh*, ed. Bonamy Dobrée and Geoffrey Webb, 4 vols. (1927–28; rpt. New York: AMS, 1967).

24. Replying to Collier's indignation at his "rewarding" Young Fashion, Vanbrugh says tartly that he has merely "help'd him to a Wife, who's likely to make his Heart ake" (*A Short Vindication of the Relapse and the Provok'd Wife*, in *Works*, I, 199).

The plays we have been considering attack essentially *literary* conventions, some of them with great success. In two cases, however, writers move beyond the realm of literary satire and produce devastating analyses of the state of marriage itself, particularly as it was practiced under the laws of the 1690s. Both deal squarely and unpleasantly with the wretched position of the woman in an unhappy marriage; neither tries to take refuge in the hierarchical verities of Cibber, the moral preachments of Charles Johnson, or the escapism of Farquhar. These later solutions were, in essence, answers to or evasions of the ugly problems so ruthlessly posed in these plays.

Thomas Southerne's *The Wives Excuse: Or, Cuckolds Make Themselves* (1691) failed on first performance and was never revived. Notwithstanding critical contempt for it from Nicoll and Dodds, John Harrington Smith hailed it as a "great play," "one of the five most considerable comedies written between 1660 and 1700," an opinion endorsed by Scouten.[25] Without bickering over the precise choice of a best five, I would certainly agree that the play ranks with *The Country-Wife, The Plain-Dealer, The Man of Mode,* and *The Way of the World.* The point is simple. The virtuous Mrs. Friendall finds that her husband is a coward and a philanderer. She then finds herself importuned by the attractive if unscrupulous Lovemore. With a struggle she beats down her inclinations and refuses him her favors. But, at the end of the play, Mr. Friendall is exposed *in flagrante delicto* with Mrs. Wittwoud before the whole company, his wife included. Husband and wife agree to separate— he happy to be free to philander, she reflecting miserably on "this hard Condition of a Woman's fate . . . I must be still your Wife, and still unhappy" (54). Southerne implies that in time she will duly succumb to Lovemore's blandishments—only, of course, to be cast aside when he tires of her.

Southerne's tone is bleakly realistic. There is no glamour here,

25. Nicoll, I, 240; John Wendell Dodds, *Thomas Southerne, Dramatist* (1933; rpt. Hamden, Conn.: Archon, 1970), p. 80; and Smith, *The Gay Couple,* p. 144. See also Sutherland, pp. 145–46, who has kind words and intelligent praise for the play. For a full analysis, see ch. 8 of Milhous and Hume, *Producible Interpretation,* forthcoming.

no benevolent high spirits. Southerne lacks that note of sad acquiescence in what he cannot change which characterizes Congreve. Like *The Plain-Dealer*, this play is an angry comment on society as the author finds it. Unlike Wycherley's play, *The Wives Excuse* is not lightened by a fairy-tale ending: no Fidelia emerges from disguise to solve the protagonists' problems in a twinkling. Critics speak of Wycherley's "angry" satire, but, despite all the bluster, *The Plain-Dealer* is a fairly cheerful play which ends on a note right out of sentimental romance. Wycherley brings a gusto to his protests which is entirely lacking in the icy clarity with which Southerne views his subject.

Mr. Friendall is a loathsome character—not exaggeratedly and melodramatically so but effectively disagreeable and repulsive. His sexual schemes have none of the exuberance one is accustomed to find in plays like *A Fond Husband* or Dryden's *Mr. Limberham*. Friendall is cold, slimy, selfish, petty, and mean. Usually such characters are relegated to secondary roles, villain or butt—Vernish in *The Plain-Dealer*, Sparkish in *The Country-Wife*. Southerne takes such a character, portrays him at full length, and makes him husband to an attractive, intelligent, decent woman. The result is a truly serious satire and a remarkably unpleasant, unsettling play. As Sutherland observes, Southerne has an exceedingly acute grasp of human motives and psychology: he studies the philanderer and notes the results instead of just putting sex games onstage for our entertainment. Southerne's urbane gentility makes a wonderful ironic cover for the morass of cuckoldry, seduction, lies, and intrigue he presents. *The Wives Excuse* is a genuine comedy of manners, one in which superficial courtliness and Southerne's famous stylistic polish simply emphasize the hypocrisy and degradation of the reality underneath.

The Wives Excuse is a problem play, and Southerne does nothing at all to disguise the lack of a resolution. Had he written *The Plain-Dealer*, he would have left Manly to starve in the gutter, thereby making the play more honest—and, we may guess, less successful. Here one is brought to realize just how wretched a marriage like the Friendalls' can be and, worse, that for the woman there is simply no escape. Prior to the twentieth century, comedies without a resolution are rare. *The Alchemist* dissolves into cheerful nothing-ness, but social order *is* reestablished. *Le Misanthrope*, a famous instance, arrives at least at a dual conclusion, critical both of soci-ety and of the man who refuses to adapt to its minimum social demands. Southerne is unwilling to soften or distract attention from the unpalatable situation he delineates. He does not even supply the harsh, macabre gaiety of Otway's comedies. *The Wives Excuse* is a dark comedy which arrives—as Bonamy Dobrée suggests "great comedy" should—on the verge of tragedy and leaves us there.[26]

Southerne remains absolutely uncompromising. Vanbrugh is willing at least to split our attention between a hopeless marital situation and a romance plot about which he is guardedly optimis-tic. *The Provok'd Wife* (1697) offers us two plots. In one we are shown an intolerably bad marriage: Sir John Brute is a loutish sot, and we do not marvel that Lady Brute is attracted to Constant, an admirable gentleman who loves her devotedly. In the contrasting romance plot, Lady Brute's niece Bellinda decides to marry Heart-free because she likes and admires him, even though he has rather little money. By no means is Vanbrugh hostile to marriage itself: rather, he is unhappily aware how horribly wrong it can go. When Constant and Heartfree debate in V, iv, they conclude that, "tho' Marriage be a Lottery in which there are a wondrous many Blanks; yet there is one inestimable Lot, in which the only Heaven on Earth is written. Wou'd your kind Fate but guide your Hand to that, . . . I . . . shou'd envy you." Heartfree replies, "And justly too: For to be capable of loving one, doubtless is better than to possess a Thou-sand. But how far that Capacity's in me, alas I know not" (I, 176). On marriage Vanbrugh is skeptical, ironic, and doubting—but not opposed. The conclusion of *The Provok'd Wife* is distinctly bleak, but, in allowing for the possibility of happiness in marriage, Van-brugh avoids the despairing bitterness which pervades *The Wives Excuse*.

The importance of marital incompatibility as a theme in Van-brugh's plays was long ago pointed out by Paul Mueschke and

26. Bonamy Dobrée, *Restoration Comedy* (London: Oxford Univ. Press, 1924), pp. 15–16.

Jeannette Fleisher.[27] There seem to be three reasons that their analysis, though often cited, has not been more fruitfully influential. First, they treat Vanbrugh almost in a vacuum, making comparisons only with a few plays by Wycherley, Congreve, and Farquhar. Second, they find two basic themes in the plays: marital incompatibility and the predicament of the younger brother in a society with a law of primogeniture. The latter is not—in my opinion—seriously treated by Vanbrugh, and the yoking discredits the valid observation. Third, Mueschke and Fleisher are dissatisfied with the ending of *The Provok'd Wife*. They are glad that Vanbrugh does not present what they term "the comedy of manners" handling of the situation—a deserved cuckolding (in the fashion of Ravenscroft, we might say). Equally, they are glad that a sentimental reform is eschewed. But they do yearn for something conclusive. "The inexorable modern problem dramatist would have forced the situation at the conclusion to its ultimate implications; divorce, or the assertion of independence on the part of the woman, à la Ibsen's Nora. Vanbrugh's rational treatment is, from this point of view, far in advance of the comic method of the Comedy of Manners, but his intention and his social vision are equally far removed from the problem play solution."

This seems unreasonable. "Divorce" in the modern sense was legally impossible; Southerne-style separation solves nothing. And, if the postcurtain sequence of events in *A Doll's House* is rather vague, what would it be here? In late seventeenth-century society, Nora's "solution" is not only not viable, it is unavailable. A married woman *could not* leave her husband save by returning to her family or becoming a kept woman. Vanbrugh has given us exactly the ending the situation demands: no exit for Lady Brute; qualified cheer in the possibility of some felicity for Bellinda and Heartfree.

Lincoln B. Faller has correctly observed that, "though both his plays end as comedies generally do, with marriages or people agreeing to marry, it can hardly be overlooked that both are more centrally concerned with marriages in the process of collapse."[28] (End-

27. "A Re-Evaluation of Vanbrugh," *PMLA*, 49 (1934), 848–89, esp. p. 855.
28. "Between Jest and Earnest: The Comedy of Sir John Vanbrugh," *Modern Philology*, 72 (1974), 17–29.

ing aside, this is true of *A Journey to London* as well.) In *The Relapse* we see the effects of human frailty upon a happily reconstructed marriage but are aware that *both* husband and wife are tempted. In *The Provok'd Wife* our sympathies are almost entirely with the wife, but, as Faller shows, she is a complex character and not without her own imperfections. "She has married Brute, as she tells us, out of 'vanity' and 'ambition' [I, 116]. She encourages Constant's attentions with no apparent guilt; despite her sense of morality, her greatest fear remains the loss of reputation." [29] Only in *A Journey to London* does Vanbrugh seem to veer excessively toward a simplistic black-and-white contrast. Vanbrugh is an acute psychologist: without having much depth, his characters nonetheless possess the motives, contradictions, and feelings which bring them to life and arouse sympathetic understanding, if not serious empathy.

Like Southerne, Vanbrugh does not want serious empathy: he is writing dark comedy, not tragedy or melodrama. Lady Brute is left stuck in a horrible and irremediable situation, but rousing floods of tears for her would do nothing beyond exercising the audience's sensibility for its own enjoyment. The play exists to analyze and question, not to make ringing emotional appeals. Like *The Wives Excuse*, and *The Way of the World* for that matter, *The Provok'd Wife* is a rather cold play. None of these writers is happy with the world as he finds it. Congreve is the most accepting of the three: he sees all the follies and imperfections clearly but tolerates what he knows cannot be changed, albeit with an underlying sense of sadness quite foreign to the airy Etherege or the boisterously gay and angry Wycherley. [30] The ways of the world are indeed not easily changed. The perception of their evils rouses Southerne to harsh and indignant cynicism (a peculiar combination) and Vanbrugh to a more resigned ironic doubt and skepticism. Their accounts of marriage in these plays represent serious satiric questionings of the institution and the role of women. Marriage is not being attacked, but both writers are dubious about its chances of success and acutely

29. Ibid., p. 22. The page reference in the quotation is changed to the Dobrée edition.

30. This half-hidden melancholy is well analyzed by Clifford Leech in "Congreve and the Century's End," *Philological Quarterly*, 41 (1962), 275–93.

alive to the problems which visibly poison so many marriages in real life. The results are dark, serious, realistic, and questioning. Not for these men the tidy solutions of the reform comedy school. They do not write to defend the status quo, and, far from glossing over its problems, they expose them with a merciless and depressing clarity.

Happy-Ending Plays

Standing in sharp contrast to these problem plays are what we might unkindly call "solution" plays. Here marital discord is treated as a problem to be resolved. Structurally, the result is closely analogous to romance comedy. At the end we are presumably to feel that warm glow which ordinarily comes from marriage and a happy-ever-after ending. We are invited to feel about marital reconciliation what we normally feel about a successful courtship. The apparent wretchedness of the couple can be used to heighten the raptures of the happy ending. Cibber's facile *Love's Last Shift* (1696), mentioned above, is the famous illustration. A better play, and one more typical of this subgenre, is Cibber's *The Careless Husband* (1704), in which Sir Charles Easy—a good man at heart—repents and reforms after a delicate hint from his wife that she has found him asleep *in flagrante delicto* with her maid, Edging. Here at least Sir Charles is basically a pleasant and attractive character: his conversion is still too facile, but we can accept his penitence quite as readily as we can the majority of rake reforms at the end of romance comedies. This light-reform formula appears regularly for decades: Taverner's *The Artful Wife* (1717) is a good example of it.

Occasionally, especially before 1700, the needed reform will be treated even more casually and actually proves only a neat way to wrap up another matter. Thus, in John Dryden, Jr.'s *The Husband His own Cuckold* (1696), a husband takes his wife's would-be lover's place at an assignation, and the shock brings her to her senses, but for the audience, the excitement of the near-cuckolding action outweighs the reform. Dilke's *The City Lady: or Folly Re-*

claimed (1696) follows the doings of Lady Grumble, "a City Lady lately remov'd into *Covent-Garden*, in all things affecting Quality": she is eventually humbled enough to accept the station in life of her husband, a rich old cit. Here attention is really on social pretension: marital discord is merely a by-product, and the reform (46) makes a tidy ending.

Reform comedy is usually far more sober than these lively, high-spirited plays. Steele's *The Tender Husband* (1705) is not really "sentimental," but the reclamation of the wife is meant to be emotionally affecting. Clerimont, Sr., driven to distraction by his wife's extravagance and gaming, sets Lucy in male disguise to tempt her. He then interrupts the assignation with drawn sword, whereupon his wife weeps, kneels, and all is well. Various changes can readily be rung on this device. In *The Bath* (1701), Durfey has a brother interrupt his sister's planned amours, protect her reputation, and send her back to her husband, lesson learned. In *As You Find It* (1703), Charles Boyle sends a wife in disguise to an assignation with her husband. The same trick appears several times, notably in Captain Charles Boadens' *The Modish Couple* (1732).[31] However silly the device can sometimes appear, one may recall that da Ponte and Mozart use it to good effect in *Le nozze di Figaro*.

In all of these cases the real issue is evaded: adultery or extravagance are forsworn, but the marriage itself is left unexamined. A few plays do at least exhibit awareness that temptation is motivated at home. William Burnaby's *The Reform'd Wife* (1700) shows us Astrea, the unhappy young wife of a nouveau riche fool, old Sir Solomon Empty, adapting herself to her married life. By the standards of the 1670s the husband richly deserves horns, and the dashing young Freeman ought to be just the man to bestow them. But though Astrea is tempted she resigns herself to duty. Several plays by Charles Johnson display this greater sense of pain and psychological acuity. *The Generous Husband* (1711) shows us rich old Carizales repenting his folly in marrying a wife of fifteen and saying

31. Lord Hervey may well be the real author. See Charles B. Woods, "Captain B——'s Play," *Harvard Studies and Notes in Philology and Literature*, 15 (1933), 243–55.

that their problems are all his fault—whereupon she is so overcome by his generosity that her discontents are stilled.[32] This may sound like sentimental slush, but let us not forget that *The School for Scandal* contains a rather exact parallel. In *The Wife's Relief, or The Husband's Cure* (1711), Johnson alters Shirley's *The Gamester*. Cynthia is the virtuous wife of Riot, a wastrel debauchee. Riot tries to seduce her friend Arbella, who consults with Cynthia and "agrees" to an assignation. Gambling, Riot loses the assignation to his friend Volatil. Cynthia tells her husband that she took Arbella's place, and he, horrified, repents. This is a neat improvement on the usual assignation trick. Johnson uses the gaming theme again in *The Masquerade* (1719), this time reforming a card-loving wife. The psychology is well handled: the wife does not mend her ways easily, and the husband does not fall into her arms at the first sign of contrition.

Reform is not, of course, limited to married persons. And, actually, reclamation from the gaming table is a device just as well used with a courting couple, as Centlivre chooses to do in *The Gamester* and *The Basset-Table* (both 1705). Here reform-oriented marital discord comedy and the post-1700 form of ordinary romance comedy run in parallel lines. Only rarely is the married state crucial to the problem which must be overcome. One of the few attempts to make it so is Cibber's *The Lady's last Stake* (1707), an interesting if uninviting experiment. The subject is a gambling, wenching husband in need of reformation, but here Cibber eschews the facile solutions of *Love's Last Shift* and *The Careless Husband*. The prologue announces that this wife is no Lady Easy. Here Lady Wronglove, cold, proud, and implacably virtuous, is maddened by her husband's ways and harasses him into behaving yet worse. In Act IV she specifically rejects and derides the solutions offered in *The Careless Husband* (44). Perhaps Cibber's own stormy domestic life helped, but he obviously had a vivid understanding of the problems of everyday life and the routine irritants which can poison a marriage; he communicates domestic misery well. But, just as we

32. Carizales has much to learn. At the outset he says, "I have purchas'd her of her Father" and calls her his "property," albeit a "costly" one. This rhetoric is quite typical of old husbands and fathers in these comedies.

seem to be approaching a "divorce" (that is, a legal separation), Sir Friendly Moral intervenes, a sententious guide, philosopher, and friend who preaches good sense, good feeling, and forgiveness. The resulting play is a ponderous, didactic bore. Nonetheless the attempt to make marital discord real—not comic, not an excuse for adultery, not just a *pro forma* reason for a heartwarming reform— suggests Cibber's desire to go beyond the facile variants on the romance pattern with which he and others had been experimenting.

Cibber got his best chance twenty years later in *The Provok'd Husband* (1728), an important and undervalued play. Vanbrugh died leaving a fragment of three and one-half acts, published as *A Journey to London*. The piece has some fine low-comic scenes and a good overall scheme (contrasting a high-life marital problem with the comic contretemps of a country family come to town). However, the construction is awkwardly handled, and one cannot really see how Vanbrugh would have ended the piece. According to Cibber, he planned a "*Catastrophe*" in which "the Conduct of his Imaginary Fine Lady" so provoked the long-suffering husband that he was actually to "turn her out of his Doors" (III, 179). In *The Provok'd Wife* Vanbrugh had studied an impossibly bad husband whose wife had no recourse; here he turns the tables, but the husband does have some recourse. How the play would have worked, dramatically and emotionally, is hard to imagine. Gay was to end his *The Distress'd Wife* (1734) by having an extravagant wife hauled off to the country, an unsatisfying ending to a weak play which tries to do some of the things Vanbrugh had attempted in *A Journey to London*.

Cibber stepped in with highly effective solutions. He saves the marriage, but only after a harrowing series of scenes and the apparent passing of the point of no return. He retains Vanbrugh's contrasting plots with the two wives running riot, eventually sending the country family back where it belongs and emphasizing the thematic relevance of Lord Townly's sister, Lady Grace ("of Exemplary Virtue"), and her admirer, Mr. Manly. From the first line Cibber focuses the play squarely on marriage: "*Lord Townly* [solus]: Why did I marry?—Was it not evident, my plain, rational Scheme of Life was impracticable, with a Woman of so different a way of Thinking?—Is there one Article of it, that she has not broke in upon?—Yes,—let me do her Justice—her Reputation" (III, 185).

The decency and misery of Lord Townly are dwelt upon throughout—though one may note that from the first speech his wife's sexual virtue is never called in question. The lady may be foolish, thoughtless, reckless, and spendthrift, but she remains chaste. In the prologue Cibber says that plays "should let you see / Not only, What you Are, but Ought to be" and that he presents "Not Scenes, that would a noisy Joy impart, / But such as hush the Mind, and warm the Heart." Lady Townly uses her husband shamelessly (for example, III, 188, 222–24). What arguments can reach her (III, 189)? None, apparently. Cibber goes so far as to suggest that Parliament is remiss in not providing for divorce on the ground of incompatibility (III, 249–50). Lord Townly determines upon legal separation—which brings his wife to her senses in a long and highly emotional scene which accomplishes a reversal. Cibber lets the lady plead background and environment as extenuating circumstances but concludes by loudly touting "The Husband's Right to Rule" (III, 252).

Is this hybrid play simply a sentimental vulgarization of Vanbrugh's design, as is usually assumed? Samuel Johnson, we might note, refers to it in terms of high praise as a laughing comedy.[33] Cibber was a slick professional dramatist: the play "worked" with tremendous success for many decades in the theatre, running well initially even against *The Beggar's Opera.* Preserving the loutish country family, polishing up the gentility of the Townly group, and concluding with heavy but not mawkish sentiment, Cibber arrives at a well-balanced combination. One might point to Dickens as a parallel example of an author whose vivid, boisterous low life offsets a sentiment rather too treacly for twentieth-century taste.

At least one contemporary found the play's pat solutions unconvincing. In an anonymous pamphlet, this "private Gentleman" argues that there was no apparent motive for the marriage in the

33. James Boswell, *The Life of Samuel Johnson*, ed. George Birkbeck Hill and L. F. Powell, 6 vols. (Oxford: Clarendon Press, 1934–50), II, 48. Cf. Goldsmith's "An Essay on the Theatre." For a good general account of the play, see Peter Dixon's introduction to his RRDS edition (Lincoln: Univ. of Nebraska Press, 1973).

first place and that there is still no basis for compatibility.[34] He takes the subject extremely seriously. "There is no doubt of it but Marriage (how witty soever the Wags may be upon it in all Seasons, and even the Men of Sense in their looser Moments) is an Institution the most serious in itself, and of the greatest Consequence to a Commonwealth of any in it" (11). Cibber, he finds, is careless of psychological consistency and contradictory in Lord Townly's threats—some of which are illegal. The objections are to superficiality, not to reform, and this author points out how closely Cibber follows Charles Johnson's pattern in *The Masquerade* and suggests—correctly—that the psychology in that play is considerably more realistic. What he overlooks is the great vividness of character in the later play, a virtue which explains its greater effectiveness in the theatre. Even this critic willingly admits that Cibber managed "to draw Tears from the Eyes of most of his Audience."

The Provok'd Husband is a vivid picture of marital disharmony. It is also a very conservative statement about the proper nature of marriage—an obnoxious one by present-day standards. "Let Husbands govern: Gentle Wives obey" (III, 254). Sir Francis Wronghead must see the need to hustle his wildly extravagant wife back to the country where she belongs. Lord Townly must learn to assert himself, his wife to submit. Lady Grace must accept Manly's "Doctrine" of marriage, which says that the male must leave off his role as lover and take up that of dominant husband (III, 192). Thus Cibber's response to disharmony is to assert a traditional solution: submission to duly constituted authority.

The only one of these plays to propose "divorce" as a really happy solution is *The Beaux Stratagem* (1707).[35] Readers will re-

---

34. *Reflections on the Principal Characters in a late Comedy Call'd The Provok'd Husband* (London: J. Roberts, 1728), esp. pp. 11, 13–14, 21.

35. A few plays end with it as a *pro forma* resolution. The Woodlys in *Epsom-Wells*, for instance, say quite cheerfully that they will get a "divorce," whatever that means. Usually, "divorce"—meaning separation—is definitely regarded as unsatisfactory. An instance is Hildebrand Jacob's *The Tryal of Conjugal Love* (1738), a one-act farce in which an old husband "tests" a hypocritical young wife. I cannot agree with Nicoll (II, 205) that the wife "rejoices" in the consequent divorce. She hates her husband, but the separation they arrange is not treated as a satisfactory resolution. This piece blends psychological realism with farce foolery in a peculiar and disconcerting way.

call the denouement. Aimwell, overwhelmed by Dorinda's goodness, exclaims, "Such Goodness who cou'd injure; I find my self
unequal to the Task of Villain; she has gain'd my Soul, and made it
honest like her own;—I cannot, cannot hurt her" (66) and promptly
confesses his villainy, whereat she exclaims "Matchless Honesty"
and calls for the priest to marry them. Fortunately the death of
Aimwell's brother has made him the wealthy viscount he pretended
to be. I venture to say that this is "sentimental" and that audiences
still like it. Meanwhile, what of Mrs. Sullen and Archer? The Sullens' unhappy marriage has been humorously but brutally drawn
for us.

> *Mrs. Sullen.*   O Sister, Sister! if ever you marry, beware
> of a sullen, silent Sot, one that's always musing, but
> never thinks. . . . He came home this Morning at his
> usual Hour of Four, waken'd me out of a sweet Dream
> of something else, by tumbling over the Tea-table, which
> he broke all to pieces, after his Man and he had rowl'd
> about the Room like sick Passengers in a Storm, he comes
> flounce into Bed, dead as a Salmon into a Fishmonger's
> Basket; his Feet cold as Ice, his Breath hot as a Furnace,
> and his Hands and his Face as greasy as his Flanel Night-
> cap.—O Matrimony!—He tosses up the Clothes . . .
> disorders the whole Oeconomy of my Bed, leaves me
> half naked, and my whole Night's Comfort is the tune-
> able Serenade of that wakeful Nightingale, his Nose.
> (12)

Sullen is a stupid, brutish sot, who is made thoroughly unattractive
in the course of the play. In an amusing inversion of a proviso scene,
the Sullens agree only that they have no use for each other (70–71).
He is delighted at the thought of being rid of her but intends to
keep her marriage portion—changing his mind only when he has
to yield to blackmail. The tag lines at the end announce that "Consent, if mutual, saves the Lawyer's Fee, / Consent is Law enough to
set you free."

This is of course entirely illegal all around. The Sullens lack grounds even for a separation, and only parliamentary decree (for which there is no legal justification) could allow either to remarry, though most readers find a clear implication that Mrs. Sullen will marry Archer.[36] Yet this flight into the completely unreal has seemed attractive and satisfying to generation after generation of play-goers. There has been scarcely a whisper of protest about illegality, immorality, sentimentality, or what have you. Genest does report an anecdote suggesting that Mrs. Oldfield (who first played Mrs. Sullen) was dubious about audience reception of this airy "divorce," yet these fears soon proved groundless.[37]

Farquhar's wishful thinking is grounded in logic and serious argument: his indebtedness to Milton was suggested long ago.[38] However illegal, this solution is highly agreeable and accords with our idea of what "ought" to be. The lack of outcry about impossibility and immorality suggests the need for caution in assuming that realism—always a vexed issue in these plays—was expected by the audience. That *The Beaux Stratagem* is escapist is undeniable, but it is delightfully so. This is humane comedy at its finest: the view of human nature it presents is benevolently skeptical—neither cynical in the old 1670s fashion nor tending to the saccharine in the manner of the "reform" mode popular after 1700. Farquhar indulges in a departure from reality, but he is not blind to it. Where he is genially self-indulgent (and aware of it), Cibber, Centlivre, Boyle, and Steele tend to be all too blindly and solemnly benevolist in their assumptions and preachments.

With the exception of Farquhar's fairy-tale solution, all of these plays arrive at a conservative answer which supports the social and

36. The text of the first quarto does *not* say that Archer and Mrs. Sullen will go off together (either married or otherwise), though the textual history certainly suggests this interpretation in eighteenth-century productions. For a detailed analysis of the interpretive possibilities—from serious social satire to plain romp—see Judith Milhous and Robert D. Hume, "*The Beaux' Stratagem*: A Production Analysis," *Theatre Journal*, 34 (1982), 77–95.

37. Genest, *Some Account of the English Stage*, II, 366.

38. Martin A. Larson, "The Influence of Milton's Divorce Tracts on Farquhar's *Beaux' Stratagem*," *PMLA*, 39 (1924), 174–78.

legal status quo. The question posed is simple: how can this marriage be saved? For saved it always is, and the problem turns out to lie not in law or marriage but in individual error which writers (Farquhar excepted) always presume to be remediable. No doubt the presumption of possible reform implies faith in the natural goodness of man. But these are not very philosophical plays, and I suspect that the prime if often unconscious motive in these marital reform comedies is the defense of an institution which psychologists still tell us is the underpinning of society as we know it. Writers assumed that marriage should work, that it must work. Reform comedy is thus a statement of faith.

From Hard to Humane Comedy

As we have seen, marital discord comedy displays two quite different structures. The more common one is a parallel to and development of romance structure, comprising a movement to reconciliation, higher harmony, personal and social felicity. The other, rare but important, springs from a recognition of the intractability of the problem, and it moves only to impasse.

Literary interest in the subject clearly stems from two sources— extrinsic social problems and dissatisfaction with the unreality of the romance convention followed in almost all late seventeenth-century comedies. From the 1670s through the 1690s, we find a trickle of antiromance comedies, and with increasing directness writers start to confront the problem of unhappy marriage.[39] The most devastating satiric attacks on marriage law and the most painfully skeptical considerations of love and marriage are a product of the nineties, a transitional period between the exuberant Carolean comedies, Tory and aristocratic in values, and the more staid Augustan comedies, generally more expressive of a bourgeois, Whig outlook. After 1700 marriage is almost never questioned as an in-

39. Occasionally one will find an antiromantic play which works by simply refusing to accept a conventional reform and marriage. Thus at the end of Durfey's *The Richmond Heiress* (1693) Fulvia, an heiress, is so disgusted by the duplicity of her fortune-hunting suitors that she renounces marriage entirely.

stitution: in comedy the issue is not whether there will be virtue and reform but how seriously and didactically they will be upheld.

The Collier crisis and the new morality are obviously involved in the change. But Jeremy Collier did not make English drama sentimental; he did not even do much to make it moral. However loudly the reformers protested, they did not constitute the theatregoing audience.[40] As that audience became more bourgeois after 1688, the "values" acceptable to it naturally changed.[41] Collier's roars simply contribute to a dramatic ethos in which a basically bourgeois ideology is stoutly maintained. Marriage, as such, could not be questioned without outraging the sensibilities of this audience. Looking back, one finds that the really serious questions raised about marriage come not from Restoration rakes upholding libertine principles but from people like Southerne, Vanbrugh, and Congreve, who would *like* to find marriage satisfactory and are distressed by their own doubts and fears.

To draw a distinction between the ethos of 1675 and 1710 is easy enough. To differentiate among the sorts of plays current after 1695 has proved a good deal harder. By contrast to the relatively harsh Carolean comedy, the "humane" influence is indeed pervasive. Even Vanbrugh, who has deep roots in the older tradition, has a tenderness of sensibility which sets him off from Wycherley or Etherege. Congreve shares it (and is consequently condemned by Rose Zimbardo);[42] Southerne does not. Yet plainly Vanbrugh and Farquhar differ considerably in tone and outlook, and both of them must be distinguished from Cibber (who exhibits a wide range all by himself) or Charles Johnson. As against the "old" hard comedy I would distinguish three basic types of "new" comedy: 1) ordinary "humane" comedy—for example, *The Careless Husband*, *The Beaux Stratagem*; 2) "reform" comedy, with a much heavier didactic em-

---

40. A point well developed by Calhoun Winton in "Sentimentalism and Theater Reform in the Early Eighteenth Century," in *Quick Springs of Sense: Studies in the Eighteenth Century*, ed. Larry S. Champion (Athens: Univ. of Georgia Press, 1974), pp. 97–112.

41. See John Loftis' *Comedy and Society*. As Loftis shows, the old Carolean forms carried over, but implicit and explicit values change, some quite quickly (moral matters), some astonishingly slowly (social prejudice against merchants).

42. *Wycherley's Drama*, pp. 7–15.

phasis—for example, *The Bath, As You Find It, The Lady's last Stake*; and 3) overtly "exemplary" comedy, of which the celebrated example is *The Conscious Lovers.*

Obviously any one play may mix plot lines of contrasting types. Thus Steele's *The Funeral* (1701) mingles a light romance story with a strictly exemplary one, harshly satirizes some scoundrels, and dissolves a dreadful marriage on the grounds of bigamy.[43] Similarly, Vanbrugh mingles elements of hard and humane comedy in all his plays. Neither Vanbrugh nor Farquhar will go all the way to reform, even a flippant one.[44] Chameleon Cibber happily produces all three kinds of the new comedy and shows in the first four acts of *Love's Last Shift* that he could have written Carolean sex comedy right along with Ravenscroft and Durfey, had he been born twenty years earlier. *The Careless Husband* is a classic illustration of superficial reform ex machina: the real point of the play is its display of gentility. *The Lady's last Stake* is about as preachy as reform comedy gets. *The Provok'd Husband* mixes a serious reform plot with an exaltedly exemplary romance, along with some excellent satire (borrowed from Vanbrugh) on the foolish country gentry. In one respect marital discord comedies tend to be atypical, since post-1700 some kind of reform is almost a sine qua non in them. Most of the straight humane comedies are romantic intrigue pieces, like Thomas Baker's popular *Tunbridge-Walks* (1703) or Centlivre's *The Busie Body* (1709).

There is a tremendous swing in these years—not from "libertine" to "sentimental" comedy but from light, satiric romance to solemn romance. In marriage comedy there is a parallel shift away from satiric deflations of romance convention and challenging problem plays as writers turn to the reform-oriented comedy which affirms the traditional status quo and papers over its problems. The earlier writers felt free to challenge, question, criticize. To ask why this freedom vanished goes beyond the scope of this essay. In brief, I would guess that it was a matter of economics. The London the-

43. Bigamy does occasionally serve as a deus ex machina solution to an apparently hopeless situation, as in Mrs. Pix's *The Innocent Mistress* (1697).

44. Farquhar has Richmore, a rake, perform a turnabout at the end of *The Twin-Rivals* (1702), but the effect is disconcerting and unconvincing.

atre was in deep financial trouble by the late 1690s; the managers were struggling to attract and hold a new audience to replace the court-oriented Carolean audience (now dying off) which flocked to see plays in the happy days of Charles II; and, under attack from religious reformers, the companies were naturally inclined to be noncontroversial. Vanbrugh and Congreve drew Jeremy Collier's hottest fire, which may seem odd. Their plays were current but were far less titillating than many others still being performed. Actually, *A Short View of the Immorality and Profaneness of the English Stage* (1698) is as much concerned with challenges to hierarchical order and proprieties as it is with smut per se. Collier is strong on providential justice, social order, respect for class and authority. I am not about to suggest that Collier successfully forbade criticism of marriage. But the movement of which he was chief spokesman was intensely conservative, and it had an inhibiting effect on all kinds of challenges to authority and traditional order. This point brings us back to a really disconcerting anomaly in eighteenth-century theatre history: audiences refused to tolerate in new plays what they continued to enjoy in old ones. Despite the turn toward "purity," the bawdy plays of the seventies continued to hold the stage. Similarly, a play like *The Provok'd Wife* remained long popular, despite the overwhelming predominance of tidy reform solutions in new plays after 1700. This double standard seems peculiar, to say the least.

Following the transition from seventeenth- to eighteenth-century comedy, almost all scholars have felt that they were tracing a decline.[45] I feel the same way yet do not want this feeling to prohibit sympathetic attention to the later plays. As a means both of epitomizing the shift and defending the potentialities of humane comedy, I want to conclude with a contrast: Dryden's *Marriage A-la-Mode* (1671) set against Fielding's *The Modern Husband* (1732). Most of my attention has been to the crucial swing point in the middle: readers may have been wondering what has become of my title limits. Neither writer, in truth, does much with marital discord, but

45. Most recently Laura Brown has made explanation of this "decline" one of her central goals in *English Dramatic Form, 1660–1760* (New Haven: Yale Univ. Press, 1981).

both do produce a single, exceptional comment, and their attitudes can usefully be compared.

Marriage A-la-Mode has been a much-admired and little-understood play. My concern is not with the complexity of the double plot but solely with the impact of the nonheroic subplot. Rhodophil and Doralice have soon tired of each other: Dryden presents a vivid if witty picture of their boredom, dissatisfaction, and readiness to stray. Enter Palamede and Melantha, engaged under parental pressure and resisting vigorously. The resulting intrigues hover close to double copulation but come to naught. The men finally realize what has been going on and nearly fight but pause to reason the matter out. They find that they can be jealous even of what they do not love. They are unwilling to give "their" women freedom, even if that is the price of having their own. Palamede has a suggestion: "What dost think of a blessed community betwixt us four, for the solace of the women and relief of the men? Methinks it would be a pleasant kind of life: Wife and Husband for the standing Dish, and Mistris and Gallant for the Desert" (79). But this, they fear, would just give rise to jealousy: however logical, open marriage is rather a strain on security. So they conclude that "we had as good make a firm League, not to invade each others propriety," and agree to stick to their own women. P. F. Vernon notes that the play is "exceptional" in failing to support the usual romantic verities about marriage, yet "the men do finally decide that some kind of social compact is necessary not to 'invade each other's propriety' (V, i). . . . At heart this is a cynical conclusion. Promiscuity is condemned only because it frustrates the possessive instinct and leads to impossible complications in society." [46]

I think this view entirely misses the complexities of Dryden's irony. He has given us a more than clear picture of a stale and unhappy marriage and a marriage arranged for economic convenience. Both are quite unsatisfactory. Yet the ways of the world are not easily changed, and the possessive instinct is not to be dismissed lightly, as Dryden well knew. Nothing in the play suggests that Dry-

---

46. Vernon, "Marriage of Convenience and The Moral Code of Restoration Comedy," p. 377.

den considers women "property." His blatant use of that term may
be a reference to the economic status of women in marriage, but
the thrust of it is a comment on the *selfishness* of man. The clear
implication is that marriage is unsatisfactory but that people must
make the best of what they cannot change. This is more than merely
"cynical": it is sad, serious, and wry, a skeptical and unhappy comment on the human condition. Predictably, the play seems to have
been misunderstood by the Carolean audience, which took the subplot as nothing more than titillation. Joseph Arrowsmith decries
the play for its smuttiness in *The Reformation* (1672?), a delightful
spoof. An anonymous commentator in *Marriage Asserted* (1674)
complains that the audience reveled in the behavior that Dryden
was attempting to satirize.[47]

Fielding's play seems a world away. Certain facts are well established. It ran well in 1732, though it was not revived. It is based
on a real-life episode and is designed as a multipronged satiric attack. The main object is the notorious "crim. con." law which allowed a husband to mulct for heavy damages anyone he could prove
had cuckolded him.[48] Fielding comments harshly on the husband
who lives on his wife's gifts from her paramour. But what really
disturbs him is the husband who makes money from his wife's
"criminal conversation" with another man—especially when there
is no way to prevent collusion on the part of the husband or even
a frame-up.[49] The husband tolerant of his wife's adultery has a potential political relevance to Sir Robert Walpole—to whom the play
is dedicated, with apparent politeness. Even John Loftis has taken
the dedication straight, but, as J. Paul Hunter has recently sug-

47. See ch. 4, sec. "The Satiric Impact of the Play," above.
48. In legal theory, husband and wife were one person—hence the wife could
not be conceived to "consent" to adultery, and so the husband could sue the man
who cuckolded him for assault or trespass. See Holdsworth, VIII, 430. One of the
ugliest aspects of "crim. con."—not abolished until 1857—was its role in parliamentary divorce. As "conditions precedent" to a parliamentary divorce, a man had *both*
to obtain an ecclesiastical separation *a mensa et thoro* and to "have recovered damages against the adulterer in an action at common law for criminal conversation"
(Holdsworth, *A History of English Law*, I [3rd ed. 1922], 623).
49. For these points see Charles B. Woods, "Notes on Three of Fielding's Plays,"
PMLA, 52 (1937), 359–73.

gested, one might well view this as a sly trick, an apparently innocuous way of bringing the very relevant Walpole to the reader's attention.[50] In Mr. and Mrs. Modern, Fielding certainly gives a pitilessly clear picture of selfish, degraded, and unhappy people. As a negative example of bad marriage, it is quite effective, as is Fielding's protest against "crim. con." The originality and daring of this play are evident if it is compared with a piece like Mrs. Haywood's *A Wife to be Lett* (1723), in which a husband accepts £2,000 for his wife's favors, but she declines to cooperate and sees that the money is returned.

My interest, however, is mainly in Fielding's treatment of Mr. and Mrs. Bellamant. They love each other and their family, and Mrs. Bellamant is clearly a paragon. Her husband, however, has fallen for Mrs. Modern and in his infatuation is lavishing money on her he can ill afford. His infidelity is exposed, but his remorse soon prompts his wife to a generous forgiveness. Charles B. Woods dismisses this story curtly as "extraneous material, which shows the influence of sentimental dramatists like Cibber and Steele." I would not be so hasty. The play seems to make at least three points beyond its attack on "crim. con." First, the bad results of an economic view of marriage are clearly shown. "Your person is mine: I bought it lawfully in the church," snaps Mr. Modern when his wife protests at public exposure for profit (58).[51] "Marriage is traffic throughout; as most of us bargain to be husbands, so some of us bargain to be cuckolds" (35). Second, the evils of a money-based society are detailed: the slimy Lord Richly thinks he can buy even Mrs. Bellamant, an expectation generated by wide experience. Finally, Fielding gives a subtle and convincing psychological portrait of Mr. Bellamant: he is realistic enough to see that a good marriage

50. John Loftis, *The Politics of Drama in Augustan England* (Oxford: Clarendon Press, 1963), p. 130, and J. Paul Hunter, *Occasional Form: Henry Fielding and the Chains of Circumstance* (Baltimore: Johns Hopkins Univ. Press, 1975), pp. 56–57.

51. References are to *The Complete Works of Henry Fielding*, ed. William Ernest Henley, 16 vols. (1903; rpt. New York: Barnes and Noble, 1967), Vol. III. For a general account of Fielding on marriage, see Murial Brittain Williams, *Marriage: Fielding's Mirror of Morality* (University: Univ. of Alabama Press, 1973).

does not preclude infatuation but also that infatuation need not destroy a good marriage.

Reading the play one can scarcely help thinking of *Amelia*. In both works Fielding attempts to convey a clear and unattractive depiction of vice, a warmly attractive picture of virtue, and a sympathetic analysis of human frailty. He is committed to a view of human nature which holds that almost everyone is reclaimable. Here Fielding is a believer, where Dryden is a skeptic. Easy assertions of human goodness and perfectibility are easy to dismiss, while bitter cynicism grounded in unhappy experience is hard to ridicule. Yet is the "sentimental" assumption behind *The Provok'd Husband* or even *The Modern Husband* any less convincing or morally satisfactory than the romance convention which tells us that rakes will stay reformed in Carolean comedy? Unlike Cibber, Fielding waves no magic wand; he would not claim that Vanbrugh's Brutes could make their marriage work. Fielding faces evil squarely—so much so that this play has the reputation of being impossibly unpleasant, degraded, and disgusting. In Lord Richly he gives a far harsher picture of the rake and adulterer than any predecessor save Southerne. The difference lies in what he believes and affirms can work for *some* people.

> *Mr. Gaywit.* My lord, I have had some experience in women, and I believe that I never could be weary of the woman I now love.
>
> *Lord Richly.* Let me tell you, I have had some experience too, and I have been weary of forty women that I have loved. (82–83)

Happiness and virtue are notoriously difficult to make interesting, but here as later Fielding does his best.

The Bellamant plot in *The Modern Husband* expresses a deeply felt ideal, one which appears in various guises in most of the later eighteenth-century marital discord comedies. Hoadly's ever-popular *The Suspicious Husband* (1747), Colman's *The Jealous Wife* (1761), the Teazle plot in Sheridan's *The School for Scandal* (1777) all defend, uphold, and support a positivistic concept of man and marriage which likes to assume that virtue and decency can usually be made to work.[52] This attitude is not, of course, exactly what we expect in "comedy," which by our usual standards should amuse and is best fitted to question, ridicule, and tear down. Just as late seventeenth-century tragedy generally fails to "do" what we want tragedy to do, so eighteenth-century comedies tend to frustrate our expectations. To make serious emotional statements without becoming ponderously preachy requires the genius behind Shakespeare's romantic comedies. Most readers prefer *Tom Jones* to *Amelia*; similarly, they are happier with *The Beggar's Opera* than with *The Modern Husband*. Yet in that play, as in *Amelia*, Fielding attempts a serious affirmation, one not to be dismissed lightly. The humane outlook is not especially amusing, and the conventions of reform comedy now seem as lifeless and simplistic as those of nineteenth-century melodrama. Yet the form seems to have satisfied a real need in its audience. We have ample testimony of the tears with which audiences greeted plays like *The Conscious Lovers* and *The Provok'd Husband*.

By present-day standards, the savage pessimism of Otway and Southerne or the wryly bitter questioning of Vanbrugh are greatly preferable to Cibber's facile resolutions or even Fielding's more realistic optimism. Yet most of us can find attractions in wishful thinking. Optimism can be pleasant indeed in the romance conventions of Congreve's *Love for Love* or the escapism of *The Beaux Stratagem*. All reasonably serious marital discord comedies start from a real and disturbing problem—and because it is real we cannot comfortably accept the tidy solutions eighteenth-century audiences evidently craved. Marital discord comedy is inherently problem comedy. It runs a wide gamut, from the sheer amusement of

52. Hoadly's play is usually treated briefly and dismissively as a sentimental comedy. For sharply differing views of it from two decidedly nonsentimental playwrights, compare Macklin's *The New Play* [*The Suspicious Husband*] *Criticiz'd, or, The Plague of Envy* (1747; Larpent MS no. 64, Huntington Library), a neat job of debunking, with Samuel Foote's sympathetic reaction in *The Roman and English Comedy Consider'd and Compar'd* (London: T. Waller, 1747).

comic strife (as in *The Devil of a Wife*) outward in one direction to satisfying resolution in romance form and on to didactic preachment; in the other direction it runs to satiric deflation of romance convention and on to bleakly powerful portrayals of a marital hell from which there can be no escape.

7

The Multifarious Forms of Eighteenth-Century Comedy

Eighteenth-century comedy is a large and untidy subject—and one that still suffers from the prevalence of misleading and derogatory clichés. Much has been written about a few of the plays and playwrights, some of it quite good. In four important respects, however, scholars are still failing to come to grips with problems inherent in the subject. First, we still lack a satisfactory sense of the structure of the period. The eighteenth century is not, theatrically speaking, an undifferentiated morass. Hence we need to take subperiods into account. Second, our understanding of the various ways in which eighteenth-century writers conceive "comedy" as a genre is fuzzy. Third, the laughing-sentimental terminology which we have inherited is an unsatisfactory way of characterizing the plays of the time. No such dichotomy can validly be drawn: in order to escape the limitations of false categories we need to establish a new terminology—one that fairly represents the aims and potentialities of the plays themselves. Finally, we need to ask just what right we have to treat stage vehicles as printed literature, and on what terms we can safely and profitably do so.

The Structure of the Period

Many scholars have a curiously unstructured concept of the eighteenth century, and Nicoll's generic discussions by half-century have provided minimal help. People have spoken loosely of the neoclassical and preromantic periods, or the Age of Pope and the Age of Johnson—concepts widely employed yet misleading in their simplistic generality. And such designations are no use to the historian of the drama. Fortunately the checkered history of the theatre does provide a reasonably clear sense of both how and why the drama developed as it did. Five fairly distinct phases appear in eighteenth-century drama. They are so obvious that I am almost embarrassed to point them out—but evidently they were not so obvious to scholars who did not have *The London Stage* to draw on, and because no one has yet said the obvious, I will go ahead and do so.

The drama of the first period I have designated "Augustan."[1] Whether this muddy term was the best choice we need not pause to debate. Chronologically, we may say that the first phase comprises the years 1708–28. The closing date is provided by the triumph of *The Beggar's Opera* and the rapid changes it triggered in the London theatre world. The opening date—provided by the new theatrical union decreed by the lord chamberlain—is a little more arbitrary. By 1708 or 1710, however, a basic change has occurred in the norms of the English drama. The hard, satiric, mostly Tory comedy of the Carolean period has gradually given way to something else—a humane and reform-minded comedy whose ideology tends to be more bourgeois and Whig. The change occurs gradually and untidily over a span of nearly thirty years. But by 1708 Congreve, Southerne, and Vanbrugh have fallen silent, and Farquhar (whose career is a minipattern of the change) is dead. The theatre was in an unhealthy state, and even after the permanent reestablishment of a second company in 1714 the managers remained stodgy, careful, and unventuresome. Staging new plays was always an expensive gamble, and in periods of stasis and noncompetition the new plays were few and mostly unexperimental. Thomas Davies tells us that Barton Booth "often declared in public company, that he and his partners lost money by new plays; and that, if he were not obliged to it, he would seldom give his consent to perform one

1. *Development*, ch. 10.

of them." [2] A. H. Scouten observes that "Booth could afford to talk in such a way so long as Nance Oldfield, Wilks, and Cibber were still helping him attract spectators; nevertheless, this attitude meant slow death for the drama." [3] There are fewer interesting plays from this period than from any other time in the century—only the lull that follows the Licensing Act is anything like as bleak. The successful new plays are mostly reprises of the tried and true by professional theatre people such as Cibber, Centlivre, and Charles Johnson.

The second phase is probably best christened the "New Wave" in eighteenth-century drama. It is triggered by the simultaneous triumphs of *The Beggar's Opera* and *The Provok'd Husband* in 1728, which brought about a startling change in the London theatre. The thirties' boom, so maddeningly truncated by the Licensing Act in 1737, reflects a sudden realization that an enormous untapped theatregoing public had grown up in London—and that it could be exploited. An explosion of theatrical activity is the immediate result. Where two companies had been cautiously coexisting we abruptly find four and five groups competing vigorously and successfully, some of them quite ready to offer new and radical plays. [4] Henry Fielding's "off-off Broadway" venture at the Little Theatre in the Haymarket is famous, if not much studied. The big patent houses, inherently conservative, were forced to compete against innovation-minded rivals: the result is a tremendous upsurge in new plays. Few of them are very good. But we must remember that Robert Walpole was able to cut off this movement before it achieved maturity. If the Carolean theatre had been suppressed in 1669—an imaginable supposition—how would we now view the products of its apprentice playwrights? The 1730s writers experiment vigorously in new play types, trying ballad opera, bourgeois tragedy, and topical revues. John Loftis, writing about the New Wave drama from a very different vantage point, sees it as finally displacing and

2. *Memoirs of the Life of David Garrick*, 2 vols. (London: Printed for the Author, 1780), I, 208.
3. *The London Stage*, Part 3, I, cxxxviii–cxxxix.
4. For a discussion, see *The London Stage*, Part 3, I, cxxxix–cxlix, and "The London Theatre from *The Beggar's Opera* to the Licensing Act" (ch. 9 below).

abandoning long-dominant "Restoration stereotypes."[5] The political and social concerns of these writers, and the multiplicity of venues, ought to have produced a glorious period in English drama. Instead, Walpole's intervention produced a profitably conservative theatre and something like a wasteland in new plays.

The third phase (1737–60) we may dub the "Lull," or the "Low Georgian" period. Given a safe monopoly, Covent Garden and Drury Lane took no chances. Shakespeare required no author's benefits and entailed less risk than something new. The greatest demand for fresh work was in afterpieces. Some considerable new plays were mounted—Thomson's *Tancred and Sigismunda* (1745), Hoadly's *The Suspicious Husband* (1747), Home's *Douglas* (1756), some Foote farces, and Garrick's early work—but though the theatres were operating profitably, one senses little vitality in the trickle of new plays. Reflecting on the state of the theatre in the 1750s, George Winchester Stone, Jr., remarks on its "quietness and regularity."[6]

Exactly why the theatre came to life so relatively abruptly circa 1760 we need not inquire here. Signs occur that both dramatists and audience were irked by the lack of new plays and by the complacent enjoyment of the monopoly by the patent theatres.[7] At all events the drama revived somewhat, and the next two decades were to see a remarkable upsurge in dramatic activity, even within the confines of the patent monopoly. This belated Silver Age may be termed the "High Georgian" period. Goldsmith and Sheridan are the luminaries, but as I have shown in detail elsewhere, they actually inherited a flourishing comic tradition.[8] Macklin's *Love a-la-Mode* (1759), Murphy's *The Way to Keep Him* (1760) and *All in the Wrong* (1761), Foote's *The Minor* (1760) and *The Lyar* (1762), Colman's *The Jealous Wife* (1761) and *The Deuce is in Him* (1763), and Garrick and Colman's *The Clandestine Marriage* (1766) are all highly successful laughing comedies that predate the appearance of

---

5. *Comedy and Society*, ch. 5.
6. *The London Stage*, Part 4, II, 741.
7. See ch. 10, sec. "The New Plays, 1759–1773," below.
8. "Goldsmith and Sheridan and the Supposed Revolution of 'Laughing' against 'Sentimental' Comedy" (ch. 10 below).

Goldsmith's *The Good-Natur'd Man* in 1768. These and a flock of
1770s plays have long been well regarded by specialists, but even
among eighteenth-century scholars the curious myth persists that
Goldsmith and Sheridan are an isolated flicker of light in the midst
of numberless and depressing sentimental comedies. In truth this
was an era of good writing and fine acting, and one offering the
scholar-reader many pleasant surprises. And in fairness, one must
say that the example of the *comédie larmoyante*, first really influential in England in the 1760s, stimulates English writers to thought
and experiment, and leads them to attempt more subtle and sympathetic character portrayal.

The High Georgian period has no sharply defined end. One
could point to Garrick's retirement in 1776 as the close of an era,
especially as his departure brought the Sheridan-Linley management into control of Drury Lane. Thomas Harris had taken over as
manager of Covent Garden two years earlier. (Sheridan and Harris
were to dominate management until 1809.) Arbitrarily, one might
point to 1780 as a terminus. By then Garrick, Colman, Macklin,
Foote, Murphy, Goldsmith, and Sheridan himself were dead or
lapsing into silence, and a new generation of writers was taking
over. Holcroft and Inchbald have very different interests and styles.
One could even make a case for concluding the High Georgian period in 1794, when the opening of the mammoth new Drury Lane
playhouse marked the end of the eighteenth-century theatre as Garrick had known it. I prefer to consider the years 1780–94 a fifth
phase, a *fin de siècle* epilogue in which we see a move toward the
norms of the nineteenth century—a move accommodated in the
rebuilding of Covent Garden in 1792 and the construction of Sheridan's Drury Lane. A few figures will show why theatre architecture
had a decided—and unfortunate—influence on comedy. In the late
seventeenth century the Drury Lane theatre probably held no more
than 800 people. In 1733 it was estimated to hold 1,000. By 1790
a series of revampings had expanded the capacity to about 2,300.
The new Drury Lane of 1794 held more than 3,600 people—with
disastrous effects on the audibility of dialogue. Covent Garden was
likewise inflated—from a capacity of some 1,400 in 1732 to about
3,000 in 1792. The Licensing Act prevented the erection of more

theatres, and in consequence the patent houses bloated themselves on their monopoly.[9] Given the difficulty of hearing dialogue clearly in such barns we cannot be surprised that ranting melodrama flourished while wit comedy languished.

The point is obvious. The eighteenth-century theatre is anything but monolithic, and one simply cannot make blanket statements. From the standpoint of the practicing dramatist, different periods offered radically different circumstances and markets. The writer whose every semiprofane wisecrack would be blue-penciled by an efficient and arbitrary censor was not going to indulge in the hijinks of the 1730s.[10] And a writer struggling to sell his play to the cautious managers of ever bigger playhouses was well advised to use proven formulas.

Concepts of Comedy

When we ask how "comedy" was conceived in the eighteenth century (leaving subperiod distinctions aside for the moment), we are confronted immediately with a conceptual difficulty. Is comedy defined by its subject and its treatment of that subject (as Aristotle suggests) or by an intrinsic structure—a movement from adversity to prosperity (as Northrop Frye tells us)—or by reference to its designed effect upon an audience (as Samuel Johnson implies when he says that *She Stoops to Conquer* achieved "the great end of comedy—making an audience merry")?[11] Subject is the most common criterion: comedy is "that branch of the drama which adopts a humorous or familiar style, and depicts laughable characters and incidents" (*OED*). But the happy-ending structure is almost always assumed: "a stage-play of a light and amusing character, with a

9. For a discussion of theatre size and finances, see the introductions to the five parts of *The London Stage*, and Harry William Pedicord, *The Theatrical Public in the Time of Garrick* (1954; rpt. Carbondale: Southern Illinois Univ. Press, 1966), ch. 1.

10. For a good account of this subject see L. W. Conolly, *The Censorship of English Drama, 1737–1824* (San Marino: Huntington Library, 1976).

11. Boswell, *The Life of Samuel Johnson*, ed. George Birkbeck Hill and L. F. Powell, II, 233.

happy conclusion to its plot" (*OED*). Johnson's *Dictionary* definition ("A dramatick representation of the lighter faults of mankind") stresses subject and implies moral point. The difficulty of justifying a happy ending for "low" or flawed characters causes eighteenth-century dramatists no end of grief. And the reward of virtue is seldom funny.

A large part of the difficulty is terminological, and reflects confusion about exactly what the critic is trying to define and discuss. Consider M. H. Abrams' well-known account of the elements of criticism. The *world* is selectively imitated by the *author*, who creates the *work*, which affects the *audience*. (In the case of drama we have an added complication: actual performance demands middlemen between work and audience.) An astonishing amount of the criticism devoted to eighteenth-century comedy has focused morbidly and reproachfully on the world-author relationship. Writers are accused of a sentimentalism that falsifies the world they show and leaves the resulting work a saccharine invitation to tears and empathy. Though "sentimental" comedy is always assumed to be affective in design, most studies have treated it as a result—a deplorable result—of the author's world view. The concept of authorial benevolence is central to Bernbaum's seminal interpretation. He tells us that the drama of sensibility "implied that human nature, when not, as in some cases, already perfect, was perfectible by an appeal to the emotions. . . . It wished to show that beings who were good at heart were found in the ordinary walks of life." [12] Such ideological study can certainly be valid and fruitful. One should not, however, take the *work-audience* relationship for granted. This is especially true in works written for a conservative commercial theatre. I shall try to pay the *work-audience* relationship proper attention in the final section of this essay. At the moment I merely want to make the point that eighteenth-century theorists seldom get beyond claiming that comedy should amuse its audience—or objecting to the inadequacy of such a view. Some of the objectors

12. Ernest Bernbaum, *The Drama of Sensibility* (1915; rpt. Gloucester: Peter Smith, 1958), p. 10.

assume that vice should be lashed; others that reform should be shown, or virtue exhibited and rewarded. A moment's reflection will tell you that no one concept of comedy could possibly encompass such diverse ends.[13]

What aims do eighteenth-century writers consider open to the author of comedies? At the beginning of the century a remarkable spread of possibilities finds critical warrant. The writer "could evoke anything between contempt and admiration for the lead characters; emphasize plot, character, or discourse; and work with radically different balances of wit, humour, satire, and example."[14] At any point during the century one can more or less duplicate this spread of views. Early in the period Addison calls ridicule "trivial" and argues that it is often used "to laugh men out of virtue" (*Spectator* no. 249), though Francis Hutcheson—a follower of Shaftesbury— accepts ridicule as a positive moral force.[15] Traditional views by no means disappear in the course of the century. William Cooke considers comedy a means for curing vice by ridicule—a commonplace in magazine commentary right into the nineteenth century. [16]

Eighteenth-century pronouncements on comedy are complicated by two major changes. First, as Draper and Gray correctly observe, writers come increasingly to "make character the essence of comedy."[17] This is true both in theory and in practice. Plot is treated as secondary. A concomitant rise in concern for "passion" encourages the rise of highly emotional *drames* and melodramas in the second half of the century. But what is the author to do with

---

13. I have demonstrated this point at length in "Some Problems in the Theory of Comedy," *Journal of Aesthetics and Art Criticism*, 31 (1972), 87–100.

14. *Development*, p. 62. For a detailed survey of theories of comedy, 1660–1710, see ch. 2.

15. *Reflections upon Laughter* (Glasgow: R. Urie for D. Baxter, 1750), pp. 32–36.

16. *The Elements of Dramatic Criticism* (London: Kearsly and Robinson, 1775), p. 145.

17. John W. Draper, "The Theory of the Comic in Eighteenth-Century England," *Journal of English and Germanic Philology*, 37 (1938), 207–23; quotation from p. 218. Charles Harold Gray, *Theatrical Criticism in London*, p. 19. On the presentation of character in this drama the reader may wish to consult Joseph W. Donohue, Jr.'s excellent *Dramatic Character in the English Romantic Age*.

his characters? The more prominent they are in his design, the more we need to know how the author regards them. The second change, a much more visible one, comes in the way characters are viewed. Edward Niles Hooker long ago pointed out that in the Restoration period "Humours . . . were follies and vices to be lashed. Though the term *humour* occurred in diverse senses during the lifetime of Dryden, still the thing in whatever guise was likely to provoke a single attitude: disapproval or contempt." [18] As Hooker noted, this attitude was changing even by 1700. Increasing sympathy for singularity and eccentricity breeds a gentler view of potential objects of ridicule. The "mighty chasm" that yawns between Swift and Sterne has been well studied by Stuart M. Tave in *The Amiable Humorist*, and the whole shift from hostile to sympathetic humor needs no recounting here.

The effect of this enormous change in sensibility is still underestimated and misunderstood. Tave was little concerned with the drama, and in part we may agree with Hooker's observation that comedy failed "to adapt itself to the new interests of the age." That Tave has to take his illustrations from art and the novel does tell us something about the drama. Theorists of comedy (as opposed to theorists of humor) stuck doggedly to the notion of ridiculing vice and folly, and to a remarkable degree writers of comedies persist in "satirizing" stock figures. The jealous husband or lover, the fop, the miser, the social climber, the country booby—all offer easy and inviting targets. But there is seldom any bite to such portrayals, which are "satire" only in a technical sense. By late seventeenth-century standards practically every writer of comedy after 1740 is "sentimental"—not because they all accept benevolent Shaftesburyite principles, or aim to evoke tears (few do), but because of a more subtle and more pervasive change in prevalent views of humours and human nature.

The chasm that yawns between Swift and Sterne likewise separates Goldsmith and Sheridan from their seventeenth-century fore-

18. "Humour in the Age of Pope," *Huntington Library Quarterly*, 11 (1948), 361–85; quotation from p. 363.

bears. One simply does not find in eighteenth-century comedy the sort of harsh, ugly, bitter criticism of society and the human condition which is to be found in the comedies of Otway and Southerne. An Aristotelian traditionalist like Thomas Twining can say in 1789 that comedy is to ridicule vicious characters,[19] but in practice this means no more than potshots at long-established sitting ducks. Foote, Murphy, and Macklin can occasionally muster some sting, but most writers—Goldsmith and Sheridan included—are robustly genial, even about their "satirized" characters. Mrs. Hardcastle is not a portrait etched in venom, nor is Lady Sneerwell.

To confuse amiable humor and "sentimentalism" is a terrible mistake. And neither can be equated with the "exemplary" bent that underlies Steele's theory of comedy.[20] I will try to sort out some of the differences in practice in the next section. The point I am trying to insist upon here is twofold. Theorists are chaotically diverse in their prescriptions—and practice by no means tidily illustrates theories. Horace Walpole's "Thoughts on Comedy" (completed about 1786) shows us the grab bag nature of thinking on the subject. Walpole likes "genteel" upper-class comedy; subordinates plot to character; can be very fussy about the working out of the "moral," but thinks *The Alchemist* Jonson's best comedy; likes the satire of *The Double-Dealer*, but delights in the feeling of *The Careless Husband*. Walpole diverges from popular taste in his scorn for obvious butts: "A Scot, an Irishman, a Mrs. Slipslop, can always produce a laugh, at least from half the audience."[21] The diversity of possibilities is evident. And whatever anyone thought comedy should be or do, William Jackson is very much to the point when he observes near the end of the century that comedies are merely amalgams of stage conventions.[22] What kinds of results such amalgamation could produce is the problem to which we must now address ourselves.

19. *Poetics of Aristotle* (London: Payne, 1789), Part I, Section viii.

20. See Shirley Strum Kenny, "Richard Steele and the 'Pattern of Genteel Comedy,'" *Modern Philology*, 70 (1972), 22–37.

21. "Thoughts on Comedy," in *The Idea of Comedy*, ed. W. K. Wimsatt (Englewood Cliffs: Prentice Hall, 1969), p. 203.

22. *Thirty Letters*, 3rd ed. (London: T. Cadell, 1795), Letter no. 14.

The Changing Play Types

Discussions of eighteenth-century comedy have long been haunted by the peculiar idea that "sentimental" comedy overwhelmed and suppressed the "laughing" comedy tradition inherited from the seventeenth century. So fine a scholar as John Harold Wilson states that at the end of the seventeenth century, comedy "turned, like a penitent prodigal, to the comedy of tears." Writing in 1974 A. Norman Jeffares tells us that in the eighteenth century "cynicism bowed to sententiousness, worldly wit gave way to worthy wisdom, and the comedy of sex was completely swamped by a flood of sentimentality." Kenneth Muir says flatly that "when we come to the middle of the century . . . the new plays were all sentimental."[23] Such views are not tenable. Twenty years ago Arthur Sherbo provided statistics from Genest to prove the overall dominance of laughing comedy—results decisively confirmed by *The London Stage*.[24]

The whole concept of sentimental comedy is in fact merely a distraction and a red herring. Anyone who has read a reasonable number of the plays usually dubbed sentimental knows that in fact they are too disparate to constitute a definable genre. To imagine that there is "something absolute" to define—a type which exists as a kind of Platonic form—is unsound and unhelpful, as John Loftis notes in a review of Sherbo's *English Sentimental Drama*.[25] None of the categories into which one can put eighteenth-century comedies remotely approaches the absolute. But granting this, we will want to find categories that overlap as little as possible. On this ground we may conclude that Nicoll's long-influential choices are unsatisfactory.

Nicoll divides eighteenth-century comedy into 1) comedy of manners, 2) comedy of intrigue, 3) comedy of humour, 4) comedy of sensibility—dubbed "sentimental comedy" in his account of the second half of the century, and 5) farce. Shakespearean adaptations

23. John Harold Wilson, *A Preface to Restoration Drama* (1965; rpt. Cambridge: Harvard Univ. Press, 1968), p. 129. A. Norman Jeffares, ed., *Restoration Comedy*, 4 vols. (London: Folio Society, 1974), I, xx. Kenneth Muir, *The Comedy of Manners* (London: Hutchinson, 1970), p. 156.

24. Sherbo, *English Sentimental Drama*, ch. 7.

25. *Modern Language Notes*, 74 (1959), 447–50.

and ballad opera he sets in separate categories altogether. The problems are obvious. As Stone observes, "Shakespearean, humours, manners, intrigue, and sentimental prove categories of some use—yet what comedy of sentiment fails to call heavily upon intrigue and manners to make it go at all?"[26] As Stone says, one may dub *The Clandestine Marriage* a comedy of manners for its satire on Lord Ogleby and the Sterlings, or a comedy of sentiment for its use of Fanny. Any decision is arbitrary. Most twentieth-century writers call *The Provok'd Husband* a sentimental comedy, yet to Samuel Johnson it seemed one of the best laughing comedies of the century. Nor should we forget that a "comedy of manners" can be as harshly critical as Fielding's *The Modern Husband* or as warmly affectionate as Goldsmith's *The Good-Natur'd Man*. A ballad opera may be as tart as *The Beggar's Opera* or as saccharine as Bickerstaff's *The Maid of the Mill*.

Messy borderlines are one thing; fundamental vagueness about categorization quite another. A large part of Nicoll's problem is that some of his distinctions are based on subject (manners, humours, intrigue—or source!), others on treatment (pathetic or musical), which are altogether different matters. More than thirty years ago John Harrington Smith tried to escape such tangles, and simultaneously free himself from the bogs of sentimentalism, by describing the change in drama between 1675 and 1710 as a transition from "cynical" to "exemplary" comedy. His study remains one of the best treatments of this drama ever written, but though it is useful, the concept of exemplary comedy is much too narrow to serve as a characterization of eighteenth-century practice in general. To say that "comedy should devote itself to recommending . . . higher ideals by framing characters who . . . exemplify them and by punishing or chastening their opposites"[27] describes well the *modus operandi* of what I am about to define as reform and exemplary comedy, but is largely irrelevant to a majority of the plays in the period. And the distinction between positive example and reform is one that seemed important to Steele—rightly so, for very differ-

26. *The London Stage*, Part 4, I, clxi.
27. *The Gay Couple*, ch. 8, esp. p. 226.

ent kinds of plays and characters can be involved. The difference is obvious when one compares the treatment of an errant wife in Charles Johnson's *The Masquerade* (1719) with the didactic display of exemplary propriety in *The Conscious Lovers* (1722).

To find descriptive terms that will work satisfactorily we need to look for a single basis on which to determine them. To look simultaneously at subject and at treatment simply breeds confusion. My very modest proposal is that we abandon the world-author nexus for the moment and turn instead to the work-audience relationship. Comedies are designed to elicit a reaction: let us categorize them on that basis. For the Augustan period we might divide as follows.

Type	Reaction to be elicited	Example
Farcical	Amused contempt; benevolent indifference	Johnson's *Love in a Chest* (1710)
Satiric	Superiority; disdain	Baker's *The Fine Lady's Airs* (1708)
Humane	Benevolent good will	Centlivre's *The Busie Body* (1709)
Reform	Strong approval; relief	Johnson's *The Generous Husband* (1711)
Exemplary	Outright admiration	Steele's *The Conscious Lovers* (1722)

A few notes and observations are in order. Both satiric and genuinely exemplary comedy are a rarity between 1708 and 1728. Bits of satire may be found in some farces—*Three Hours After Marriage*, for example—and in many of the humane comedies that are the norm in this period. By contrast with the "hard" Carolean comedy, almost all of these works are "soft." One may quibble over whether a given Centlivre play is humane or reform comedy, but in comparison with the norms of 1675 a decisive shift has occurred. Obviously a given play may comprise plot lines that would be classified differently. In *The Provok'd Husband* the Townly plot is a high-life reform; the Lady Grace–Manly plot is purely exemplary;

and the Wronghead plot is a sharp satire on country "gentry." Because reform is a crucial part of the two most conspicuous story lines, it seems to me to characterize the play.

The principal types of Augustan comedy are humane and reform. Humane comedy is the dominant type right through to 1780.[28] After that, under increasing pressure from musical comedy, it gradually evaporates and changes. Its humorous and farcical elements are carried on in the afterpiece tradition, and its more serious concern with its characters is absorbed into serious comedy and the *drame*. Humane comedy is characterized by its essential good humor, even where it is satiric. As an extreme instance of the contrast we may take *The Country Girl*, Garrick's 1766 adaptation of Wycherley's *The Country-Wife* (1675). Wycherley's play leaves the impression that the author is showing up the hypocrisy dominating London life: Margery learns that lying is necessary to survival. Garrick's version leaves the audience to delight in a traditional romantic plot in which youth and love triumph over age and avarice. Unlike the old "hard" comedy of the Carolean period, the humane comedy never presents bitter or cynical acceptance of an unsatisfactory status quo. Even *The Beggar's Opera*, with its strong satiric leanings, has no essential bite and ugliness. Its incipient despair is offset by an essentially comic perspective. The indignation and contempt which Southerne, Wycherley, or even Congreve can elicit is lacking. This distinction need not imply a value judgment. Cynicism can be cheap and true humanity profoundly moving. To take noncontroversial instances we might contrast the raucous political satire of *Eastward Hoe!* with the blithe pastoralism of *As You Like It*.

The Beaux Stratagem (1707) is a quintessential example of humane comedy. Its sunny country air and affectionate treatment of its characters put it a world away from *The Country-Wife* or *The Souldiers Fortune*. Aimwell's celebrated *volte-face* and confession

28. I should explain that I am employing the term "humane" in a sense slightly different than that proposed by Shirley Kenny in her "Humane Comedy" essay. Her definition is postulated on matters of character, dialogue, and plot; mine on reaction elicited. And she considers substantially all early eighteenth-century comedies humane, including those I define as reform and exemplary types. I agree that vis-à-vis Carolean norms all of these plays may be called humane, but beyond that basic distinction my reform and exemplary categories are designed to supply necessary subdivisions.

in Act V have been denounced as sentimental mush, and the fairy-tale solution of genuine and ugly marital problems between the Sullens removes any semblance of social realism. But do we want to see something else happen? I think not. Centlivre's long-popular *The Busie Body* (1709) is an excellent illustration of a play whose characters and plot devices simulate those of Carolean plays, but whose cheery high spirits rob it of the gritty ugliness an earlier writer might have found in similar elements. Addison's *The Drummer* (1716) was considered an important sentimental comedy by French and German writers later in the eighteenth century,[29] but has been largely ignored in this century. The play is in fact an enjoyable and farcical romp, set off from other such works only by the seriousness and affection with which Addison presents Sir George Truman (presumed dead), his loyal wife, and his devoted steward, Vellum. Such sentiment as the play may be said to possess consists in genuinely virtuous characters and a lack of "studied Similes and Repartees," as Steele terms them in his 1716 preface. The joking use of a fake ghost, and the gusto of Addison's satire on the fortune-hunting Tinsel, give the play a tone far from the saccharine ponderousness one might expect from most critics' dismissive descriptions. Three of the characters are exemplary, but by no means is this a sentimental play in the terms defined by Sherbo: it does not exaggerate sentiment or invite excessive emotional response from the audience.

Critics have often called humane comedies sentimental if the successful denouement relies on the voluntary yielding of the blocking figure. Colman and Garrick's *The Clandestine Marriage* (1766) is an excellent illustration of such a case. If Lord Ogleby's heart were not genuinely and honorably touched by Fanny, he would not intervene to set all right. Critics often ridicule such presumption of the essential goodness of the human heart (to paraphrase Bernbaum)—but are we to assume that the illustration of disinterested feeling automatically renders a play contemptible? Or even sentimental? Surely the way in which the author uses this feeling to affect the audience is a far more significant indicator of the nature

29. See Nicoll, II, 199.

of his play. John Kelly's *The Married Philosopher* (1732) has a design very similar to Garrick and Colman's play, and has likewise been condemned for sentimentality. Young Bellefleur's firmness and nobility under the threat of disinheritance by his ranting uncle is the sort of thing people sneer at in Cumberland, and the uncle's giving way at the end, though not pat, does presume some essential decency. But the play as a whole, despite its over-long speeches, presents lively contretemps and amusing characters.

The conventions of the humane comedy, and the ways it could be viewed in its own day, are well summed up in Dr. Benjamin Hoadly's *The Suspicious Husband* (1747) and the controversy it stirred.[30] Almost always dismissed as sentimental, this immensely popular play is full of racy intrigue, bedroom encounters, and bawdy propositions. Mr. Strictland's jealousy is sharply satirized, but Ranger's exuberant womanizing is left unpunished. At the play's end he remains an "extravagant rake" on the loose. Hoadly leaves no doubt that Ranger's dissipated ways are foolish and unsatisfying—indeed he has Ranger tell us so in the soliloquy with which he opens the play. "Let me reflect a little—I have set up all Night. I have my Head full of bad Wine, and the Noise of Oaths, Dice, and the damn'd tingling of Tavern Bells; my Spirits jaded, and my Eyes sunk into my Head: and all this for the Conversation of a Company of Fellows I despise. . . . Honest *Ranger*, take my word for it, thou art a mighty silly Fellow."

Steele might have suggested that Ranger be brought to an appropriate state of penitence, and rewarded with a virtuous heiress.[31] Hoadly is satisfied to let us enjoy the rake's schemes—frustrating them for the duration of the play—while letting us see that though Ranger is no model, neither is he a liar or a scoundrel. Mrs. Strictland is indeed an exemplary character, and the two pairs of

30. For a hostile contemporary response, see Macklin's *The New Play Criticiz'd* (Huntington Library, Larpent MS no. 64).

31. Foote addresses precisely this point in *The Roman and English Comedy Consider'd and Compar'd*, pp. 29–30. "Could not . . . the Author throw this Youth, in the Course of his Nocturnal Rambles, into some ridiculous Scene of Distress, which might, with Propriety, have reclaim'd him[?]" His reply is that the "amiable Beauties" of Ranger's character allow us to overlook "Blemishes in his Conduct" without tempting us to emulate his follies.

young lovers are virtuous enough, but nothing in the play invites emotional excess. "No Tears, I beg. I cannot bear them" says Mr. Strictland at the height of the reconciliation scene. Garrick, we may note, scored a great and highly profitable triumph in this play— acting the insouciant Ranger. And it appears that the author had the actor in mind when he wrote the part.[32]

If a basic dichotomy is to be drawn, it must rest not on the presence of virtuous characters but rather on the kind of action presented and the sort of response it seems designed to elicit. The standard pattern of the humane comedy generally involves a romance plot. Reform comedy most often presents a marital situation. In the case of *The Suspicious Husband* we do see a satire on jealousy, concluded with the cure of the offending party. One might say the same of a great many "Restoration" comedies, which conclude with the rake mending his ways and receiving his heiress. In most such cases, however, the reform is essentially *pro forma*. What makes the end of Shadwell's *The Squire of Alsatia* (1688) remarkable, and prophetic of eighteenth-century forms, is the serious didactic and emotional weight placed upon the reformation. Plays that make reform prominent and crucial in their basic design seem to me to fall in a special category.

Reform comedy may be as tidily facile as Cibber's *The Careless Husband* or as ponderous and preachily didactic as his *The Lady's last Stake* (1707). Such plays tend to be unrealistically optimistic marital tracts, though Steele's *The Lying Lover* (1703) and Centlivre's *The Gamester* (1705), for example, make similar points in romance plots. Charles Johnson's *The Generous Husband*, *The Wife's Relief*, and *The Masquerade*, and the Cibber-Vanbrugh *Provok'd Husband* are well-known instances of this kind of play. By no means, however, can we say that reform comedy is sentimental comedy, if by that designation we mean a work that presumes the goodness of human nature. Hildebrand Jacob's *The Prodigal Reform'd* (1738; Part 1 of *A Nest of Plays*) is an instructive illustration. Young Severn must be reclaimed from a life of dissipation: fortunately his heart "is yet sound and uncorrupted." Told that his father has died

32. *The London Stage*, Part 3, II, 1287.

at sea and that he is now a pauper, young Severn quickly learns that his loving mistress is a heartless and mercenary whore, his bosom friends a pack of sneering spongers. His distress is of course artificial, and his father soon reappears, bearing a rich heiress. But young Severn has learned his lesson: other people are *not* necessarily as kind, decent, and honest as he is. Quite a sentimental moral! Reform comedy is indeed as various as humane comedy. It grows out of Shadwell's late didactic humours comedies, and in it we may discern the roots of the serious comedy of the latter half of the eighteenth century.

The humane and reform types I have been illustrating are dominant in the Augustan period and indeed persist well into the second half of the century. During the 1730s boom they are joined by a flock of relatively topical political, social, and literary satires—a set of works well illustrated by Fielding's *Historical Register*, *Modern Husband*, and *Author's Farce.*[33] Such works were successfully squelched by Walpole, and throughout the Low Georgian period the standard types are repeated with minor variations. Many of the best plays are afterpiece farces by Foote. In the High Georgian period some alteration in terminology becomes necessary. The influence of *comédie larmoyante* and rising concern with social and moral problems produce plays that cannot always be properly discussed as "comedy." For want of a better term I will refer to the type as "serious comedy," but some account of the checkered history of its classification is necessary to indicate the nature and complexity of the subject.

Serious comedy has been little studied. Many of the relevant

33. Fielding's plays remain astonishingly neglected, in large part because of their social and political topicality. For some account of his comic and satiric theory and strategy, the reader may consult W. R. Irwin, "Satire and Comedy in the Works of Henry Fielding," *English Literary History*, 13 (1946), 168–88; A. E. Dyson, "Satiric and Comic Theory in Relation to Fielding," *Modern Language Quarterly*, 18 (1957), 225–37; William B. Coley, "The Background of Fielding's Laughter," *English Literary History*, 26 (1959), 229–52; J. Paul Hunter, *Occasional Form: Henry Fielding and the Chains of Circumstance*, chs. 2 and 3; Jean B. Kern, "Fielding's Dramatic Satire," *Philological Quarterly*, 54 (1975), 239–57; and Jack D. Durant, "The 'Art of Thriving' in Fielding's Comedies," *A Provision of Human Nature: Essays on Fielding and Others*, ed. Donald Kay (University: Univ. of Alabama Press, 1977), pp. 25–35.

plays have been called sentimental, and most students of sentimental drama have been hostile to it. Indeed one of the best of them, Arthur Sherbo, says explicitly that sentimental drama "is a debased literary genre": consequently his whole study is a history of what he terms artistic degeneracy. Nicoll (whose categories Sherbo follows) is almost alone in trying to discern subtypes in sentimental comedy—surely a necessary proceeding, when we consider the diversity of the works so categorized. It is evident, he says, "that three distinct tendencies are to be traced in the comic literature of this type. There are the relics of the Cibberian Genteel comedy. . . . there is the often mawkishly pathetic theatre of Cumberland, intent upon raising a sigh and calling forth a tear; and there is the more revolutionary humanitarian drama which is seen at its best in the plays of Mrs. Inchbald and of Thomas Holcroft."[34]

This division seems awkward and incomplete. To begin with, the whole idea of "genteel comedy"—plays that depict the manners and conversation of an upper-class world—is muddled and largely irrelevant. Many critics assume that a genteel comedy must be an exemplary comedy. This assumption is easy to make for several reasons. Traditional comedy invites us to laugh at or despise low characters. Presented with graceful, witty, often wealthy persons of rank, we tend to be favorably impressed and take them as models. Steele certainly suggests in *Spectator* no. 65 that this is what happens when we see a Dorimant in *The Man of Mode*, and he bitterly denounces the play as a tempting picture of an altogether false ideal. Horace Walpole, for whom the play "shines as our first genteel comedy," reminds us that "when Addison [to whom he attributed *Spectator* no. 65] . . . anathematised this play, he forgot that it was rather a satire on the manners of the court, than an apology for them."[35] As Walpole suggests, genteel comedy must thus be distinguished from exemplary. As the class, wealth, and gentility of the characters rise, we cannot easily view them as we do the rogues of Alsatia—but we are not to presume that the author is giving us a model. *The Man of Mode*, *The Careless Lovers*, and *The Conscious*

34. Nicoll, III, 153–54.
35. "Thoughts on Comedy," p. 198.

Lovers are all genteel comedies—and they are, respectively, satiric, reform, and exemplary comedy. "Genteel" refers to subject and presentation, not to designed response, and is therefore not a category in the classification I am proposing.

Nicoll's second category—the "mawkishly pathetic theatre of Cumberland"—is both unduly hard on that much abused writer and simplistic, for it runs together emphasis on delicate feelings (of the sort used and satirized by Hugh Kelly) and the use of distress to evoke suspenseful empathy—the basis for what becomes the nineteenth-century *drame*. Nicoll's third category—humanitarian drama—again confounds semidistinct types, running together the moral and social concerns that seem to me to separate a play like Holcroft's *Duplicity* from Inchbald's *Every One Has His Fault*.

The inadequacy of traditional terminology is manifest. We may even ask whether reform and exemplary plays, past a certain point, are properly to be discussed as comedy at all. To move the pity and empathy of the audience—let alone its admiration—is sufficiently distinct from the traditional aims of comedy conceived in Aristotelian terms to make the resulting works essentially distinct in kind. If we appeal to the plays of Shakespeare, a theorist like Elder Olson will tell us that *As You Like It*, *Twelfth Night*, and even *Much Ado* are not comedies but romances.[36] The influence of *comédie larmoyante* after 1760 is a further complication. Earlier writers sometimes speak with pride of eliciting tears from an audience, but the sensibility to be found in the plays of Frances Sheridan, Hugh Kelly, and Cumberland is new and distinctive. Their work blurs the differences in subject and sensibility which separate comedy from tragedy—and it definitely aroused the hostility of writers with more traditional views of comedy. Goldsmith and Sheridan, among others, do certainly react against a heavy emphasis on sensibility, a reaction perhaps most delightfully embodied in Foote's *The Handsome Housemaid; or, Piety in Pattens* (1773).[37]

36. *The Theory of Comedy* (Bloomington: Indiana Univ. Press, 1968).
37. Extant as Larpent MS no. 346 and Folger MS D.a.48. First printed by Samuel N. Bogorad and Robert Gale Noyes in *Samuel Foote's "Primitive Puppet-Shew" Featuring "Piety in Pattens": A Critical Edition*, published as a special issue of *Theatre Survey*, 14 (1973), no. 1a.

English theorists never altogether caught up with the developments of theatrical practice, but Diderot offers us some useful distinctions in his essay "On Dramatic Poetry" attached to *Le Père de famille* (1758). "Gay comedy . . . has for its object ridicule and vice; serious comedy . . . has for its object virtue and the duties of man." To these types he adds tragedy dealing with domestic affliction and that grander tragedy that presents "public catastrophes." [38] Diderot's defense of *comédie sérieuse* is impassioned. He urges the attractions of serious concernment with the subject on the part of the audience, and emphasizes sincerity, sensitivity, and the goodness of human nature. We need not suppose, however, that only a benevolist can write *comédie sérieuse*. The association of eighteenth-century "sentimental" comedy with belief in the goodness of human nature is a matter of fact, but Diderot makes a terribly obvious point: comedy and tragedy are not absolutes. In *Le Fils naturel* he attempted to write a drama "between comedy and tragedy": in *Le Père de famille* he splits the difference between that midpoint and comedy.[39] One can easily find English precedent for late eighteenth-century ventures into *comédie sérieuse*. A number of late seventeenth-century plays merely designated "A Play" on the title page anticipate this pattern. Southerne's *The Disappointment* (1684) and Durfey's *The Banditti* (1686) are obvious examples. Despite this early move to get away from the designation "comedy," no satisfactory terminology evolved by which the efforts of serious but nontragic dramatists could be properly distinguished.

Had Horace Walpole's little essay possessed the catchiness of Goldsmith's, our inherited views of eighteenth-century comedy might be very different indeed—and a good deal more in line with reality. Walpole fully comprehends the difference between what he terms "merry comedy" and "serious comedy," pointing to *Le Misan-*

38. Denis Diderot, "On Dramatic Poetry," appendix to *Le Père de famille* (1758). Translation by John Gaywood Linn in *Dramatic Essays of the Neoclassic Age*, ed. Henry Hitch Adams and Baxter Hathaway (New York: Columbia Univ. Press, 1950), pp. 348–59.

39. Burgoyne's popular *The Heiress* (1786) is a lightened adaptation of this play. In type it is really more a humane than a serious comedy, but its style delighted the fastidious Horace Walpole, who declared it "the best modern comedy" (Letter to Lady Ossory, 14 July 1787).

thrope as "a pattern" for the latter. Sentimental comedy—or as he specifically calls it, *comédie larmoyante*—Walpole understands as a deliberate attempt to create a new, intermediate form.

> I do not take the *comédie larmoyante* to have been so much a deficience of pleasantry in its authors, as the effect of observation and reflection. Tragedy had been confined to the distresses of kings, princesses, and heroes; and comedy restrained to making us laugh at passions pushed to a degree of ridicule. . . . I should therefore think that the first man who gave a *comédie larmoyante*, rather meant to represent a melancholy story in private life, than merely to produce a comedy without mirth. If he had therefore not married two species then reckoned incompatible, that is tragedy and comedy, or, in other words, distress with a cheerful conclusion; and instead of calling it *comédie larmoyante*, had named his new genus *tragédie mitigée*, or, as the same purpose has since been styled, *tragédie bourgeoise*; he would have given a third species to the stage.[40]

Some forty years ago Fred O. Nolte argued that pathetic comedy and domestic tragedy are both parts of a *drame bourgeois* movement which grew throughout Europe during the eighteenth century.[41] I am suspicious of the tidiness of Nolte's ideas about evolution, but his perspective does put *comédie sérieuse* in more comfortable company than it usually enjoys. Voltaire, Kotzebue, and Lessing (who was quite hostile to *pathetic* comedy) make more interesting comparisons for Cumberland and Holcroft than do some of their English contemporaries.

If we ask what types are commonly tried in the High Georgian and *fin de siècle* periods, we will see that though the English drama has changed slowly, the change is real. Farce, satiric, and humane comedy are all flourishing (examples are *Piety in Pattens*, Murphy's *The Way to Keep Him*, and Burgoyne's *The Heiress* respectively). However, in place of the reform and exemplary categories which

40. "Thoughts on Comedy," p. 204.
41. *The Early Middle Class Drama (1696–1774)*, New York University Ottendorfer Memorial Series of Germanic Monographs, no. 19 (Lancaster, Pa.: no publisher, 1935).

suffice early in the century, we must distinguish at least four types of English *comédie sérieuse*.

Type of serious comedy	Emotion sought	Example
Drama of sensibility	Exhibition of genteel feeling to rouse delicate empathy	Inchbald's *Lovers' Vows* (1798)
Pathetic drama	Happy-ending exhibition of distress to rouse suspenseful empathy	Holcroft's *The Deserted Daughter* (1795)
Moral melodrama	Exhibition of folly or error to rouse didactic distress	Holcroft's *The Road to Ruin* (1792)
Humanitarian problem drama	Exhibition of social problems to rouse didactic empathy	Cumberland's *The Jew* (1794)

There are two basic tendencies within serious comedy. They are not mutually exclusive, but as a rule one or the other predominates. One is a stress on feelings (whether pathos in *The Deserted Daughter* or generosity in *The West Indian*); the other is a drive toward the arousal of an explicitly moral response. The difference is well illustrated in a comparison of Edward Moore's *The Gamester* (1753; technically a bourgeois tragedy) with Holcroft's *Duplicity* (1781), a work that, as its author admits in his preface, is significantly indebted to Moore's play. What one remembers about *The Gamester* is the harrowing misery of Beverley and his wife. They are made sympathetic characters, and though one certainly recognizes Beverley's culpability, one cannot help sympathizing with him in his woe. Upon reflection one may indeed conclude that gambling is bad, but the play itself is a vehicle for the presentation of affecting distress. In *The British Theatre* Mrs. Inchbald severely criticizes it on precisely these grounds. To make gambling repulsive, she says, Moore should have made his gamester not "an object of pity" but one "of detestation." [42] Holcroft contrives a happy ending after teaching his gamester a lesson. (In design his play is very close indeed to Mrs. Centlivre's *Gamester* of 1705, itself indebted to Shirley's *Gamester* of 1633. *Plus ça change* . . .) Holcroft leaves us good will toward the erring Sir Harry Portland, but he is careful not to distract our attention from the potentially dire results of the vice he is attacking. Because of the rather gratuitous demise of Beverley we must call Moore's play a bourgeois tragedy—but the difference we see here is between pathos and what Dougald MacMillan has termed sentimental satire.

The rise of the social form of serious comedy is a crucial factor in differentiating the dominant type of the High Georgian period from that of the *fin de siècle* years. This rise of "social" concern in comedies usually dismissed as sentimental has been well discussed by Dougald MacMillan in an important and neglected article. [43] "The course of serious comedy, however, began to turn more and more toward the representation of situations and persons from everyday life. The tone of genteel sensibility characteristic of Kelly and the sentimental pathos played up by Cumberland . . . *began to give place to an attitude of sentimental satire*, if such a term can be used."

This point, implicit in Nicoll's excellent account of Mrs. Inchbald, is of great importance for any true understanding of the so-called sentimental comedy. In the work of Inchbald, Holcroft, and Frederick Reynolds (to cite the best-known cases) we see serious criticism of genuine social and moral evils. Critics' reluctance to concede much merit to these works seems odd, when one considers the relative esteem in which Kotzebue's problem plays are held. The sentimental satire on which many of the serious comedies rely has been little studied and poorly understood. By the standards of those accustomed to the angry, biting satire of Wycherley, Otway, or

42. Elizabeth Inchbald, ed., *The British Theatre*, Vol. 14 (London: Longman, 1808).

43. "The Rise of Social Comedy in the Eighteenth Century," *Philological Quarterly*, 41 (1962), 330–38. Quotation from page 336, italics added. MacMillan was evidently unaware of Nolte's study, which covers some of the same ground.

Southerne, or the witty, cutting criticisms of Congreve or Vanbrugh, sentimental satire seems ponderous and preachy. Satire that
lacks the spice of "Tory gloom" disconcerts us: the sentimental satirists are basically optimists about human nature, however severely
they show up vice and evil.

Why did the lighter forms of mainpiece comedy languish toward the end of the century? A large part of the answer lies in the
tremendous appeal of musical comedy. Ballad opera enjoyed a major revival in the 1760s, and the concomitant rise of the burletta
gave legitimate comedy stiff competition. The direction in which
audience taste was tending is obvious in figures supplied by Charles
Beecher Hogan.[44] Of the twelve most frequently staged mainpieces
in the years 1776–1800, four were Shakespeare plays (*Hamlet,
Macbeth, The Merchant of Venice,* and *Romeo and Juliet*). Only
two were contemporary legitimate comedies: Sheridan's *The School
for Scandal,* and Hannah Cowley's *The Belle's Stratagem* (1780).
The other six (in descending order of popularity) were all musical comedies of one sort or another: *The Beggar's Opera,* Bickerstaff's *Love in a Village* (1762), Sheridan's *The Duenna* (1775), the
younger Colman's *Inkle and Yarico* (1787), the elder Colman's *The
Spanish Barber* (1777), and Cobb's *The Haunted Tower* (1789).
Caught between the delights of musical comedy and the continuing appeal of farcical afterpieces, traditional mainpiece comedy
stagnated.

At this point we might reflect briefly on the ground just cov-
ered. The account of differing types of serious comedy just concluded should serve as a reminder of precisely what I mean by
"multifarious." Not only are several quite different sorts of comedy
written during each period of the century, but each one has its own
set of diverse potentialities. The long-standing tendency, dictated
by inherited terminology, to categorize plays as laughing or sentimental has largely obscured the diversity of play types actually
common in the period. Within this rather confusing spread of possibilities, however, we find dramatists after the Licensing Act ex-

44. See *The London Stage,* Part 5, I, clxxi–clxxiii.

tremely conservative. Despite the hundreds of new plays, shifts in common types occur so slowly that they are perceptible only when they are considered against at least a decade of time, and often much longer. As Joseph Donohue observes, "the first instinct of the English repertory theatre is to rely on the tried and proven. Its second instinct is to seek out the new, especially if only slightly different. . . . A glance through any season . . . reveals the dominance of the known commodity."[45] Indeed the sheer unoriginality of almost all eighteenth-century comedies is so striking, and the theatrical reasons for it so evident, that we can scarcely avoid inquiring exactly what our knowledge of the theatrical circumstances of these plays should do to our critical perceptions of them.

Visualizing the Plays in Performance

Critics have almost unanimously preferred the harsh, skeptical comedy of the late seventeenth century to the "new" comedy that supplants it. Eighteenth-century comedy is not, on the balance, very "sentimental," though it is good-humored. The dominant humane comedy tradition is definitely grounded, in theory and in practice, in the concept of "laughing" comedy. And though some of the serious comedies do indeed indulge in bathetic emotion, many of the plays of that sort are honest, well-crafted works. The real ground of objection to eighteenth-century comedy is not to sentimentality or false emotion—rather, it is to unimaginative use of stereotyped elements.

Anyone who has read a hundred comedies from the High Georgian period should be painfully aware of just how essentially unoriginal even the plays of Goldsmith and Sheridan prove to be in type, characters, and comic devices. The repertory theatres mounted new plays grudgingly and exercised extreme caution in what they

---

45. *Theatre in the Age of Kean* (Oxford: Blackwell, 1975), p. 84. Donohue provides a useful account of the repertory ca. 1800, explaining the way serious comedy shades into the nineteenth-century melodrama—a subject beyond my scope here.

chose. Of course the Licensing Act is at least partly responsible for the problem. "Great comedy" (in Bonamy Dobrée's phrase)[46] can be hostile, subversive, and genuinely obnoxious to prevailing politics and mores. Scholars long spoke of the Grundyizing effect of the middle-class audience and the censor, but the really influential factor is the restriction to two patent theatres. A smaller, independent theatre could try to cultivate its own audience—perhaps one with minority tastes. The bloated patent houses naturally catered to the taste of the lowest common denominators. Television networks today make a legitimate parallel.

No period produces floods of great works. One may fairly say in defense of eighteenth-century comedy that it offers us many excellent plays of all types—if we are allowed to judge by the standards of the theatre for which they were written. Eighteenth-century comedy is nonelitist, and in truth it is not very literary. Lack of interpretive complexity and profundity characterizes humane comedy, reform comedy, farce, and the various sorts of serious comedy alike—and it has been a perpetual irritant to scholars, who like to be able to get their teeth into something substantial. The delightful farce tradition which flourishes in this period, always alive and well in afterpieces, offers the literary scholar little to do. Farce can be chronicled, and its constituent elements pointed out, but even a Leo Hughes cannot really bring it to life on the page. At the other extreme serious comedy tends to date badly. Social mores and contemporary issues quickly lose their fascination for an audience, especially when handled in a quasi-realistic setting. The very seriousness and realism for which Dougald MacMillan commends late eighteenth-century comedy now work against it. Moral earnestness is no substitute for the delights of literary technique in the eyes of a scholarly interpreter.

We must face an unpalatable fact bluntly. Though there are many fine eighteenth-century comedies of diverse types, interpretive studies of them have usually been depressingly sterile. Most of the comedies simply need no explication—a fact which has left

46. *Restoration Comedy*, ch. 1.

scholars doing the unnecessary, or trying to place comedies in relation to largely imaginary concepts of sentimentalism. The complexities and ambiguities which allow critics to bicker endlessly and
happily over Wycherley and Congreve are lacking even in Goldsmith and Sheridan. Sheridan's language has delighted scholars, partly
because it makes him far more readable than, say, Murphy. But
what else are we to do with Sheridan? He can be praised (falsely)
for returning to Restoration norms, or for doing battle against
overwhelming tides of sentimentalism—and has been, *ad nauseam*.
Heaven knows I do not mean to dispraise Sheridan, whose plays
delight me both as a reader and as a theatregoer. But as a literary
critic I find him an unappealing subject. *The Rivals* is a wonderful
play, and one which has maintained its appeal for me through the
four productions I have seen. But I have no doubt what it "means,"
or how to respond to it. The only really fruitful criticism I have
seen of it is Mark Auburn's, a study that looks to stage history and
promptbooks as a key to possible meanings in performance.[47]

This brings us to a question. To what extent are these plays
properly considered written literature? Certainly they were almost
always published, and the reading public's demand for a popular
play "was virtually inexhaustible," as Hogan remarks.[48] Ten editions of *The Road to Ruin* were called for in 1792; *Lover's Vows*
achieved eleven in 1798. Older plays were steadily reprinted, and
the popularity of Bell's *British Theatre* and other such collections is
solid evidence of the enormous demand for reading texts. Some
authors did revise for publication. The 1710 edition of Congreve
shows a systematic attempt by the author to present his plays in
literary rather than theatrical form. Much later in the century the
availability of Larpent MSS allows us to determine differences between acted and printed texts. Richard Bevis points out, for example, that a great deal of the sentimentalism which clogs Kelly's
The School for Wives (1773) was in fact not spoken in performance, but was evidently considered welcome by the novel readers

47. "The Pleasures of Sheridan's *The Rivals*: A Critical Study in the Light of
Stage History," *Modern Philology*, 72 (1975), 256–71.
48. *The London Stage*, Part 5, I, clxxv.

of the day.[49] We cannot safely assume that what we read in play quartos was always what the audience saw in the theatre.

Despite the obvious popularity of published play texts, most of them now seem to lie pretty dead on the page. This is, I think, a function both of the theatre system that bred them and of the way we go about reading them. The poetic richness of Shakespeare, the plot intensity of Jacobean city comedy, the linguistic polish of Vanbrugh, and the verbal gags of Wilde all work to satisfy the reader. So do the character depths of Ibsen, and Shaw's quasi-novelistic descriptions—the latter obviously designed for reading. But eighteenth-century comedies do not develop the features which make for good reading, and in consequence we see them at a crushing disadvantage.

Just as John Styan would have us visualize Shakespeare in performance, so we need to re-create the circumstances of eighteenth-century theatrical performance as we read. Even many teachers of this drama seem disturbingly vague about the physical characteristics and operation of eighteenth-century playhouses. The way the changeable scenery worked, the size of a particular theatre at a particular date, and the identity of the actors for a given play are facts readily available to anyone.[50] Drury Lane of 1710 is not Drury Lane of 1780, and the importance of understanding the physical characteristics of the theatre is painfully evident if one reads Harley Granville-Barker's hostile and uncomprehending account of Wycherley.[51]

The reader should not forget that the text he is reading was in fact merely the largest element in what often amounted to a variety show. A normal night included preliminary music, a prologue, a mainpiece, entr'acte singing and dancing, and an afterpiece. From

49. *The Laughing Tradition: Stage Comedy in Garrick's Day* (Athens: Univ. of Georgia Press, 1980), pp. 34–39.

50. For help in these realms, see Edward A. Langhans, *Restoration Promptbooks* (Carbondale: Southern Illinois Univ. Press, 1981); Richard Southern, *Changeable Scenery* (London: Faber and Faber, 1952); Donald C. Mullin, *The Development of the Playhouse* (Berkeley: Univ. of California Press, 1970); and Richard Leacroft, *The Development of the English Playhouse* (London: Eyre Methuen, 1973).

51. Harley Granville-Barker, *On Dramatic Method* (1931; rpt. New York: Hill and Wang, 1956), ch. 4.

the very start of the century the managers were forced to supplement dramatic offerings with anything they thought might help the box office take. In April 1703, for example, Drury Lane offered Southerne's popular *Oroonoko* with the following additions:

> ... several Italian Sonatas by Signior Gasperini and others. And a new Entertainment of Instrumental Musick compos'd by Mr. *Keller*, in which Mr. *Paisible*, Mr. *Banister*, and Mr. *Latour* perform some extraordinary Parts on the Flute, Violin, and Hautboy, with several new Dances by Mr. *Du Ruel*, and Mrs. *Campion*. Likewise the famous Mr. *Evans*, lately arriv'd from *Vienna* ... will Vault on the manag'd Horse, where he lyes with his Body extended on one Hand in which posture he drinks several Glasses of Wine with the other, and from that throws himself a Sommerset over the Horses head, to Admiration. (*Daily Courant*)

The atmosphere of the eighteenth-century theatre was closer to Barnum and Bailey than to Bayreuth.

Aware of this carnival atmosphere, the reader should try to see the play as it was originally mounted. We might liken the imaginative effort involved to reading music. A passably skilled musician can "hear" a work in his head as he reads the printed page, even when dealing with a complex orchestral or operatic score. A work like Bach's *Art of the Fugue* has technical fascinations that a Schubert quartet does not, however delightful to hear. But in either case, to enjoy "reading" the work, one must actively re-create the piece. Likewise the reader of a play needs to see and hear, at least in his head. We should block out the action as we go along, moving the actors about, and imagining the costumes and changeable scenery which are so important in this theatre. A reader can "see" stage movements and scene shifts, hear the speeches as they would be spoken, and respond to the personality and technique of well-known and pleasing actors. In a repertory theatre one sees the same actors again and again, and there is a special pleasure in seeing how they will adapt themselves to different roles, and in returning to savor the details of an interpretation one knows well. To read a playtext from this period without an appreciation of the actors who mounted it—and for whom it was usually specifically tailored—is to rob oneself of one of the best ways of understanding the potentialities of the roles.

Know the actors is an excellent piece of advice for readers. Such visualization is of course much easier if one has examples to work with. The cinemagoer who has seen Max von Sydow in a dozen parts has a great advantage in re-creating a sense of the cinematic experience from the scrappy bits of the published screenplay of *The Seventh Seal*. Or consider another parallel. First read the score and libretto of *The Magic Flute*. Then listen to a recording. Then watch the Bergman film two or three times. Then return to the score and libretto. They should come to life. Similarly, when one has seen a fine performer in a shallow role—Martyn Greene as the Lord Chancellor in *Iolanthe*—it should electrify one's sense of the part. We have ample testimony that Garrick did this for a host of roles—Ranger in *The Suspicious Husband* among them.

We cannot bring the eighteenth century back to life, and most of us would not want to. But we can cultivate a sense of theatrical circumstances and a producer's eye. So doing we can understand why these plays worked so well in the theatre—and also help ourselves enjoy them. My final point may prove controversial, but I think it important. To read eighteenth-century comedy without regard for the actors' "subtext" is to leave most of it at an uninteresting level. What we find in these playscripts is seldom profoundly meaningful; rather, we see here vehicles that offer good theatrical potentialities for skilled performers to elaborate on. Literary interpreters must deal with intrinsic and demonstrable meanings. But a performance that does so will be leaden indeed. A production I saw of *The Way of the World* in 1976 was precisely that. It played what was on the page—giving the effect of a note-perfect and quite expressionless musical performance. No competent director would want to restrict his actors to the letter of the page. As readers—not as interpreters—we need to cultivate the kind of imagination which goes into production. Only then will these comedies regain for us the vitality that made them such effective stage vehicles in their own setting.

8

"The World is all Alike": Satire in The Beggar's Opera

The Beggar's Opera has been much enjoyed but imperfectly understood: critics have called it everything from an eighteenth-century *Pinafore* to a harsh and vehement satire. The difficulty of arriving at an accurate characterization is evident in Ian Donaldson's excellent study, in which he concludes that the work is both "a sentimental lollipop" and "a terse social fable."[1] To relish Gay's high spirits and many palpable hits is easier than to explain what the whole business adds up to. Behind the farcical plot are several obvious kinds of appeal—political satire, gibes at Italian opera, the delightfully incongruous combinations of words and tunes, the social mockery, the parody of romance. Almost every critic has been struck by the work's "satiric" character, and most would agree with Edgar Roberts' assertion that "one must remember that it is above all a satire."[2] If this is true—and I agree that it is—then presumably we should be able to say what objects are attacked, how, and to what ends. This turns out to be easier said than done.

What is the point of *The Beggar's Opera*? Is there a point? Is there a "message"? Is there something less conceptually explicit to be "learned"? How should the audience respond to the work? Are

1. *The World Upside-Down*, p. 182.
2. *The Beggar's Opera*, ed. Edgar V. Roberts (Lincoln: Univ. of Nebraska Press, 1969), p. xxvi.

message and tone at odds? Despite some excellent criticism on *The Beggar's Opera* critics remain surprisingly and disconcertingly divided on elementary interpretive problems. Consequently a reinvestigation from a new angle seems in order. The key issue is the standards of judgment that are to be applied to the characters, events, and sentiments of this pseudo-opera. Response to the work must depend heavily on the standards brought to it, since the play itself does not present us with explicit values and judgments. Evidently Gay either assumed that the audience would know what standards to apply (and hence would know how to "read" his inversions), or intended to leave at least some part of his audience puzzled and uneasy. In practice, audiences always seem to have supplied standards of judgment—or to have felt that none were needed. From both internal and external evidence, however, I am going to argue that *The Beggar's Opera* is a more radical and subversive enterprise than any ordinary kind of satire. Whatever Gay and his Scriblerian friends may have thought he was doing, the work became a satire that systematically undercuts itself, and in the process negates the values necessary to serious satire.

Gay's Subject: The Problem of Satiric Objects

If *The Beggar's Opera* is a satire, what does it attack? The assault, such as it is, turns out to be multipronged, and most critics have taken refuge in the multiplicity of the satiric targets. The objects involved are 1) politics, in particular Walpole; 2) Italian opera; 3) literary forms, especially comedy of sentiment, tragedy, and the happy-ending convention in opera; 4) society's structure and conventions. We are left to decide how serious Gay's "attack" is in each case, and whether a quarter scoop from each subject adds up to a whole satire.

The political references need not be demonstrated anew. Our question is their purpose. At one extreme C. F. Burgess argues that the play is an attempt to "indoctrinate" the audience with Tory views couched in an *à clef* satire. According to this reading,

"Newgate" means "Whitehall," Macheath is George II, Lockit is Foreign Minister Townshend, Lucy is the Countess of Suffolk, and Peachum is Walpole—who admittedly appears in other guises as well.[3] The reading is simplistic and procrustean, but it gives us a hypothesis: the object is political indoctrination, with the ultimate hope of seeing the rascals turned out.

An immediate caution should be sounded about such *à clef* identifications. Gay does establish certain linkages: Walpole/ Macheath; Walpole/Peachum; Lucy and Polly and the divas quarrel; Lucy and Polly with Walpole's wife and mistress, and so forth. But whether the characters are meant to be "portraits" is much to be doubted. The general parallels established, Gay seems to have left the rest to the audience's imagination. And as Gagey shrewdly notes, "even Gay may have been surprised at the numerous allusions read indiscriminately into his lines by the contemporary public."[4] Indeed one of the most often-cited "particular hits" has turned out to be no hit at all. The famous quarrel between Walpole and Townshend is described in detail by Schultz and many others as the basis for the "collaring scene" (II, x) between Lockit and Peachum.[5] Alas, the satiric hit is chronologically impossible: *The Beggar's Opera* was premiered in January 1728, and the quarrel occurred in 1729.[6] Let the explicator beware.

Did *The Beggar's Opera* have significant political consequences? Was it meant to? Bertrand Goldgar has refuted D. H. Stevens' claim that Walpole responded to the piece by mobilizing a public relations apparatus. Subsidy of government newspapers and attacks on such opposition journals as the *Craftsman* and *Mist's Journal* seem to have been part of a larger conflict, rather than a

---

3. C. F. Burgess, "Political Satire: John Gay's *The Beggar's Opera*," *Midwest Quarterly*, 6 (1965), 265–76.

4. Edmond McAdoo Gagey, *Ballad Opera* (1937; rpt. New York: Blom, 1968), p. 45. This is a good illustration of the Wallace principle (see ch. 1, above, sec. "Content and the Meanings in Drama").

5. William Eben Schultz, *Gay's "Beggar's Opera": Its Content, History and Influence* (New Haven: Yale Univ. Press, 1923), pp. 186–87.

6. See Jean B. Kern, "A Note on *The Beggar's Opera*," *Philological Quarterly*, 17 (1938), 411–13.

direct response to Gay.[7] The practical results of *The Beggar's Opera* did not go beyond provoking a lot of talk. And whether Gay imagined that more might come of his satire is questionable at best. Stevens very plausibly suggests that the immediate occasion for Gay's political hits in the piece is bitter disappointment on the part of the Tories in 1727 when George II ascended the throne and promptly made his peace with Walpole—thus frustrating Tory hopes for a return to power and patronage. Stevens concludes that Gay "could have no feeling he was altering . . . the course of political events. . . . His motive was revenge, not reform." This is an important conclusion, and one running directly counter to Burgess' hypothesis. There are many punitive hits at Walpole, but they are essentially miscellaneous and incidental to the play as a whole. And Gay does almost nothing actively to promote the Tory cause.

That *The Beggar's Opera* had a political impact cannot be denied. The amount of fuss in the papers is clear proof that people saw the work in political terms—though as Goldgar notes, the government papers took the position that an "innocent" piece had been "explained into a *Libel*" by the opposition press. Walpole cannot have enjoyed the hullabaloo, however, and he was stung enough to ensure that *Polly* remained unacted. Critics sometimes express surprise at this suppression, seeing little in the work of any political import whatever. But as Gagey rightly observes, however free from direct allusion, *Polly* presents Macheath debased into the pirate Moreno—a coward and scoundrel who is deservedly hanged at the end—and "in the popular mind" Macheath "had become fully identified" with Walpole. Further, Macheath's "desertion of Polly, the faithful wife, for the dissolute Jenny Diver could only relate to Walpole's connection with Molly Skerrett."[8] Thus in contemporary eyes *Polly* might seem far from harmless. Whether the hits were more than a casual bit of snide commentary and wishful thinking seems questionable, but the second time around Walpole played safe.

7. David Harrison Stevens, "Some Immediate Effects of *The Beggar's Opera*," *The Manly Anniversary Studies in Language and Literature* [no editor] (Chicago: Univ. of Chicago Press, 1923), pp. 180–89; Bertrand A. Goldgar, *Walpole and the Wits* (Lincoln: Univ. of Nebraska Press, 1976), esp. pp. 69–74.

8. Gagey, p. 51.

To assess the political satire in *The Beggar's Opera* fully we need to ask just how specific the attacks are. Is the play "topical" or "general"? Ulrich Weisstein berates Gay for over-topicality while praising Brecht's *Dreigroschenoper* as "a universal satire that makes little reference to the contemporary German situation."[9] But just how topical is *The Beggar's Opera*? Making a systematic search for connections and allusions, Schultz came up with so few that he was driven to call Gay's attack "general, rather than specific."[10] True, Brecht's Mackie has no individual political referent, while Gay's does. Yet Gay does no more than establish a set of suggested character references, and that not on a one-to-one basis; he then lets the audience draw its own inferences. Singularly little of the action in the play has any factual relation to Walpole. Knowledge of the parallel greatly enriches the play, but the general attack on statesmen embodied in Macheath and Peachum seems quite as effective as that in Brecht's version. By translating Walpole into this fantasy, Gay debases and smears him, and does it so skillfully that the audience relishes the trick. But I must agree with Stevens in finding neither high purpose nor even practical political design in the piece.

Politics have had more than their share of attention as the center of satiric import. Italian opera is equally obviously *a* satiric object—but is perhaps even less the target of serious attack. In setting up a *beggar's* opera—using pop tunes, burlesquing arias, pathetic prison scenes, farewell scenes, divas' squabbles (in particular those between Faustina and Cuzzoni), and in general mocking the silly conventions of a form enjoying a fad—Gay plainly has a specific satiric object in view. His purpose, however, remains questionable. Was this a serious attempt to drive Italian opera off the stage, as early critics often say? Bertrand Bronson, who did much toward identifying the particular hits, thinks not. "There is little probability that Gay intended a serious attack upon Italian opera, and he may even have been somewhat appalled at the amount of damage caused by his play. For his ridicule does not go beyond poking af-

---

9. "Brecht's Victorian Version of Gay: Imitation and Originality in the *Dreigroschenoper*," *Comparative Literature Studies*, 7 (1970), 314–35.

10. See Schultz, pp. 178–97, for a catalogue of allusions and contemporary opinion on the point.

fectionate fun at conventions which, like most conventions objectively regarded, have their ludicrous side."[11] Gay had, of course, written the libretto of *Acis and Galatea*, which Handel set to music about 1719. If he had any real animosity toward the Italian opera, no one has yet shown it.

On a more general literary plane, we can readily agree that though the overall form of the piece is controlled by its being a burlesque travesty of serious opera, there is along the way plenty of reference to pathetic comedy and tragedy. Gay's weird generic amalgam comes as no surprise to readers of his *The What d'ye Call It* (1715), for Gay was well-practiced at standing genres on their heads and mixing them up. Here we have serious opera revamped into low-burlesque, given a Gilbert and Sullivan farce plot, and infused with flippant bon mots. Because of the insistence on inversion, the burlesque is more than simple travesty. Opera is lowered by its social level here, but Gay busily insists that Macheath is "a great man," and to have the characters assume a status not altogether usual for their rank gives them a kind of claim to take themselves seriously enough for opera, whatever *we* may think. Clinton-Baddeley observes of *The What d'ye Call It* that Gay puts high sentiment into the mouths of the low, but does something more than simple parody because he insists on sobriety and straight faces in presenting even the most outrageous jokes.[12] The same technique is crucial to *The Beggar's Opera*. So well does Gay counterfeit the appropriate sentiments that even a hard-headed critic like Ian Donaldson can find Polly's sticky sentiments genuinely affecting, despite the presence of obvious ironies.[13]

The majority of the satiric hits in the play are social. To say

11. Bertrand H. Bronson, "*The Beggar's Opera*," in *Studies in the Comic* (Berkeley: Univ. of California Press, 1941), pp. 197–231. The extreme position on anti-opera satire has been taken by Arthur V. Berger in "*The Beggar's Opera*, the Burlesque, and Italian Opera," *Music and Letters*, 17 (1936), 93–105. For a rebuttal, see William A. McIntosh, "Handel, Walpole, and Gay: The Aims of *The Beggar's Opera*," *Eighteenth-Century Studies*, 7 (1974), 415–33. For the best account of operatic context, see Lowell Lindgren, "*Camilla* and *The Beggar's Opera*," *Philological Quarterly*, 59 (1980), 44–61.

12. V. C. Clinton-Baddeley, *The Burlesque Tradition in the English Theatre After 1660* (1952; rpt. New York: Blom, 1971), pp. 44–45.

13. Donaldson, *The World Upside-Down*, pp. 161, 174.

merely that high life and low life are inverted is incomplete. Mrs. Peachum can say indignantly of Macheath, "What business hath he to keep Company with Lords and Gentlemen? he should leave them to prey upon one another?" (I, iv).[14] But despite the elaborate insistence that Macheath's gang is courageous, industrious, truthful, and honorable (II, i), or Peachum's *sententiae* ("Business is at an end—if once we act dishonourably"—II, x), we recognize that the thieves and fences prey upon one another every bit as much as do lords and gentlemen. The Peachums' view of marriage, [15] the indignantly righteous view of lawyers ("The Lawyers are bitter Enemies to those in our Way. They don't care that any Body should get a Clandestine Livelihood but themselves"—I, ix), the happy acknowledgment of a truth: "Money well timed and properly applied, will do anything" (II, xii)—all radically dislocate our normal views. Yet to assume that Polly and Macheath are "good" and the Peachums "evil" would be simplistic and wrong. Macheath, however dashingly he is often played in the theatre, is a lying scoundrel, and though Polly can wallow quite convincingly in pathetic sentiment, she is at times given the iciest realism: "A Girl who cannot grant some Things, and refuse what is most material, will make but a poor hand of her Beauty, and soon be thrown upon the Common" (I, vii)—followed by the brutal truths of Air VI.[16] Gay does not romanticize low life.

If there is a central satiric purpose in *The Beggar's Opera*, it probably lies in the realm of money and social injustice. Sven Armens has argued at length that the theme of money and its misuse is the key to the whole work.[17] The "communistic" elements were

14. All quotations are from the first edition (1728).

15. "Do you think your Mother and I should have liv'd comfortably so long together, if ever we had been married?" (I, viii). "*Polly.* I did not marry him (as 'tis the Fashion) cooly and deliberately for Honour or Money. But, I love him. *Mrs. Peach.* Love him! worse and worse! I thought the Girl had been better bred" (I, viii). "The comfortable Estate of Widow-hood, is the only hope that keeps up a Wife's Spirits. . . . Hang your Husband, and be dutiful" (I, x).

16. The astonishing inconsistencies and fluctuations in the characters and our perceptions of them are well analyzed by Patricia Meyer Spacks in *John Gay* (New York: Twayne, 1965), pp. 148–51.

17. *John Gay, Social Critic* (New York: King's Crown Press, 1954), pp. 55–71.

noted long ago by William Empson, and there is no denying their presence. However, we must beware of easy assumptions. Armens surveys the "socialistic" prescriptions of Macheath's merry band of Robin Hoods ("We are for a just Partition of the World. . . . We retrench the Superfluities of Mankind"—II, i) and comments: "Gay's utilitarianism is revealed again in this passage: money should be a fluid item of exchange: it should be apportioned with some measure of equality." Now Gay may well be for greater equality of wealth, but let us remember the source of these fine sentiments—a gang of thieves justifying their depredations. Whatever our final conclusion on Gay's views about justice, our first response should clearly be amusement at this piety. Overall, we may agree with Armens that "the *implied* moral commentary" on society in *The Beggar's Opera* is "vehement."[18] Every character is to some degree evil or corrupt. Government, professions, and aristocracy are cheerfully savaged. But it is *cheerfully*, and any "vehement" satire is strictly by implication. How should the audience feel? Would it—should it—conclude with Armens that Gay is preaching against the corrupting influence of a "city" environment on the pure nature of man?

Is the purity of the "country" ever asserted or implied in *The Beggar's Opera*? What evidence are we offered (there or elsewhere) for Shaftesburyite sympathies in Gay? He is more tolerant of human frailty than Swift, but is he preaching benevolism in a roundabout way? A "vehement" satire on the state of society would require a conviction that reform was possible (persuasive), or would be an angry expression of disgust and despair (punitive). I can see almost nothing in our extensive records of eighteenth-century reactions to suggest that the audience took it either way. Quite to the contrary, delight and amusement seem to dominate the reactions, along with a few moralistic grumbles about making highwaymen too attractive. Swift talks about the "job" to be done by *The Beggar's Opera*,[19] and borrowing this term Ronald Paulson says that

18. Armens, p. 71 (italics added). For another "hard" reading see Isaac Kramnick, *Bolingbroke and His Circle* (Cambridge: Harvard Univ. Press, 1968). A more moderate version of this position is taken by Peter Elfed Lewis in his excellent edition (Edinburgh: Oliver and Boyd, 1973).

19. Swift to Gay, 28 Mar. 1728: "The Beggars Opera hath knockt down Gulliver, I hope to see Popes Dullness knock down the Beggars Opera, but not till it

"the 'job' is a *sine qua non* of satire,"[20] but what exactly is Gay seeking to accomplish? If Gay was trying to make Walpole look ludicrous or contemptible he was fairly successful—but satire on Walpole is only a peripheral element. If Gay was preaching social reform, the best we can say is that his audience seems not to have noticed. A satisfactory account of *The Beggar's Opera* is not to be had from examination of its satiric targets. Our next step, therefore, must be to turn to the peculiar generic form in which Gay embodied his satire.

Gay's Generic High Jinks

The Beggar's Opera, though unique among Gay's works, is far from being an isolated freak. It was just one of Gay's eleven dramatic ventures, being preceded by two farces, two comedies, a tragedy, and a pastoral, and followed by two ballad operas, a comedy, and a farce. Gay was a thoroughly experienced playwright and an old hand at satiric burlesque. One cannot "explain" *The Beggar's Opera* from the rest of the canon, but a brief survey may help us understand the dramatic habits of mind which underlie it.

Gay's first dramatic venture, unperformed, is *The Mohocks* (1712).[21] As the dedication "To Mr. D***" makes plain, Dennis' frigid *Appius and Virginia* (1709) is in the author's sights. Dennis gets his lumps, and Thomas B. Stroup suggests that Gay took a passing swipe at Milton's sublime grandiosity, which had recently been hailed by both Addison and Dennis.[22] The burlesque amounts to straight travesty in the fashion of Duffett's *The Mock-Tempest* or *Psyche Debauch'd*. And it quickly gets forgotten once the plot is launched and Gay develops the farcical possibilities: the Mohocks

---

hath fully done its Jobb." *The Correspondence of Jonathan Swift*, ed. Harold Williams, 5 vols. (Oxford: Clarendon Press, 1963–65), III, 278.

20. *The Fictions of Satire* (Baltimore: Johns Hopkins Univ. Press, 1967), pp. 3–4.

21. See the analysis by Peter Lewis, "Another Look at John Gay's 'The Mohocks,'" *Modern Language Review*, 63 (1968), 790–93.

22. "Gay's *Mohocks* and Milton," *Journal of English and Germanic Philology*, 46 (1947), 164–67.

haul the hapless watchmen into court on the charge of being Mohocks. Lewis correctly observes that "the criminal gang, presented at a courtly assembly with its own emperor, strict protocol, allegiances, and standards of conduct, certainly foreshadows Macheath's band." But no one has argued that there is any real bite to the "topical satire" (F. W. Bateson's phrase). Gay tugs Dennis' tail with a slick Scriblerian preface, and the stylistic burlesque is initially skillful, but the whole piece amounts to a whimsical, farcical trifle. There is technique aplenty in this "Tragi-Comical Farce"; the purpose is slight.

Gay has a knack for seeing several sides of a question, a talent that robs him of satiric consistency and fervor, but which contributes greatly to his chameleon skill as a mimic. The next two ventures into comic drama find him both wholeheartedly adopting, and then subverting, the generic norms of his day. *The Wife of Bath* (1713) is a standard exercise in dramatic carpentry. Bateson grumpily calls it "a rubbishy comedy on conventional lines," and is offended by "Chaucer, metamorphosed into a Queen Anne gallant."[23] Such a view is too harsh: Gay gives us solid second-rate Cibber, with epigrammatic frosting.

The What d'ye Call It (1715), long successful, is a minor masterpiece. A "Tragi-Comi-Pastoral FARCE," it mocks all three forms, with copious glancing references at popular plays and generic norms. The preface is a straight-faced imitation of Dennis' ponderous, firstly-secondly style. What we are shown is a country revel: Sir Roger superintends the performance of a play he has ordered produced— with ghost—"both a Tragedy and a Comedy and a Pastoral too: and if you could make it a Farce, so much the better—and what if you crown'd all with a spice of your Opera?" Despite this "frame" beginning, critics have been surprisingly ready to take seriously the country bumpkins' tragicomedy then enacted. Nicoll finds a strong pathetic-sentimental element, and Bateson feels that "the pathos is only more affecting because of a suspicion of irony which keeps it

---

23. F. W. Bateson, *English Comic Drama, 1700–1750* (1929; rpt. New York: Russell and Russell, 1963), ch. 5.

fresh and sweet." [24] Pope does indeed report that the "common people of the pit and gallery received it at first with great gravity and sedateness, some few with tears; but after the third day they also took the hint, and have ever since been very loud in their clapps." [25] Nonetheless, Lewis is surely correct in finding the piece the systematic burlesque it was reportedly designed to be. [26]

A harshly realistic view of "pastoral" life pervades the piece, which bluntly displays legal injustice and the brutal workings of the Press Act. Never, however, are we allowed to forget that we are watching Sir Roger's ludicrous play-served-to-order. At the outset, the frame tells us that Squire Thomas (Sir Roger's son) has impregnated Kitty (daughter of Sir Roger's steward). In the play, Squire Thomas acts Thomas Filbert, the countryman falsely accused of impregnating Dorcas (acted by Kitty). This strong linking of "reality" and "play" is established right at the start. The play proceeds in jingling couplets (ludicrously out of fashion in drama) which undercut the genuine social criticism.

> [*Aunt*] O Tyrant Justices! have you forgot
> How my poor Brother was in *Flanders* shot?
> You press'd my Brother—he shall walk in white,
> He shall—and shake your Curtains ev'ry Night.
> What though a paultry Hare he rashly kill'd,
> That cross'd the Furrowes while he plough'd the Field?
> You sent him o'er the Hills and far away;
> Left his old Mother to the Parish pay,
> With whom he shar'd his Ten Pence ev'ry Day.
>
> (I, i)

The complaint is serious, but the presentation is not. Similarly the

24. Nicoll, II, 197–98. Bateson, p. 85. Nicoll discusses the play under the heading "Comedies of Sensibility," though he admits "satirical" tendencies.

25. Letter to Caryll, 3 March 1715. *The Correspondence of Alexander Pope,* ed. George Sherburn, 5 vols. (Oxford: Clarendon Press, 1956), I, 283. "The hint" is presumably Scriblerian sponsorship.

26. Peter Elvet [*sic*] Lewis, "Gay's Burlesque Method in *The What D'Ye Call It,*" *Durham University Journal,* n.s. 29 (1967), 13–25.

five ghosts of victims of judicial injustice (including an embryo) are handled so jokingly as to remove any real sting.

In Act II Peascod is to be shot as a deserter; the surprise arrival of a reprieve at the last instant foreshadows *The Beggar's Opera.* The scene then shifts to Kitty's preparations for suicide—attended by a "Chorus of Sighs and Groans." She faints at the crucial moment, is doused by her attendants, and recovers to imagine herself turned into a stream—a neat debunking of the convention of the heroine fainting and imagining herself in heaven. Catastrophe prevented, marriage ensues. Here it is performed by a real parson— and Squire Thomas finds himself united in earnest to the girl he has debauched. With this lovely twist on the mock/real marriage so often employed in comedies, Gay achieves "poetic justice."[27]

Like Fielding's *Tom Thumb* to come, *The What d'ye Call It* mimics and distorts generic models rather than concentrating on travesty of a particular work—as Gay had set out to do in *The Mohocks* and as Fielding was to manage so brilliantly in *The Covent-Garden Tragedy,* a demolition of Philips' *The Distrest Mother.* As in *Tom Thumb,* the satiric object is the style, not the subject. Obviously a burlesque may use inflated style to mock the subject, as in *The Rape of the Lock,* or conversely to debase the style, as in *The Splendid Shilling.* Thomas Filbert as Hero, his tear-jerking farewell scene with Kitty, Peascod's sentimental laments on the scaffold (as it were), are all good take-offs on standard elements in pathetic tragedies. But the importance of the play for us lies in its kaleidoscopic quality. Critics often say that tragedy and comedy are "outlooks" or "attitudes" toward a subject. Gay, we find, is quite capable of presenting more than one outlook per play. *Tom Thumb* is a more effective burlesque, largely because it sticks to one vantage point. Gay chooses to give us abortive tragedy, subverted comedy, debased pastoral—all set into what turns out to be farce, albeit with halfway serious social implications. But however obvious the *fabrication*[28] of the elements mocked, so well are they limned that

27. See G. S. Alleman, *Matrimonial Law and the Materials of Restoration Comedy,* ch. 4. A close parallel is Durfey's *The Marriage-Hater Match'd* (1692).

28. I am employing this term almost as Hugh Kenner uses "counterfeit." See *The Counterfeiters* (Bloomington: Indiana Univ. Press, 1968).

fleetingly we can respond as to the thing itself. Or at least our response is both to the thing itself and to the mocking of it. Here we are never left in any doubt about Gay's views of his subjects, despite the superficially "close resemblance between *The What D'Ye Call It* and its targets."[29] When we get to Polly Peachum as sentimental heroine we are in far murkier waters—but we will do well to remember Gay's skill at deadpan counterfeiting of clichés.

This same fabricative power is evident in *Three Hours After Marriage* (1717), in which Gay was assisted by Pope and Arbuthnot. Little need be said about this *jeu d'esprit*. In form, it is a straight comedy, as the title page dubs it. Coarse, vigorous, full of situational farce, the play has been discussed mostly for its personal satire and its stormy reception in the theatre.[30] The lampooning of John Dennis as Sir Tremendous is superb. The female writer Phoebe Clinket is good fun, whether she represents Lady Winchelsea or (less probably) Susanna Centlivre. Why, however, should the Scriblerians turn to writing such coarse-grained stuff? The key question is whether we are seeing watered down Durfey sex-comedy or hyped-up Centlivre.

Because Gay and his friends provide no overt signs of burlesque intention, the audience might well take the play straight. We are given no leading preface, and no rehearsal or play-within-play frame to direct our response. The hits at Phoebe Clinket's play in Act I are good satire, but do not suggest that the whole piece is a spoof. Even the most outrageous and delightful piece of nonsense, the would-be seducers of Dr. Fossile's new young wife having themselves delivered to his museum in the guise of a mummy and an alligator respectively, is straight out of Ravenscroft's long-popular *Anatomist*. The odd twist at the end, dissolving the marriage, is flippantly handled, but is no more implausible than its romantically

29. The description is Lewis' (p. 15), the qualifier mine.
30. See especially George Sherburn, "The Fortunes and Misfortunes of *Three Hours After Marriage*," *Modern Philology*, 24 (1926), 91–109; William Henry Irving, *John Gay, Favorite of the Wits* (Durham: Duke Univ. Press, 1940), pp. 147–64; and John Harrington Smith's Augustan Reprint Society facsimile edition (1961), as well as the edition (using the original act division) by Richard Morton and William M. Peterson (Lake Erie College Studies, Painesville, Ohio, no. 1), also published in 1961.

treated equivalent in Mrs. Pix's *The Innocent Mistress*. But the key to the play is its relation to other drama circa 1717: it coarsens and exaggerates the standard devices of Cibber-Centlivre style "intrigue" comedy. As Lewis concludes, "although *Three Hours After Marriage* is usually described as a farce, it should be clear that the authors succeed in pushing the typical farcical incidents of intrigue comedy to the point at which even these become so ridiculous that they are transformed into burlesque."[31] The results can certainly be enjoyed as what they purport to be—a farcical intrigue comedy, which leaves Lewis a bit disappointed. Our only real hint at something different comes from Gay's signing the "Advertisement" and suggesting that the piece is a Scriblerian production. Just as we would refuse to take "straight" a sticky pastoral claimed by Swift, or an anti-dissenter tract signed by Defoe, so we know better than to take *Three Hours After Marriage* for what it so successfully counterfeits.

In *The Mohocks* Gay sets out to burlesque a single work; in *The What d'ye Call It* he mocks generic conventions with burlesque deflation; in *Three Hours* he and his helpers pull off a subtle joke by letting the audience take seriously what the authors consider a satiric exaggeration of a trivial form. In all three John Dennis suffers the slings and arrows of outrageous Scriblerians: Gay is a deft lampooner. And in light of this talent, his reputation for namby-pambyness is astonishingly inappropriate. There is bite in these plays, though they are really no more than satiric entertainments. Good burlesque requires skill at counterfeiting—and Gay has it to an almost disconcerting extent. *The Shepherd's Week* (1714) is a good nondramatic example. So well does Gay adopt Philips' style that even with Pope's explanation of the object, and Trowbridge's lucid exposition of the details of the technique, so careful a critic as Forsgren can be left uncertain about the satirical impact of the poems.[32]

In all of these cases the objects satirized are literary and to a

31. Peter Elfed [*sic*] Lewis, "Dramatic Burlesque in *Three Hours After Marriage*," *Durham University Journal*, n.s. 33 (1972), 232–39.

32. Pope to Caryll, 8 June 1714; Hoyt Trowbridge, "Pope, Gay, and *The Shepherd's Week*," *Modern Language Quarterly*, 5 (1944), 79–88; Adina Forsgren, *John*

lesser extent personal. In each case an attack is conducted by means of manifest fiction (in these cases burlesque—distorted "imitation") upon recognizable particulars—either specific works or well-known current literary conventions and persons. The point of the satire is plainly punitive rather than persuasive. Dennis felt the harpoon deeply, but Gay writes more to amuse his clique than to hurt Dennis. Scriblerian productions (which do not really include the major works of Pope and Swift) are meant both for the world and as an in-group joke. However cutting, however nasty, however much resented, Scriblerian Club satire is raillery: the writers play their game mostly for pleasure. Indeed, this may account for some of the venom in others' responses: to be denounced or debunked by an angry moralist is bad enough, but to be cut up for fun by a group of malicious elitists is intolerable.

Returning to *The Beggar's Opera* at this juncture, we need to ask, generically, what it is. If a satire, then a satire on what? If a ballad opera—the usual designation—then just what did that mean in 1728? Only very recently has anyone insisted on the importance of realizing that at the time of the premiere, there was no such genre, and that consequently the piece must have seemed extremely disconcerting. "When we call *The Beggar's Opera* a ballad opera, we should remember that this is a retrospective category. . . . Unlike his imitators, Gay was being extremely provocative and was deliberately creating uncertainty in devising an opera that not only departed from current expectations of opera but also flouted existing operatic paradigms so ostentatiously."[33] Finding models and analogues for *The Beggar's Opera* has proved remarkably difficult.[34] We are left to conclude—given the lack of either generic guidance or clear internal values—that Gay was deliberately trying to disorient his audience, to frustrate expectations, and to deprive

---

Gay: "Poet of a Lower Order" (Stockholm: Natur och Kultur, 1964), [Vol. 1], pp. 105–13, 163–67.

33. Peter E. Lewis, "The Uncertainty Principle in *The Beggar's Opera*," *Durham University Journal*, 72 (1980), 143–46.

34. See Carolyn Kephart, "An Unnoticed Forerunner of 'The Beggar's Opera,'" *Music and Letters*, 61 (1980), 266–71.

them of stock responses. This is hardly what we expect of an Augustan satirist. And of course the strategy works less well once ballad opera has become a familiar phenomenon.

Clearly, Gay was burlesquing the form of Italian opera. His "subject" is social class, conventions, and attitudes (and secondarily contemporary politics, music, and literature), satirized through incongruous imitation of the "high" in a low social setting. On these points, there is relatively minor ground for disagreement. But the attitude toward the material is heavily colored by what Empson calls "the stock device of the play . . . a double irony."[35] No doubt the intricacies of this double irony account in large part for the radical divergencies of critical views of the work. But to make sense of it, we will have to decide what our attitude toward the material ought to be.

Gay's Self-Negating Satire

Most interpreters of *The Beggar's Opera* make some sort of assumption—either from external sources or by extrapolation from the text—about what sort of satirist Gay was. The common assumptions are 1) Gay soft, 2) Gay hard, 3) Gay the message-monger, and 4) Gay mixed.[36] Only the last really seems to make sense.

The classic account of the soft Gay—derived from his poems—is Sutherland's. Gay's personality enters heavily: he was "gentle, good-natured, indolent, lovable in the extreme, shiftless, impracticable, innocent, volatile, a sort of Augustan Peter Pan"—not, in short, the sort of man who would be a serious thinker or a hard-hitting social critic.[37] Surveying Gay's poetry, Sutherland concludes that we cannot look to him for "'criticism of life' . . . he produced *objets d'art*, delicate, formalized, artificial, glazed and polished by

35. William Empson, *Some Versions of Pastoral* (1935; rpt. London: Chatto and Windus, 1968), p. 210.

36. For a brief analysis of trends in recent criticism, see Arthur Sherbo, "John Gay: Lightweight or Heavyweight?" *Scriblerian*, 8 (1975), 4–8.

37. James Sutherland, "John Gay," in *Pope and His Contemporaries: Essays Presented to George Sherburn*, ed. James L. Clifford and Louis A. Landa (Oxford: Clarendon Press, 1949), pp. 201–14.

his poetic diction, and removed from actuality by a process of refin-
ing and idealizing." "Life was indeed a jest to Gay . . . [he] remained slightly aloof from human concerns." "Gay's tendency is
always, if not actually to idealize, to soften and harmonize." In *The
Beggar's Opera* Gay is clearly less "remote" from the "guzzling,
sweating, jostling crowd" than he is in his poems. But one can fairly
say that Gay serves us potentially nasty subjects with humorous
élan—including acceptance of judicial murder, bigamy, and attempted poisoning. This lightness of touch even in serious matters
convinces Schultz (a very thorough student of Gay's texts and references) that "there are no traces of anger. . . . At least a large part
of the satire . . . should be considered as belonging to the class of
general ridicule which is represented by the pungent *Pinafore*.[38]

At the opposite extreme are the hard-line interpreters. John
Preston sees a "hard cutting edge" to the satire which makes it far
more truly destructive than Fielding's more openly derogatory ironies.[39] Bateson similarly stresses "cynicism" and negativism in Gay's
view of his material. Armens is the principal spokesman for the
hard interpretation. In his view Gay is no "elegant trifler," but rather
a serious and angry social critic engaged in bitter protest against
entrenched injustices. To a "concerned" modern critic this ought
perhaps to be so. At times indeed Gay will land a hard satiric blow
in the midst of all his foolery and repartee. When at the end the
beggar complies "with the taste of the town" and supplies a reprieve, he comments: "Had the Play remain'd as I at first intended,
it would have carried a most excellent Moral. 'Twould have shown
that the lower Sort of People have their Vices in a degree as well as
the Rich: And that they are punish'd for them."

In a few flashes like this one the play may seem to be what
Armens wants it to be. This is really something like *Dreigroschenoper*: a harsh satire whose heavy-handed pessimism invites indignation and an affirmation of the possibility of change. Gay produces nothing of the sort. Nevertheless, Armens' attempt to make
him over into a junior Swift is not surprising: Goldsmith and Sterne

38. Schultz, *Gay's "Beggar's Opera*," pp. 178–79.
39. "The Ironic Mode: A Comparison of *Jonathan Wild* and *The Beggar's
Opera*," *Essays in Criticism*, 16 (1966), 268–80.

have both attracted similar reinterpretations.[40] All three writers have elements that invite such treatment, without as a whole sustaining a "Swiftian" outlook. No doubt Gay would be a greater writer if he were more like Swift—but then *The Beggar's Opera* would be far less jolly.

That Gay delivers some shrewd blows is true enough. But how much of a "message" emerges from the play? The debate over alleged encouragement of vice in general and highwaymen in particular raged through the eighteenth century.[41] The notorious altered ending of 1777—in which Macheath is given a compromise sentence of three years at hard labor—seems to have satisfied no one. The desire for a positive "moral" has been resisted by most critics: Gay is pretty hard on moral-mongering at the end of the play, as we have just seen. Hazlitt arrived at the comfortable conclusion that "the moral of the piece is to show the *vulgarity* of vice"—a tidy formulation approved by the eminent editors of a widely used textbook.[42] Granting that vice does appear vulgar here, I am still inclined to doubt that an audience thinks much about the matter.

Probably the most systematic attempt to find a message as such is Edgar Roberts'. Rejecting the socialist-egalitarian position of Armens as interpretively exaggerated and biographically improbable, Roberts appeals to the views of Pope and Swift and suggests that Gay writes against "arbitrary law," seeking reform "within the system."

> Gay's obvious sympathy for Macheath and the gang indicates a basic assumption . . . that genuine goodness can be brought out only through a sensitive and responsible social system. In the eighteenth-century world, it was considered a paternal duty for the upper class to nurture the lower classes. . . . *The Beggar's Opera* argues satirically that arbitrary and self-seeking

40. See Robert H. Hopkins, *The True Genius of Oliver Goldsmith* (1969), and Melvyn New, *Laurence Sterne as Satirist* (1969).

41. Schultz, ch. 21, gives a convenient survey.

42. Hazlitt, "On The Beggar's Opera," in *The Round Table* (1817). Cf. *Eighteenth-Century English Literature*, ed. Geoffrey Tillotson, Paul Fussell, Jr., and Marshall Waingrow (New York: Harcourt-Brace, 1969), pp. 518–19.

enforcement of laws baffles human potential by directing men away from the cultivation of goodness into the channel of survival by any means, including crime.[43]

Two obvious questions need to be raised. First, is Gay indulging in sociological explanations of crime, or is he just using criminals to besmirch the governing class? Second, Macheath is a representation of Walpole, and hence not so very sympathetic, on that count among others. And if we take Macheath seriously as an unhappy victim "driven" to crime by the present governmental and social situation, are we really to believe that Gay argues for social justice by showing us the woes of "Walpole"?

The more sympathetic we are to criminal-Macheath, the less effective is the satiric identification with Walpole-Macheath. Wondering "What's to be done?" one might draw the sort of conclusion Roberts does, but where in the play does Gay ever suggest or imply anything of the sort? If serious purpose must be conceived as residing in a moral, one is safest in following Dr. Johnson, who dismisses both charges of encouraging vice and Swift's praise "for the excellence of its morality, as a piece that 'placed vices of all kinds in the strongest and most odious light.'" Johnson argues that such responses are "exaggerated," and that "the play . . . was plainly written only to divert, without any moral purpose."[44] If we may accept a less clear and tidy purpose as nonetheless serious, we can look for a middle position.

Since Gay can with some plausibility be read either as "hard" or "soft," to insist that he is wholly one or the other is foolish. To ask whether we are dealing with a *Dreigroschenoper* or a *Pinafore* misses the obvious: Gay gives us a bit of both. Gagey illustrates the critic's dilemma. Gay can verge on the Swiftian (as in Lockit's comment: "Of all Animals of Prey, Man is the only sociable one"— III, ii). Behind all the burlesque and wit "seems to lurk a negative philosophy of disillusion which colors the opera with an all-pervading cynicism." But this misanthropic Tory gloom is greatly "obscured"

43. *The Beggar's Opera*, ed. Edgar V. Roberts, p. xx.
44. "John Gay," *Lives of the Poets.*

by "the brilliancy of Gay's wit, the rapid gusto of his scenes, and the uncertainty of whether to take him seriously or not."[45] This is a excellent formulation of what has seemed to be a fundamental ambiguity in this play. Ian Donaldson analyzes this dichotomy more closely, noting "the variousness" of Gay's appeal and his "odd ability to be at once ironic and sentimental," the product of "multiple vision." Donaldson suggests that Gay gives us a Hobbesian vision of a world dominated by self-interest, while simultaneously "as an ironic alternative" displaying "the sentimental Shaftesburian view of things."[46] I cannot quite agree that "Gay's counterfeiting is such that it is possible to believe that one is watching an orthodox sentimental drama": Gay is always careful to remind us that we are luxuriating in a pretense, as in Polly's imagining Mac's execution at the end of Act I. But if we agree with Donaldson that *The Beggar's Opera* is both "lollipop" and "terse social fable," we have then to ask what the fable signifies and why it has been amalgamated with a lollipop.

Does Gay use sugar-coating to make a harsh satire palatable? The idea is plausible, but if we cannot decide what is being savaged, the hypothesis breaks down. The best answer is surely "human nature," here coolly depicted as part of the Hobbesian jungle world. The constant reiteration of images comparing human and animal life[47] exerts a powerful direct and subliminal effect—yet to what end? As Spacks concludes, there is "no reforming zest," and though "our reaction is technically a reaction to satire . . . the satire is an-

45. Gagey, *Ballad Opera*, pp. 42–43. Naturally our response is affected by the nature of any particular production. In this connection, we may wonder about the significance of the eighteenth-century traditions of women playing Macheath; productions using child actors; and performances with men playing the female roles and vice-versa. How appropriate are such stunts to hard satire or a serious "message" play?

46. Donaldson, *The World Upside-Down*, esp. pp. 161, 167, 171, 175, 177, and 182.

47. Jenny likens Macheath to a cock attended by hens (II, Air V). Filch is likened to "a shotten Herring" (III, iii). Macheath calls women "Decoy Ducks" and "Beasts" (II, v). Lucy pictures Macheath as a rat she can throw "To the Dog or Cat,/ To be worried, crush'd, and shaken" (II, Air IX). Men are compared to hooked fish and trapped birds (III, Air V), and likened to "Pikes, lank with Hunger, who . . . bite their Companions and prey on their Friends" (III, Air III).

imated less by moral fervor than by a bittersweet perception of the persistent follies of the race"[48]—the satirist's included, we may add.

In what remains the best general account of *The Beggar's Opera*, Bertrand Bronson, convinced of the "serious implications" of the total conglomeration, defines them in terms of a single central point: "*The world is all alike!* That is the final lesson of Gay's satire."[49] Indubitably this *is* Gay's "moral," and yet on reflection it seems a distinctly odd one. Just what sort of *satire* ends in this moral? If we are actually to accept it, and Bronson feels that we are, then *Gay has at a stroke demolished the very basis for "satire" in the Swiftian sense*—a fundamental assumption of superiority by the satirist, a conviction of differences, of right and wrong. If "the world is all alike," the satirist included, then there is nothing the satirist can really be *for*. Hence satiric perceptions that seem to be a basis for profound (even Swiftian) pessimism lose most of their sting, and we are left with a disconcertingly flippant cynicism.

The Beggar's Opera is certainly an "attack" upon recognized particulars carried out by means of what Edward Rosenheim calls manifest fictions. But reflecting on the lack of indignation, and the leveling moral, one should come to see that the multiple undercuttings of Gay's satire represent an unusual, even a peculiar, authorial attitude toward the material presented. Here we find no savage indignation, no aloof superiority, no self-righteous Popean preachments. When we cast our nets for "implied norms" behind the satire, we come up empty. Gay's attitudes toward his subjects are a curious mixture of wry acceptance and constitutional distaste. The characters he shows us are nasty rogues, and the Hobbesian picture of nature they give us is horrible, if reflected upon. But their smug and sanctimonious view of themselves is irresistibly comic: Gay has a sharp eye for pride and self-delusion. We respond much less negatively than we might to the characters, largely because there are really no victims in the story. Gay's delightful flippancy would be hard to maintain in the face of genuine persecution and pathos.

48. Spacks, *Gay*, pp. 127, 166.
49. Macheath uses this phrase near the end of the play (III, xiv) when he discovers to his astonishment and indignation "that even our Gang can no more trust one another than other People."

If Gay wanted us to loathe and despise the scoundrels, he would have to show them doing some real harm. The tone of *The Beggar's Opera* does odd things to our perception of the satirist who stands behind it.

This brings us back to the "figure of the satirist." In dramatic burlesque, the author stands aloof, unless he chooses to write in a spokesman, as Fielding occasionally does. In "direct" verse satire, like much of Pope's, the impact depends heavily on the "voice" of the authorial persona. Maynard Mack, in a widely cited analysis, sees three distinguishable "voices" in Pope's formal satires: the plain, good man; the ingenue; and the indignant public defender—a self-proclaimed hero and moral arbiter. Using these categories, Patricia Spacks has analyzed Gay's satiric poems (principally the epistles, the five eclogues, and the two series of fables) and argues that

> as satires these works are strangely unconvincing. . . . [The persona] seems to feel himself all too deeply involved in the world he nominally criticizes. There is no separation between satirist and target. . . . The poet observes and understands human weakness, finds it comic though pathetic, and because of his own lively sense of pleasurable involvement in the general irrationality cannot be bitter or fierce. The satirist's function is to censure, to lash; Gay does neither.[50]

Professor Spacks notes that Gay's usual "voice" is that of the naïf, and that he "rarely achieved the high tone of the public defender of the right; struggling toward such heights, he falters again and again. . . . Gay's major problem was to find an appropriate stance, a public role which would make satire fully possible."

Unlike his fellow Scriblerians, Gay does not hold himself apart from what he views: the result is a perpetually unstable and uncomfortable satirist's perspective. Hence *The Beggar's Opera* is not just a satire on various political, social, and literary objects, but a satire wryly deflated by its author's self-deprecatory negativism. Probably this posture, the satirist standing on his own trapdoor, is as natural

---

50. Patricia Meyer Spacks, "John Gay: A Satirist's Progress," *Essays in Criticism*, 14 (1964), 156–70. Cf. Maynard Mack, "The Muse of Satire," *Yale Review*, 41 (1951), 80–92.

to Gay as the tramp was to Charlie Chaplin: both are uncomfortable when pushed into grander status, just as both can luxuriate in the incongruously pathetic-sentimental. When Gay inflates himself from the ingenue-beggar poet into the serious role of Poet-Spokesman for *Polly*, he becomes a third-rate imitation of Pope, uncomfortably committed to a stance he has no faith in. There the multiple ironies evaporate and simplistic black and white distinctions between the corrupt Macheath and the noble savages yield clear but trivial morals. Gay is not Prince Pope, and when he tries to be he falls flat on his face.[51]

If we recognize the essential self-deprecation of the satire in *The Beggar's Opera*, certain critical observations about the play make more sense. A number of recent scholars seem to me to have been very close to this crucial realization without following up the implications of their own discoveries. Thus Spacks sees Gay's "self-involvement" with his satiric subjects in the poems, but does little to explore the possibilities of this perception for *The Beggar's Opera*. Armens comes right to the verge of a major breakthrough in his summation when he says that Gay felt "it his duty to live up to the satirist's calling," though he recognized that there were no remedies for the evils he attacked.[52] This is a terribly serious admission, coming from the greatest champion of Gay's serious import. Is Gay the satirist simply a dog baying at the moon? Anguish and despair in the face of the intractability of the evils contemplated could be powerful (if not useful), but what evidence have we that Gay was masking nihilistic despair with mocking laughter? The "bittersweet" duality noted by Spacks seems related, rather, to a wryly comic realization of the satirist's inability to defend his own position.

Bateson recognized the negativism and concluded that "Gay had become fat and middle-aged; he had lost his ideals and his

---

51. For a useful overview see Howard Erskine-Hill, "The significance of Gay's drama," in *English Drama: Forms and Development*, ed. Marie Axton and Raymond Williams (Cambridge: Cambridge Univ. Press, 1977), pp. 142–63. Erskine-Hill points out that "Far from seeing man in 'One clear, unchanged and universal light' (*An Essay on Criticism*, line 71), these plays are aware that the thing perceived depends on the approach of the perceiver," and he stresses their "kaleidoscopically shifting perspectives" (p. 162).

52. Armens, *John Gay, Social Critic*, p. 226.

illusions, and their place had been taken by personal spite and a cheap cynicism borrowed, without being understood, from Swift and Pope." [53] This seems decidedly unfair. It ignores Bateson's own perception of Gay's ironical "stereoscopic ability to assume at one time two or more points of view." Worse, it implies that Gay did not believe in, or even understand, the outlook he expressed. In fact, his comic-sardonic disillusionment is highly typical of himself, and quite uncharacteristic of Pope or Swift. They can be angry, negative, or despairing, but almost never are they flippantly cynical without meaning to provoke a contrary reaction. Does Gay want us, à la Brecht, to reject the cynicism, to cry out against his claim that "the world is all alike"? Let the critic prove it who can. Did Gay assume that his audience would read conventional judgments into the work? One cannot prove the contrary, but if the host of topsy-turvy inversions are to be taken seriously, then the resultant "uneasiness" and "disorientation" stressed by Peter Lewis and other recent critics seem to argue strongly against such an assumption.

Far from embodying "cheap cynicism," *The Beggar's Opera* actually cuts deeper and more dangerously than the more "committed" satires of Swift, Pope, and Fielding. For where those authors savagely attack the bad, Gay undermines our easy and uncritical faith in the good. John Preston accurately remarks that *Jonathan Wild* "leaves intact and essentially unchanged the roles of high and low," while "Gay's irony threatens our faith in the qualities we most admire: honesty, honour, friendship, loyalty, and love." [54] Even this, ironically enough, we are to find funny—though not entirely so. To be made to realize that "the world is all alike" is both risible and sobering. The implications are serious enough, but they are also a dead end, for as Armens himself could see, there are no remedies.

The Beggar's Opera remains technically a satire in form and method, but Gay very deliberately eschews the "job" which ought to be its sine qua non. The results are not the kind of political,

---

53. Bateson, *English Comic Drama*, pp. 97–98. The comment is directly concerned with *Polly*, but is applied generally to Gay in the later 1720s. The following quotation is from p. 102.

54. Preston, "The Ironic Mode," p. 279.

social, or literary manifesto-denunciation we find in the *Dunciad*, *Gulliver*, or *The Historical Register*. Gay embodies in his mock-opera a pessimistic world view which is wry and self-deprecatory rather than despairing. The philosophical implications, while undeniably bleak, are leavened with tolerance, humanity, and a keen sense of the ludicrousness of it all. What we find then is satire in form and ostensible purposes, but carried out in such a way as to negate the satiric stance in the very process of the "attack." These results represent a delicate, perhaps an unconscious balance: that *The Beggar's Opera* remained sui generis, an isolated monument despite a host of imitations, is no surprise.

9

The London Theatre From The Beggar's Opera *to the Licensing Act*

Few decades are as exciting to the theatre historian as the ten seasons between the premiere of *The Beggar's Opera* in 1728 and the passage of the Licensing Act in 1737. New theatres, violent management upheavals, labor strife, aggressive competition, and the introduction of important new forms make each season a fresh adventure. Historians of the drama, in contrast, have found this period much less interesting. The unprecedented success of *The Beggar's Opera* and *The Provok'd Husband* during the season of 1727–28 stimulated a tremendous upsurge in theatrical activity and hastened changes in long-stagnant play types. Good professional playwrights take time to develop, however, and no major writer had emerged from his apprenticeship before Walpole put an end to the competition that fostered new plays. Consequently, few important plays were written in these years, and knowledge of what was to happen in 1737 inevitably dampens the critic's enthusiasm for studying developments that will go nowhere.

During the 1730s we see in the new plays a decisive move away from what John Loftis calls the Restoration stereotypes[1]—a move definitely slowed by the Licensing Act but, I shall argue, by no means insignificant for the evolution of English drama during the eighteenth century. Given the vitality of the theatrical activity and the

1. *Comedy and Society*, esp. ch. 3.

new forms being explored, the lack of a full dramatic history is surprising. Nicoll simply lumps the plays of this decade together with others of the 1700–1750 period, and the *Revels History* touches on little more than Fielding. There are some useful specialist studies (particularly those by Loftis, Goldgar, and Kern),[2] but we have as yet nothing like a full treatment of the plays.

The present essay is a kind of prolegomenon to such a study. My objects here are three-fold: 1) to sketch the nature of the influence exerted by theatrical circumstances, 2) to indicate the directions in which drama and theatre were moving, and 3) to reevaluate the effects of the Licensing Act. This essay is neither an account of the theatrical background per se (a desideratum supplied by A. H. Scouten in 1961 in his introduction to Part 3 of *The London Stage*) nor a sketch of the history of the drama in these years (still needed, but definitely a subject for a book). In a sense, I am trying to re-create the vantage point occupied by writers working for the London theatre in the decade before the Licensing Act, unconscious of approaching doom. Why did they write what they did? How did "the market" look to a bright young writer/manager like Fielding? In what direction was the London theatre moving?

To ask what might have evolved had there been no Licensing Act, or had it taken a different form, is not mere self-indulgence. In the theatre of the 1730s we can see both the possibility of great vitality and change, and the conservative repertory basis on which the theatres operated in Garrick's day. To decry the Licensing Act is easy enough, but we cannot really understand its effect unless we have studied the movements of the thirties and made some estimate of where they might have taken the London theatre. I will argue, indeed, that the most damaging effects of the Licensing Act were largely unrelated to government censorship, but stem, rather, from managerial habits deeply entrenched in the London theatre well before 1737. The tragedy of the Licensing Act is not censorship but restriction to two patent theatres. This restriction meant little or nothing to the government once Fielding had been put out of busi-

2. Loftis, *Comedy and Society*; Goldgar, *Walpole and the Wits*; Jean B. Kern, *Dramatic Satire in the Age of Walpole, 1720–1750* (Ames: Iowa State Univ. Press, 1976).

ness, but the patent house managers naturally seized upon it for their own ends and used it to suppress all competition. The inevitable effect of this exercise in self-interest was the choking off of the supply of new drama that had started to flourish so promisingly after the success of *The Beggar's Opera*.

The Theatrical Situation in 1727–28

A young writer just starting his career—Fielding, for example—faced an uphill battle if he hoped to support himself as a dramatist. He had exactly two potential venues for his work, neither of them known for championing unknown writers, or indeed for undertaking new plays from any source. Drury Lane was run by the celebrated Triumvirate (Robert Wilks, Barton Booth, and Colley Cibber), Lincoln's Inn Fields by the pantomime-minded John Rich. Neither theatre had any commitment to contemporary drama. Only a handful of new plays had been staged each season since the government-mandated Union of 1708. The reopening of a second theatre in December 1714, after the accession of George I, allowed Rich to put his father's patent to use again, but made little difference to the prospects of getting new plays staged. Neither theatre had been more than moderately profitable in the nearly fifteen years since competition had resumed in 1714, and both houses had settled comfortably into a pattern of nonaggressive coexistence.

A brief survey of the two theatres' repertory in 1726–27 (believed to have been Fielding's first season in London)[3] will make plain just how conservative, even stagnant, these theatres had become. They opened the season by politely playing on alternate nights from the beginning of September to the last Saturday in October. During this season Drury Lane performed a total of sixty-five plays (only one of them new) on a total of 173 nights.[4] The one new play, James Moore-Smythe's *The Rival Modes*, a derivative and old-

3. Wilbur L. Cross, *The History of Henry Fielding*, 3 vols. (1918; rpt. New York: Russell and Russell, 1963), I, 55–56.
4. In these figures I am counting only mainpieces.

fashioned love-chase comedy, lasted 6 nights and was never revived. Hardly an inspiration to budding dramatists! Lincoln's Inn Fields countered with fifty plays on a total of 166 nights. Four of these plays were new, but two of them lasted only 2 nights each, and another managed 4.[5] Philip Frowde's *The Fall of Saguntum* had a good initial run (11 nights), but was mounted only once more this season and never revived.

The conservatism in the theatres' repertory policy is made even clearer if we break their plays down into period of origin.

Table 1: *Mainpieces Performed in the Season of 1726–27*

	DL			LIF		
Pre-1660	11		(17%)	9		(18%)
1660–94	26		(40%)	16		(32%)
1695–1707	23		(35%)	16		(32%)
1708–20	3		(5%)	4		(8%)
Post-1720	2	(1 new)	(3%)	5	(4 new)	(10%)
	65			50		

Thus at Drury Lane only 8 percent of the plays staged had been written within the past twenty years, and thirty-seven of them (57 percent) were more than thirty years old. Even that figure does not tell the whole story, since most of the plays from the 1660–94 period predate the Union of 1682. We should remember that Wilks, Cibber, and Booth were naturally predisposed to the flock of plays written in the decade after 1695, having created roles in many of them. Rich's company had no such direct tie to turn-of-the-century repertory. Nonetheless the figures at Lincoln's Inn Fields are only slightly less discouraging. Both theatres had a set of Shakespeare-era warhorses, and both relied heavily on stock plays of the Carolean period. Likewise both relied almost equally on the flock of "perennial favorites" written around the turn of the century at the height of the competition between Drury Lane and the rebel actors

5. Anon., and unpublished, *The Savage*; David Lewis, *Philip of Macedon*; Leonard Welsted, *The Dissembled Wanton*. None was revived.

at Lincoln's Inn Fields under Betterton.[6] We should note also that sixteen plays were in both theatres' repertories in 1726–27,[7] occupying a total of 80 nights at the two theatres.

One of the most striking facts about both repertories is the small number of performances of any single play. Drury Lane did not perform a single old play more than five times; six plays enjoyed five performances each (*The Albion Queens, Cato, The Careless Husband, The Committee, The Relapse, Tamerlane*). Six plays managed four performances each (*2 Henry IV, Love for Love, The Provok'd Wife, Rule a Wife, Sir Courtly Nice, The Way of the World*). Twenty-three were given three performances each; all others one or two. At Lincoln's Inn Fields (which kept a smaller active repertory) the picture is only slightly different. Two plays enjoyed seven performances (*The Confederacy* and *The Country-Wife*) and one had six (*The Prophetess*). Three plays managed five nights (*The Beaux Stratagem, Merry Wives, The Mistake*), and seven had four nights. Only seven more achieved three nights; the rest one or two. The situation at Lincoln's Inn Fields this season differed principally in that the theatre enjoyed a striking success with a revival of *Camilla* (1706), a translated Italian opera which had been off the stage for ten years. *Camilla* received a startling twenty-five performances.

Of the plays performed three times or more, only three had been written since the Union of 1708—Centlivre's *The Busie Body* (1709), Philips' *The Distrest Mother* (1712), and Bullock's *The Woman's Revenge* (1715—an adaptation of a 1680 Behn adaptation). The other post-1708 plays in the repertory were Addison's *Cato* (1713), Rowe's *Jane Shore* (1714), and Addison's *The Drummer* (1716). The one post-1720 play in the repertory was *The Con-*

---

6. See Shirley Strum Kenny, "Perennial Favorites: Congreve, Vanbrugh, Cibber, Farquhar, and Steele," *Modern Philology*, 73, No. 4, Part 2 [Friedman *Festschrift*] (1976), S4–S11, and Judith Milhous, *Thomas Betterton and the Management of Lincoln's Inn Fields.*

7. Aesop, *The Beaux Stratagem, The Country-Wife, Hamlet, Julius Caesar, King Lear* (Tate), *Macbeth, The Old Batchelour, The Orphan, Oroonoko, The Provok'd Wife, The Recruiting Officer, Richard III, The Rover, The Spanish Fryar,* and *Tamerlane.*

scious Lovers (1722), whose author was of course Sir Richard Steele, one of the patentees at Drury Lane. One may fairly say that the prospects for aspiring playwrights were bleak.[8]

Thus far our consideration has excluded afterpieces, but they do not in fact much change the position. Neither company offered an afterpiece at even half its performances this season. (In many cases, of course, entr'acte singing and dancing were offered instead.) Drury Lane mounted seventy-four afterpiece performances in 173 nights. Five old standbys occupied a total of 8 nights, all in the benefit season.[9] Thurmond's long-popular *Harlequin Dr. Faustus* ran throughout the season, and the house got good runs from Thurmond's *Apollo and Daphne or Harlequin's Metamorphosis*, *The Miser*, and *Harlequin's Triumph*. Thus Drury Lane's new afterpieces were all written by an insider—its dancing master. At Lincoln's Inn Fields 77 nights of afterpieces were split among twelve plays, but 32 were devoted to Theobald's new *The Rape of Proserpine*. The afterpiece tradition had not really established itself until 1715: hence most afterpieces were relatively recent. The boom in pantomime started by John Rich, however, meant that the theatres were far from anxious to secure legitimate two-act comedies.

One might ask why, under these circumstances, the theatres bothered to mount *any* new plays. Barton Booth complained that Drury Lane lost money on new plays, and said that "if he were not obliged to it, he would seldom give his consent to perform one of them."[10] What "obliged" the managers to it? There seem to be at least four factors. First, new plays bred publicity. The newspapers were increasingly full of theatrical news and gossip in the 1720s, and new plays had news value. Second, the public evidently wanted *some* variety. Third, the importunities of writers were hard to resist

8. They seem even bleaker upon further examination. Centlivre and Rowe were established professional playwrights by 1708; Christopher Bullock was an actor at LIF; Addison was one of the great names in early eighteenth-century literature.

9. *The Strollers* (3), *The Stage-Coach* (2), *The School-Boy*, *Hob*, *The What d'ye Call It*.

10. Booth's complaint was reported by Thomas Davies. See ch. 7, sec. "The Structure of the Period," above.

all the time, and the theatres cannot have lost much on most new plays.[11] And fourth, there was always the hope of a hit. We have no box-office reports for Drury Lane in 1726–27, but those for Lincoln's Inn Fields show an enormous fluctuation in the take— from £14 (*A Fond Husband*, 30 November) to £210 (*Aesop*, 18 February). In the latter case the theatre was benefitting from *The Rape of Proserpine*. The theatre grossed a phenomenal £200 each of the first eight nights this afterpiece was performed. Expenses ran about £50 a night at this time, and many days the theatre took in less or very little more. A success with a new play, or a lucky revival like *Camilla*, was eagerly sought.

Unless a theatre chose to offer a new play "New Dress'd," or it required special new scenery, investment in a new play was more a matter of time and trouble than money. The author still received only profits from the third night (and third nights thereafter during the first run). The nuisance, however, was considerable. The norm throughout the season was for each theatre to mount six different mainpieces each week. As a rule they did not repeat any play within two weeks except during first runs of new plays. Learning the lines and rehearsing a new script likely to survive all of three nights (on the average) was not, therefore, a welcome proposition on top of the usual demands of the repertory system.

Another reason that managers may have been chary of new plays—or quickly became so after 1728—is the vague legal status of such plays. If a successful new play could forthwith be pirated by the opposition it represented much less potential advantage than if it remained the exclusive property of the company which first mounted it. Rights to plays had been a sore subject back in 1660,[12] and the matter had never really been settled. The Carolean arrange-

---

11. Extant figures from Rich's company suggest that curiosity often gave the theatre a decent house the first night, and the author's friends generally made the third night productive of house charges or better. Second nights were often quite unprofitable—so much so that on occasion the second night was canceled or made the author's benefit.

12. See Robert D. Hume, "Securing a Repertory: Plays on the London Stage, 1660–1665," *Poetry and Drama, 1570–1700: Essays in Honour of Harold F. Brooks*, ed. Antony Colman and Antony Hammond (London: Methuen, 1981), pp. 156–72.

ment had been that pre-1660 plays were divided (very unequally) by the lord chamberlain; new plays belonged exclusively to the company which first performed them. The Union of 1682 gave the United Company rights to all plays. After the rebellion of 1695 both companies performed old plays and had exclusive right to new ones, but this distinction collapsed with the actor transfers of 1706 and the new Union of 1708. Between 1714 and 1728 Drury Lane and Lincoln' Inn Fields refrained from poaching each other's new plays, but this appears to have been a matter of private cooperation. There seems to have been no legal barrier to a competitor's buying a copy of the play and rushing it into production—as a nonpatent company at the Haymarket was to do in 1728 with *The Beggar's Opera.*

The season of 1727–28 opened without any sign that it would differ notably from the dozen that preceded it. The two companies alternated politely until the coronation of George II (11 October), an event which brought the *beau monde* to town earlier than usual and made daily performance worthwhile. The overall repertory patterns carry on what we saw in 1726–27. Drury Lane mounted sixty-three plays (three of them new) in 188 nights. Of the sixty revived plays only six were not performed there in 1726–27—that is, fifty-four were carried over. At Lincoln's Inn Fields fifty-nine plays (two of them new) were mounted in 194 nights, but eighteen of the revivals (totaling 35 nights) were not in the 1726–27 repertory.[13] Sixteen plays (totaling 64 nights) appeared in both companies' repertories. As in the previous season, the offerings were heavily weighted toward older plays. (See Table 2, next page.)

Once again the post-1708 plays were anything but adventurous: *Cato, The Distrest Mother, Jane Shore, The What d'ye Call It,* and *The Conscious Lovers* at Drury Lane; *The Busie Body, A Bold Stroke, The Drummer, Woman's Revenge, Thomyris,* and *The Wife's Relief* at Lincoln's Inn Fields. *Thomyris*—a translated Italian opera of 1707—was an unsuccessful attempt to repeat the success of *Camilla* the previous year.

These figures effectively mask the startling developments of the

13. Many of these revivals were for benefit performances.

Table 2:   *Mainpieces Performed in the Season of 1727–28*

	DL		LIF	
Pre-1660	13	(21%)	8	(14%)
1660–94	24	(38%)	22	(37%)
1695–1707	18	(29%)	19	(32%)
1708–20	4	(6%)	6	(10%)
Post-1720	4 (3 new)	(6%)	4 (2 new)	(7%)
	63		59	

season. On 10 January Drury Lane opened the Vanbrugh-Cibber *Provok'd Husband*, which ran an astonishing twenty-eight times in succession and another nine times later during the season. Several days into the initial run Lincoln's Inn Fields opened *The Beggar's Opera*, which ran thirty-two times without interruption and might have gone longer had it not extended into the benefit season. The total of sixty-two performances at Lincoln's Inn Fields this season was unprecedented in the entire history of the London theatre.[14]

The success of *The Beggar's Opera* demonstrated conclusively that there was a large, hitherto almost untapped audience in London. It had pulled into the theatre not only a multitude of repeat attenders but also a large group of potential and occasional theatregoers who could perhaps be induced to attend regularly. But how? Neither company had ever shown much disposition to engage in aggressive promotion. Both had been content to make moderate profits with an ultraconservative repertory policy that attracted a solid cadre of regular theatregoers. The key question in the spring of 1728 was whether Drury Lane and Lincoln's Inn Fields would change their stodgy ways in response to a radically altered theatrical situation. Neither company moved vigorously to exploit it. Drury Lane seems initially to have viewed *The Beggar's Opera* as a kind of freak misfortune that would run its course. At Lincoln's Inn Fields John Rich simply settled down to enjoy his golden goose without much thought for the morrow.

14. The closest thing to it is *The Constant Couple* at the turn of the century, which reputedly achieved fifty performances in five months. There are, however, no exact performance records with which to check this total.

The Challenge of the Little Haymarket, 1728–1730

The first sign that someone was prepared to capitalize aggressively on the situation created by the triumph of *The Beggar's Opera* is a pirate production at the Little Haymarket. Not much is known of this theatre. Built in 1720 by John Potter, it was evidently neither large nor fancy.[15] For eight seasons it had been occupied by an ever-shifting succession of foreign troupes, amateurs, and musicians. As early as 1721–22 Aaron Hill broached a scheme to use the Little Haymarket as the venue for a third English company.[16] The idea came to naught, but even at that date someone was convinced that there was room for competition in London.

During the season of 1727–28 the Little Haymarket was principally occupied by a Signora Violante, whose troupe offered everything from acrobatics and rope dancing to a pantomime called *The Rivals*. The first hint of a more direct kind of competition for the patent theatres was the premiere of John Mottley's *Penelope* on 8 May. This is the first of many *Beggar's Opera* imitations—a comic ballad opera of London low life which survived only three nights. Starting in late May a "New Company of English Comedians" began to offer occasional performances of standard repertory pieces—*The Orphan*, *The Drummer*, *Tamerlane*, *The Spanish Fryar*, and *Richard III*. Summer performances of this sort were by no means unknown at the Little Haymarket, but late in June an extraordinary event occurred. For Monday 24 June "a New Company who never appeared on that Stage before" advertised *The Beggar's Opera* "All the Songs and Dances set to Musick, as it is perform'd at the Theatre in Lincoln's-Inn-Fields."[17] We have, unfortunately, no idea who managed this company or who performed in it. Lincoln's Inn Fields had given "positively" its last performance of Gay's piece the previous Wednesday, and it offered only a very sketchy summer season.

---

15. The reported cost of the building was £1,000. By contrast Dorset Garden cost £9,000 in 1671, and Drury Lane about half that in 1674. For a convenient account of London theatre buildings (with comparative charts on dimensions, cost, capacities, etc.) see Edward A. Langhans, "The Theatres," in *The London Theatre World*, pp. 35–65.

16. See *The London Stage*, Part 2, II, 637.

17. All performance data is drawn from Parts 2 and 3 of *The London Stage*.

(Drury Lane offered none at all.) We do not know, for example, whether some of the summer performers at the Little Haymarket were moonlighting from Lincoln's Inn Fields. Nor have we any idea whether Rich acquiesced in this transfer. I am inclined to doubt it. Rich had refused to let his performers use *The Beggar's Opera* for their benefits that spring, and the fifteen performances given at the Little Haymarket suggest a distinctly profitable venture. Unless Rich was somehow getting a cut, this production represents the first major breach in the de facto agreement to let each company retain exclusive rights to successful new plays.

The season of 1728–29 saw the two patent theatres operate pretty much as before in most respects, but it is remarkable for the appearance of full-fledged competition. For the first time since 1642 there was a third company of import in London. The Little Haymarket operated only 115 nights (plus concerts) versus 195 for Drury Lane and 157 for Lincoln's Inn Fields. And it ran only twenty-three plays (versus sixty-eight and forty-eight respectively). But there could be no doubt in anyone's mind that the Little Haymarket intended direct competition. Its first performance was *The Beggar's Opera* (8 October), a work already staged six times that fall in its original Lincoln's Inn Fields venue, most recently on 4 October.

The repertory at the Little Haymarket for 1728–29 is an odd amalgam. The company staged single performances of such standard pieces as *The Recruiting Officer, Oroonoko, The Beaux Stratagem,* and *Tamerlane,* and offered two and three performances of others (*The Spanish Fryar, The Orphan, Venice Preserv'd*). They revived three pieces which had been out of the repertory ten to twenty years—*Don Carlos* (one night), *The Lunatick* (three), and *The Metamorphosis* (five). Some twenty-five nights were occupied by old plays, and fifteen more by *The Beggar's Opera.* The rest of the season (more than 60 percent of the nights) was devoted to new plays, singly and in combination. The company tried some ten new pieces (including afterpieces), and it had major successes with three of them. *The Humours of Harlequin* (twenty-six performances) is merely the sort of thing John Rich prospered on. But Coffey's *The Beggar's Wedding* (thirty-four performances) is a successful follow-up on Gay's ballad-opera form, and Samuel Johnson of Cheshire's *Hurlothrumbo* (thirty-three performances) is a wonderful piece of satiric nonsense.[18]

Against this innovative fare, Drury Lane and Lincoln's Inn Fields ran pretty much the mixture as before.

Table 3: Mainpieces Performed in the Season of 1728–29

	DL			LIF		
Pre-1660	15		(22%)	9		(18%)
1660–94	22		(32%)	16		(33%)
1695–1707	21		(31%)	14		(29%)
1708–20	6		(9%)	6		(12%)
Post-1720	4	(2 new)	(6%)	4	(3 new)	(8%)
	68			49		

Examination of the new plays, however, affords clear proof that Drury Lane had been deeply traumatized by *The Beggar's Opera.* Both of its new mainpieces were ambitious ballad operas and their failure must have been a decided disappointment. Cibber's *Love in a Riddle* was damned by faction in two nights;[19] Charles Johnson's *The Village Opera* lasted only four.[20] A ballad-opera afterpiece, *The Lover's Opera*, had a slow start but did enter the repertory. Drury Lane's one major success this season was *Perseus and Andromeda*, a fancy pantomime which was performed more than forty times. By way of competition Lincoln's Inn Fields proved remarkably conservative. Its three new mainpieces were all tragedies. Richard Barford's *The Virgin Queen* and Eliza Haywood's *Frederick, Duke of*

18. The other new plays were Mottley's *The Craftsman* (6), *The Quaker's Opera* (4), *The Lottery* (6), *The Royal Captives* (1—lost), Odell's *The Smugglers* and *The Patron* (1), and Cibber's *Damon and Phillida* (1—but later a successful afterpiece for many seasons). *Damon* was also performed at Drury Lane and Bartholomew Fair.

19. Revamped as an afterpiece it later enjoyed considerable success as *Damon and Phillida.*

20. Nicoll, II, 242, calls *The Village Opera* "a great success," but beyond the initial four nights at Drury Lane the only record of revival I find is a brief run at the Haymarket in 1729–30.

Brunswick-Lunenburgh are heroic-conspiracy pieces that lasted only three nights apiece. Samuel Madden's *Themistocles*, a somewhat turgid patriot drama, managed nine. A ballad-opera afterpiece, *Hob's Opera*, found little support. The successful experimentation in 1728–29 was carried out at the Little Haymarket.

The pattern of the 1729–30 season repeats that of 1728–29, save for the addition of Goodman's Fields to the scene (discussed in the next section). The patent houses stuck with their usual policies while the Little Haymarket (playing more sporadically) experimented. During 1729–30 Drury Lane tried a bit of everything. Another ballad-opera mainpiece flopped (Odingsells' *Bayes' Opera*), and the company had very modest luck with a pair of ballad-opera afterpieces (*Patie and Pegie* and *The Stage Coach Opera*). Two tragedies (Martyn's *Timoleon* and Thomson's *Sophonisba*) had good initial runs, and a comedy (Miller's *Humours of Oxford*) managed six nights. Four new pantomimes found little favor. But Drury Lane was feeling the need to compete more energetically. At Lincoln's Inn Fields Rich countered with a new ballad opera, *Momus turn'd Fabulist* (a considerable success), and his own version of *Perseus and Andromeda* (with more than fifty performances, a success even greater than Drury Lane's).

The Little Haymarket presents a marked contrast. Running 100 nights, it used pre-1720 plays only 6 times. Its great successes were Fielding's *The Author's Farce* and *Tom Thumb* (which ran 28 straight times together). To be sure, the smaller capacity and lower overhead of the Little Haymarket were more conducive to lengthy runs, but this second successful season of competition made plain that there was a market for something other than repertory warhorses.

Competition from Goodman's Fields, 1729–1732

The Little Haymarket represented competition for the patent theatres via different repertory policy; Goodman's Fields represented competition via different location. In October 1729 Thomas Odell opened a theatre in a converted workshop in Ayliffe Street, Goodman's Fields.[21] This was plainly an attempt to reach an audience in east London for which the patent theatres were relatively remote. All the signs point to its being an immediate success. Scouten records a report that house charges were only £16 per night, and that the company generally played to houses of about £60 its first year, never below £50.[22]

The initial strategy at Goodman's Fields was to offer a repertory essentially similar to that of the patent houses, but to do it in a location where a well-drilled company of beginners and journeymen would have an audience to itself. In 188 nights during 1729–30 Goodman's Fields mounted thirty-eight mainpieces (four of them new). Of their thirty-four old plays all were repertory pieces, and all but two were in the current repertory at Drury Lane, Lincoln's Inn Fields, or both that season.[23] Goodman's Fields simply took the most attractive of the patent theatres' shows and made them available closer to home. Recent hits such as *The Beggar's Opera* and *The Provok'd Husband* were performed six and seven nights respectively this season. Instead of running plays like *Hamlet* or *The Recruiting Officer* once or twice or four times in a season, Goodman's Fields ran them eight or nine, and it ran far fewer plays just once or twice.

Goodman's Fields did exhibit a definite preference for the more modern part of the patent theatres' repertory. It ran some old favorites—*Hamlet, Merry Wives, Othello, Rule a Wife*—and some of the Restoration standbys (*The Old Batchelour, Venice Preserv'd, The Spanish Fryar*), but the figures show a clear tilt toward the eighteenth century.

---

21. Scholarship on Goodman's Fields remains scanty. The study most often cited, Frederick T. Wood's "The Goodman's Fields Theatre," *Modern Language Review*, 25 (1930), 443–56, is marred by some serious errors and has been entirely superseded by Scouten's introduction and calendar in Part 3 of *The London Stage*.

22. *The London Stage*, Part 3, I, xxi–xxii.

23. The two exceptions were Farquhar's *The Inconstant* (last revived at Drury Lane in 1723) and Centlivre's *The Man's Bewitched* (out of the repertory since 1709).

Table 4:   *Mainpieces in the Repertory, Season of 1729–30*

	DL		LIF		GF	
Pre-1660	11	(17%)	9	(16%)	4	(10.5%)
1660–94	22	(35%)	18	(31.5%)	8	(21%)
1695–						
1707	18	(29%)	17	(30%)	10	(26%)
1708–20	6	(9.5%)	7	(12%)	9	(24%)
Post-1720	6	(9.5%)	6	(10.5%)	7	(18.5%)
	63		57		38	

In other words, approximately 20 percent of the mainpieces mounted at Drury Lane and Lincoln's Inn Fields were written in 1708 or later, as opposed to more than 40 percent at Goodman's Fields. This pattern continued at Goodman's Fields during 1730–31 and 1731–32. One sign that it ceased to rely on novelty and had to compete more directly, however, is a rapid rise in its employment of afterpieces. In its first season it used afterpieces only 33 nights, in its second 96, in its third 132.

One inevitable result of Goodman's Fields' reliance on a repertory that overlapped its competitors' so heavily was a number of direct collisions, and even more near misses. Prior to 1728 such overlapping is a rarity, except for *Tamerlane* on King William's birthday. By 1729–30 there are a lot of cases in which two or more of the theatres performed the same play within a week or two. To what extent this represents herd instinct, and to what extent malice, we have no way to tell.

The most striking feature of the Goodman's Fields operation is its conservative repertory policy. The most important of its new plays is Fielding's *The Temple Beau*, and it had fairly good luck with Ralph's *The Fashionable Lady* (a burlesque opera), both in its first season. After that its premieres are few and unsuccessful.[24] That the house could succeed in direct competition with the established theatres—and its productions seem to have been on a par with those at the patent houses—is testimony to the skill with which Goodman's Fields was managed, even when allowance is made for its

24. In 1730–31 Goodman's Fields mounted *The Cynick* (3 nights) and *The Earl of Essex* (4); in 1731–32 *The Footman* (5) and *The Jealous Husband* (3).

different location. By 1731–32 Henry Giffard had become manager for Odell, and he seems to have been an outstanding manager. Scouten points out some of his virtues and innovations—rigorous training for young performers, skillful promotion, good public relations, changing casts until a show was at its best, and so forth.[25] These things do not show up in a performance calendar, but they go a long way toward explaining how Goodman's Fields could compete with the giants.

The Haymarket venture tells us that there was a market in London for innovative contemporary drama—a market which had been ignored by Rich and the Triumvirate. The success of Goodman's Fields tells us that the patent theatres were not exhausting the audience demand for more traditional dramatic entertainment. In these circumstances London must have seemed ripe for larger and better theatres, and perhaps even for more companies.

The State of the Repertory and the Trends in New Plays, 1728–1732

The effect of competition on the patent houses is obvious when we survey their offerings in the early thirties. In 1730–31 Drury Lane mounted sixty-seven mainpieces for a total of 192 nights; seven of the plays were new. Lincoln's Inn Fields did fifty-four mainpieces over 178 nights, six of them new. The thirteen new mainpieces at the two patent houses is by a considerable margin the largest total since well before the union of 1708. Of the new plays only *The London Merchant* (initially a summer production at Drury Lane) was a major success, but David Mallet's *Eurydice* managed 14 nights at Drury Lane. Lincoln's Inn Fields had less luck with new plays, but responded to changing circumstances by picking up recent plays from other theatres' repertories. For the first time Lincoln's Inn Fields staged *The Conscious Lovers* (1722), and it mounted Fielding's *The Coffee House Politician* (Little Haymarket, 1730, under the title *Rape upon Rape*). In 1731–32 Drury Lane tried five new main-

25. *The London Stage*, Part 3, I, lxxx–lxxxv.

pieces (only *The Modern Husband* was a success), Lincoln's Inn Fields just one—but by that time Rich was putting his money and energy into the building of his new Covent Garden theatre.

By 1731–32 the influence of the Little Haymarket was in temporary decline, although the reasons for this decline cannot be given with confidence. Any attempt at a detailed study of the company fails for lack of information. We do not know its managers, its earnings, or its expenses. We cannot be at all certain how complete our performance calendar is, and our roster of the performers is not always complete. We cannot even be sure how many distinct groups used the premises each season. From the number and regularity of the performances over a span of three seasons, we can deduce significant success. But why the company reduced its activity so markedly in 1731–32, for example, we simply do not know. We have records of twenty-six plays over eighty-five nights in 1730–31, with six new plays. In 1731–32 the totals fall to seventeen in forty, three of them new.

We can make some guesses. A company relying heavily on new scripts has to find good ones, or at least popular ones. Fielding had a substantial part in the Little Haymarket's early success. By 1731–32 he was sufficiently established that his work was in demand at the major houses. With increased competition the other theatres (including Goodman's Fields) were readier to consider new scripts, and perhaps the Little Haymarket tended to get last choice. Cross suggests that the Little Haymarket declined because of "threatened if not actual interference by the government."[26] There is some evidence for this (for example, interference with a performance 20 August 1731), but how important a factor this was we cannot be certain. Whatever the reasons, the Little Haymarket slipped back into relative obscurity in 1731–32.

The full significance of the competition inaugurated by the Little Haymarket in 1728, however, did not become visible until after 1730 and was not restricted to new plays. A brief analysis of the 1731–32 season will suggest the changed nature of the London the-

26. Cross, *The History of Henry Fielding*, I, 114–15.

atre milieu. Of the fifty-eight plays offered at Lincoln's Inn Fields, twenty-three were in the active repertory at Drury Lane this season—an increase of 50 percent over the norm in the mid-1720s. Both companies performed *The Beggar's Opera* and *The Provok'd Husband,* and Lincoln's Inn Fields started doing *The London Merchant,* premiered at Drury Lane just the preceding summer. Both patent companies continued to rely heavily on pre-1708 classics, but the following figures are significant.

Table 5: Post–1720 Mainpieces (Including New Plays) Offered Each Season by the Patent Companies

	DL	LIF	TOTAL
1726–27	2 (3%)	5 (10%)	7 (6%)
1727–28	4 (6%)	4 (7%)	8 (6.5%)
1728–29	4 (6%)	4 (8%)	8 (7%)
1729–30	6 (9.5%)	6 (10.5%)	12 (10%)
1730–31	8 (11%)	11 (20%)	19 (16%)
1731–32	10 (16%)	7 (12%)	17 (14%)

More than half the total is new plays, and much of the balance represents a few plays repeated each season. Even so, we learn from this a) that competition from the Little Haymarket definitely pushed the patent houses to mount some new plays, and b) that concomitantly they noticeably increased the proportion of contemporary plays in the repertory. The absolute numbers are not great in either plays or performances, but the contrast with the mid-1720s is striking, the more so when we remember that few of the new plays ever amounted to anything. Of forty-one new mainpieces tried at the patent houses between 1728 and 1732 only five survived significantly beyond one season.[27] The effect of the Little Haymarket was precisely what a believer in free enterprise would predict. When pushed by a competitor, the patent houses bestirred themselves.[28]

27. *The Double Falsehood* (barely), *The Provok'd Husband, The London Merchant, The Beggar's Opera,* and *Momus turn'd Fabulist.*

28. Another clear indicator of increased competition is the rise in the number of afterpieces. Drury Lane offered 143 afterpieces in 197 nights, Lincoln's Inn Fields 132 in 172 during 1731–32. We must remember that as a rule neither house ordi-

One is, unfortunately, less inclined to rejoice at the upsurge in new plays after one has read them. Of course much the same could be said of the new plays written in the first few years after 1660. Our immediate concern, however, is with the state of the market. In the first four seasons after the triumph of *The Beggar's Opera* a wide variety of play types were tried—with varying and quite unpredictable success. By mid-1732 a new phase in the boom was in prospect. Two important new theatre buildings were nearing completion; reliance on new scripts was on the upswing; impending management changes at Drury Lane suggested that it might adopt an even more venturesome approach; and enough new plays had been mounted to give aspirant writers something to go on. Surveying the efforts of the previous four seasons, a would-be dramatist might reasonably have drawn the following conclusions.

1. Music—especially ballad opera—was "in." Counting afterpieces, some thirty-five ballad operas had been tried in four years. After 1730 the trend was clearly away from mainpieces, which were relatively expensive and hence a greater risk in time, trouble, and money. The vogue for low-life subjects died quite quickly, and ballad opera moved toward pantomime and farce. *Momus turn'd Fabulist* (LIF, December 1729) and *The Fashionable Lady, or Harlequin's Opera* (GF, April 1730) were early indicators. The major successes of the past two years bore out this trend. The Coffey-Mottley *The Devil to Pay* (DL, August 1731),[29] and Fielding's *The Lottery* and *The Mock Doctor* (DL, January and June 1732) are musicalized farce.

Perhaps contrary to expectation, Rich had made little effort to follow up *The Beggar's Opera* with more ballad opera. Prior to 1730–31 Drury Lane and the Little Haymarket had mounted six ballad operas each, as had Lincoln's Inn Fields. Goodman's Fields

---

narily played afterpieces during the first run of a new play; a few shows (e.g., *The Beggar's Opera*) normally stood by themselves; and benefits often added singing and dancing instead of an afterpiece.

29. For a disentanglement of the complex history of this popular piece, see Arthur H. Scouten and Leo Hughes, "*The Devil to Pay*, a Preliminary Check List," *University of Pennsylvania Library Chronicle*, 16 (1948), 15–24.

had tried just one.[30] But in 1730–31 and 1731–32 Lincoln's Inn
Fields and Goodman's Fields did two ballad operas apiece, and the
Little Haymarket one, while Drury Lane tried ten new ones, a couple
of them ambitious mainpieces like *The Jovial Crew* and *Highland
Fair.* One must grant that Drury Lane's persistence paid off: despite
a string of disappointments, they found some popular and profitable afterpieces. Rich's relative lack of interest in ballad opera
probably reflects his understanding that it was increasingly aimed
at the market he already reached with pantomime.

    2. Pantomime continued "in" with a vengeance. The enor-
mous and continuing popularity of several mid-1720s pantomimes
(*Jupiter and Europa, The Necromancer, Harlequin a Sorcerer, Apollo
and Daphne,* and *The Rape of Proserpine,* at Lincoln's Inn Fields;
Harlequin Dr. Faustus, another version of *Apollo and Daphne,* and
Harlequin's Triumph at Drury Lane) naturally encouraged the development of more such pieces. There are two reasons that great
numbers of them did not inundate the stage. First, they were both
expensive and complicated to stage, and hence a risk. Second, audiences were so willing to see the same few over and over that managers did not need to take such a risk very often. As with ballad
operas we find Drury Lane far more aggressive than Lincoln's Inn
Fields in trying new shows: eight versus three. Goodman's Fields
also tried three, the Little Haymarket just one. The two versions of
Perseus and Andromeda flourished; so did Drury Lane's *Cephalus
and Procris.*

    3. Tragedy was relatively easy to get staged, but not likely to
achieve much popularity. Dramatists—and to some degree managers—were caught in a bind. Critical precepts pointed in one direction, audience preferences in another. Anyone reading periodical
criticism in these years finds all sorts of demands for moral serious-

---

30. Fiske says that "Goodman's Fields was not at first able to find enough
singers," but in 1732 began to stage ballad operas with vigor. In fact, Goodman's
Fields mounted *The Fashionable Lady* in April 1730 (in its first season), and in July
the company got up *The Beggar's Opera* and *The Stage Coach Opera.* For a good
discussion of "Ballad Opera 1728–1736" see Roger Fiske, *English Theatre Music in
the Eighteenth Century* (London: Oxford Univ. Press, 1973), ch. 3.

ness, historicity, poetic justice, conformity to decorum and the rules, and so forth.[31] That writers ought to compose such pieces, and that managers should produce them, were widely accepted propositions. Unfortunately—or perhaps fortunately—audiences seldom showed much disposition to support the results.

In practice, there are at least six clearly distinguishable types of serious drama being written at this time. The most numerous are 1) heroic-intrigue tragedies, and 2) "Roman" or pseudo-classical tragedies. By this time the heroic-intrigue mode was pretty tired, but authors still cranked out such works with great regularity. Barford's *The Virgin Queen*, Jeffrey's *Merope*, Walker's *The Fate of Villainy*, and Ralph's *The Earl of Essex* are examples. The Roman plays—in a genre much indebted to *Cato* (1713)—include such pieces as Johnson's *Medea*, Mallet's *Eurydice*, and Sturmy's *Sesostris*. The best of them is undoubtedly Thomson's *Sophonisba*. 3) A subcategory of the Roman play is perhaps best termed "patriot drama," a subgenre which was to gain popularity in the later years of the Walpole administration. In these years Madden's *Themistocles* and Martyn's *Timoleon* are the principal examples. Political topicality (even just in theme) seems to have been a significant advantage. 4) A few providential tragicomedies were still getting written—for example, Theobald's *Double Falsehood* (whose modest success was surely the result of the alleged Shakespearean connection) and Cooke's *Triumphs of Love and Honour*. 5) Pathetic plays by Southerne and Rowe remained extremely popular in the repertory, but new ones are few in number at this time. Bellers' *Injured Innocence* is an example. 6) Finally, one promising new development is the "fate play." Wandesford's *Fatal Love*, Hill's *Athelwold*, and Lillo's *The London Merchant* are early examples. The key to this subgenre is circumstances that create a psychological crisis for the leading characters. Its roots lie in pathetic drama; Southerne's *Fatal Marriage*, still very popular on the stage in the 1730s, is an obvious ancestor. Roman plays tend to be emotionally frigid, the heroic-intrigue plays emptily heated. The purely pathetic plays depict mis-

31. For a convenient survey, see Charles Harold Gray, *Theatrical Criticism in London to 1795*, chs. 1 and 2.

ery simply to arouse sympathy. The fate plays are more interesting because of their greater emphasis on character. Unlike the Roman plays they tend to have characters who are to some degree believable.[32]

A writer's best chance with a tragedy was Drury Lane or Lincoln's Inn Fields, which mounted nine and seven respectively in these years. By contrast the Little Haymarket tried four, and Goodman's Fields just two. Both of Goodman's Fields' efforts, and two of those at the Little Haymarket, were heroic-intrigue plays. Drury Lane was more venturesome than Lincoln's Inn Fields in new tragedies. Drury Lane (if we count the summer company) sponsored two of the fate plays, two providential tragicomedies, a pathetic play, a patriot drama, and three Roman plays. Drury Lane was, interestingly, the only house *not* to mount a heroic-intrigue play. Lincoln's Inn Fields, by contrast, tried four of them, along with a patriot drama and a pair of Roman plays. Thus in this period Drury Lane was clearly the most adventurous and successful house for tragedy— not that it made any money for its pains.

4. Comedy was not flourishing. With the riches of the seventeenth century to draw upon, the managers had little enthusiasm for bothering with new mainpieces, and since the most successful afterpieces were pantomimes and ballad operas they underwrote no great number of two-act comedies either. For such comedies as there are, however, the theatres exhibit quite different partialities. "London social comedy" was principally the province of Drury Lane, which put on such plays as *The Provok'd Husband*, *The Modish Couple*, and *The Modern Husband*, as well as lighter London comedies like *Love in Several Masques* and *The Lover*. The Little Haymarket tried a couple of light London comedies but had an obvious bias in favor of topical comedy (*The Craftsman*, *The Smugglers*, *Rape upon Rape*) and farce (*The Author's Farce* and several which were not published). Lincoln's Inn Fields, in clear contrast, had little use for comedy of any sort. Rich tried just one London social comedy (Kelly's *The Married Philosopher*) and a pair of undistinguished

32. For detailed accounts of the "Roman," "Othellian" (pathetic), and "fate" genres see Bonnie Nelson, *Serious Drama and the London Stage, 1729–1739* (Salzburg: Salzburg Studies in English, 1982).

farces. Goodman's Fields mounted a trio of London comedies (*The Temple Beau* was the only success) and what appear to be a pair of afterpiece farces (lost). Surveying these rather limited offerings a young writer could conclude with no difficulty that "serious" comedies should be offered to Drury Lane, farces and topical pieces to the Little Haymarket.

5. Burlesque was proving decidedly popular. *Hurlothrumbo*, *Tom Thumb* (and later *The Tragedy of Tragedies*) had done incredibly well, and the Little Haymarket specialized in such things, having also mounted such works as *The Cheshire Comicks*, *Jack the Giant-Killer*, *The Welsh Opera*, and *The Blazing Comet*. The first major burlesque mounted elsewhere was Fielding's *Covent Garden Tragedy*, put on at Drury Lane in June 1732. Its production was a clear sign that Drury Lane was ready to steal the thunder from pesky non-patent competitors.

Overall, our hypothetical young writer might reasonably conclude that legitimate comedy was not flourishing, mainpiece ballad opera had shot its bolt, and tragedy needed a new twist to get away from its clichés. Burlesque and topical material had become good bets. Farcical ballad opera afterpieces were in demand. For the writer with grander literary aspirations patriot drama and fate tragedy were the best possibilities.

We are hampered in any attempt to analyze the tastes of the four theatre managements by not knowing who (if any one person) was making decisions at the Little Haymarket. Goodman's Fields was unadventuresome with new plays in these years and did not mount many in any case. Rich put on more new plays at Lincoln's Inn Fields than his reputation might lead one to expect, especially in the realm of tragedy, but he seems to have been both conservative in taste and a somewhat unskillful judge of quality.

Granting that the Little Haymarket provided the stimulus, Drury Lane comes out surprisingly eclectic and forward-looking in this little survey. Colley Cibber—who read most of the scripts submitted to Drury Lane—has often been ridiculed for refusing *The Beggar's Opera*, but we might reflect in his defense that he was no fool and cannot have been unaware of its anti-Whiggish tenor. Perhaps he would have swallowed his Whig principles and pocketed the cash had he anticipated its success, but in the circumstances one can hardly sneer at his turning down so very odd a work, especially one so liberally freighted with matter obnoxious to Cibber's high-life friends. At all events, the evidence suggests that Drury Lane was being intelligently managed in the seasons we have just surveyed. Little as Cibber may have liked Fielding, Drury Lane was quite ready to produce his plays in the spring of 1732.

The Opening of Covent Garden and the Second Phase of Competition, 1732–1736

In the fall of 1732 several events occurred that were to have major impact on the theatrical scene in London. Henry Giffard opened a new and better Goodman's Fields theatre. John Rich opened his fancy new Covent Garden theatre. And in the course of four months the Triumvirate management that had guided Drury Lane for twenty seasons dissolved and disappeared. In none of the three cases was the full effect immediately apparent.

The new Goodman's Fields theatre opened 2 October 1732 with *1 Henry IV*. It was relatively small and inexpensive, but by all accounts a superb venue for plays.[33] The architect was Edward Shepherd (who also designed Covent Garden for Rich). The exterior dimensions were approximately 90 by 52 feet; the cost was £2,300 plus whatever Giffard himself invested. Scouten calculates capacity at about 707, or circa £67 at regular prices. There is no better proof of the success of the first Goodman's Fields theatre than Giffard's readiness to build more elegant quarters and the ease with which he found twenty-three people willing to invest £100 in the venture. The elegant interior decoration suggests a comfortable budget. The new theatre did not, of course, make any essential change in the competitive balance in London: it simply replaced a make-shift venue. Its importance lies in its demonstration of the viability of the third full-time company.

33. For the best account of the theatre see *The London Stage*, Part 3, I, xxiii–xxvii.

Covent Garden was an altogether fancier enterprise. The exterior dimensions were 117 by 62 feet, the cost about £6,000. Capacity has been variously estimated, but was about 1,300 to 1,400. At advanced prices Rich could hope to gross more than £200 a night with something close to a full house. Covent Garden was new, handsome, fancily rigged for pantomime spectacle, and blessed with excellent acoustics. It was, interestingly, essentially identical to Lincoln's Inn Fields in capacity.[34] When Rich opened his new house, 7 December 1732, he became proprietor of two large and well-rigged theatre buildings in the West End. What would he do with Lincoln's Inn Fields? Several possibilities must have occurred to Rich. He could rent the building (or sell it outright) for nontheatrical purposes. He could rent it out to freelance groups and musicians, as the Little Haymarket had been used in the 1720s. He might simply operate it himself as a second venue for his company. Or conceivably he could find a new opera company ready to rent it. There is evidence that all four possibilities were real.[35]

How seriously Rich considered opening a second company at Lincoln's Inn Fields we have no way to tell, but he definitely tried the experiment of competing for the holiday custom in 1732–33 by running the two theatres simultaneously during the Christmas and Easter seasons.[36] The figures preserved in *The London Stage* suggest moderately profitable operation, but the detailed analysis by Hughes and Scouten also shows why Rich had difficulties with this scheme. His company was big, and at Christmas Covent Garden was in the middle of a long run of *The Beggar's Opera* (twenty nights, starting 16 December), but even so he needed certain performers in both places. He had not only to do some recasting but to rush some people half a mile from one theatre to the other. To operate both theatres on a regular basis Rich would have had substantially to enlarge his roster of performers, thereby increasing his

34. For details on the construction and features of Covent Garden see *The London Stage*, Part 3, I, xxvii–xxxii.

35. See Paul Sawyer, *The New Theatre in Lincoln's Inn Fields* (London: Society for Theatre Research, 1979), esp. pp. 22–24.

36. For a detailed account see Leo Hughes and Arthur H. Scouten, "John Rich and the Holiday Seasons of 1732–3," *Review of English Studies*, 21 (1945), 46–52.

financial commitments and risk. Would the demand support another West End venture? With the benefit of hindsight we may guess that it would have: Giffard, after all, decided to move to Lincoln's Inn Fields in 1736. But for whatever reasons Rich refrained from extending himself further.

The possibility of an opera tenant was genuine. "English opera" had languished since the rage for Italian opera hit London with *Camilla* in 1706 and the arrival of Handel in 1711. Since then the Royal Academy of Music had gone spectacularly broke, and Handel's company, reconstructed in 1729, was none too healthy. English composers, surveying the situation and noting the vogue for ballad opera, naturally wondered whether the time was ripe for a change. *Amelia* (by Carey and Lampe) had scored a success at the Haymarket in the spring of 1732. During the season of 1732–33 five more "English operas" were mounted (as well as the Little Haymarket's *Opera of Operas* burlesque in May 1733). None managed more than six nights, but the idea of an English revival was clearly in the air.[37] Arne's advertisement of 22 February 1733, announcing English opera performances at Lincoln's Inn Fields, refers to him as "Proprietor of English Operas" and requests "Encouragement from the Town." The experiment fizzled, but the Lincoln's Inn Fields theatre remained available. In due course it was to be occupied by Giffard's Goodman's Fields company for the last season before the Licensing Act.

Meanwhile at Drury Lane the stability of the Triumvirate gave way to chaos almost overnight during the summer of 1732. Steele had died in 1729, and the actor-triumvirs then applied for a patent in their own names. This they got in April 1732. In July Barton Booth, long ailing and inactive, sold half his share to a theatrical dilettante, young John Highmore. On 27 September Robert Wilks died, and his wife promptly made the painter John Ellys her representative. A month later the wily Colley Cibber "rented" his share to his ambitious son Theophilus for £442 per annum (plus a twelve

---

37. See Fiske, pp. 130–45. The Little Haymarket tried *Brittania* (Lediard and Lampe, with highly innovative scenic trappings; and *Dione* (Gay and Lampe). Lincoln's Inn Fields mounted *Teraminta* (Carey and Smith), *Rosamond* (Addison and Arne), and *Ulysses* (Humphreys and Smith).

guinea per week salary for acting). Thus by 1 November 1732 the Drury Lane management had passed into new hands.

Unfortunately, the new managers could agree on practically nothing. The civil war that followed is among the most publicized of eighteenth-century theatrical broils and need not be rehearsed in detail here. Suffice to say that in March 1733 Colley Cibber prudently sold out to Highmore (outraging his son in the process), and by May Theophilus had led an actor revolt against the patentee. Highmore retained physical possession of the theatre, and so Theophilus led the actors off to perform at the Little Haymarket in 1733–34. Highmore kept Drury Lane running with a stopgap company, and he persuaded Rich to join him in an attempt to put their nonpatent competitors out of business via the courts. This proved entirely unsuccessful, and bad publicity to boot. During the winter Highmore sold out to another amateur dabbler, John Fleetwood, and Fleetwood negotiated with Theophilus Cibber for the return of the rebel actors. By March 1734 a treaty of sorts had been concluded and the Drury Lane company reassembled.[38]

The results of this upheaval were various and deleterious. The actors were bitter about having to serve a gentleman amateur. On his side Fleetwood was unhappy with the terms he was compelled to accept in order to reclaim his principal actors. At bottom, the issue was simple: who should run the theatre? The Triumvirate had come into power as a result of an elaborate conspiracy against the tyrannical Christopher Rich in 1709.[39] Rich's son John (allowed to use the patent again in 1714) was at least a performer, albeit a hard-nosed and tightfisted manager. The Triumvirate had a gentleman-partner from 1712 on—first the Tory William Collier and then the Whig Steele. Could less distinguished actors be patentees? Or license holders? The actors' rebellion of 1695 (led by the great Thomas Betterton) gave precedent for granting a license "at

38. For a fuller account see *The London Stage*, Part 3, I, lxxxix–xciii; and Richard Hindry Barker, *Mr Cibber of Drury Lane* (New York: Columbia Univ. Press, 1939), ch. 9.

39. On the elaborate machinations which had resulted in John Rich's father being put out of business, see Judith Milhous and Robert D. Hume, "The Silencing of Drury Lane in 1709," *Theatre Journal*, 32 (1980), 427–47.

pleasure" to an actor-cooperative. But was a license necessary at all? The operation of the Goodman's Fields company—owned and run by an actor—seemed to suggest otherwise.

We cannot be sure exactly what possibilities were explored by the various parties in this ruckus. Fleetwood definitely owned a controlling share in the patent and held rights to the Drury Lane theatre and its stock of costumes and scenery. He also had the capital necessary to operate such a venture. Theophilus Cibber and his friends may well have felt that in the long run they could not compete effectively from the Little Haymarket, just as Betterton's company had been hampered by the cramped old Lincoln's Inn Fields theatre and lack of capital after 1695. The third Lincoln's Inn Fields, vacated by Rich, would have given them a competitive venue, but since they would have been competing directly with Covent Garden, Rich probably did not want to rent to them. The upshot was a sour peace and a return to Drury Lane. Exactly ten years later another actor rebellion took place (organized by Garrick and Macklin). In the meantime the inexpert and penurious Fleetwood was in control of the Drury Lane repertory. The results were anything but pleasing to playwrights.

A survey of repertory and new plays in these years is complicated by the chaotic events just reviewed. "Drury Lane" does not signify a stable management or even a single company. Likewise the Little Haymarket in much of 1733–34 is occupied by what was previously the heart of the Drury Lane company, though of course managerially one is not talking about anything like the Drury Lane company as it had existed up to July 1732. The situation is further complicated by the woes of Handel's opera company, which had performed about fifty times each season in the King's Theatre, Haymarket, since reopening in 1729. A series of squabbles between management and singers led, irrationally, to the establishment of a second Italian opera company in London for 1733–34. As one opera company had been unprofitable, two of them naturally found the going difficult.[40] In 1734–35 the splinter company took over

40. For some background and financial specifics, see Judith Milhous and Robert D. Hume, "Box Office Reports for Five Operas Mounted by Handel in London, 1732–1734," *Harvard Library Bulletin*, 26 (1978), 245–66.

King's and Handel moved in with John Rich. During the spring Rich sometimes put on plays at Lincoln's Inn Fields while Handel was using Covent Garden. This curious dual arrangement at Covent Garden continued through 1736–37 and somewhat complicates any attempt to compare Rich's repertory with his offerings early in the thirties.

To get a clear idea of the developments in new plays and the various theatres' repertory policies we will have to make two brief surveys, one of seasons, the other of genres. Overall, the repertory offerings remain fairly constant during the mid-thirties. The proportion of pre-1660s, Restoration, turn of the century, and contemporary plays holds fairly steady at each theatre.

The pattern in season-by-season competition is clear. Following the opening of Covent Garden and the new Goodman's Fields, and during the heated competition generated by the actor rebellion of 1733–34, all of the theatres were active in producing new shows. A high proportion, however, were afterpieces. Table 6 (next page) shows vividly the pattern of new productions in these seasons. For the sake of comparison I have carried it on through 1737–38. A peak of competition was reached in 1732–33, despite Drury Lane's relative inactivity under its squabbling new management. By 1735–36 the patent theatres are visibly settling back into conservative patterns. Neither Fleetwood nor Rich had been having much luck competing with new plays, and they seem to have agreed, tacitly or otherwise, not to compete on that basis. As they reduced their offerings of new plays Giffard picked up some of the slack, a pattern he was to continue in 1736–37 when he moved to Lincoln's Inn Fields and into more direct competition with the patent houses.

Turning from theatres to genres we find a rapidly changing pattern.

1. In tragedy Drury Lane continued to be the principal sponsor, despite the shifting management, mounting five of the twelve new ones. Heroic intrigue tragedy lost its numerical dominance, and the four examples did not captivate the public (Havard's *Scanderbeg*; Bond, *The Tuscan Treaty*; Theobald, *The Fatal Secret*; Lillo, *The Christian Hero*). Duncombe's *Junius Brutus* (DL) did nothing

Table 6:   New Plays Mounted in London 1732–33 to 1737–38

	DL	CG	GF	HAY	LIF	TOTALS
1732–33	1 T 1 C 7 ap	1 E.op. 2 b.op.mp 2 T 2 ap	1 b.op. 1 T 3 ap	2 E.op. 2 C 1 trav.op. 3 ap	3 E.op.	17 mp 15 ap
1733–34	2 C 1 T 5 ap	2 C 1 ap	3 ap	1 C 2 top. C 3 ap	1 ap	8 mp 13 ap
1734–35	2 T 2 C 6 ap	2 C 4 ap	2 ap	1 ap	2 C	8 mp 13 ap
1735–36	1 C 1 ap	4 ap	1 T 1 b.op. 1 hist. 1 ap	1 top.C 2 C 1 T 6 ap	1 T 1 past.op. 3 ap	10 mp 15 ap
1736–37*	1 C 3 ap	1 T	[vacant]	1 T 1 C 1 top.C 1 b.op. 2 burl. 7 ap	2 C 1 T 1 hist. 4 ap	12 mp 14 ap
1737–38	1 C 1 T 2 ap	1 C 2 T 1 ap	[closed]	[closed]	[closed]	5 mp 3 ap

*Goodman's Fields company moved to Lincoln's Inn Fields

Abbreviations: ap = afterpieces   mp = mainpieces
                       b.op. = ballad opera past. op. = pastoral opera
                       burl. = burlesque   T = tragedies
                       C = comedies   top.C = topical comedy
                       E.op. = English opera trav. op. = travesty opera
                       hist. = history play

to encourage managers to try more Roman plays. As might have been predicted, several fate plays were mounted, though only Lillo's *Fatal Curiosity* (Little Hay, 1736) was a real success. Johnson's *Caelia* (DL, 1732) failed in one night, though it deserved to do better. Sterling's *Parracide* (GF, 1736) and Hewett's *Fatal Falsehood* (DL, 1734) found no vogue at all. Two translations from Voltaire by Aaron Hill did surprisingly well. *Zara* managed fifteen straight nights at Drury Lane in January 1736—though it got produced only after a success at York Buildings the previous summer. Goodman's Fields responded by putting on *Alzira* later in the spring of 1736, and it found some favor.

2. In comedy we find that Drury Lane and Covent Garden averaged four per season between them; Goodman's Fields shunned the form both in mainpieces and afterpieces; the Little Haymarket tried a couple each year, most of them pretty farcical. Of twenty-seven examples from these four seasons I would class seven as London social comedy, six as light London comedy, ten as farce, four as miscellaneous or unclassifiable because lost. Of the twenty-seven only four proved even moderate successes: Fielding's *The Miser* (DL, 1733), *The Intriguing Chambermaid* (DL, 1734—ap), and *Don Quixote in England* (Little Hay, 1734), and Miller's *The Man of Taste* (DL, 1735). Covent Garden ran a lot of afterpiece farces in 1735 and 1736. Given their uniform lack of success this is a bit hard to understand. Straight comedy was not selling.

3. Ballad opera (almost entirely in afterpiece form) continued to get produced at a brisk clip. Gay's *Achilles* (a mainpiece at CG in 1733) enjoyed some twenty performances but did not become a repertory piece. *The Harlot's Progress* and *The Livery Rake* (a pair of DL afterpieces in 1733) gave good service. Rich got some topical mileage out of *The Stage Mutineers* (CG, July 1733), poking fun at Drury Lane's troubles. Henry Carey's *The Honest Yorkshireman*, after a rocky time getting produced at all, proved a popular addi-

41. On the bizarre production history of this piece, and what it tells us of theatre management in 1734–35, see Arthur H. Scouten and Leo Hughes, "The First Season of 'The Honest Yorkshireman,'" *Modern Language Review*, 40 (1945), 8–11.

tion to the repertory.[41] Some twenty ballad operas, however, fell almost immediately into oblivion. Drury Lane tried ten, Goodman's Fields six, Covent Garden and the Little Haymarket five apiece. Managers were still hopefully accepting them in 1735 and 1736, but the vogue had definitely faded.

4. Burlesque continued to be the special province of the Little Haymarket, which had some successes and some flops. Carey's *Chrononhotonthologos* (an imitation of *Tom Thumb*) found only moderate favor, as did *Tumble-Down Dick*. *Queen Gin* proved ephemeral. Neither the Little Haymarket with *The Beggar's Opera Tragedized* (1734) nor Covent Garden with *Macheath in the Shades* (1735) caught the audience's fancy. Proof that burlesque still offered great possibilities was afforded only by Fielding's *Pasquin* (Little Hay, March 1736), which managed a stunning sixty-four performances by the end of the summer. It sparked what appears to have been an immediate imitation at Covent Garden called *Marforio* (10 April—anon., lost), but despite an advertising appeal "to those who have paid a Visit to his Brother Pasquin" the piece lasted only one night.

5. Pantomime rolled on. Fully half of the ten new ones were produced at Drury Lane, and only one at Covent Garden. Goodman's Fields and the Little Haymarket tried two apiece. As in earlier years, old favorites so well satisfied the audience that there was no urgent demand for new ones.

Surveying the state of affairs from the vantage point of the summer of 1736, a writer would hardly have felt euphoric about the prospects. There was clearly a large market for theatre in London. Drury Lane, Covent Garden, Goodman's Fields, and the Little Haymarket had all offered substantial seasons in 1735–36 (along with the Opera of the Nobility at King's), and the previous season a French company had played more than 110 nights at the Little Haymarket. But Drury Lane was proving decidedly unadventurous under Fleetwood, and Rich was ready to follow his lead. The pattern suggests that Drury Lane and Covent Garden had decided that they could get by without many new plays, regardless of what Goodman's Fields or the Little Haymarket chose to do. Whether they would have flourished with this policy in the face of aggressive competition is a question rendered academic a year later by the passage of the Licensing Act.

The End of an Era and the Significance of the Licensing Act

To the theatre historian, aware of the imminence of the Licensing Act, there is a special poignancy to the season of 1736–37. But at the time it seemed a season like any other. The principal change was Giffard's decision to move his company from Goodman's Fields to Lincoln's Inn Fields. Giffard tried a few performances in Rich's old theatre in September and October 1736. Within three weeks he was denying that the move was permanent,[42] but it became so. Four factors seem significant in this move. First, Lincoln's Inn Fields was bigger. It seated something close to double the capacity of Goodman's Fields. Second, at Lincoln's Inn Fields Giffard could charge the same prices as Drury Lane and Covent Garden: Goodman's Fields and the Little Haymarket had generally charged about a shilling less for each category of seat. Third, Giffard must have been convinced that he could pull in a good enough audience in the West End to make it worth his while to pay Rich rent for Lincoln's Inn Fields. And fourth, Rich must have been convinced that regular competition at Lincoln's Inn Fields would not reduce his take at Covent Garden. This is eloquent testimony to the managers' estimate of the demand for theatrical entertainment in London.

Drury Lane and Covent Garden operated conservatively, and Giffard not a great deal less so. Drury Lane put on one new mainpiece and four new afterpieces. Covent Garden chose to put on no new plays of any sort. The repertory breakdown seems very familiar. Performance figures supplement the tale this tells. Drury Lane mounted fifty-five plays over 195 nights, Covent Garden fifty over 128. Covent Garden also housed Handel's opera company, however, and it accounted for 53 more performance dates.[43] Lincoln's

---

42. *London Daily Post and General Advertiser* (13 Oct, 1736): "We are assured Mr Giffard will very shortly open the Theatre in Goodman's-Fields, notwithstanding the many false and invidious Reports of his having intirely left that part of the Town." Quoted in *The London Stage*, Part 3, II, 606.

43. This total includes five performances of *Alexander's Feast* and some oratorio performances in Passion Week.

Table 7:   Mainpieces in the Repertory, Season of 1736–37

	DL		CG		LIF		HAY	
Pre-1660	13	(24%)	11	(22%)	3	(6%)	1	(6%)*
1660–94	16	(29%)	14	(28%)	13	(27%)	3	(19%)
1695–1707	15	(27%)	16	(32%)	16	(33%)	4	(25%)
1708–20	5	(9%)	4	(8%)	7	(14%)	1	(6%)
post-1720	6	(11%)	5	(10%)	10	(20%)	7	(44%)
		(1 new)†				(4 new)		(5 new)‡
	55		50		49		16	

*The one pre-1660 play is *King John*, mounted as a hit at Cibber. See Emmett L. Avery, "Fielding's Last Season with the Haymarket Theater," *Modern Philology*, 36 (1939), 286–87.

†Does not include four new afterpieces.

‡Does not include ten new afterpieces.

Inn Fields tried forty-nine plays over 147 nights. Some 63 theatrical performances took place at the Little Haymarket (a few of them by a "Company of Volunteers"). Only 10 of these dates, however, featured plays more than one year old—that is, of the nine older plays, only one was given twice. Because the Little Haymarket used some pieces (for example, *The Historical Register*) as both mainpieces and afterpieces, figures exactly equivalent to the other companies are hard to calculate, but we may say that in this final season the Little Haymarket staged fifteen new titles. Several of these works are lost, and a number are nothing more than topical skits, but the energy and intensity of the operation is impossible to miss.[44] The great success was of course *The Historical Register* (34 performances), but *Eurydice Hiss'd* (18) is a gem of an afterpiece, and *The Dragon of Wantley* (4 nights at the end of the season) became an enduring success.

The degree to which the Little Haymarket's offerings were anti-Walpole in 1730 and 1731 remains a subject of debate. Political allusions can certainly be deduced from *Tom Thumb*, for instance,[45] but there is little evidence that the original audiences saw

44. No full account of Fielding as manager has ever been written. The best account of his operation at the Little Haymarket in 1736–37 remains Emmett L. Avery, "Fielding's Last Season with the Haymarket Theater," *Modern Philology*, 36 (1939), 283–92.

45. See Sheridan Baker, "Political Allusion in Fielding's *Author's Farce, Mock Doctor*, and *Tumble-Down Dick*," *PMLA*, 77 (1962), 221–31.

the piece in these terms. Wilbur Cross saw the Little Haymarket as highly political, and his views have been influential. Bertrand Goldgar's more skeptical view, however, should remind us not to make easy assumptions, or to read the aggressive politics of 1736–37 back into the early thirties.[46] There can be no doubt, however, that Fielding was gunning for Walpole in 1736 and 1737.

All the evidence suggests that Fielding expected to continue his theatrical activities. Indeed, there are signs that he was planning to expand his operation. Emmett L. Avery was the first scholar to find a proposal for erecting a new theatre—a proposal which in all probability came from Fielding. The *Daily Advertiser* for 4 February 1737 contains an ad stating that "Whereas it is agreed on between several Gentlemen to erect a New Theatre for the exhibition of Plays, Farces, Pantomimes, &c." builders are invited to propose plans to the undertakers by 2 May. Site size is given (an irregular plot 120 feet on the north, 130 feet on the west, 110 feet on the south), and certain features are specified—for example, "the Stage to be 30 Feet wide at the first Scenes").[47] A brief letter in the same paper 19 February says almost in so many words that this theatre is planned for Fielding's company: "it is intended for a Company of Comedians every day expected here, late Servants to their Majesties Kouli Kan and Theodore, who in the meantime will entertain the Town in true English manner, at the New Theatre in the Hay-Market." Fielding subsequently advertised his company in precisely these terms. As Avery observes, "the principal reason for thinking that Fielding may not have made the original proposals for a new theatre is that the notice specifies pantomime as one form of entertainment to be offered in the playhouse, and Fielding satirized rather than produced pantomime." This is quite true, but need not be considered a serious objection to the attribution of these proposals to Fielding. Pantomime would have been expected by potential investors, and Fielding could point out that the Little Haymarket had just mounted *The Defeat of Apollo*, a burlesque of pantomime.

46. Bertrand A. Goldgar, *Walpole and the Wits*, ch. 4.
47. Emmett L. Avery, "Proposals for a New London Theatre in 1737," *Notes and Queries*, 182 (1942), 286–87.

What came of these proposals we do not know. Fielding had evidently dropped the idea by early May, since in his "Dedication to the Publick" of *The Historical Register* he says "The very great Indulgence you have shown my Performances at the little Theatre, these two last Years, have encouraged me to the Proposal of a Subscription for carrying on that Theatre, for beautifying and enlarging it, and procuring a better Company of Actors. If you think it proper to subscribe to these Proposals, I assure you no Labour shall be spared, on my Sides to entertain you in a cheaper and better Manner than seems to be the Intention of any other." J. Paul de Castro, replying to Avery's note, says flatly that "Fielding could have been in no financial position in 1737 to acquire an interest in a newly constructed theatre, as he was probably liable under an existing lease for the Little Theatre in the Haymarket." And he goes on to say that it is "inconceivable that Fielding could propose embellishments to the theatre in 1737 were he a mere tenant at will."[48] These objections will not stand serious scrutiny. First, there is no evidence that Fielding was tied to a long-term lease at the Little Haymarket. Second, while he certainly did not have the money to erect a new theatre for himself, Rich and Giffard had raised money for new theatres by selling shares, and as London's most popular living playwright Fielding had every reason to think that he could do the same. Third, while Fielding would not have raised funds to make major improvements in a structure in which he was a mere tenant at will, he might well have done so if John Potter had given him a long-term lease.

We are free to conclude that in the spring of 1737 Fielding was expecting to stay in business and was casting about for ways and means to establish himself in a more secure and permanent managerial position. At the age of thirty, with a family to support, he had every reason to want to run his own theatre. An author's earnings were exceedingly unpredictable, and Fielding had scant love for Fleetwood, Rich, and Giffard. At this time, says Cross, "the drama . . . was to Fielding more than a means of support; it was his soul; it was his life."[49] What better way to indulge his passion

48. J. Paul de Castro, in *Notes and Queries*, 182 (1942), 346.
49. Cross, *The History of Henry Fielding*, I, 235.

and support his family than run his own theatre? Giffard had succeeded. Why not Fielding? To be sure, there were some clouds on
the horizon. A bill to regulate the theatre more strictly had failed
in 1735,[50] but rumors of another attempt were in the air by February 1737. A bill which might have served such a purpose was
given its first reading on 9 March, and on 25 March an essay de-
nouncing the "projected Restraint on the Number of Playhouses"
appeared as the last of the *Daily Journal*'s "Occasional Prompter"
series. It has only very recently been attributed to Fielding, but
plausibly so.[51] Fielding was certainly indignant, and had reason to
be worried, but the specter of government intervention had loomed
and receded before.

Far from drawing in his horns this spring, Fielding became
brasher than ever before. Along with *The Historical Register* he
mounted such obvious hits at the administration as *The Rehearsal
of Kings* (lost) and Lacy's *Fame*. There is some evidence that Fielding meant to get bolder yet. On 25 May he advertised to start
the 30th

> *Macheath turn'd Pyrate; or Polly in India.* An Opera. Very
> much taken, if not improv'd from the famous Sequel of the
> late celebrated Mr Gay. With a New Prologue, proper to the
> Occasion. And after the Run of that, the Town will be enter-
> tain'd with a new Farce of two Acts, call'd *The King and Titi;
> or The Medlars.* Taken from the History of Prince Titi, Origi-
> nally written in French, and lately translated into English.[52]

Walpole had of course got Gay's *Polly* banned before performance,
and Fielding's proposing to mount what appears to be an adaptation of *Polly* was tantamount to daring Walpole to try to do some-

50. See *The London Stage*, Part 3, I, xlix–l. The long-standing belief that the
first attempt at such a bill occurred in May 1733 is founded on a misdated letter.
See Vincent Liesenfeld, "The 'First' Playhouse Bill: A Stage Ghost," *Theatre Notebook*, 31, no. 2 (1977), 9–12.
51. See Thomas Lockwood, "A New Essay by Fielding," *Modern Philology*,
78 (1980), 48–58.
52. Quoted in *The London Stage*, Part 3, II, 675. For a discussion of *The King
and Titi* see Avery, "Fielding's Last Season," pp. 290–91.

thing about it. The bill now known as the Licensing Act had its first reading on 24 May. Whether Fielding took alarm at this juncture we cannot be sure. The Little Haymarket had performed *The Historical Register* Tuesday, Wednesday, and Thursday May 17–19, and again Monday the 23rd. Perhaps, as Avery suggests, Fielding "simply closed the theater." This is possible, but hardly in keeping with Fielding's aggressive posture that spring. Other bills had been read and come to naught, and the Licensing Act was not formally approved by Parliament and the king until 21 June. There is, in fact, some evidence that the government effectively silenced Fielding in late May. In a letter to the lord chamberlain dated 7 January 1737 [that is, 1737/8] John Potter (proprietor of the Little Haymarket) says, "In order to prevent what was Intended to be Represented in my theatre in May last it was your Grace's pleasure to declare I should meet with a Reward for such dutifull Behaviour and I have read the promise of Sir Robt Walpole to the same purport."[53] This sounds very much as though Walpole, not content to wait for the pending act to take effect, took steps to shut Fielding down before he could stage *Macheath turn'd Pyrate*.

The story of the passage of the Licensing Act is too well known to need review here.[54] Likewise the effects of the act hardly need fresh rehearsal. As Table 7 shows, there was an immediate and precipitate decline in productions of new plays. From twelve new mainpieces (and fourteen afterpieces) in 1736–37 the total falls to five new mainpieces (and three afterpieces) the following season. Only a bare trickle of new plays achieved performance in the next decade: in the first seven years of the forties Covent Garden mounted exactly three new mainpieces. No more need be said of this.

We should, however, reflect on exactly what the Licensing Act demanded. Walpole wanted to put an end to satiric harassment from

53. Published by J. Paul de Castro (n. 48, above).
54. P. J. Crean's "The Stage Licensing Act of 1737," *Modern Philology*, 35 (1938), 239–55, has been almost entirely superseded by Scouten's introduction to Part 3 of *The London Stage*, I, xlviii–lx. For an addendum to Scouten's account of attempts to evade the act, see Emmett L. Avery and A. H. Scouten, "The opposition to Sir Robert Walpole, 1737–1739," *English Historical Review*, 83 (1968), 331–36.

Fielding. Had he merely demanded that all scripts receive the assent of the lord chamberlain (or his deputy) all the theatres would probably have fussed about the censorship, and Fielding might well have exercised all his ingenuity in trying to see what he could slip past the censor. By making the act double-barrelled—that is, demanding both censorship and a restriction to patent houses—Walpole both ensured Fielding's elimination as a theatrical pest and helped persuade the patent theatres to accept the irritation of censorship. Given their lack of interest in staging new plays, Fleetwood and Rich must have felt that a bit of censorship was a small price to pay for getting rid of two popular and effective competitors.

The real bane in the Licensing Act was not censorship but the restriction in the number of theatres. Fielding—if he was indeed the author of the "Occasional Prompter" essay—seems to have understood this perfectly and gone right to that point. He protests against "Castration," but the crux of his position is an objection to the "projected Restraint on the Number of Playhouses." Censorship was, in fact, widely accepted as reasonable and even desirable in the eighteenth century.[55] Censorship would certainly have ensured that something like *The Historical Register* did not get performed. But not all governments are as apt for satire as Walpole's in its later years, and reviewing the plays of the thirties one will find no great number which would have fallen foul of a censor. There is potent irony in the fact that during the next hundred years the government showed almost no interest in the number of theatres in London: the letter of the law was insisted upon by the owners of the two patent companies. As Scouten points out, the lord chamberlain raised no objection to Giffard's reopening Goodman's Fields for the 1740–41 season. Giffard was put out of business again when the patent company managers went to court and complained.[56] What blighted English drama after 1737 was less the Licensing Act than the ruthless

55. A point well made by L. W. Conolly in *The Censorship of English Drama, 1737–1824*, and by Calhoun Winton, "Dramatic Censorship," in *The London Theatre World*, pp. 286–308.

56. This cooperation to preserve a "just monopoly" persisted for decades. For an account of Sheridan and Harris working together to frustrate all attempts at competition see Joseph Donohue, "The London Theatre at the End of the Eighteenth Century," in *The London Theatre World*, esp. pp. 340–45.

protection of their monopoly by the patent company managers. The restriction to two theatres was bad enough; the corollary was just as bad, for inevitably the patent theatres expanded their capacity, ultimately making themselves fit only for spectacle and melodrama.[57]

Some form of censorship was probably unavoidable, but the restriction to two legitimate theatres had effects out of all proportion to Walpole's original intention, and was by no means inevitable. What, we might ask, would the London theatre have been like at mid-century with censorship but no other restrictions? On the basis of what we have seen in the thirties, we might guess at something like the following: 1) Drury Lane, specializing in legitimate classic theatre with a heavy bias toward pre-1708 plays; 2) Covent Garden, much the same, but with more emphasis on music and pantomime; 3) King's, for Italian opera and concerts; 4) Goodman's Fields (or Lincoln's Inn Fields), run in the Giffard style, offering a conservative repertory with an eighteenth-century emphasis; and 5) the Little Haymarket, doing mostly contemporary and experimental scripts.

What we actually find in the fifties and sixties is a watered-down form of such a spread. There is no "third" legitimate theatre, and the Little Haymarket is occupied by Foote only in the summer season. The conservative basis on which the big patent houses operated after 1737 is clearly anticipated by their modus operandi in the 1720s, and again by the patterns toward which they gravitated during the mid-thirties. Under most managers this was probably their natural bent, and in many ways it is quite defensible. There is every reason to believe, however, that they could have made money with their classic repertory with or without competition from the likes of the Little Haymarket. Big houses in New York are not beggared by off-Broadway ventures.

In conclusion, we need to ask briefly what we are to make of the evolution of play types between 1728 and 1737. Was the drama going somewhere? Did the Licensing Act destroy such developments as we have found, or did writers adapt and carry on?

57. For a brief discussion see ch. 7, sec. "The Structure of the Period," above.

1. The ballad opera boom had burned itself out by the mid-thirties. It did, however, give the London theatre a tremendous push toward fuller utilization of music, and the burletta tradition which flourished later in the century is clearly an outgrowth of tastes inculcated by ballad opera.

2. Political comedy was booming in 1737, and the Licensing Act effectively squelched it. Only occasionally did a play with genuine political significance get by the censor—Sheridan's *The Critic* is an obvious example. The taste for topical material and satire, however, continued unchecked, and in due course Foote learned to capitalize on these predilections, working around the limitations imposed by the censor. Foote is no Fielding, but can we imagine Foote appearing and flourishing without Fielding before him?

3. The "fate tragedy" that seemed to be developing so promisingly in the mid-thirties did not really survive the Licensing Act. Admittedly we have only a few examples, and no one can say that the form would necessarily have taken hold and flourished in England. The fate tragedy did prove influential on the Continent, and its serious treatment of character under stress appears again in English drama later in the century, though more in various forms of *comédie sérieuse* than in tragedy proper.[58]

4. Comedy—other than farce—seems mostly to have been treading water in the thirties. The rakish norms of the Carolean era are finally swamped, but nothing very distinctive replaces them. There are signs, however, of the emergence of a new mode of humane comedy, perhaps best dubbed "London social comedy." We see it in some of Fielding's plays (*The Modern Husband, The Old Debauchees, The Universal Gallant*), in John Kelly's *The Married Philosopher*, and in James Miller's plays (particularly *The Mother-in-Law* and *The Man of Taste*). To define this social comedy fully is beyond my scope here, but in brief its essence is a view of the characters as part of a group. The viewpoint—the fundamental ideology—of Carolean comedy is that of the individual making a necessary accommodation to the society in which he must live. The

58. For a discussion of *comédie sérieuse* in England see ch. 7, sec. "The Changing Play Types," above.

fundamental ideology and viewpoint of eighteenth-century social comedy is that of the *honnête homme* in harmony with his society. There are, to be sure, preachy moral comedies in the seventeenth century, and rakish figures in eighteenth-century comedies, but there is a basic shift of values. The change is gradual and hard to pin down, but Loftis is surely correct in seeing the 1730s as the swing point in a basic change in the values and stereotypes of comedy. Is this a shift from "satiric" to "sentimental" comedy? Certainly not. Pathos, patheticism, and example are no more dominant in the drama of the thirties than they were a generation earlier.

How much effect did the Licensing Act actually have? An immense effect, but in certain respects less than one might have thought. Political drama was made nearly impossible, but most of the other developments of the thirties carry on—albeit in slow moving and watered-down form. The twenty years of near stasis following 1737 might be likened to the Commonwealth period: there is no sharp break between 1642 and 1660, and nor is there between the drama of the 1730s and that of the 1760s. Censorship was a misfortune but not necessarily a major one. The dire misfortune was the limitation to the patent theatres. Eighteenth-century drama turns stodgy not because of sentimentalism, or bourgeois audiences, or censorship, but because without competition the theatre managers saw no reason to risk money on new plays, and certainly not on experimental ones.

10

Goldsmith and Sheridan and the Supposed Revolution of "Laughing" against "Sentimental" Comedy

The cliché is venerable: Goldsmith and Sheridan rebelled against a dominant "sentimental" comedy and tried to revive "laughing" or satiric comedy. Their model was supposedly "Restoration" comedy purged of its indecencies. In recent years two amendments to this view have become routine. First, the sentimental was admittedly not completely dominant—a point first made decisively in 1957 by Arthur Sherbo in *English Sentimental Drama*. Second, Goldsmith and Sheridan are said to be themselves significantly infected by the "prevailing" sentimentalism. Standard reference works (such as Nicoll's *History*) repeat the cliché, or a modification of it, and despite a variety of recent objections the view is still current. For example Samuel L. Macey speaks of "the Aristophanic mood of two great English writers, to whom Nicoll very properly refers as '*the reactionaries*, Goldsmith and Sheridan.'" [1]

Critical opinion has long been colored by a desire to see rebellion against the sentimental. The present rather low estimate of the two writers results from the opinion that they failed to carry their

---

1. "Sheridan: The Last of the Great Theatrical Satirists," *Restoration and Eighteenth Century Theatre Research*, 9 (Nov. 1970), 35–45. The reference is to Nicoll, III, 135.

revolution through. This valuation is not my concern here. My aim is to suggest that the perspective given by the concept of a struggle to reassert laughing against sentimental comedy is quite misleading. To begin with, Goldsmith and Sheridan produce very different sorts of plays from very different premises. For another, the notion of attempted "return" is widespread—but return to *what*? Goldsmith is not Congreve; Sheridan is often seen as a failed Congreve. But as Harold Love remarks, it is unfair to judge people by the distance by which they failed to write *The Way of the World*.[2]

Inevitably, our view of the two writers is influenced by the terms of Goldsmith's famous "Comparison between Laughing and Sentimental Comedy." But he refers favorably there to Vanbrugh and Cibber: oddly enough, the same critics who believe fervently in Goldsmith's "revolution" also tend to consider Cibber the father of sentimental comedy. The meaning of this reference will therefore bear some investigation. More generally, I think we need to be very suspicious of an uncritical acceptance of the terms of Goldsmith's essay. What precisely he means and what we mean by "sentimental" needs clarification. Critics vary considerably in their interpretation of "the last age" which is to be restored. Certainly too the relationship of the plays of Goldsmith and Sheridan to those of their contemporaries and predecessors can profitably be reconsidered, especially in the light of the performance records now available in *The London Stage*. Starting then from a reexamination of the "Comparison," I want to enquire how the plays of Goldsmith and Sheridan fit into the pattern of new comic productions between 1760 and 1780 and whether the traditional revolutionary hypothesis can be considered accurate or adequate.[3]

2. Review of the Regents Restoration Drama Series, *AUMLA*, 27 (1967), 106–8.

3. Since the original form of this essay appeared in 1972 there have been some heartening signs that scholars are ready to abandon the long-standing cliché that Goldsmith and Sheridan rebelled against a dominant "sentimental" drama. In a pair of important books published in 1977 John Loftis and Mark Auburn both present views of Goldsmith and Sheridan in their context which are substantially in accordance with mine. See Loftis, *Sheridan and the Drama of Georgian England* (Oxford: Blackwell, 1977), and Auburn, *Sheridan's Comedies: Their Contexts and Achievements* (Lincoln: Univ. of Nebraska Press, 1977).

Goldsmith's "Essay" and Its Context

Exactly what does Goldsmith *say* in his famous "Essay on the Theatre," what does he insinuate, and—perhaps as important—what do we infer from it?[4] Quite probably, the piece is essentially a puff to prepare the way for *She Stoops to Conquer*, first staged two months after the essay's appearance. Rhetorically, the essay is unquestionably a brilliant performance—so much so that both its actual content and its enormous critical influence have gone almost unquestioned, even among scholars who are thoroughly familiar with the theatre history of the period. Is the essay, the basis for most modern views of late eighteenth-century theatre history, an accurate account of dramatic trends? The answer is no, and in fairness to Goldsmith one must say that it was probably meant to be nothing of the sort. Writing in the heat of the moment, he seems to have been reacting excessively to very temporary phenomena. No insult to Goldsmith is intended when I say that modern critics have taken a piece of ephemeral journalism far too seriously.

He opens with the assertion that tragedy has "of late . . . given way to Comedy."[5] This is true: new comic mainpieces were not being mounted during the 1750s, but around 1760 we find a marked shift in taste. The 1760s see a flood of new comedies, both mainpieces and afterpieces, and one of our principal objects must be to see what sorts of plays these were. Very well—comedy (defined as a "natural portrait of Human Folly and Frailty") is in vogue, and Goldsmith poses a basic question: "Whether the Exhibition of Human Distress is likely to afford the mind more Entertainment than that of Human Absurdity?" Here he loads his terms: if *entertainment* is the writer's sole object, absurdity is indeed to be preferred. But not many writers would have gone along with Goldsmith's implicit disavowal of moral purpose, and indeed, the very "authorities" to whom Goldsmith promptly applies all consider the "ridic-

4. We presume that the essay is Goldsmith's. It appeared anonymously in the *Westminster Magazine*, 1 January 1773, and was first ascribed to him in 1798 by Thomas Wright, printer of the magazine. But the ascription has not, I believe, ever been seriously questioned.

5. All quotations from the essay are from *The Collected Works of Oliver Goldsmith*, ed. Arthur Friedman, 5 vols. (Oxford: Clarendon Press, 1966), III, 209–13.

ulous" to have a moral as well as an entertainment function. By stretching his case here and emphasizing absurdity, Goldsmith is preparing the way for his later disposal of the claim that "Sentimental Pieces do often amuse us."

The third paragraph is a masterpiece. It opens with an appeal to Aristotle, who is quoted as saying that comedy is "a picture of the Frailties of the lower part of Mankind," while tragedy deals with the "Misfortunes of the Great." With authority thus judiciously insinuated, Goldsmith announces that comedy must stick to "Low or Middle Life," and asks whether "an exhibition of its Follies be not preferable to a detail of its Calamities?" Who can disagree with Aristotle? And who wants genuine *Calamities* in a comedy? However, we should pause long enough to reflect that we do not find "Princes or Generals" in *False Delicacy* or *The West Indian*. Nor do those works introduce calamities more severe than those in *The Good-Natur'd Man*, *The School for Scandal*, or *Tom Jones*—though they dwell more on attendant sentiments. Nonetheless, Goldsmith seizes triumphantly on his distinction—follies vs. calamities—to ask: "Which deserves the preference? The Weeping Sentimental Comedy, so much in fashion at present, or the Laughing and even Low Comedy, which seems to have been last exhibited by Vanburgh [*sic*] and Cibber?"

This key passage suggests a) that sentimental comedy—however defined—is the dominant genre at present, and b) that the sort of play Goldsmith approves of was produced by Vanbrugh and Cibber, whatever that means. The first claim I will take up in detail in the next section. The second is an important and astonishingly neglected hint at what Goldsmith had in mind. In discussing the antecedents of "laughing" comedy, critics have pulled forth playwrights from Greene, Lyly, and Shakespeare to Congreve and Farquhar—without, as far as I am aware, stopping to think about the one specific reference Goldsmith gives us. It could mean either of two things—Vanbrugh and Cibber separately, or their collaborative play, *The Provok'd Husband* (1728).[6] Either possibility is fascinat-

---

6. The play was not a collaboration in the usual sense. Vanbrugh died leaving a fragment (published as *A Journey to London*, 1728), which Cibber revised and

ing. Critics of H. T. E. Perry's generation (for example, Bernbaum) thought of Cibber's *Love's Last Shift* (1696) as the "first" senti- mental comedy, and though that idea is thoroughly exploded, an aura of the sentimental persistently clings to Cibber. By Bernbaum's standards, Vanbrugh would be an odd bedfellow, for his *The Re- lapse* (1696) was long viewed as a last-gasp attack on the new mode by an adherent of the older, satiric school. This is simply not true: relapse or no, Vanbrugh's fifth-act resolution is almost identical to Cibber's, relying on the same facile reversals of character. Both in these plays and later ones, Vanbrugh and Cibber are closer to late Shadwell than to Etherege and Congreve—an interesting observa- tion in light of the many claims for Goldsmith and Sheridan's at- tempt to "restore" Restoration comedy.

I believe, however, that Goldsmith was more probably refer- ring to *The Provok'd Husband*. Boswell's *Life of Johnson* records that Johnson considered *The Good-Natur'd Man* the best comedy which had appeared since *The Provok'd Husband*, and further, that Croaker was the best comic character of recent years.[7] Now the Vanbrugh-Cibber play had been extremely popular, and though Goldsmith does not mention the fact, it continued to be so through- out the 1760s and early 1770s. It is an entertaining work, but a highly moral one. Indeed, by almost any common definition, *The Provok'd Husband* is a *sentimental* comedy, and so recent a scholar as George Winchester Stone unhesitatingly classifies it as such.[8] There is a delicious irony here: Goldsmith is triumphantly proposing to restore the glory of the English stage by imitating what most of us would cheerfully classify as a sentimental comedy!

The confusion here rests on the term "sentimental." *The Pro- vok'd Husband* is not identical in type to *False Delicacy*, and Gold- smith can quite reasonably approve the one and disapprove the other. Nonetheless, the confusion should give us pause. Our every- day definitions are not adequate here. And however we want to

---

expanded. Both versions are printed in *The Works of Sir John Vanbrugh*, ed. Dobrée and Webb.

7. *The Life of Samuel Johnson*, ed. George Birkbeck Hill and L. F. Powell, II, 48.

8. *The London Stage*, Part 4, I, clxiii.

define "sentimental," we do not escape the fact that if Goldsmith seriously proposes to use *The Provok'd Husband* (or even Vanbrugh and Cibber separately) as a generic model, he cannot have been doing quite what most critics have assumed he was attempting. Goldsmith's antecedents will bear another look, and we must refrain from jumping to conclusions about where his sympathies really lay.

When Goldsmith returns to his argument from his sweeping rhetorical questions, it is to make a more extended excursion into the authorities. From them we learn "that as Tragedy displays the Calamities of the Great; so Comedy should excite our laughter by ridiculously exhibiting the Follies of the Lower Part of Mankind." Again Goldsmith stresses his calamity/folly distinction, quoting Boileau to the effect "that Comedy will not admit of Tragic Distress." This sort of argument had long been used against tragicomedies. When *The Winter's Tale*, for example, was finally revived by Garrick in 1756, it was as a three-act adaptation. But Goldsmith's position was old-fashioned. His aesthetic would have condemned much of Shakespeare, but his contemporaries were evidently receptive to Charles Macklin's revolutionary tragic portrayal of Shylock—a clear case of transforming what had long been a buffoon's part into a figure of "terrifying ferocity" (Francis Gentleman's phrase) within a comic context. Further, Goldsmith holds firmly to the idea that an audience can sympathize seriously only with the "Great"— a notion contradicted in practice by the success of eighteenth-century "domestic" tragedies. Actually Goldsmith is trying hard to associate "sentimental" comedy with "*Tradesman's Tragedy*." The rhetorical device is neat: define a radical division between comedy and tragedy; associate the comedy you don't like with tragedy; and that comedy is invalid—*q.e.d.* Goldsmith never once, however, *names* a sentimental play or playwright. This omission is significant: *False Delicacy* (supposedly his *bête noire*) is certainly not *The Gamester*. One does not have to like *The Suspicious Husband*,[9] *The Conscious Lovers*, *False Delicacy*, *The West Indian*, and *The School for Wives*,

---

9. Benjamin Hoadly's comedy (1747) was the most popular "sentimental" comedy in the 1747–76 period.

to see that Goldsmith is far from describing them accurately when he implies that sentimental comedy is a bastard version of tragedy. His sharp criticism of "accidental distress" of "mean" characters could be turned around and applied to *The Vicar of Wakefield.* Goldsmith might reply that his novel is a satiric burlesque of accidental distress and excessive sensibility.[10] Perhaps so, but Kelly can rightly maintain that he is displaying *false* delicacy.

Goldsmith is heavy-handedly dogmatic: "notwithstanding this weight of authority, and the universal practice of former ages, a new species of Dramatic Composition has been introduced under the name of *Sentimental* Comedy." Here, as throughout the essay, he hides behind vaguely cited authority, and exaggerates the "universal practice" of former ages. We should not let our prejudices against "sentimental" comedy obscure his distortions. "Since the first origin of the Stage, Tragedy and Comedy have run in different channels, and never till of late encroached upon the provinces of each other." The tragicomedies of Fletcher and Dryden were no longer much on the stage, so perhaps Goldsmith can be excused for overlooking them, but Shakespeare was in the midst of a tremendous revival in the mid-eighteenth century, and his works constantly exhibit the encroachment Goldsmith complains of. Terence is the only example of such "approaches" he offers, but he is said always to stop short of the "downright pathetic"—a disputable claim. And Goldsmith promptly twists again: "All the other Comic Writers of antiquity aim only at rendering Folly or Vice ridiculous, but never exalt their characters into buskined pomp." In his "Dedication to Detraction" (of *The Choleric Man*, 1775) Cumberland rightly cites Varro and Menander as practitioners of the outright pathetic. And who among Steele, Hoadly, Kelly, Cumberland, or others *does* try to exalt his characters into buskined pomp? We may complain of namby-pambyness, excessive emotionalism, and lack of laughter, but to suggest that they are writing domestic tragedies is silly.

10. Goldsmith's novel has been read this way by Robert H. Hopkins, *The True Genius of Oliver Goldsmith* (Baltimore: Johns Hopkins Univ. Press, 1969), and Robert Julian Griffin, "Goldsmith's Augustanism: A Study of his Literary Works," Diss. Univ. of California, Berkeley, 1965.

Both forms play to sensibility, but then so do *Tristram Shandy* and *The Deserted Village*.

Stepping back from the laughing-sentimental dichotomy may help clarify the issues involved. The authorities Goldsmith loves to brandish are basically agreed on the satiric and corrective function of comedy: it was to "instruct and please" by "holding the glass" to a society in need of satiric correction. Critics occasionally remark on the similarity of Goldsmith's position to that taken by John Dennis in his "Remarks on *The Conscious Lovers*" (1723), in which he insists loudly that laughter and ridicule are the defining features of comedy.[11] To some extent, one can see Goldsmith carrying on a longstanding quarrel about the nature of comedy. Stuart M. Tave makes the important point in *The Amiable Humorist* that between 1650 and 1750 there is a drastic overall shift in the dominant concept of humor: Hobbesian ridicule largely gives way to a more benevolent sympathy. Many late seventeenth-century comedies rely on a very unsympathetic view of their protagonists, many of whom are sharply satirized. Toward the end of the century, an increasing number of lead characters reform piously or become semi-exemplary, as in Shadwell's last plays. To say simply that unsympathetic humor gives way to sympathetic, and satirized characters to exemplary, is inaccurate: exemplary comedy can be found in the 1660s, and Fielding, for instance, is no purveyor of pious milksop heroes.[12] Nevertheless, the overall change that Tave defines must be taken into account in any discussion of mid-eighteenth century comedy.

Goldsmith's dichotomy is far simpler than the complex factors involved will allow. 1) Modern critics have tended to see the difference between laughing and sentimental comedy as the difference between bawdy Restoration plays and moral eighteenth-century ones. Piety can certainly be irritating, but many moral comedies are still satiric—for example, Colman's *The Jealous Wife* (1761). 2) Likewise, we tend to think of "sentimental" comedy as founded on an excessive and drippy belief in the goodness of human nature. Res-

11. *The Critical Works of John Dennis*, II, 251–74.
12. For a fuller discussion, see my *Development*, ch. 2.

toration comedy expresses Hobbes, sentimental comedy Shaftesbury. But then Goldsmith, Fielding, and Sterne, though not syrupy
devotees of Shaftesbury, are certainly not Hobbesian pessimists: all
three have benevolist sympathies and can get a good deal of mileage out of sensibility. 3) Hence one must make at least a three-way
distinction among laughter *at* a character; sympathetic laughter;
and serious empathy. Wycherley elicits the first; Goldsmith and Sterne
mostly the second; Cumberland moves closer to the third—but then
so, very often, does Shakespeare. 4) Turning from types of response
to character to sorts of plays, we can see several types: serious satire (*The Plain-Dealer*), friendly satire (*The Good-Natur'd Man*),
empathetic satire (*The West Indian*), and actual exemplary comedy
(*The Conscious Lovers*).

The difference between the sentimental and the exemplary is
important. The former refers to the sort of treatment the material
is given; the latter concerns the view we are to take of the lead
characters.[13] Steele came increasingly to write exemplary comedy:
like his Restoration predecessors he claimed to instruct his audience but, unlike them, he proposed to do so by positive rather than
negative example. An exemplary character, as the name implies, is
held up as an example for emulation. This is emphatically not true
even of so admired a character as Belcour in *The West Indian*. A
character we like immensely can do foolish things, even if he is
basically "good," and our response will be sympathetic amusement. Tom Jones and Parson Adams are examples. Given a sympathetic (if realistic) view of human nature, an author will produce
neither savage satire nor pious examples of virtue. An exemplary
character may strike us as "sentimental" in the sense that such beings
seem a weak-minded self-indulgence, but there is little necessary
connection between ideal characters and the common features of
what we generally think of as sentimental comedies.

13. In a useful essay, Arthur Friedman has made a similar sort of distinction
between "sentimentalism" as it appears in the *kind of characters* and "sentimentalism" characterized by its *effect on the audience*. "Aspects of Sentimentalism in
Eighteenth-Century Literature," *The Augustan Milieu: Essays Presented to Louis A.
Landa*, ed. Henry Knight Miller, Eric Rothstein, and G. S. Rousseau (Oxford: Clarendon Press, 1970), pp. 247–61.

Arthur Sherbo's cautious and sensible investigation of the "sentimental" shows that no clear-cut genre can be isolated. Sentimental traits appear in varying degrees. Typically, these traits amount to eschewal of humor and the bawdy, repetition and prolongation of certain kinds of scenes, and an emphasis which brings sensibility to the fore.[14] Sentimentalism amounts to a certain kind of handling of material. Remove Sterne's humor and bawdy, and he would be left quite a sentimentalist. Most modern critics do not care for this side of Sterne, a fact which may account for some recent attempts to make him into a sort of latter-day Jonathan Swift. Sterne's wit, his bawdy, his ability to laugh at his own emotional indulgences, may make his radical sensibility palatable to us, but they should not obscure his "sentimental" side.

Goldsmith fiercely attacks the good characters of "sentimental" comedy, but we should see that the goodness does not constitute the sentimentality. "All the Characters are good, and exceedingly generous . . . and though they want Humour, have abundance of Sentiment and Feeling. If they happen to have Faults or Foibles, the Spectator is taught not only to pardon, but to applaud them, in consideration of the goodness of their hearts; so that Folly, instead of being ridiculed, is commended."

In short, Goldsmith says that sentimental comedy presents characters for approval who should be satirized. Perhaps the twentieth-century reader is inclined to agree—"by all means consign sentimental comedy to perdition." But let us remember that among the characters whose faults and foibles we pardon for goodness of heart are Parson Adams, Tom Jones, Uncle Toby, Charles Surface, and Goldsmith's own Honeywood. These characters are not as namby-pamby as Belcour, but their faults and foibles *are* pardoned; we feel not contempt but benevolent delight and sympathy for them.

Goldsmith says that comedy is to elicit laughter, and that the source of laughter is ridicule. Exactly fifty years earlier, Dennis had indignantly denounced Steele's attempt "to introduce a Joy too ex-

14. See Sherbo, *English Sentimental Drama.* I am simplifying a complex description here.

quisite for Laughter." But the swing toward benevolism and sensibility had changed the dominant theory of humor. Growing delight in pathetic and sympathetic humor allowed for empathy with characters who would once have been cruelly derided. Tave calls Cervantes and Shakespeare the old masters in this form, and Sterne the great modern example. Don Quixote and Falstaff are perfect cases of our pardoning egregious faults. My point here is simply that we have to be gullible to go along with Goldsmith's denunciation of pathos and sympathy in comedy.

Whatever may be wrong with the plays of Kelly and Cumberland from our point of view, the problem is not their admission of pathos and sympathetic humor. Goldsmith would have it that the essence of comedy is laughter through ridicule, but such a notion fits Shakespeare, Cervantes, Fielding's novels, and Sterne very badly indeed. The authorities he appeals to have little application to humor and comedy as they were being practiced in the eighteenth century. But Goldsmith thunders on, setting up straw objections and triumphantly demolishing them. If men are entertained by sentimental comedy, why object? Answer: true comedy would entertain more. Why not let comedy make men weep? Answer: because tragedy could just as well make men laugh. One sneering argument is allowed in favor of sentimental comedy: any fool can write trite sentiments. Perhaps that jibe can be allowed some merit.

Enjoying Goldsmith's blasts at "Bastard Tragedy," we forget to ask precisely what he is talking about. Consider his famous example: "A friend of mine who was sitting unmoved at one of these Sentimental Pieces, was asked, how he could be so indifferent. 'Why, truly,' says he, 'as the Hero is but a Tradesman, it is indifferent to me whether he be turned out of his Counting-house on Fish-street Hill, since he will still have enough left to open shop in St. Giles's.'"

Two observations occur to me about this brilliant passage. First, I find it curious that no one has ever identified the play referred to. I cannot do so myself, and would not be surprised to learn that Goldsmith had fabricated the whole damning example.[15] Second,

15. Following a comment in a letter by David Garrick to George Steevens (13 Jan. 1775) critics have sometimes assumed that Goldsmith was sniping at Cumberland's *The Fashionable Lover*, but I have never found this claim convincing. For a

clearly the type of this example has no application at all to the well-known "sentimental" plays against which critics presume Goldsmith was writing. His repeated snarls at "Tradesman's Tragedy" could apply to something like *The London Merchant*, but certainly not to *False Delicacy* or *The West Indian*. Some skepticism about the general applicability of Goldsmith's construct seems justified when he turns out to be so extraordinarily vague about what precisely he purports to be describing.

The conclusion of the essay strikes a bathetic note. "Humour at present seems to be departing from the Stage." The audience may soon "sit at a Play as gloomy as at the Tabernacle." But worse may follow. "It is not easy to recover an art when once lost; and it would be but a just punishment that when, by our being too fastidious, we have banished Humour from the Stage, we should ourselves be deprived of the art of Laughing." This last histrionic suggestion can be ignored. But Goldsmith clearly implies that—as of January 1773—laughter and amusement are being driven out of the theatre. Garrick's brilliant prologue for *She Stoops to Conquer* (March 1773) dramatizes the same idea.

> *Enter Mr. Woodward, dressed in black and holding a Handkerchief to his Eyes.*
> Excuse me, Sirs, I pray—I can't yet speak—
> I'm crying now—and have been all the week!
>
> .   .   .   .
>
> The Comic muse, long sick, is now a dying!
>
> .   .   .   .
>
> Who deals in *sentimentals* will succeed!
> Poor *Ned* and *I* are dead to all intents,
> We can as soon speak *Greek* as sentiments!
>
> .   .   .   .
>
> I give it up—morals won't do for me;
> To make you laugh I must play tragedy.

---

detailed denial of the supposed allusion see Oliver W. Ferguson, "Sir Fretful Plagiary and Goldsmith's 'An Essay on the Theatre,'" in *Quick Springs of Sense: Studies in the Eighteenth Century*, ed. Larry S. Champion (Athens: Univ. of Georgia Press, 1974), 113–20.

Goldsmith, we learn, is the doctor who may yet save the patient—a neat conceit. One question remains: is this gloomy picture of theatrical fashion anything like accurate?

The New Plays, 1759–1773

To the uninitiated reader, Goldsmith's essay suggests that Congreve, Vanbrugh, and Farquhar are being forced off the stage by *The Conscious Lovers*. To be sure, Goldsmith actually says nothing of the sort. He names no names, and so we tend to supply them.[16] Such a view is too silly to attribute to Goldsmith: *The Conscious Lovers*, after all, preceded his essay by precisely half a century, and the works of the late seventeenth-century playwrights had stayed popular. Consider the season of 1772–73, during which Goldsmith's "Essay" appeared. *The London Stage* records performances of *The Provok'd Wife* (three of them); *The Beaux Stratagem* (eight); *The Recruiting Officer* (three); *The Double-Dealer* (two); *The Plain-Dealer*; *Love for Love*; *The Inconstant* (two); *The Rehearsal* (five). Laughing comedy has not yet disappeared. *The West Indian* (a 1771 smash hit) does receive eleven performances; Goldsmith's own *She Stoops to Conquer* runs up seventeen performances, despite a premiere late in the season (15 March). *The Conscious Lovers* comes out with three. *False Delicacy* manages exactly one performance—and is advertised as "Not acted for 3 years."[17]

Thus although Goldsmith casts himself in the role of heroic defender of an old faith crumbling under the onslaught of depraved modern fashions, we may feel some doubts. Three questions in particular arise. 1) If humor is being "banished" from the stage, presumably performance records will show a significant decline in both new "laughing" comedies and in productions of old ones. We now

16. That Goldsmith himself sometimes thought this way we can deduce from other works. "The audience now sit uneasy at the sprightly sallies of Vanburgh [*sic*] or Congreve" ("On the Present State of our Theatres," *Works*, III, 54). "The works of Congreve and Farquhar have too much wit in them for the present taste" (*Vicar of Wakefield*, ch. 18).

17. *The London Stage*, Part 4, III, 1711. The next performance of *False Delicacy* was a full ten years later, in the 1782–83 season.

have full records available: is this indeed true? 2) Given Johnson's remark about *The Provok'd Husband* and the probability of Goldsmith's referring to it in his essay, we need to ask what precisely Goldsmith meant by "sentimental" in the context of the 1760s, when the boom in sentimental comedy allegedly developed. 3) More broadly, we need to evaluate Goldsmith's apparent implication that no new "Laughing and even Low" comedy was produced between 1728 and 1768.[18]

The year 1728 produced not only *The Provok'd Husband* but also *The Beggar's Opera* (ten performances in 1772–73)—certainly a satiric, laughing comedy, unless a caviller calls it a musical. During the 1730s Fielding produced a dazzling array of savagely satiric and uproariously funny comedies and farces. Perhaps he was too farcical and political for Goldsmith's taste—but several of his plays were regularly performed between 1747 and 1776, among them *The Intriguing Chambermaid*, *The Lottery*, *The Miser*, *The Mock Doctor*, and *The Virgin Unmask'd*. Goldsmith is not the only man to ignore Fielding. For some reason (topicality perhaps) he has never received a full, modern, study of his plays, and when his work appears in anthologies, *The Tragedy of Tragedies* is usually chosen. Had Goldsmith been a snooty Congrevean, he might have considered Fielding too unrefined to deserve notice—but his own plays certainly verge on the farcical. Perhaps because drama survey courses tend to hop from Congreve to Goldsmith and Sheridan (with a brief shudder over *The Conscious Lovers*), the myth persists of an eighteenth-century bog of sentimental drama with a brief pseudo-Restoration flicker in the 1760s and 1770s. Of course this is nonsense: the 1730s was one of the liveliest periods in English theatre history, and sentimental comedy was not precisely the mainstay. The Licensing Act of 1737 put an end to freewheeling experimentation; hence the 1740s and 1750s are not a prime period for new comedies. Goldsmith's implication that nothing of import was produced between Farquhar and the late 1760s (save perhaps *The Provok'd Husband*) is ridiculous, but we may grant that prior to 1760

18. Any such investigation is necessarily plagued by terminology. For discussion of the problem see *The London Stage*, Part 4, I, clxi–clxii, and ch. 7, above.

the theatres were following a pretty conservative policy. Complaints about this are evident in pamphlet literature:[19] basically, the managers were not risking much on new productions. The period 1760–80 is altogether livelier. In light of Fielding and Gay and the dearth of sentimental comedies between the 1720s and the 1760s, we can safely concentrate on the later period.[20]

Frederick T. Wood notes that after a prolonged dry period, "the revival [of sentimental comedy] reached its zenith during the years 1760–1767." "For the next seven years sentimentalism in drama was furiously assailed, and there grew up in opposition to it a school of writers who strove to bring back to the theatre something of the older spirit of the Comedy of Manners. The first blow was struck in Goldsmith's *The Good-Natur'd Man*."[21] This view is basically shared by Bernbaum and Nicoll: sentimental comedy revives between 1750 and 1767; suffers a counterattack 1768–73; and enjoys a final and decisive triumph 1773–80 and thereafter, despite the efforts of Sheridan. In fairness to Nicoll, one must note that he is far too learned to fall prey to this view in its worst form, and is perfectly aware that many writers other than Goldsmith and Sheridan worked in nonsentimental modes. Some scholars seem oblivious to this fact. In a much-quoted essay, DeWitt Croissant says flatly that sentimental comedy was dominant throughout the eighteenth century.[22] Kenneth Muir asserts that "when we come to the middle of the century . . . the new plays were all sentimental."[23]

---

19. For example, Edward Purdon's *Letter to Garrick on Opening the Theatre* (1759), and an article in the *Weekly Magazine* (1 Jan. 1760), discussed in *The London Stage*, Part 4, II, 741.

20. Even Frederick T. Wood has to struggle to uncover examples between Steele and 1760—and he finds practically every play sentimental which is moral or exhibits a belief in the goodness of human nature, including plays by Macklin and Colman and Gay's *Beggar's Opera*. See Wood's "Sentimental Comedy in the Eighteenth Century," *Neophilologus*, 18 (1932–33), 37–44, 281–89.

21. Wood, pp. 285, 286.

22. "Early Sentimental Comedy," *Essays on Dramatic Literature: The Parrott Presentation Volume*, ed. Hardin Craig (Princeton: Princeton Univ. Press, 1935), pp. 47–71.

23. *The Comedy of Manners*, p. 156. Muir's work is a good example of the persistence of the views outlined at the start of this chapter. In a book aimed at students, he says that the plays of Goldsmith and Sheridan "represent an attempt to

The common concept of the theatrical situation is aptly summed up by Robert J. Griffin, in a fine thesis on Goldsmith already cited: *The Good-Natur'd Man* (1768), "did not begin to stem the tide of sentimental comedies then gushing across the English stage."[24]

Presumably a close study of performance records in *The London Stage* will tell us precisely what plays constituted this flood. In this period the two theatres together usually put on only four or five new mainpieces per year, and roughly as many afterpieces. Even so, a piece-by-piece survey would be tedious—many of the new productions are tragedy, opera, or burletta—but we can easily survey the relevant pieces.

1759–60

Macklin, *Love a-la-Mode*. A humours farce which was exceptionally popular throughout the period (1760–80). Afterpiece.

Murphy, *The Way to Keep Him*. A satiric comedy of manners which long remained extremely popular. Originally an afterpiece, it was rewritten in 1761 as a five-act mainpiece (with an added subplot) in a more "sensible" vein.[25]

1760–61

Foote, *The Minor*. A vigorous satire on a good-hearted libertine; long an immense success. Its dramatized introduction is a kind of manifesto for satiric comedy.

Colman, *The Jealous Wife*. Another immense success. One of the major satiric comedies of the period; discussed below.

Colman, *Polly Honeycombe*. An extremely successful afterpiece. A trenchant satire on the sentimental novel mode; discussed below.

Macklin, *The Married Libertine*. A lively, humorous comedy with

---

return to the comic tradition of the seventeenth century," even though "there is a residue of sentimentality in both Goldsmith and Sheridan" (pp. 156–57).

24. Griffin, "Goldsmith's Augustanism," p. 144. Such a view can be found in full flower by 1812. See Stephen Jones' continuation of the *Biographia Dramatica*, 3 vols. (London: Longman, 1812), III, 263–64, s.v. "She Stoops to Conquer." There is no hint of this view in Isaac Reed's 1782 edition.

25. For texts see Arthur Murphy, *"The Way to Keep Him" and five other plays*, ed. John Pike Emery (New York: New York Univ. Press, 1956), and Richard W. Bevis, ed., *Eighteenth Century Drama: Afterpieces* (Oxford: Oxford Univ. Press, 1970). It was the mainpiece version which held the stage.

a vein of sentimental moralizing. The play ran nine nights against claque opposition and was not revived. *The London Stage* (Part 4, II, 841) quotes one "H. F." who suggested revisions: "The scenes wherein Lady Belville is solemn, grave complaining and moral may be much abbreviated. . . . Pray consider whether that serious, moral and sentimental part in the character of Angelica might not be curtailed, or entirely omitted." More such suggestions follow—all aimed at removing the moral and sentimental parts in the interest of popularity.

Murphy, *All in the Wrong*. A very popular manners comedy.

Murphy, *The Citizen*. A farce which remained extremely popular throughout this period.

Reed, *The Register Office*. A farce (afterpiece); a steady, continued success.

1761–62

Whitehead, *The School for Lovers*. A mainpiece which had a good run of thirteen nights its first year, and was a modest, steady success for several seasons. A translation from the French. According to Bernbaum, this play inaugurates the sentimental revival. The prologue does speak of drawing tears from the audience.

Foote, *The Lyar*. A humours intrigue which was very popular after a few slow seasons.

1762–63

Mrs. Frances Sheridan, *The Discovery*. A fairly lively sentimental comedy which was a considerable success its first season, achieving seventeen performances (helped by Garrick's acting, according to Nicoll—III, 139), but quickly lost favor, managing only six more performances in this period.

Bickerstaff, *Love in a Village*. A popular, spritely comic opera.

1763–64

Mrs. Sheridan, *The Dupe*. Sentimentally inclined; hissed, quickly dropped, and not revived.

Murphy, *No One's Enemy but his Own*. A humours comedy; hissed and not revived.

Murphy, *What We Must all Come to*. A brisk humours comedy.[26]

Colman, *The Deuce is in Him*. A long-popular and very funny satire on platonic love.

1764–65[27]

Mrs. Griffith, *The Platonic Wife*. Limped through six nights.

Bickerstaff, *The Maid of the Mill*. A tremendously successful comic opera: twenty-nine performances the first season, revived frequently throughout the period. Bernbaum calls it a major sentimental document. The play is a dramatization of *Pamela* with Mr. B. transformed into Lord Aimworth, a model of propriety. Perhaps more saccharine than sentimental.

1765–66

Kenrick, *Falstaff's Wedding*. A flop.

Mrs. Griffith, *The Double Mistake*. Ran a few nights its first month; not revived. Bernbaum says that "the fact that *The Double Mistake* succeeded in spite of its artistic blemishes shows how completely sentimentalism had for the time recaptured the theatrical public" (p. 218)! A moderately sentimental play.

Garrick and Colman, *The Clandestine Marriage*. A tremendous and lasting success; discussed below.

---

26. For the circumstances under which this play was initially damned, see Howard Hunter Dunbar, *The Dramatic Career of Arthur Murphy* (New York: Modern Language Association, 1946), pp. 164–72. Revived under the title *Marriage a-la-Mode*, and in 1776 as *Three Weeks After Marriage*, it seems to have been a passable success.

27. Another play which definitely deserves notice is Macklin's *The Man of the World*, a brilliant and devastating comedy of manners in a strictly satiric mode. Performed in Dublin in 1764 (as *The True-born Scotchman*), the play was refused a license in London in 1770 and 1779 on political grounds. The first London performance was in May 1781; first publication was in 1792. For stage history the play is unimportant save as an example of what the censor would not pass. But it also shows that in the mid-1760s someone was capable of writing first-rate satiric comedy. Sir Pertinax Macsycophant is one of the great comic creations of the century. On Macklin's play, see Dougald MacMillan, "The Censorship in the Case of Macklin's *The Man of the World*," *Huntington Library Bulletin*, no. 10 (1936), 79–101, and his introduction to the Augustan Reprint Society facsimile edition (Los Angeles, 1951).

1766–67

Garrick, *The Country Girl.* An insipid adaptation of *The Country-Wife,* which nonetheless remains in the manners mode. For Garrick, it was not popular, though it achieved a steady trickle of performances.

Colman, *The English Merchant*—an adaptation from French sentimental comedy. According to Nicoll (III, 140), this is "one of the most representative sentimental dramas." No particular success initially, it was revived occasionally during this period.

Murphy, *The School for Guardians.* A vigorous comedy of manners; dropped after a few performances.

1767–68

Kenrick, *The Widow'd Wife.* A namby-pamby, emotion-oriented play which managed a few performances its first season, and just one the next year.

Kelly, *False Delicacy.* A major success; discussed below.

Goldsmith, *The Good-Natur'd Man.* A fair success; discussed below.

According to the hypothesis engendered by Goldsmith's essay, we should find a flood of sentimental comedies in this group, and observe the virtual disappearance of "true" comedy. Such a claim has been made by Bernbaum. "In the six years ending with 1767, the temporary supremacy of true comedy [he is referring to the farces of Foote, Macklin, and Murphy in the 1750s] was thus overthrown, and seven successful sentimental comedies were produced. In no previous period had the genre been so dominant and prolific." Distinguishing between comic opera and domestic comedy, he adds: "such were the two varieties of sentimental comedy that between 1762 and 1767 almost monopolized the stage." [28] So Goldsmith implies, but will the case bear scrutiny? Obviously my list of plays above is drastically selective, but it does include all of the plays Bernbaum sees fit to put forward, and since he was making a systematic search for the sentimental, I think we may assume that I am not misrepresenting his case.

28. Ernest Bernbaum, *The Drama of Sensibility,* pp. 222–23.

In practice, the "flood" turns out to amount to about one new production a year, and some of those arguable. Few afterpieces are sentimental, but if we count them in, roughly seven of ninety new productions are "sentimental comedy"; counting mainpieces alone, approximately seven of forty. A case could be made for counting more comic operas as sentimental, but then a couple of Bernbaum's examples are debatable. We may ask, too, what he means by "successful." Consider his instances one by one. 1) *The School for Lovers.* After a good first season, a steady, quiet success. 2) *The Discovery.* A considerable success in its first season—then quick oblivion. 3) *The Maid of the Mill.* A great and lasting success. Sentimental in exhibiting exemplary characters, not in Goldsmith's sense. 4) *The Double Mistake*—essentially a flop. 5) *The Clandestine Marriage.* A tremendous and lasting success, but in my opinion, not a sentimental comedy in Goldsmith's sense or any other. 6) *The English Merchant*—no real success, though revived occasionally. 7) *The Widow'd Wife*, which limped through one season.

Consider now some plays Bernbaum does not discuss.[29] 1) *The Way to Keep Him*—a vast success. 2) *The Jealous Wife*—one of the great mainpiece successes of the decade. 3) *Polly Honeycombe*—the most popular comic afterpiece of the decade (excluding pantomimes and the like). 4) *All in the Wrong*—very popular. 5) *The Citizen*—a long-successful farce. 6) *The Deuce is in Him*—a perennially popular satire on platonic sentiment. 7) *The Country Girl*—despite purification (Horner disappears) a disappointment for Garrick. 8) *The School for Guardians*—like *The Double Mistake*, dropped after a few performances.

With the exception of *Polly Honeycombe*, I have largely ignored afterpieces. Even so, to make a case for growing dominance of sentimental comedy would be difficult. Some laughing comedies fail (*No One's Enemy but his Own; The School for Guardians*),

---

29. Bernbaum tries hard to call three earlier plays sentimental: Macklin's *Love a-la-Mode*, Foote's *The Minor*, and especially Joseph Reed's *The Register Office.* I agree with Nicoll in thinking otherwise. All three were great and lasting successes—testimony to audience enjoyment of humours and satiric farces. *The London Stage*, Part 4, II, 861, points out that Reed's play met trouble with the licenser over profanity and *double entendre*.

but so do some sentimental comedies (*The Double Mistake; The Widow'd Wife*). What are the major successes of the decade, prior to the 1767–68 season?—farces by Macklin, Foote, Murphy, and Colman; the great mainpiece successes are *The Jealous Wife* and *The Clandestine Marriage*. Whitehead's *The School for Lovers* is the one clearly sentimental play which did well and continued to do so after its first season. Bickerstaff's *Maid of the Mill* may well be deemed generally "sentimental," but it is scarcely sentimental comedy in the usual senses. We find then that "flood" is a rather exaggerated description of the flow of sentimental comedies, and further, that with an occasional exception, they were not doing well in the theatre. Conceivably we are merely expecting sentimental domination too soon, misled by Bernbaum. Myth has it that *False Delicacy* (allegedly an epitome of sentimental slop) ruined Goldsmith's chances for a hit with *The Good-Natur'd Man*. This is far from accurate. Goldsmith's play achieved eleven performances its first season (versus seventeen for *False Delicacy*), and the author's nights brought him some £340, which added to his publisher's fee (a very respectable £50) gave him one of his most profitable ventures ever.[30] Comments on the sensational success of *False Delicacy* generally ignore an important point: it was a flash in the pan. Kelly's play was offered seven times in the next two seasons, and once more three years later. Compared to *The Jealous Wife* at the beginning of the decade, or *The Clandestine Marriage* in roughly the same period, Kelly scored only a very ephemeral success.[31] We may note too that although it was premiered a month later in the season, *The Clandestine Marriage* ran as many nights (seventeen) its first year, and almost as many again the next. In short, Kelly's success was far from unprecedented and it did not last.

Two questions obviously deserve notice. Are *The Jealous Wife* and *The Clandestine Marriage* arguably sentimental comedies? And if not, why does Goldsmith utterly disregard their existence in his "Essay"? About the former no doubt arises. Even Bernbaum (who

30. See Ralph M. Wardle, *Oliver Goldsmith* (Lawrence: Univ. of Kansas Press, 1957), p. 182.
31. *The Good-Natur'd Man* did only a bit worse: three performances in 1770–71 and one in 1773.

can find sentimentalism in some pretty odd places) says flatly that the play is an amusing attempt at "high comedy." *The Clandestine Marriage*—a collaboration between Garrick and Colman—is arguable. To call it simply a sentimental play would be misleading: trenchant social satire makes the designation ridiculous. Yet tears and fainting, rigid moral decorum, and an appeal to the goodness of human nature all seem like a sentimental taint to some readers. Sherbo, a cautious and careful authority, refuses to classify the play outright, but in two places quotes evidence to distinguish it from the French *comédie larmoyante*.[32] Personally, I agree with Stone that satire outweighs sentiment and makes the play a brilliant comedy of manners, though admittedly a highly moral one with a good deal of sensibility.

Given the tremendous popularity of such plays as *The Jealous Wife, The Way to Keep Him, Polly Honeycombe,* and *The Clandestine Marriage,* why should Goldsmith apparently ignore their existence? One conjecture seems highly plausible: Goldsmith felt himself badly treated by Garrick and Colman, the two playhouse managers. His failure to acknowledge their plays is quite possibly simply a matter of personal dislike and jealousy. And we should recall that in an ephemeral piece of journalism, Goldsmith can scarcely be expected to take a broad, historical view. As I will try to show below, he was very probably upset about the apparent trend in taste during the season in which a play of his own was to be staged.

According to Bernbaum's scheme, the years 1768–72 see an "attack" on sentimental comedy. Lest the reader feel I am flogging a dead horse, let me point out that Sherbo (chapter 7) uses these same chronological divisions and descriptions—albeit skeptically. Again, I find little evidence for the generalization. Both sentimental and nonsentimental comedies are mounted regularly, with varying success. The major sentimental plays are as follows. 1) Mrs. Griffith, *The School for Rakes,* 1769: an adaptation of Beaumarchais which ran well for a year and then managed only two isolated performances. 2) Cumberland, *The Brothers,* 1769: a solid success over

32. Sherbo, pp. 8, 85, 150.

a number of seasons. But I would agree with Leo Hughes that this play is really a prototypical melodrama which looks forward to the end of the century; the reward of virtue seems incidental.[33] 3) Kelly, *A Word to the Wise*, 1770: a high-minded attack on libertinism which was forced off the stage on political grounds and had no run at all. 4) Cumberland, *The West Indian*, 1771: a vast and lasting success. 5) Cumberland, *The Fashionable Lover*, 1772: a pro-Scotch imitation of *The West Indian* which had a good run for a year and then petered out with a few more performances. 6) Mrs. Griffith, *A Wife in the Right*, 1772: actionless, laden with delicate feeling, and a complete flop. 7) William O'Brien, *The Duel*, 1772: a flop.

The major laughing comedies of the 1768–72 period are as follows: 1) Foote, *The Devil Upon Two Sticks*, 1768: a long-standing success which contained many hits at excess sentiment. 2) Colman, *Man and Wife*, 1769: ran well for five years. 3) Whitehead, *A Trip to Scotland*, 1770: a vigorous satire on the eloping girl and sentimental literature. Interestingly, this play did extremely well: it ran far better in the 1770s than Whitehead's sentimental *School for Lovers* had in the 1760s. 4) Three plays by Foote, *The Lame Lover* (1770), *The Maid of Bath* (1771), and *The Nabob* (1772), were respectively a flop, a passable success, and a hit. 5) Garrick, *The Irish Widow*, 1772: a considerable, lasting success.[34]

What we find, then, is a mixed picture. The most popular comedy of the period immediately preceding Goldsmith's "Essay" is indubitably *The West Indian*. On the other hand, laughing comedies were, on the average, doing much better than sentimental comedies. *The Devil Upon Two Sticks, Man and Wife, A Trip to Scotland, The Nabob,* and *The Irish Widow* were all solid, lasting successes. Foote and Whitehead, indeed, achieved their success by satirizing sentimentality. Granted, these are not great plays. But our question is stage history, not merit. Nonsentimental comedies are

33. Leo Hughes, *The Drama's Patrons* (Austin: Univ. of Texas Press, 1971), p. 186.

34. Mention should be made of Foote's *A Sentimental Comedy; or Piety in Pattens* (otherwise known as *The Handsome Housemaid*), 1773, a brilliant parody of the *Pamela* mode. First offered as a "puppet show," this piece was adapted as an "entertainment" and appeared on the legitimate stage a number of times. Apparently it was very popular: see the *Biographia Dramatica* (1812), III, 150–56.

being produced with great success right through the decade before Goldsmith's essay. That most critics have never heard of these plays, much less read them, does not mean that they did not exist and were not significant.

To carry the account of new productions through the 1770s is an endeavor which goes beyond the scope of this essay. It is sufficient to say that the tale is much as before. Some sentimental plays did well—for example, Kelly's *The School for Wives*, 1773—but the great successes of the decade are laughing comedies: *The School for Scandal*, *The Duenna*, *Bon Ton*, and of course *She Stoops to Conquer*. Cumberland himself tried his hand at an out-and-out laughing comedy—*The Choleric Man* (1774).[35] To deny the presence of sensibility and a benevolent view of human nature in much of this drama would be idle. These elements are central to *The West Indian* and prominent in *The School for Scandal*. The impact of the *comédie larmoyante* on some minor playwrights is evident enough. A widespread rage for extreme sensibility is obvious in novels of these years—Sterne's not least among them—and perhaps there is more than just coincidence in the appearance of *The West Indian* and *The Man of Feeling* in the same year—1771. But to say that there was not a strong vein of laughing comedy flourishing throughout the period 1760–80 is ridiculous. Whether he cared to admit it or not, Goldsmith was writing for a theatre in which several distinguished, popular writers of laughing comedies were active—Murphy, Macklin, Colman, Garrick, and Foote.

I have restricted my detailed consideration to a fairly narrow period, but my findings are corroborated in three broader studies. Working from Genest, Arthur Sherbo compares the runs and revivals of selected sentimental and nonsentimental plays between 1750 and 1780. His conclusions, arrived at from a different perspective, agree precisely with mine: despite some considerable sentimental successes, "the non-sentimental plays easily prove more popular," especially when lasting success and revivals are considered.[36] Sherbo

35. Not a success. For a modern edition of this work (an adaptation of Shadwell's *The Squire of Alsatia*) see Olaf S. Olson's unpublished dissertation, New York Univ., 1968.

36. Sherbo, ch. 7, esp. pp. 159–60.

(who had to work without *The London Stage*) finds his evidence producing this generalization for the whole period.[37] My more detailed investigation has shown that even in the 1760–73 period sentimental comedy never achieved even a temporary dominance.

A corroborative overview, with the advantage of precise performance figures, is offered by George Winchester Stone, Jr., in his introduction to Part 4 of *The London Stage*.[38] Stone breaks down performances at each playhouse (Drury Lane and Covent Garden) as tragedy or comedy, and then further into categories: Shakespeare, Heroic, Pseudo-Classic, Pathetic, and Pseudo-Romantic, for tragedy; Shakespearean, Humours, Manners, Intrigue, and Sentiment, for comedy. For the period 1747–76, Stone finds 10,545 performances of mainpieces (5,179 comedies; 3,412 tragedies; 1,954 "miscellaneous"—operas, history plays, and so forth). Of these, 1,074 are claimed to be "sentimental" comedy within Stone's notion of that elusive category. "Manners" comedy claims 1,942 performances; Shakespeare's comedies 737; intrigue comedy 914; humours 512. In short, by this system, sentimental comedy accounts for about 10 percent of mainpiece performances, while manners comedy alone comes close to 20 percent. These figures are all the more impressive in that they are restricted to mainpieces. Almost invariably, of course, a short afterpiece was added—usually two acts. Stone's figures show that pantomime and outright farce were much the most popular forms for afterpieces.

The afterpiece tradition is the principal subject of an excellent study by Richard Bevis.[39] Working from his own categories and judgments, Bevis comes up with figures which bear out Stone: 8–9 percent sentimental comedy. Two other points seem worth raising. Bevis, working with the Larpent MSS, makes the interesting point

37. Sherbo adds an interesting table (p. 161) which shows that in and after Bernbaum's period of final "triumph" for sentimental comedy, 1775–1800, there were 500 performances of sentimental plays in 2,319 acting days. Since Sherbo was intentionally generous in his view of the sentimental canon, the smallness of the figure is impressive—between 20 and 25 percent.

38. I, clxii–clxix.

39. *The Laughing Tradition* (1980). The original form of this chapter cited the thesis from which Bevis developed his book: "The Comic Tradition on the London Stage, 1737–1777," Diss. Univ. of California, Berkeley, 1965.

that apparently much of the sentiment and moralizing found in the printed version of Kelly's successful *School for Wives* was omitted in stage presentation. This fact should remind us that using printed quartos as evidence of stage performance is not the safest proceeding in the world. It also raises the possibility that authors, aware of what was wanted by a novel-reading public, added sentimental material for publication. The second point is less speculative. Bevis' study should remind us that if Goldsmith genuinely thought that humor and low comedy were in danger of disappearing from the English stage, he must have had an invariable habit of leaving the theatre immediately after the mainpiece—as well, of course, of invariably going to the wrong mainpieces. Fewer than 5 percent of the afterpieces could be construed as sentimental: a huge number are manners satire, farce, or laughable lampoonery.[40]

Considering the popularity of contemporary laughing comedies in this period, we should not be surprised to find that older comedies were doing well. Restriction to two theatres in London meant that classic plays constituted a large part of the repertory. With performance records easily available in *The London Stage*, elaborate documentation seems unnecessary, but a few examples will be suggestive.[41] Of pre-1760 comedies, the following were particularly popular: Hoadly's *The Suspicious Husband* (1747), *The Beaux Stratagem*, *The Conscious Lovers*, *The Provok'd Wife*, *The Provok'd Husband*, *The Beggar's Opera*, *Every Man in His Humour*, Foote's *The Englishman in Paris* (1753).

More particularly, let me expand a point I made at the start of this section. In the season of Goldsmith's "Essay" he could have seen (among others) the following: Fielding's *The Miser* (three times), *The Beggar's Opera* (fifteen), *The Busie Body* (six), *Twelfth Night* (six), *The Provok'd Wife* (three), *Every Man in His Humour* (five), *The Beaux Stratagem* (eight), *The Rehearsal* (five), *Rule a Wife* (ten),

40. Bevis, whose study should be read by anyone interested in this subject, demonstrates at length that the threat to comedy came not from sentimentality but from farce, vaudeville, spectacle—the *illegitimi* which bulked so large at the end of the century. The point is reinforced by the performance records in Part 5 of *The London Stage*.

41. Convenient tables can be found in appendix C of Harry William Pedicord's *The Theatrical Public in the Time of Garrick*.

The Recruiting Officer (three), *Much Ado About Nothing*, *The In-constant* (two), *The Provok'd Husband* (four), *As You Like It* (two), *The Alchemist* (two), *She wou'd and She wou'd not* (two), *The Committee* (two), *Volpone* (two), *Love's Last Shift*, *The Double Gallant*, *The Double-Dealer* (two), *The Funeral*, *The Plain Dealer* (Bickerstaffe alteration), *Love for Love*. All considered, the older plays were doing far better than might have been expected. Social or manners comedy tends to date quickly, and most of these plays are seventy-five years old or more. Tastes had changed, especially with respect to "decorum" of several sorts. This led, of course, to adaptations of Congreve, Wycherley, and Vanbrugh calculated to make their work inoffensive.[42] The wonder is that these plays held the stage as well as they did after 1720.[43]

Before turning to a consideration of the place of the plays of Goldsmith and Sheridan, I want to survey briefly the historical pattern we have been considering. Goldsmith's whining about the disappearance of humor from the stage is plainly nonsense. A strong comic tradition is doing well throughout the later 1750s and 1760s with the work of Murphy, Foote, Macklin, Garrick, and Colman. At the same time, we can see a flurry of interest in the "sentimental," however one may want to define that term. Personally, I see no way to make a sharp distinction between the laughing and the sentimental: some cases are clear-cut, others not. Part of the sentimental vogue—and there is a sentimental vogue, in the novel as much as in the drama—is fed by importation from French drama. Some distinctions are important. "Moral" versus "immoral" comedy:

42. On this subject see Hughes, *The Drama's Patrons*, ch. 4; Charles Harold Gray, *Theatrical Criticism in London to 1795*; Emmett L. Avery, *Congreve's Plays on the Eighteenth-Century Stage*, appendix I, and "The Reputation of Wycherley's Comedies as Stage Plays in the Eighteenth Century"; and ch. 2, sec. "The Judgment of Posterity, 1700–1776," above.

43. Admittedly, some of them had been tinkered with. *Every Man in His Humour* and *Rule a Wife*, for example, were laundered by Garrick. (See Pedicord, ch. 4.) Revision for the sake of purity and poetic justice was not always welcomed: see the *Town and Country Magazine*'s scorching review of Edward Thompson's new ending for *The Beggar's Opera*, in which Macheath is sentenced to three years at hard labor (Oct. 1777).

in this period, everyone is pretty well moral. "Genteel" versus "low" comedy: this differentiation is in part related to the satiric/exemplary division. Satiric versus sympathetic humor: even in ostensibly satiric writers, we find a good deal of latitude for sympathy.

I would not go so far as to suggest that the laughing-sentimental distinction is unreal.[44] Plainly *The Jealous Wife* is not of a kind with *False Delicacy*, nor *The Clandestine Marriage* with *The West Indian*. But the differences are of degree. All are moral; all are basically genteel; all contain a good deal of satire. Much of the point of *False Delicacy* is ridicule of excessive sensibility, though some of the point is blunted by the author's obvious admiration for sensibility itself.[45] And *The West Indian*, despite its author's extreme benevolism, remains and was intended as a very funny play. A well-known line from Garrick is often quoted about it—"I rejoice that you wept at ye West-Indian"[46]—but a newspaper writer gives a more balanced view: "at a comedy I expect and love to laugh; and I took up the pen to make my acknowledgments to an author who has gratified his inclination,—who has introduced laughter without dismissing sentiment,—and who has showed morality and mirth to be far from incompatible."[47] A laughing comedy may be strictly moral without introducing the benevolent view of human nature (*The Way to Keep Him*), or it may postulate a basic good nature (*The Clandestine Marriage*), or that good nature may be dwelt upon to the point that sentiment becomes a major feature of the play (*The West Indian*). Despite the undoubted fad for sensibility around 1770 (as much associated with novels as with plays), Thorndike is

44. See Robert John Detisch, "High Georgian Comedy: English Stage Comedy from 1760–1777," Diss. Univ. of Wisconsin 1967; and Joseph James Keenan, Jr., "The Poetics of High Georgian Comedy: A Study of the Comic Theory and Practice of Murphy, Colman, and Cumberland," Diss. Univ. of Wisconsin 1969.

45. A good discussion of Kelly's play can be found in Joseph W. Donohue, Jr.'s *Dramatic Character in the English Romantic Age*, pp. 113–18.

46. Letter to John Hoadly, 9 May 1771. *The Letters of David Garrick*, ed. David M. Little and George M. Kahrl, 3 vols. (Cambridge, Mass.: Harvard Univ. Press, 1963), II, 739.

47. *Whitehall Evening Post* (9 Feb. 1771), cited in Stanley Thomas Williams, *Richard Cumberland: His Life and Dramatic Works* (New Haven: Yale Univ. Press, 1917), pp. 76–77.

certainly correct in asserting that no such thing as "a well defined species" ever emerges.[48]

According to Nicoll (and Sherbo approves his scheme), "three distinct tendencies" appear in sentimental comedy. "There are the relics of the Cibberian genteel comedy, aiding in the intensification of that 'high' note in comedy against which Goldsmith raised the flag of rebellion; there is the often mawkishly pathetic theatre of Cumberland, intent upon raising a sigh and calling forth a tear; and there is the more revolutionary humanitarian drama which is seen at its best in the plays of Mrs. Inchbald and of Thomas Holcroft."[49] Some of this I find worrisome. Justice is certainly not done Cumberland—who is, we should note, an ardent and admirable champion of victims of social prejudice. His efforts on behalf of West Indians, the Irish, the Scotch, and later the Jews, definitely place him in the tradition of humanitarian playwrights who were so popular in the last twenty years of the eighteenth century. Another questionable point is the association of Cibber with "genteel" comedy. Goldsmith, after all, appears to connect at least one of his efforts with "Laughing and even Low Comedy." Genteel (often meaning exemplary) comedy I would associate more with Steele. No need to split hairs, however. We can agree that at least three "tendencies" mark what is commonly called sentimental comedy. One sort—an early development—stresses genteel, semi-exemplary characters. *The Conscious Lovers* is one instance; Hoadly's immensely popular *The Suspicious Husband* is another—a play on the "Restoration" model, carefully purged of its immorality. A second possibility is emphasis on sensibility. Naturally, this tends to be "genteel." As in the novel, sensibility (much of it imported from France) shows a flurry of activity around 1770: Kelly, Cumberland, and Goldsmith all reflect it and (in varying degrees) satirize it. Even in the case of Goldsmith's Honeywood, though, we sympathize too much with the benevolent character to feel that he is severely undercut—and Goldsmith rewards him with girl and fortune at the

48. Ashley H. Thorndike, *English Comedy* (New York: Macmillan, 1929), p. 413. Despite its age, Thorndike's treatment of drama, 1760–1780 (ch. 17), remains helpful.

49. Nicoll, III, 153–54. Cf. Sherbo, p. 143.

end. The third possibility is serious social argument, generally based on either faith in the goodness of human nature or a firm belief in its corrigibility. Cumberland moves strongly in this direction. To the reader who finds spontaneous reform obnoxious in every "sentimental" play from *Love's Last Shift* on, it will be little comfort to reflect that Honeywood, Cumberland's Belcour, and Sheridan's Charles Surface are all presented and rewarded in essentially similar fashion. "Sentimentalism" in this context boils down to a matter of how much the author revels in the sensibility he presents. To mock it and love it at the same time is no great trick, as the reader of *The Vicar of Wakefield* should be well aware.

Quite plainly, the implications of Goldsmith's "Essay" are misleading. What about his conception of sentimental comedy? Lacking particular examples, we have to deduce the characteristics. These appear to be: 1) genteel characters; 2) "Insipid Dialogue"; 3) pathetic scenes; 4) characters who are "good, and exceedingly generous." Certain contradictions appear. Goldsmith first declaims against noble characters in comedy, and later sneers at titled heroines and a "Hero with a Ribband," but then he thunders at Tradesman heroes. And as far as good-hearted characters go, Goldsmith's own plays are full of them, not to mention his other works.[50] About insipid dialogue and pathetic scenes, Goldsmith has a good point: a play in which they are emphasized has a markedly different tone from one in which they are not. To a considerable degree, this is the difference between *False Delicacy* and *The Good-Natur'd Man*—similar plays in many respects.

The social level of characters is a matter which puzzles me. Neither tradesmen nor Lords and Ladies are common in the "sentimental" plays of the 1760s. Possibly Goldsmith means that he dislikes "exemplary" characters—though he certainly puts plenty of attractive and likeable characters in his own plays. Or perhaps he means that insipidly virtuous characters are a bore—he does speak for "Character or Humour." This last would be an essentially valid point. Morality and gentility often combine to make charac-

50. For example, Young Marlow's noble speech to the supposed barmaid in *She Stoops to Conquer* (Act IV): "I can never harbor a thought of seducing simplicity that trusted in my honour. . . . "

ters in Georgian comedy rather bland; one of the strengths of Goldsmith and Sheridan is the memorable humours of such characters
as Croaker, Tony Lumpkin, and Mrs. Malaprop. Of course fine
humours characters also appear in the plays of Colman, Foote,
Macklin, and Murphy, so Goldsmith was hardly reviving a lost art.

Indeed, humor was very far from disappearing from the stage,
either in new plays or revivals. "Sentimental comedy" means various things at various times, and certainly cannot be sharply and
unequivocally differentiated from "laughing" comedy in the period
1760–80. Both varieties often turn on the assumption of the goodness of human nature. Most generally, we can say that Goldsmith
and Sheridan inherited a strong and continuing laughing comedy
tradition.

In light of this conclusion, one may well ask why Goldsmith
wrote the essay he did. Any answer must be speculative, but I think
a fair guess can be made. Goldsmith was about to have a fairly
farcical mainpiece produced, and certain apparent trends in taste
could have given him considerable cause for alarm. In the preceding months *The West Indian* continued to run well, and Cumberland's *The Brothers* and *The Fashionable Lover* were performed.
The last two had outrun their popularity, but to Goldsmith, it may
well have seemed that a tidal wave of Cumberland was sweeping
the stage. He did not care for Cumberland anyway,[51] and could
recollect the circumstances in which the bailiff scene in *The Good-
Natur'd Man* had been hissed: "Our audiences . . . having been
recently exalted on the sentimental stilts of *False Delicacy* . . . regarded a few scenes in Dr. *Goldsmith's* piece as too low for their
entertainment, and therefore treated them with unjustifiable se-

51. See Goldsmith's poem, "Retaliation," *Works*, IV, 352–59. Cumberland had
rejected the doctrine of original sin, a position as obnoxious to Goldsmith as Goldsmith's position on the drama proved to be to the benevolist Thomas Holcroft. In
the preface to his play *Duplicity: A Comedy* (London, 1781) Holcroft objects to the
emphasis on "humour alone" in *She Stoops*, and states that "the intention of this
Comedy is of a far nobler nature than the mere incitement of risibility:. . . I would
rather have the merit of driving one man from the gaming-table, than of making a
whole theatre merry" (pp. iv, vi)—and he goes on to admit the similarity of his
comedy to Moore's *Gamester*.

verity." [52] Goldsmith did not want to repeat with Cumberland what he had suffered with Kelly. That portion of the "Essay" directed against faultless characters and insipidity does seem aimed—a little unfairly—at Cumberland.

What about the references to Tradesman's Tragedy? Here again reference to productions in the fall of 1772 seems helpful. The most conspicuous eighteenth-century domestic tragedies are Lillo's *London Merchant* (1731) and the plays of his follower, Edward Moore. Both enjoy a small flurry in the early 1770s. *The Gamester*,[53] quiescent since the mid-1750s, suddenly comes to life, and in November, Drury Lane revived Lillo's play for the first time in two years. (Covent Garden had been playing it right along.) To a writer morbidly conscious of every ripple on the surface of the pond of taste, one swallow does a summer make. And in the new *Westminster Magazine* Goldsmith had an outlet receptive to a gloomy view of the theatre.[54] But we should not take exaggerations made in the heat of the moment too seriously. At this point we can usefully turn from the myth extrapolated from Goldsmith's essay to consider his own plays.

Goldsmith and Sheridan in Context

The widespread notion that Goldsmith and Sheridan are "reactionaries" is central to the old myth of a revolution against sentimental

---

52. *Biographia Dramatica*, ed. Isaac Reed, 2 vols. (Dublin, 1782), II, 139.

53. Not to be confused with Garrick's *The Gamesters* (an adaptation from Shirley), put on with success that same fall.

54. In the first issue an anonymous reviewer flays the pantomime put on with *The London Merchant* on 26 December, and laments that "The Stage seems now buried in universal darkness" (oddly enough, he finds the reign of Queen Anne the high point of English playwriting!). The *Westminster* is consistently severe: even *She Stoops* gets only grudging approval. The *Town and Country* seems more attuned to popular taste. It praises the "just and noble sentiments" of *The Fashionable Lover* (Jan. 1772), but gives *The Nabob* high praise for its "sufficiently general" satire, and giving "the follies and vices of the times . . . all their glare of ridicule and deformity" (July 1772). The reviewer shows no signs of avidity for sentiment: he finds the chaste diction and noble sentiments inadequate compensation for the "want of incident

comedy. Such a view is fed by the opening of Goldsmith's preface to *The Good-Natur'd Man*: "When I undertook to write a comedy, I confess I was strongly prepossessed in favour of the poets of *the last age*, and strove to imitate them." [55] Well, he himself has said it, and presumably it is greatly to his credit—but what does he mean?

Allardyce Nicoll glosses this passage as follows. "By 'the last age' Goldsmith means the age of Shakespeare; to Shakespeare he looked when Sheridan sported with Congreve. Goldsmith's real objection to the sentimental comedy is that it is too 'genteel' and does not admit of 'nature' and 'humour'. Sheridan preferred to see wit on the boards of the theatre. Goldsmith endeavours to revive the spirit of *As You Like It* where Sheridan strives to create another *Way of the World*." [56]

I have doubts about this. Sheridan wrote four original plays (including a comic opera), but only one could be viewed as a would-be *Way of the World*. How Nicoll arrives at *As You Like It* as a model for Goldsmith I cannot imagine. *The Good-Natur'd Man* is a boisterous, low, city comedy with gross humours characters like Croaker. *She Stoops to Conquer* is indeed a "country" comedy, but its farcical high spirits seem a long way from Shakespeare's play. Nicoll elaborates by saying that Goldsmith is "full of those *mots de caractère* and *mots de situation* in which Shakespeare had delighted. Goldsmith has been compared to Farquhar, but his spirit is earlier still. Without the romantic pastoralism, it is close to the mood which is prevalent in the works of Greene and Lyly and the young Shakespeare." [57]

"Spirit" and "mood" are difficult to judge with precision. What Nicoll apparently intuits I do not feel at all. Goldsmith does not write romantic high comedy; he believes in humours and amiable satire, and says so. Nor do I find much hint in Goldsmith's other writing that he looked to Shakespeare as a model. Certainly Ri-

and variety of character" in Mason's *Elfrida* (Nov. 1772), and he damns O'Brien's *Duel* as a "languid" imitation of French comedy which deserved its failure (Dec. 1772). If the *Town and Country* is at all indicative of middle-of-the-road taste, laughing comedy had little to fear.

55. *Works*, V, 13 (italics added).
56. Nicoll, III, 158.
57. Ibid., 159–60.

cardo Quintana, in a useful survey of Goldsmith's dramatic criticism, finds little.[58] Quintana concludes that "in comedy his preference . . . was for Congreve, Vanbrugh, and Farquhar, the latter being his favorite." The comparison with Farquhar makes very good sense to me.[59] His later plays combine ridicule with moral lead characters. Like Goldsmith he can move comfortably into a cheerful country setting; wit is not a leading characteristic of his plays. Given Goldsmith's well-documented admiration for Farquhar, I find that writer a plausible candidate as a referent for "poets of the last age." More plainly than Vanbrugh or Congreve, he mixes essentially good-humored satire with basically good-hearted characters.[60]

The time of Shakespeare seems rather a long way back to stand as the "last age" for a man born about 1730 and come to maturity around 1750. But the turn of the century playwrights—Congreve, Farquhar, Vanbrugh, and Cibber—might well be called of the "last age" by a man who was a child when the last play of the last of them was produced. In the same preface, Goldsmith decries "*genteel comedy*" and a "too delicate" public taste, going on to complain of the "very elevated and sentimental" French comedy with its excessive "refinement." In short, Goldsmith is opposing an excess of sensibility and refinement at the expense of humour in characters. Most certainly, he is not speaking in favor of hard-line satire on the early Restoration model. This position is in line with his later admiring reference to the "Laughing and even Low" comedy of Vanbrugh and Cibber. That reference is welcomed by critics with no more enthusiasm than Darwin was greeted by the Church of England. Who wants to find a beastly sentimental monkey among the ancestors of one of our favorite eighteenth-century dramatists? Even Quintana makes no mention of the point. But Goldsmith is looking for vigorous humours characterization while wanting more

58. "Oliver Goldsmith as a Critic of the Drama," *Studies in English Literature*, 5 (1965), 435–54.

59. The comparison with Farquhar has been fully argued by George H. Nettleton, *English Drama of the Restoration and Eighteenth Century* (New York: Macmillan, 1914), p. 286.

60. Compare Aimwell's confession ("Such goodness who could injure! I find myself unequal to the task of villain . . . ") in Act V of *The Beaux Stratagem* with the similar scene in *She Stoops* (n. 50, above).

"decency" (his term) than Vanbrugh's plays possess, and a less "coarse and licentious" spirit than even Farquhar exhibited.[61] At the same time, he disliked both the exemplary comedy of Steele and the excessive gentility of contemporary French-influenced comedy. Humours characters are seldom genteel. Many of Cibber's plays, like late Shadwell, seem to be something like what Goldsmith wanted. "Goodnatured" seems to sum up Goldsmith's notion of comedy well. In this respect, he is much less a follower of late seventeenth-century satiric practice than is a writer like Arthur Murphy.[62] Goldsmith is in the slightly awkward position of wanting comedy to be both "perfectly satirical yet perfectly goodnatured" at the same time.[63] This duality of aim appears clearly in a division of opinion about *The Good-Natur'd Man.* Some critics find it essentially sentimental; others see it as a devastating satire on sentimentality.[64] Of

61. For Goldsmith's views, see *An History of England*, 2 vols. (London: Newbery, 1764), II, 139–40, and James Prior, *The Life of Oliver Goldsmith*, 2 vols. (London: John Murray, 1837), II, 160. For discussion, see Quintana (n. 58, above), p. 445.

62. Consider, for example, Murphy's essays in *The Gray's-Inn Journal*, nos. xc, xci, xcii, and xciii, on "Ridicule in Comedy," "Comedy of Humours," "The Ingredients of Comedy," and "The Methods of Burlesque Humour" (editor's titles). Murphy states that ridicule is "the essence of comedy," and quotes Congreve, Shadwell, and Ben Jonson. These essays have been conveniently reprinted in *The Lives of Henry Fielding and Samuel Johnson, Together with Essays from the Gray's-Inn Journal*, introduction by Matthew Grace (Gainesville: Scholars' Facsimiles and Reprints, 1968). Quotation from p. 196. Many of Murphy's plays bear out this theory. His prelude *News from Parnassus* (1776) is an especially mordant swipe at sentiment. Speaking through Boccalini, Murphy argues that social satire is the business of comedy, and that the managers should even "be sparing of alterations" except where actual indecency is involved, since "the form in which the fathers of the drama left their works, shews their own frame and thought, and ought to be respected." *The Works of Arthur Murphy, Esq.*, 7 vols. (London: T. Cadell, 1786), IV, 389–424, esp. 421–24.

63. Review of *The Connoisseur*, in the *Monthly Review*, May 1757.

64. Critics who find the play essentially sentimental include Bernbaum, Nettleton, Nicoll, Thorndike, and Bevis. Robert B. Heilman makes the opposite case in "The Sentimentalism of Goldsmith's *Good-Natur'd Man*," *Studies for William A. Read*, ed. Nathaniel M. Caffee and Thomas A. Kirby (Baton Rouge: Louisiana State Univ. Press, 1940), pp. 237–53. Robert Griffin takes the same position. For a typical middle-of-the-road view, see Allan Rodway, "Goldsmith and Sheridan: Satirists of Sentiment," *Renaissance and Modern Essays Presented to Vivian de Sola Pinto*, ed. G. R. Hibbard (London: Routledge, 1966), pp. 65–72.

course if "sentimental" means good-humored and benevolent, the play is something of both. Goldsmith satirizes extravagant benevolence. Honeywood is severely chastised for his "follies," "weakness," "credulity," and the "prostitution" of his mind—*but* even Sir William speaks of "splendid errors" and the "natural charms" of his nephew's mind when he is summing up the case at the end of the play. We do rather like Honeywood, even while we laugh at him, and we are glad to see him rewarded richly at the end of the play. (Almost precisely the same thing could be said about Cumberland's Belcour.) In what remains one of the best general views of Goldsmith, W. F. Gallaway, Jr., argues that while he had a strong natural sensibility, he recognized the necessity of prudence, and so could admire characters like the Primroses without considering them desirable models for imitation.[65]

Undoubtedly the best analyses of *The Good-Natur'd Man* are those by Ricardo Quintana and Oliver W. Ferguson. Quintana says (unfortunately without much specific reference to other plays) that the work is "a typical Georgian comedy" in its form. Ferguson concludes that "If Goldsmith's play is read on its own terms and not as the opening shot in a battle against the sort of comedy represented by *False Delicacy*, it will be seen that *The Good Natur'd Man*, like Kelly's play, is a conventional specimen of English comedy in the third quarter of the eighteenth century."[66] I agree: Goldsmith's blend of satire, humours characters, morality, and geniality seem to me very much of the sort we find in *The Way to Keep Him* (five-act version), *The Jealous Wife*, and *The Clandestine Marriage*. Even more, the blend is reminiscent of *The Provok'd Husband*—or even *False Delicacy*. The Cibber-Vanbrugh play has a clear moral "Design" touching on "the Peace and Happiness of the Married State," as Cibber says in his dedication to the queen. The Prologue announces that "Plays should let you see/Not only, What you Are,

65. "The Sentimentalism of Goldsmith," *PMLA*, 48 (1933), 1167–81.

66. Quintana, "Goldsmith's Achievement as Dramatist," *University of Toronto Quarterly*, 34 (1965), 159–77; Ferguson, "Antisentimentalism in Goldsmith's *The Good Natur'd Man*: the limits of Parody," *The Dress of Words: Essays on Restoration and Eighteenth Century Literature in Honor of Richmond P. Bond*, ed. Robert B. White, Jr. (Lawrence: Univ. of Kansas Libraries, 1978), pp. 105–16.

but Ought to be." The serious scenes are not such "that would a noisy Joy impart,/But such as hush the Mind, and warm the Heart." The split plot (a Vanbrugh habit) balances the hilarious follies of the Wronghead family against the courtly polish of the Townly group—country bumpkins with money versus town gentry. Both groups are upset by a wife's folly, so thematically the play is well unified. The country group, from Sir Francis to his servant Moody ("an Honest Clown"), consists of humours characters with a vengeance. The high characters comprise three exemplary characters (Lady Grace is actually dubbed "of Exemplary Virtue" in the Dramatis Personae description) plus Lady Townly, whose immoderate (but chaste) indulgence in the pleasures of the town is in need of correction. Satire and humor abound—*The Provok'd Husband* is indeed a delightful play—but nobility, sentiment, and pathetic scenes are also much in evidence. Lady Townly's repentance and her husband's nobly forgiving all make a scene with a strong calculated appeal to sensibility. Personally, I find this play little more "sentimental" than *The Jealous Wife* or *The Clandestine Marriage*, but it certainly contains some of the elements Goldsmith declaims against— insipid dialogue and titled characters, for example.

A number of particular elements in Goldsmith's two plays are reminiscent of *The Provok'd Husband*. The use of humours characters is similar—Croaker and his wife, the country bumpkin role of Tony Lumpkin. The themes of marital discord and a foolish wife generously treated are plain in *She Stoops*. Benevolent father figures and friends turn up on all sides in all three plays. More broadly, all three combine a genial spirit and humorous, almost farcical foolery, with more serious issues of morality and character which are resolved in a moral and benevolent fashion. Lady Townly repents utterly; even Lofty confesses fulsomely in *The Good-Natur'd Man*; Miss Nevile is too high-minded to be deceitful and Marlow the soul of honor in *She Stoops*. A minor parallel, but perhaps a telling one in terms of spirit, can be found in the attitude taken toward the resolutions of *She Stoops* and *The Provok'd Husband*. Goldsmith has made the most of Marlow's magnanimity and Miss Nevile's scruples. Complications disappear, and happy endings are dispensed—only to be mildly mocked by Mrs. Hardcastle's comment: "Pshaw, pshaw, this is all but the whining end of a modern novel." Joseph Donohue rightly calls this a "burlesque of the happy ending,"[67] yet Goldsmith contrives to delight in what he satirizes. Cibber displays the same kind of ironic self-consciousness on the last page of *The Provok'd Husband*.

> *Lord Townly.* Never were Knaves and Fools better dis-
> pos'd of.
> *Manly.* A sort of Poetical Justice, my Lord, not much
> above the Judgment of a Modern Comedy.
> *Lord Townly.* To heighten that Resemblance, I think,
> Sister, there only wants your rewarding the Hero of the
> Fable, by naming the Day of his Happiness.

Cibber and Goldsmith are not sensibility-mongers of the most de-termined sort, but each is glad to have his cake and eat it too. What they gently mock, they also thoroughly enjoy.

As I suggested in the last section, laughing and sentimental comedy are not distinct entities. Rather, these designations suggest different emphases or polarities possible in comedy, and different writers employ and combine them in various ways. Johnson's ref-erence to the Vanbrugh and Cibber play and Goldsmith's probable allusion to it make a wry comment on twentieth-century inclina-tions to see laughing and sentimental as entirely opposite for by most classifications, *The Provok'd Husband* is a sentimental play. Another modern inclination is to yoke Goldsmith and Sheridan to-gether. They happen, of course, to be the only two playwrights of the later eighteenth century who are read by any but specialists, and so perhaps the connection is natural, but I do not think it a happy one.

Nicoll is one critic who sees a considerable difference between the two. He justifies the linkage on the grounds that the two "joined issue . . . against one common enemy."[68] This view is simply the old notion of joint "revolution" against sentimental comedy. But did

---

67. Donohue, *Dramatic Character in the English Romantic Age*, p. 124.
68. Nicoll, III, 158.

the two join forces? I am not aware that anyone has ever demonstrated influence on Sheridan by Goldsmith, or found evidence that
they consciously made a common cause. If such a case can be made,
someone should do so. I do not pretend to have made an exhaustive
search on a peripheral subject, but I have found no grounds for it.
Goldsmith was dead before Sheridan started writing, and Sheridan
apparently does not refer (in his *Letters*, for example) significantly
to Goldsmith. Both to some degree satirize sentiment: Goldsmith's
Honeywood, Sheridan's Lydia Languish and Joseph Surface are instances. But if this constitutes "common cause," some other plays
and writers should be added. Colman's *Polly Honeycombe*, Foote's
The Devil Upon Two Sticks, Whitehead's *A Trip to Scotland* were
all considerable successes, and all are explicitly satires on romance-
sentimentalism.

Sheridan's prologue for the tenth night of *The Rivals* does suggest on his part a conscious opposition to the "sentimental." The
speaker asks if comedy should be expected to teach or preach, points
to the Figure of Comedy, and says

> Must we displace her? And instead advance
> The Goddess of the woeful countenance—
> The Sentimental Muse! . . .
> She'll snatch the dagger from her sister's hand:
> And having made her votaries *Weep a flood*,
> Good Heav'n! she'll end her Comedies in blood.

To take this literally would be silly. The rhetoric of prologues and
epilogues is notoriously a trap for the unwary. But the similarity of
this passage to Garrick's prologue for *She Stoops* two years earlier
does suggest the obvious—that both plays were viewed as part of
a tradition of skepticism about extreme sensibility.

Various "sources" for *The Rivals* have been proposed.[69] Here

---

69. See Miriam Gabriel and Paul Mueschke, "Two Sources of Sheridan's *The
Rivals*," *PMLA*, 43 (1928), 237–50. After surveying other suggestions, they propose
Garrick's *Miss in her Teens* (1747), and Colman's *The Deuce is in Him* (1763).
Recent studies by John Loftis and Mark Auburn (n. 3, above) have both concluded
that *The Rivals* is constructed from the commonplace materials of Georgian comedy.

I am less concerned with particular sources than with the *type*. Years ago I was struck by how similar Sheridan's first effort is to Ben Jonson's *Every Man in His Humour*: both plays are essentially compounds of humours characters. I now find that P. Fijn van Draat has claimed Jonson's play as an actual source for Sheridan's.[70] His case seems to me strained and unconvincing, but I persist in seeing a general parallel. In a way this may seem far-fetched: the two plays come 175 years apart. On the other hand, humours plays were common enough in this period, and *Every Man in His Humour* (slightly revised by Garrick) was revived with great success throughout the 1760s and 1770s. Sheridan could easily have seen it often.

Whether this is idle speculation or not, we can say with assurance that *The Rivals* satirizes both excessive sensibility (in Faulkland) and romantic novel nonsense of the sort vaguely termed "sentimental" (in Lydia Languish). Indeed, the latter plot line appears to be a takeoff on Colman's *Polly Honeycombe*,[71] a debt which places Sheridan's play squarely in a satiric tradition whose nonexistence Goldsmith so loudly bewails. Sheridan's next production, *St. Patrick's Day, or The Scheming Lieutenant* (a two-act humours farce, 1775), again suggests his place as a contemporary dramatist, for it is of a type long produced successfully by Murphy (*The Apprentice, The Upholsterer, The Citizen*, and *Three Weeks After Marriage*—the last "premiered" in 1776), Colman (*Polly Honeycombe, The Deuce is in Him*), Macklin (*Love a-la-Mode*), and Garrick (*Miss in her Teens, Lethe*).

The same point—Sheridan's contemporaneity—must be drawn from his third piece, *The Duenna* (1775). This jolly comic-intrigue opera is very much a part of a popular tradition. Bickerstaff's *Love in a Village* (1762), *The Maid of the Mill* (1765), *Lionel and Clarissa* (1768), and *The Padlock* (1768) were particularly successful

---

Loftis stresses connections to *Polly Honeycombe*; Auburn points particularly to parallels with plays of Frances Sheridan and Mrs. Griffith.

70. "Sheridan's *Rivals* and Ben Jonson's *Every Man in His Humour*," *Neophilologus*, 18 (1932), 44–50.

71. Bevis comments on this point, *Afterpieces*, p. 136.

forebears. Like Bickerstaff, Sheridan is capable of having his happy ending turn on a "sentimental" premise.

> *Jerome.* Why, gad take me, but you are a very extraor-
> dinary fellow, but have you the impudence to suppose
> no one can do a generous action but yourself? Here
> Louisa, tell this proud fool of yours, that he's the only
> man I know that wou'd renounce your fortune; and by
> my soul, he's the only man in Spain that's worthy of it—
> there, bless you both, I'm an obstinate old fellow when
> I am in the wrong; but you shall now find me as steady
> in the right.[72]

Quite a turnabout for a father who was a very obstinate old fellow indeed.

Sheridan's reputation as a "reactionary" rests on one play— *The School for Scandal* (1777). The dazzling verbal polish of its surface is indubitably reminiscent of Congreve, as Sheridan's contemporaries acknowledge.[73] The details of this debt are hard to document. Sheridan left no handy essay, and his letters yield nothing. Tradition has it that "one of his first plans on assuming the management of Drury Lane was to revive the comedies of Congreve. . . . In this way he . . . prepared his actors and his audience for the great comedy which, even then, was still uncompleted."[74] Conceivably so—but the revival (no real success) was started under Garrick's management, and was carried on by both houses. Emmett Avery quotes Thomas Davies' *Memoirs of the Life of David Garrick* (1780) to the effect that Sheridan acted on Garrick's advice.[75]

72. *Sheridan's Plays*, ed. Cecil Price (London: Oxford Univ. Press, 1975), p. 161.

73. R. Crompton Rhodes' introduction in *The Plays and Poems of Richard Brinsley Sheridan*, 3 vols. (Oxford: Oxford Univ. Press, 1928), II, 5–19, conveniently collects some contemporary opinions.

74. Ibid., 5.

75. Avery, *Congreve's Plays*, p. 125. The situation is not clarified by Avery's apparent confusion about which Sheridan. The revisions of Congreve for this revival were apparently carried out by Thomas Sheridan, but the inheritor of the management was Richard Brinsley.

Indubitably it was *Thomas* Sheridan who carried out a revision of *The Double-Dealer* for Garrick.

More to the point are some particular observations. Horace Walpole calls *The School for Scandal* the best play since *The Provok'd Husband*.[76] Given the reclamation of a frivolous but chaste wife, the social satire, and both plays' high-spirited good humor, the comparison again seems apt. The treatment of Charles Surface (not to mention Lady Teazle) has long given rise to charges of sentimental contamination. A useful general consideration of the play's mode has been made by Andrew Schiller.[77] His central point is sound: the form of the play is Congrevean "in its outward aspects," but the spirit and substance are so different that it becomes another sort of play altogether. Schiller calls it "a kind of bourgeois morality play," "a typical product of its Age . . . [which] reflects accurately the tastes of the very moment." These are strong words, but justified: the conception and handling of character is more in keeping with *The Jealous Wife* or *The Clandestine Marriage* than with *The Way of the World*. Some sense of the difference can be seen by comparing *The School for Scandal* with *A Trip to Scarborough* (also 1777)—Sheridan's revision of Vanbrugh's *The Relapse* (1696). The latter is avowedly an attempt to make a Restoration comedy decent enough to satisfy contemporary taste. Unlike Garrick's *The Country Girl*, the result is not a gutted corpse. Even after Sheridan's ministrations, *A Trip to Scarborough* retains an earthy vigor, and its characterizations and satire an edge, quite lacking in the sparkling, genial, good-humored *School for Scandal*.

The difference lies not in morals and decorum but in the whole view of character. Vanbrugh and Congreve take a harsh view even of their lead characters; Sheridan, like Goldsmith, is fundamentally more sympathetic to his heroes. Charles Surface's benevolent nature and his uncle's namby-pamby delight in it are inconceivable in the world of a Vanbrugh or Congreve comedy. To claim that Sheridan is a "reactionary" is to place extraordinary weight on one

76. Letter to Robert Jephson, 13 July 1777. *The Letters of Horace Walpole*, ed. Mrs. Paget Toynbee, 16 vols. (Oxford: Oxford Univ. Press, 1904), X, 82.

77. "*The School for Scandal*: The Restoration Unrestored," *PMLA*, 71 (1956), 694–704.

aspect of one play, while ignoring the substance and spirit of his whole output—including that one play.

In sum, we should recognize that "sentimental" comedy is a complicated phenomenon comprising some fairly disparate sorts of plays. At no point in the third quarter of the eighteenth century was it—in any or all of its manifestations—dominant or anywhere close to dominant. Sufficient clamor may someday help deflate a hardy cliché. Hence, my close examination of the 1760s was made with the idea of judging the climate in which Goldsmith's essay and plays appeared. Theatrical fashion in the short run may look quite different to those living in the middle of it than it does to those with a hindsight knowledge of what was going to happen. A five-year trend is immensely important to a practicing dramatist and even a six-month's fad may mean the difference between success and failure. To the stage historian, it may be merely a microscopic wiggle in the history of taste. The terms in which Goldsmith casts his "Essay on the Theatre" have been accepted in an uncritical way by people who should know better. The "Essay" does not make a great deal of sense internally and it provides no clear references to contemporary plays. One of the few clear references it does contain has been studiously ignored. Who wants to tie Goldsmith to Cibber, of all people?

The advantage of Goldsmith's "Essay" lies in its presenting a magnificently clear, simple, and satisfying pattern against which to view later eighteenth-century drama. Evil, illegitimate sentimental comedy is forcing humor off the stage; noble, true-hearted Goldsmith (and Sheridan) make an heroic effort to revive true comedy, an effort which is, alas, doomed to fail after giving a brief flicker of light in the midst of universal darkness. Unhappily, all this is quite untrue. Despite the development of interest in various sorts of "sentimental" plays during the 1760s, Goldsmith and Sheridan inherited a thriving comic tradition which continued full blast around them. Murphy, Foote, Macklin, Colman, and Garrick made a very considerable group indeed. To say that Goldsmith and Sheridan represent a "return" to earlier modes is to ignore the huge amounts that they took from the thriving comic theatre of their own time.

To say that the two of them (along with several of their illustrious but now unread contemporaries) reacted against excessive emphasis on sensibility is perfectly accurate. But the old "revolutionary" hypothesis is bunk.

INDEX

Some single and peripheral references are omitted.

Bottle; *Recruiting Officer, The*; *Sir Harry Wildair*; *Stage-Coach, The*; *Twin-Rivals, The*

Fashionable Lady, The (James Ralph), 284, 288, 289n

Fashionable Lover, The (Richard Cumberland), 322n, 334, 342, 343n

Fatal Curiosity, The (George Lillo), 300

Fatal Discovery, The (1698; anon.), 68

Fatal Falsehood, The (John Hewitt), 300

Fatal Friendship (Catherine Trotter), 67, 68

Fatal Love (Osborne Sydney Wandesford), 290

Fatal Marriage, The (Thomas Southerne), 71, 189, 290

Fatal Secret, The (Lewis Theobald), 298

Fate of Capua, The (Thomas Southerne), 24, 67, 69

Fate of Villainy, The (Thomas Walker), 290

Feign'd Friendship (1699; anon.), 68

Female Prelate, The (Elkanah Settle), 36, 116

Female Rebellion, The (1659; "H.B."), 183

Female Vertuoso's, The (Thomas Wright), 182

Female Wits, The (1696; anon.), 35

Ferguson, Oliver W., 323n, 347

Fickle Shepherdess, The (1703; anon.), 69

Fielding, Henry, 216, 271, 272, 320, 326; *Amelia*, 212; critics' comments on comedies by, 231n; as ironist, 261; *Joseph Andrews*, 13; later success of plays by, 325; plays accepted by Cibber, 293; relationship to Little Haymarket, 286, 303–7; as satirist, 34, 268; *Tom Jones*, 172, 212, 315; views on marriage, 210n. See also *Author's Farce, The*; *Covent Garden Tragedy, The*; *Don Quixote in England*; *Eurydice Hiss'd*; *Historical Register for the Year 1736, The*; *Intriguing Chambermaid, The*; *Lottery, The*; *Love in Several Masques*; *Miser, The*; *Mock Doctor, The*; *Modern Husband, The*; *Old Debauchees, The*; *Pasquin*; *Rape upon Rape*; *Rehearsal of Kings, The*; *Temple Beau, The*; *Tom Thumb*; *Tragedy of Tragedies, The*; *Tumble-Down Dick*; *Universal Gallant, The*; *Virgin Unmask'd, The*; *Welsh Opera, The*

Fine Lady's Airs, The (Thomas Baker), 226

Fleetwood, John, 305, 308; as manager of Drury Lane, 296–97, 298, 301

Fletcher, John, 80n, 318; See also *Chances, The*; *Custom of the Country, The*; *Humorous Lieutenant, The*; *Maid's Tragedy, The*; *Rule a Wife and Have a Wife*; *Scornful Lady, The*; *Sea Voyage, The*; *Valentinian*; *Wild Goose Chase, The*

Fond Husband, A (Thomas Durfey), 52, 90, 160n, 192, 276; attitudes toward marriage in, 186; blatant sex comedy, 53, 57, 87, 169; critical reaction to, 109; Downes' comments on, 92; as favorite of Charles II, 14, 86; rake hero in, 134, 143, 152, 159; revived, 73; success of, 51

Foote, Samuel, 217, 218, 231, 309, 330, 342; debt to Fielding, 310; as literary satirist, 34–35, 223; *The Roman and English Comedy Consider'd and Compar'd*, 212n, 229n; success noted, 332, 335, 338, 354; on *Suspicious Husband*, 212n. See also *Devil Upon Two Sticks, The*; *Englishman in*

Index

Levin, Richard, 26, 28, 39

Lewis, Peter E.: on Gay, 252n, 254, 255, 257n, 258, 259n, 268

Libertine, The (Thomas Shadwell), 133, 174

Licensing Act, 22, 77, 216, 238; discussed, 270–72, 302–11; effect on competition, 218, 240, 309–11; effect on repertories, 79, 240, 325

Like Father Like Son (Randolph; adapt. Aphra Behn), 117

Lincoln's Inn Fields: new plays presented 1732–38, 299; performance figures, 1736–37, 302–3; Rich at, 272, 294

—mainpieces: 1726–27, 273; 1727–28, 278; 1728–29, 281; 1729–30, 284; 1730–31, 285; 1731–32, 287; 1736–37, 303

Lindgren, Lowell, 250n

Lionel and Clarissa (Isaac Bickerstaff), 351

Little Haymarket Theatre, 285, 309; discussed, 280–82; mainpieces presented during 1736–37 season, 303; new plays presented 1732–37, 299; performance figures for 1736–37 season, 303; temporary decline, 286

Livery Rake, The (Edward Phillips), 300

Lockwood, Thomas, 306n

Loftis, John, 4, 10, 14n, 22n, 37; on audience composition, 46; on Augustan audience values, 205n; on drama in 1730s, 77; on eighteenth-century comedy, 9, 216, 224, 270, 271, 311n; on Goldsmith and Sheridan, 313n, 350–51n; on *Modern Husband*, 209, 210n

London Cuckolds, The (Edward Ravenscroft), 50, 58, 94, 160n; audience reaction to, 53, 60, 166; dropped from repertory, 79; presentation of marriage in, 96, 169, 186; rake hero in, 134, 139; 152; in repertory, 66, 73; as sex farce, 57, 143, 159

London Merchant, The (George Lillo), 6, 287, 343n; as didactic drama, 8; as domestic tragedy, 323, 343; as "fate" play, 290; success of, 285

Lottery, The (Henry Fielding), 281n, 288, 325

Love, Harold, 10n, 49, 313

Love a-la-Mode (Charles Macklin), 217, 327, 331n, 351

Love and a Bottle (George Farquhar), 20, 156, 159, 160n, 175

Love at a Loss (Catharine Trotter), 69, 157

Love Betray'd (William Burnaby), 69, 71

Love for Love (William Congreve), 10, 20, 54, 70, 212, 274, 324, 338; revived, 76n; success of, 66

Love for Money (Thomas Durfey), 63

Love in a Chest (Charles Johnson), 226

Love in a Riddle (Colley Cibber), 281

Love in a Village (Isaac Bickerstaff), 238, 328, 351

Love in a Wood (William Wycherley), 25, 29, 155, 159

Love in Several Masques (Henry Fielding), 291

Love in the Dark (Sir Francis Fane), 156

Lovejoy, A. O., 15

Love Makes a Man (Colley Cibber), 69

Lover, The (Theophilus Cibber), 291

Lover's Opera, The (W. R. Chetwood), 281

Lovers' Vows (Elizabeth Inchbald), 236, 241

Love's a Lottery (Joseph Harris), 68

Love's Contrivance (Susanna Centlivre), 69

Love's Last Shift (Colley Cibber), 10, 160n, 167, 170, 190n, 198, 206;

Index

Woods, Charles B., 197n, 209n
Word to the Wise, A (Hugh Kelly), 334
Wright, James, 173; *Country Conversations*, 173n
Wycherley, William, 46, 82, 88, 108, 136, 310; as Court Wit, 146; critical opinion on plays by, 140, 147, 204, 241; degree of reality in plays by, 109, 195; Granville-Barker on, 242; harshness of world view in plays by, 205, 231, 237; later adaptations of plays by, 338; presentation of libertinism in plays by, 175. *See also Country-Wife, The*; *Love in a Wood*; *Plain-Dealer, The*

Xerxes (Colley Cibber), 68

Zara (Voltaire, trans. Aaron Hill), 300
Zimansky, Curt A., 181n
Zimbardo, Rose A., 83, 136n, 205

Robert D. Hume is Professor of English at Pennsylvania State University. One of the country's most prolific scholars of eighteenth-century English literature, he is the author of numerous articles and reviews in the field. His books include *Dryden's Criticism* (1970); *"The Country Gentleman": A "Lost" Play and Its Background* (edited with Arthur H. Scouten, 1976); *The Development of English Drama in the Late Seventeenth Century* (1976); *The Frolicks: or The Lawyer Cheated* (edited with Judith Milhous, 1977); *The London Theatre World, 1660–1800* (edited, 1980); and *Vice Chamberlain Coke's Theatrical Papers, 1706–1715* (edited with Judith Milhous, 1982).